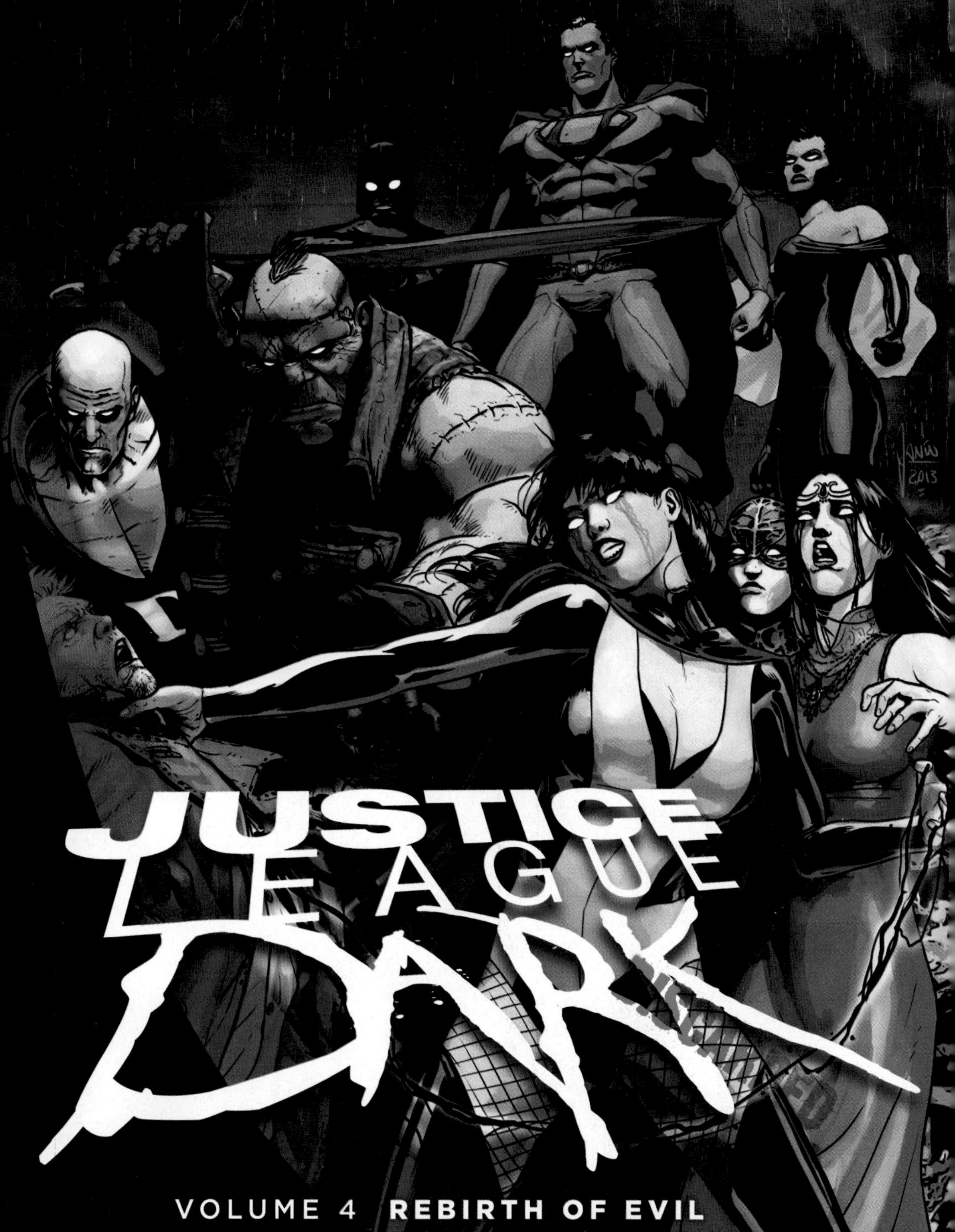

JUSTICE LEAGUE DARK

VOLUME 4 **REBIRTH OF EVIL**

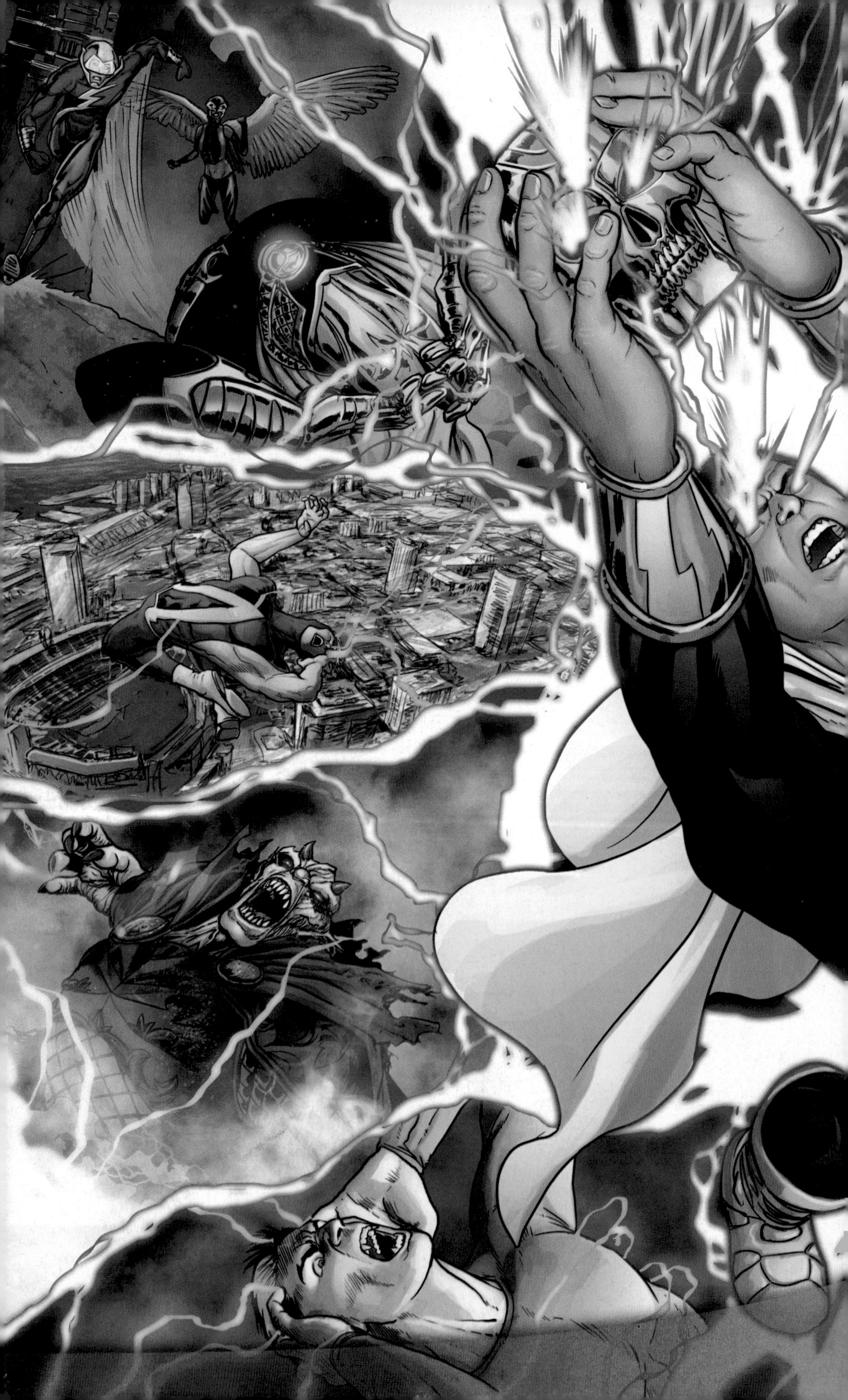

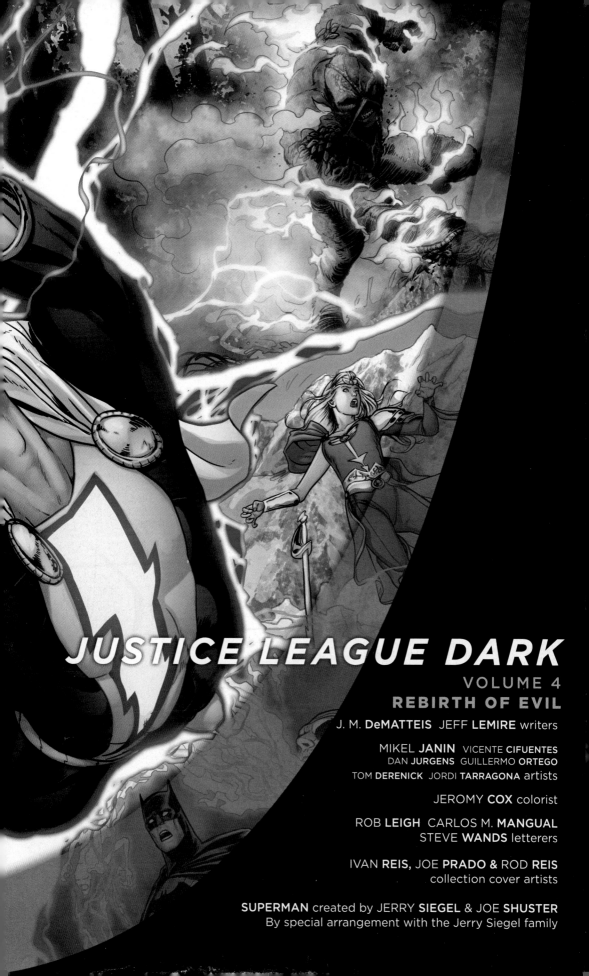

JUSTICE LEAGUE DARK

VOLUME 4
REBIRTH OF EVIL

J. M. DeMATTEIS JEFF LEMIRE writers

MIKEL JANIN VICENTE CIFUENTES
DAN JURGENS GUILLERMO ORTEGO
TOM DERENICK JORDI TARRAGONA artists

JEROMY COX colorist

ROB LEIGH CARLOS M. MANGUAL
STEVE WANDS letterers

IVAN REIS, JOE PRADO & ROD REIS
collection cover artists

SUPERMAN created by JERRY SIEGEL & JOE SHUSTER
By special arrangement with the Jerry Siegel family

BRIAN CUNNINGHAM Editor – Original Series   KATE DURRÉ Assistant Editor – Original Series
ROBIN WILDMAN Editor   ROBBIN BROSTERMAN Design Director – Books   ROBBIE BIEDERMAN Publication Design

BOB HARRAS Senior VP – Editor-in-Chief, DC Comics

DIANE NELSON President   DAN DIDIO and JIM LEE Co-Publishers   GEOFF JOHNS Chief Creative Officer
AMIT DESAI Senior VP – Marketing and Franchise Management
AMY GENKINS Senior VP – Business and Legal Affairs   NAIRI GARDINER Senior VP – Finance
JEFF BOISON VP – Publishing Planning   MARK CHIARELLO VP – Art Direction and Design
JOHN CUNNINGHAM VP – Marketing   TERRI CUNNINGHAM VP – Editorial Administration
LARRY GANEM VP – Talent Relations and Services   ALISON GILL Senior VP – Manufacturing and Operations
HANK KANALZ Senior VP – Vertigo and Integrated Publishing   JAY KOGAN VP – Business and Legal Affairs, Publishing
JACK MAHAN VP – Business Affairs, Talent   NICK NAPOLITANO VP – Manufacturing Administration   SUE POHJA VP – Book Sales
FRED RUIZ VP – Manufacturing Operations   COURTNEY SIMMONS Senior VP – Publicity   BOB WAYNE Senior VP – Sales

JUSTICE LEAGUE DARK VOLUME 4: REBIRTH OF EVIL

DC Comics, 1700 Broadway, New York, NY 10019
A Warner Bros. Entertainment Company.
Printed by RR Donnelley, Owensville, MO, USA. 7/18/14. First Printing.

ISBN: 978-1-4012-4725-6

Library of Congress Cataloging-in-Publication Data

Lemire, Jeff.
Justice League Dark. Volume 4, The rebirth of evil / Jeff Lemire ; illustrated by Mikel Janin.
pages cm. — (The New 52!)
ISBN 978-1-4012-4725-6 (paperback)
1. Graphic novels. I. Janin, Mikel, illustrator. II. Title. III. Title: Rebirth of evil.
PN6728.J87L48 2014
741.5'973—dc23
2014011630

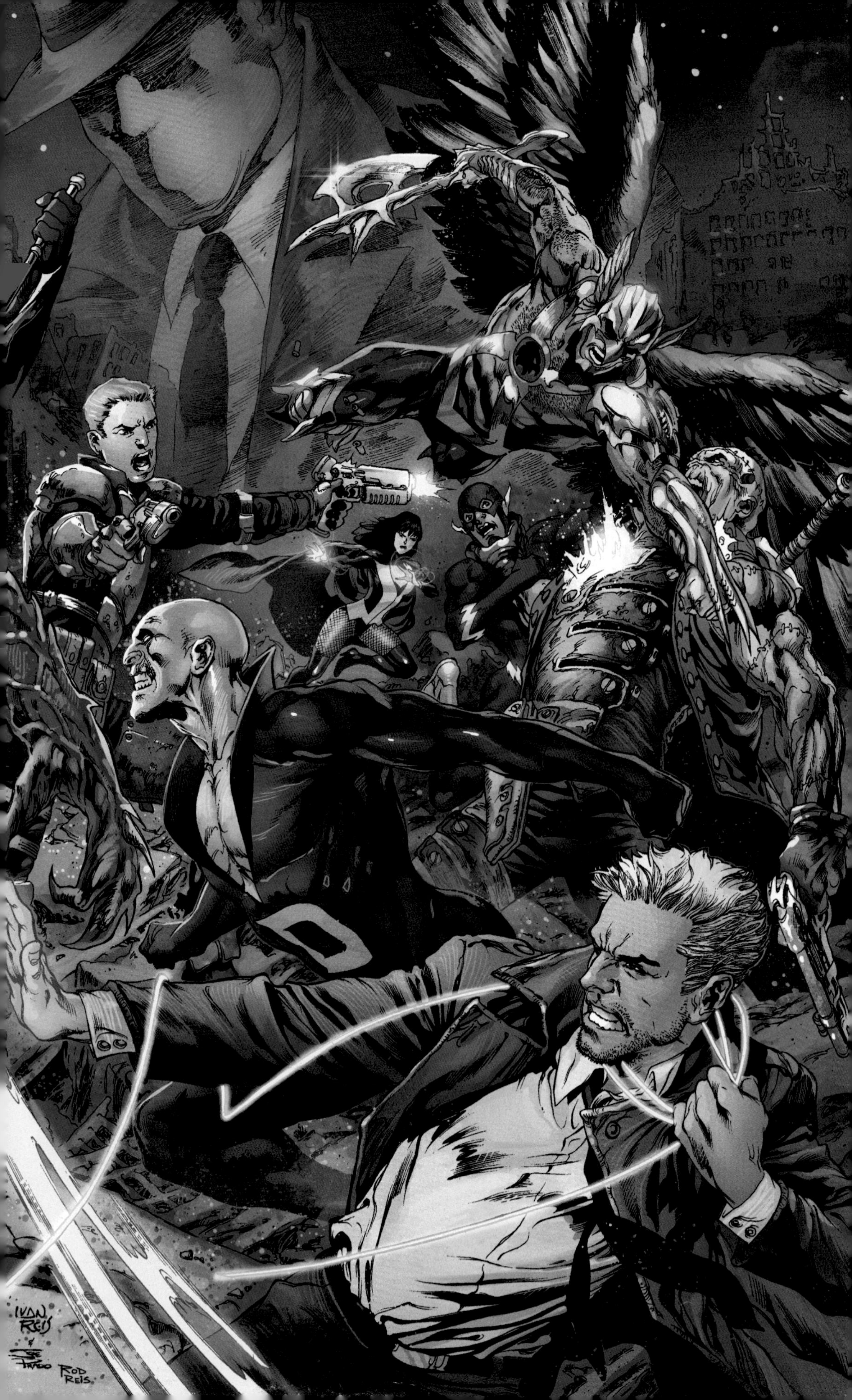
IVAN REIS
ROD REIS

JEFF LEMIRE
writer

MIKEL JANIN
artist

IVAN REIS, JOE PRADO & ROD REIS
cover artists

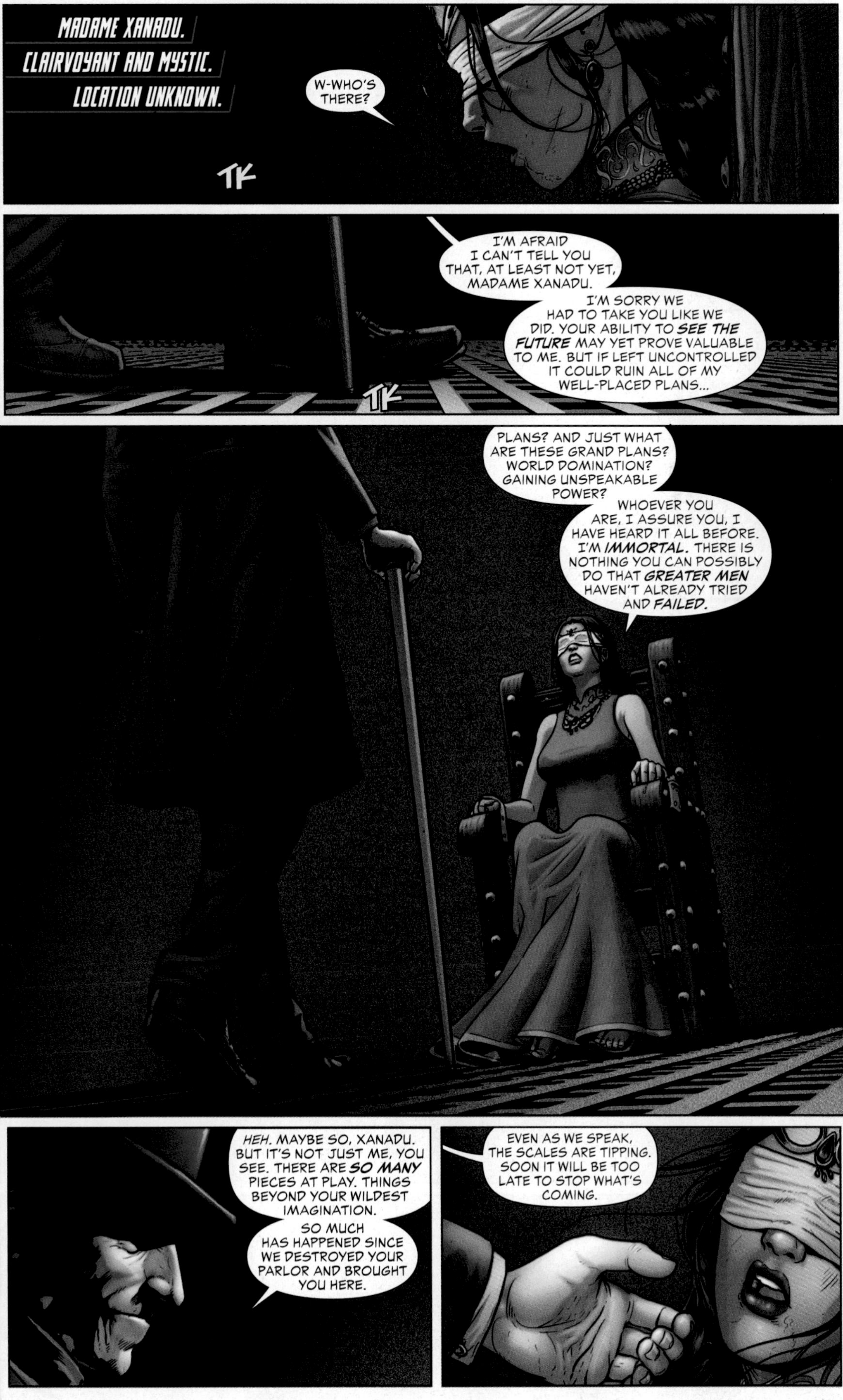
MADAME XANADU.
CLAIRVOYANT AND MYSTIC.
LOCATION UNKNOWN.
W-WHO'S THERE?
TK
I'M AFRAID I CAN'T TELL YOU THAT, AT LEAST NOT YET, MADAME XANADU.
I'M SORRY WE HAD TO TAKE YOU LIKE WE DID. YOUR ABILITY TO SEE THE FUTURE MAY YET PROVE VALUABLE TO ME. BUT IF LEFT UNCONTROLLED IT COULD RUIN ALL OF MY WELL-PLACED PLANS...
TK
PLANS? AND JUST WHAT ARE THESE GRAND PLANS? WORLD DOMINATION? GAINING UNSPEAKABLE POWER?
WHOEVER YOU ARE, I ASSURE YOU, I HAVE HEARD IT ALL BEFORE. I'M IMMORTAL. THERE IS NOTHING YOU CAN POSSIBLY DO THAT GREATER MEN HAVEN'T ALREADY TRIED AND FAILED.
HEH. MAYBE SO, XANADU. BUT IT'S NOT JUST ME, YOU SEE. THERE ARE SO MANY PIECES AT PLAY. THINGS BEYOND YOUR WILDEST IMAGINATION.
SO MUCH HAS HAPPENED SINCE WE DESTROYED YOUR PARLOR AND BROUGHT YOU HERE.
EVEN AS WE SPEAK, THE SCALES ARE TIPPING. SOON IT WILL BE TOO LATE TO STOP WHAT'S COMING.

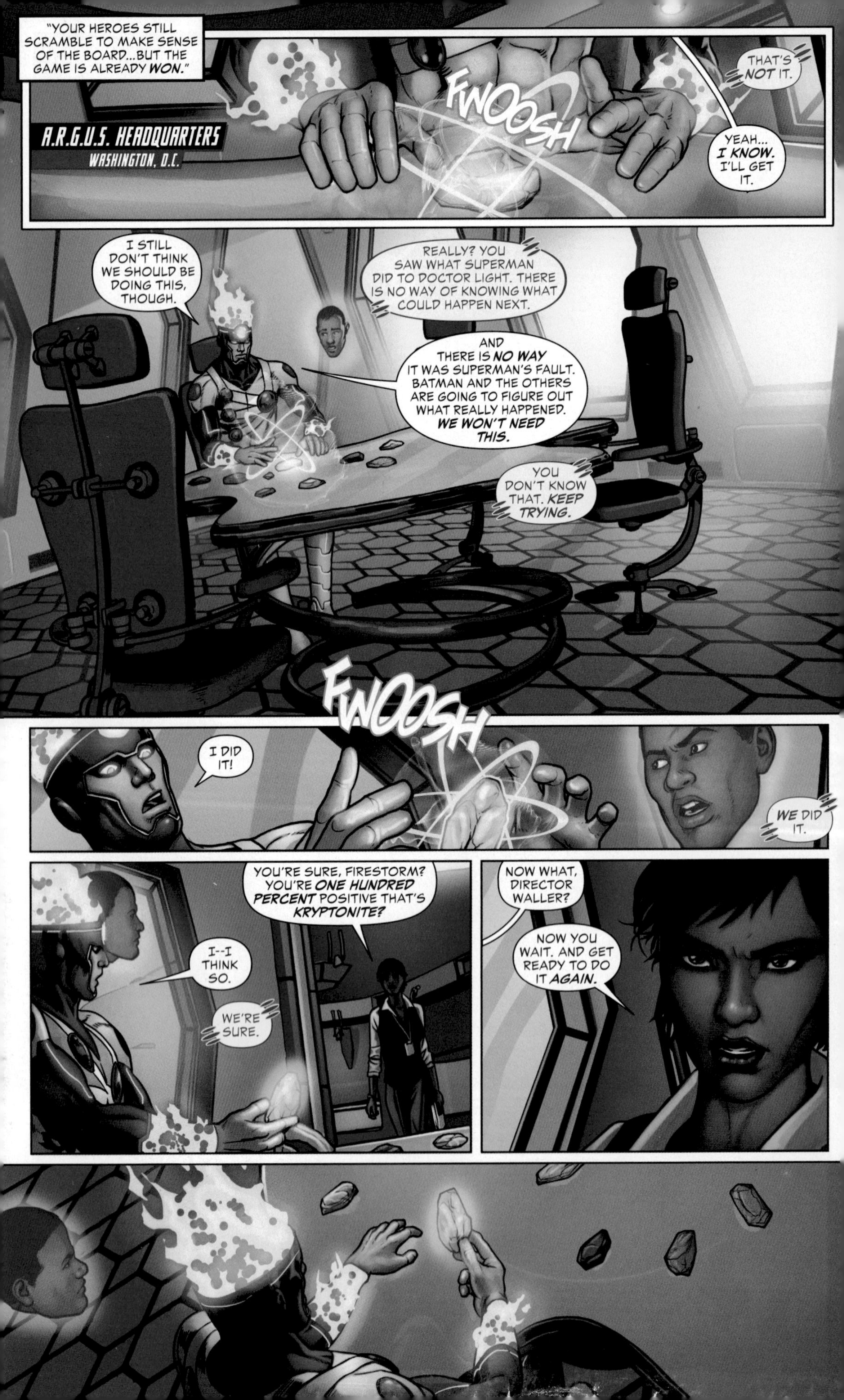
"YOUR HEROES STILL SCRAMBLE TO MAKE SENSE OF THE BOARD...BUT THE GAME IS ALREADY WON."
A.R.G.U.S. HEADQUARTERS
WASHINGTON, D.C.
FWOOSH
THAT'S NOT IT.
YEAH... I KNOW. I'LL GET IT.
I STILL DON'T THINK WE SHOULD BE DOING THIS, THOUGH.
REALLY? YOU SAW WHAT SUPERMAN DID TO DOCTOR LIGHT. THERE IS NO WAY OF KNOWING WHAT COULD HAPPEN NEXT.
AND THERE IS NO WAY IT WAS SUPERMAN'S FAULT. BATMAN AND THE OTHERS ARE GOING TO FIGURE OUT WHAT REALLY HAPPENED. WE WON'T NEED THIS.
YOU DON'T KNOW THAT. KEEP TRYING.
FWOOSH
I DID IT!
WE DID IT.
YOU'RE SURE, FIRESTORM? YOU'RE ONE HUNDRED PERCENT POSITIVE THAT'S KRYPTONITE?
I--I THINK SO.
WE'RE SURE.
NOW WHAT, DIRECTOR WALLER?
NOW YOU WAIT. AND GET READY TO DO IT AGAIN.

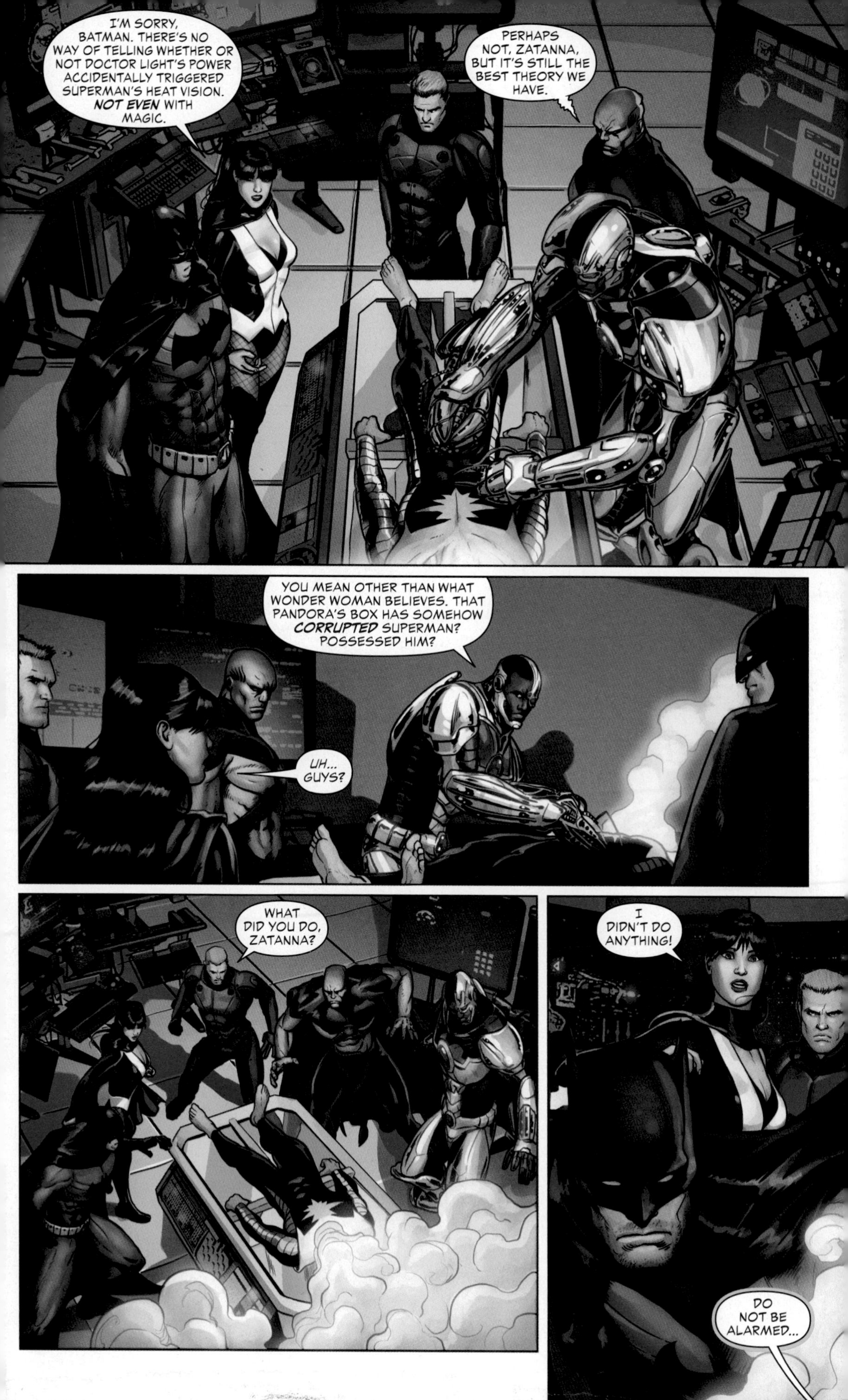
I'M SORRY, BATMAN. THERE'S NO WAY OF TELLING WHETHER OR NOT DOCTOR LIGHT'S POWER ACCIDENTALLY TRIGGERED SUPERMAN'S HEAT VISION. *NOT EVEN* WITH MAGIC.
PERHAPS NOT, ZATANNA, BUT IT'S STILL THE BEST THEORY WE HAVE.
YOU MEAN OTHER THAN WHAT WONDER WOMAN BELIEVES. THAT PANDORA'S BOX HAS SOMEHOW *CORRUPTED* SUPERMAN? POSSESSED HIM?
UH... GUYS?
WHAT DID YOU DO, ZATANNA?
I DIDN'T DO ANYTHING!
DO NOT BE ALARMED...

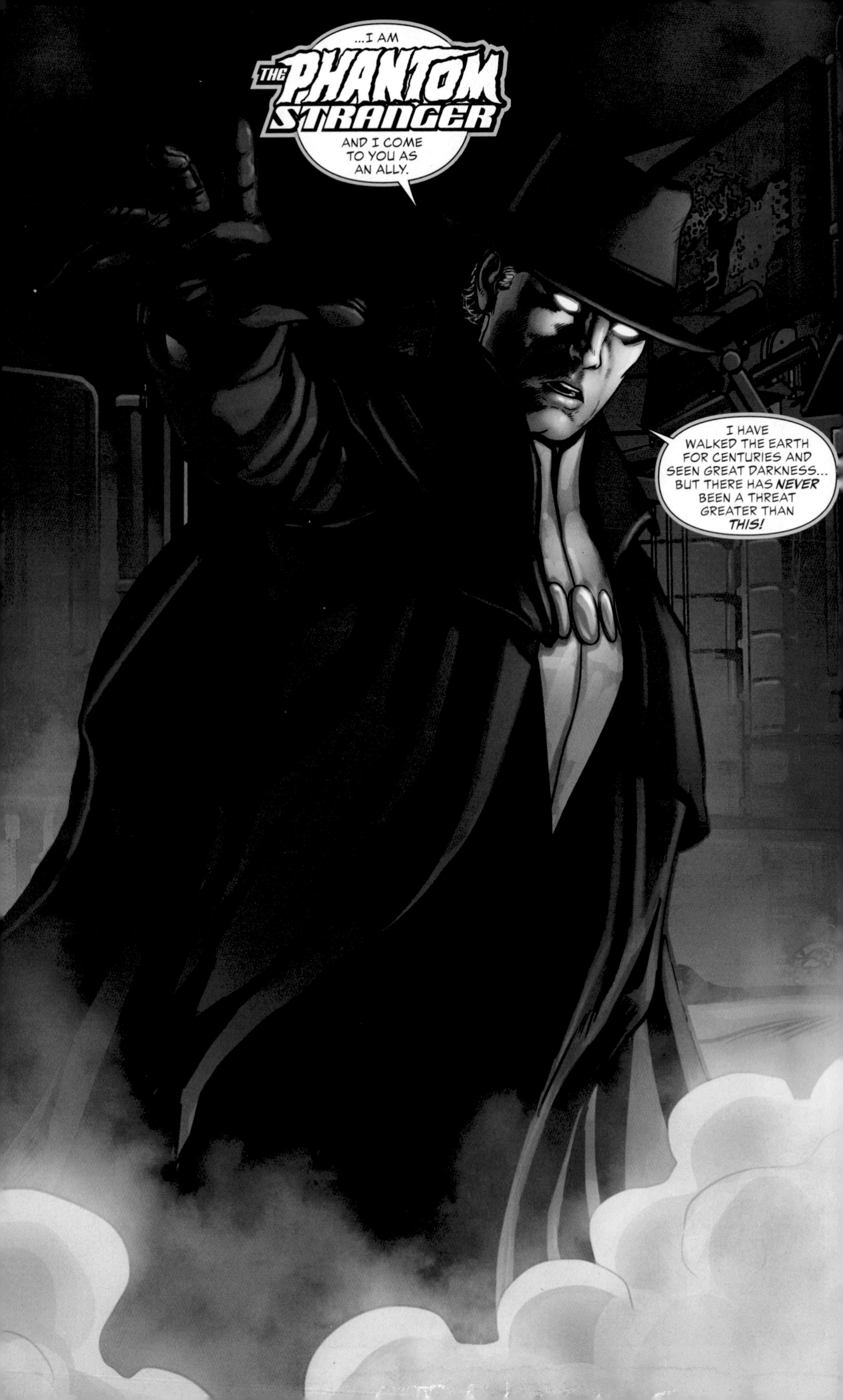
...I AM THE PHANTOM STRANGER AND I COME TO YOU AS AN ALLY.
I HAVE WALKED THE EARTH FOR CENTURIES AND SEEN GREAT DARKNESS... BUT THERE HAS NEVER BEEN A THREAT GREATER THAN THIS!

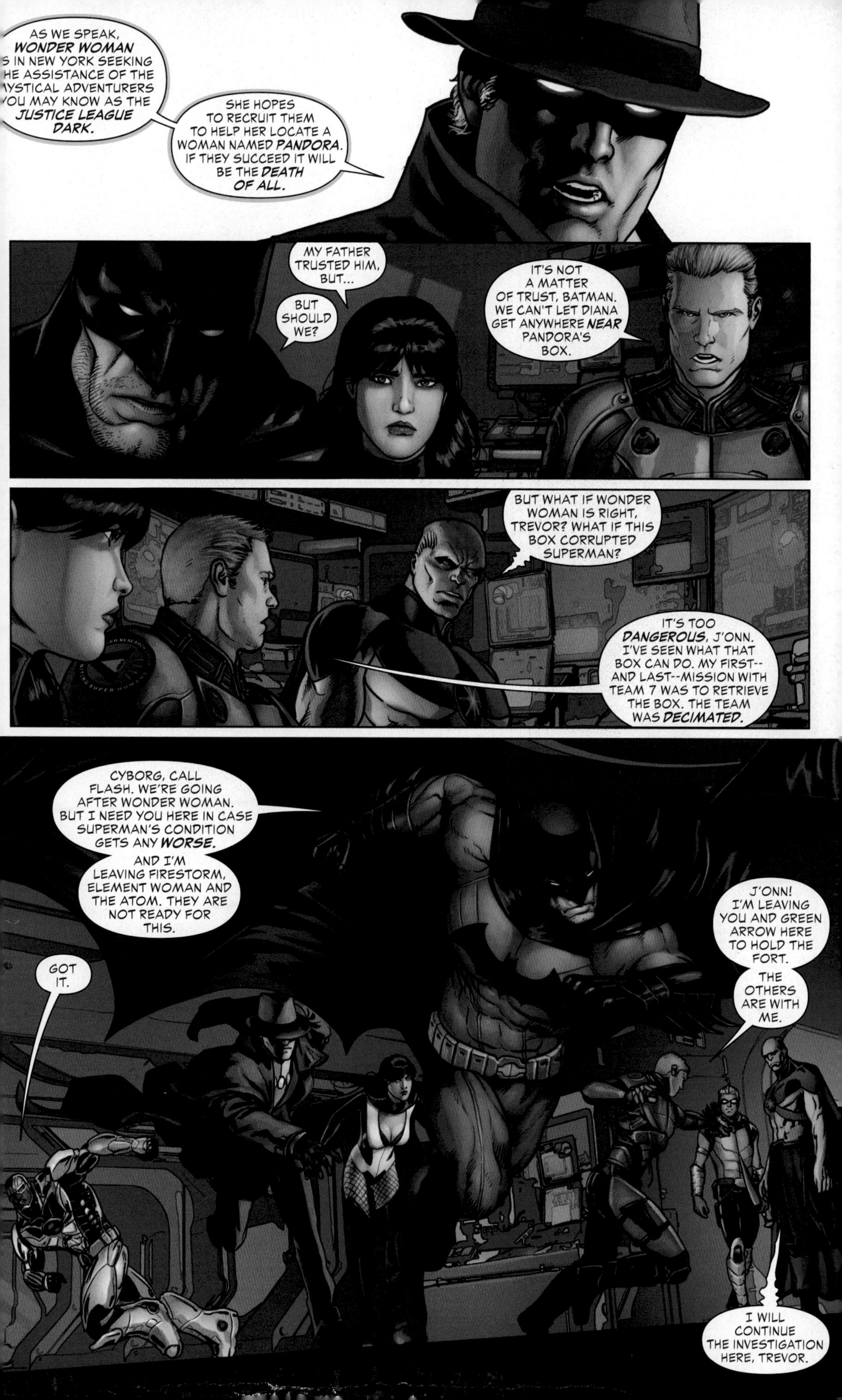
AS WE SPEAK, WONDER WOMAN IS IN NEW YORK SEEKING THE ASSISTANCE OF THE MYSTICAL ADVENTURERS YOU MAY KNOW AS THE JUSTICE LEAGUE DARK.
SHE HOPES TO RECRUIT THEM TO HELP HER LOCATE A WOMAN NAMED PANDORA. IF THEY SUCCEED IT WILL BE THE DEATH OF ALL.
MY FATHER TRUSTED HIM, BUT...
BUT SHOULD WE?
IT'S NOT A MATTER OF TRUST, BATMAN. WE CAN'T LET DIANA GET ANYWHERE NEAR PANDORA'S BOX.
BUT WHAT IF WONDER WOMAN IS RIGHT, TREVOR? WHAT IF THIS BOX CORRUPTED SUPERMAN?
IT'S TOO DANGEROUS, J'ONN. I'VE SEEN WHAT THAT BOX CAN DO. MY FIRST--AND LAST--MISSION WITH TEAM 7 WAS TO RETRIEVE THE BOX. THE TEAM WAS DECIMATED.
CYBORG, CALL FLASH. WE'RE GOING AFTER WONDER WOMAN. BUT I NEED YOU HERE IN CASE SUPERMAN'S CONDITION GETS ANY WORSE.
AND I'M LEAVING FIRESTORM, ELEMENT WOMAN AND THE ATOM. THEY ARE NOT READY FOR THIS.
GOT IT.
J'ONN! I'M LEAVING YOU AND GREEN ARROW HERE TO HOLD THE FORT.
THE OTHERS ARE WITH ME.
I WILL CONTINUE THE INVESTIGATION HERE, TREVOR.

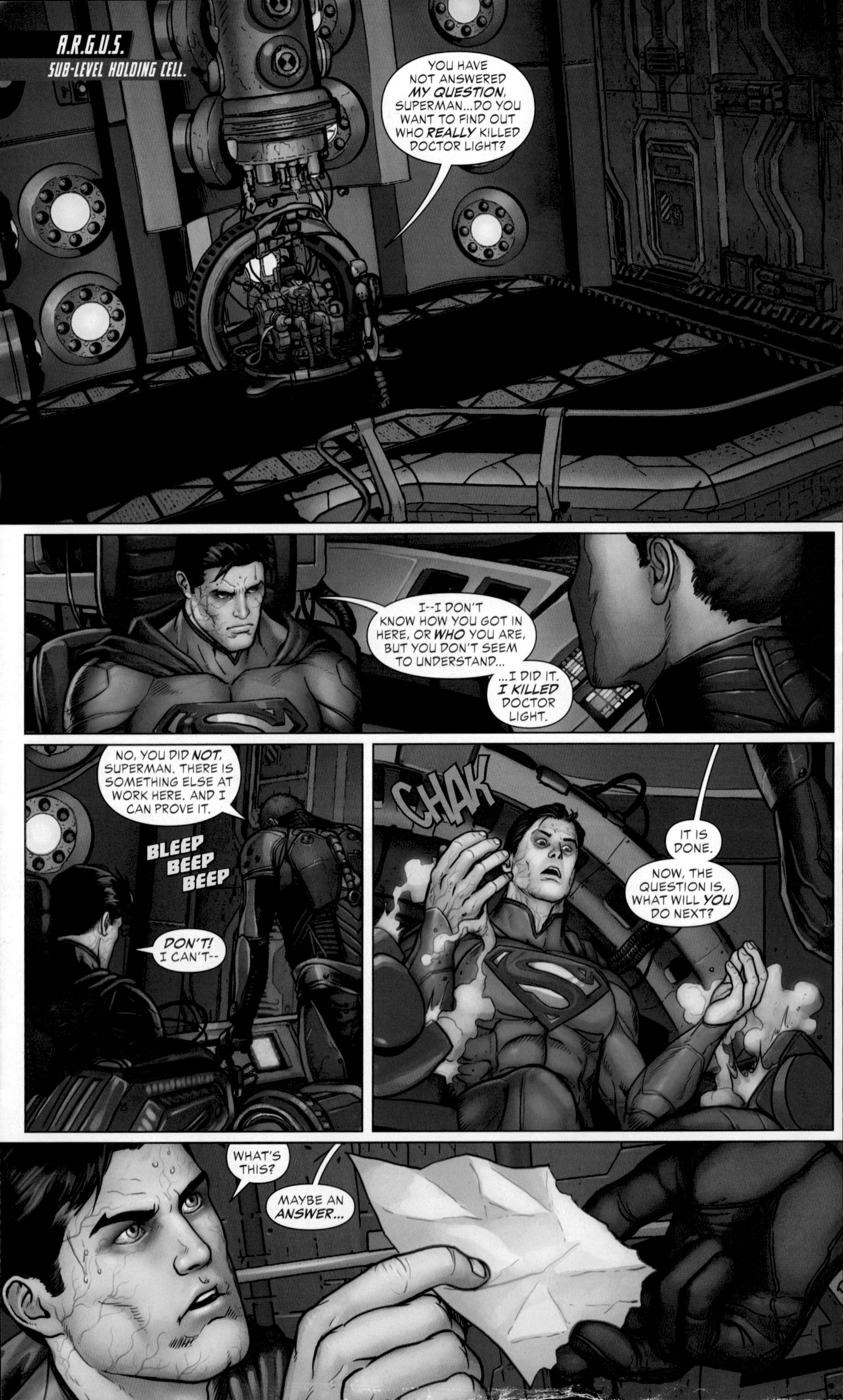
A.R.G.U.S.
SUB-LEVEL HOLDING CELL.
YOU HAVE NOT ANSWERED MY QUESTION, SUPERMAN...DO YOU WANT TO FIND OUT WHO REALLY KILLED DOCTOR LIGHT?
I--I DON'T KNOW HOW YOU GOT IN HERE, OR WHO YOU ARE, BUT YOU DON'T SEEM TO UNDERSTAND...
...I DID IT. I KILLED DOCTOR LIGHT.
NO, YOU DID NOT, SUPERMAN. THERE IS SOMETHING ELSE AT WORK HERE. AND I CAN PROVE IT.
BLEEP BEEP BEEP
DON'T! I CAN'T--
CHAK
IT IS DONE.
NOW, THE QUESTION IS, WHAT WILL YOU DO NEXT?
WHAT'S THIS?
MAYBE AN ANSWER...

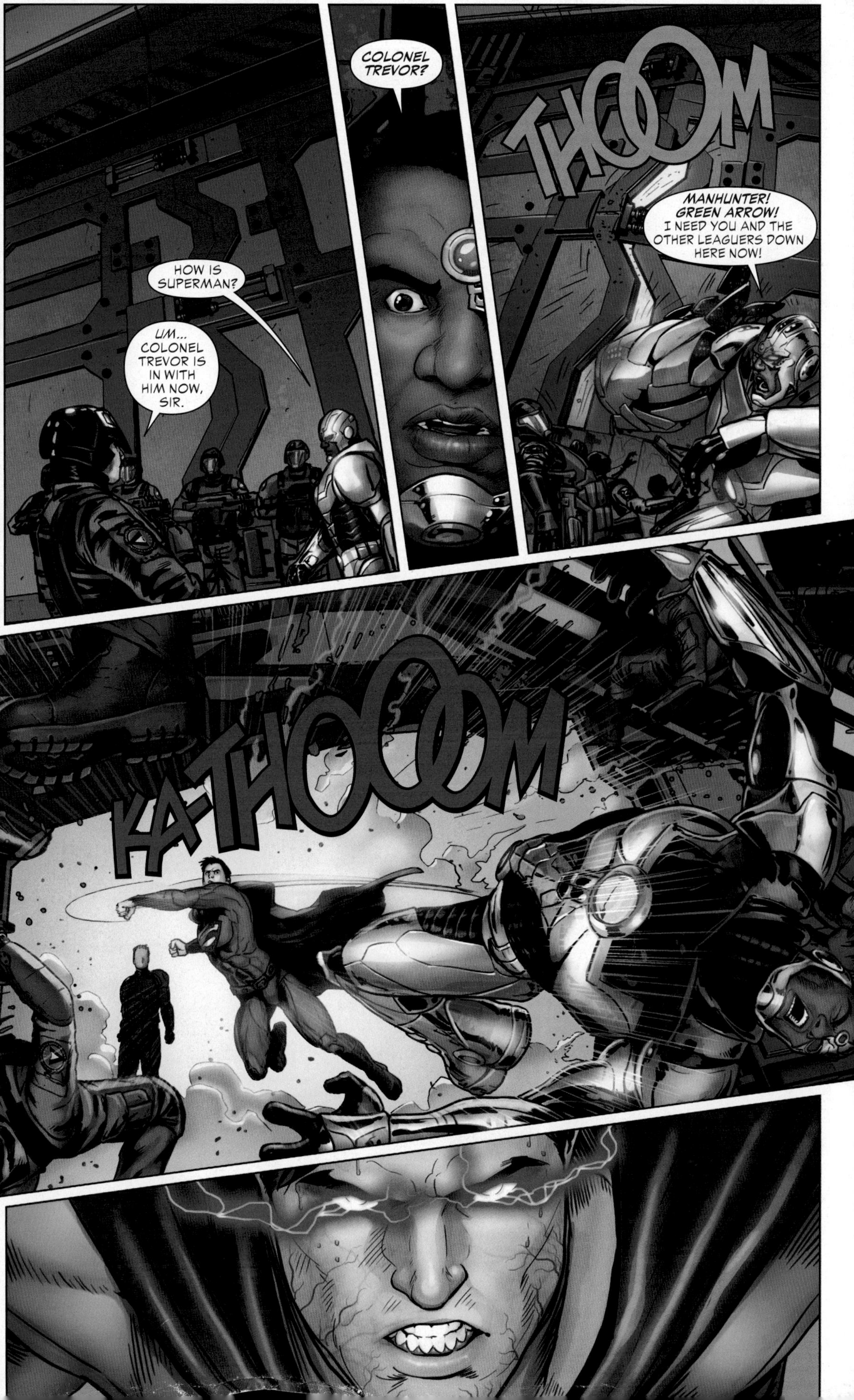
HOW IS SUPERMAN?
UM... COLONEL TREVOR IS IN WITH HIM NOW, SIR.
COLONEL TREVOR?
THOOOM
MANHUNTER! GREEN ARROW! I NEED YOU AND THE OTHER LEAGUERS DOWN HERE NOW!
KA-THOOOM

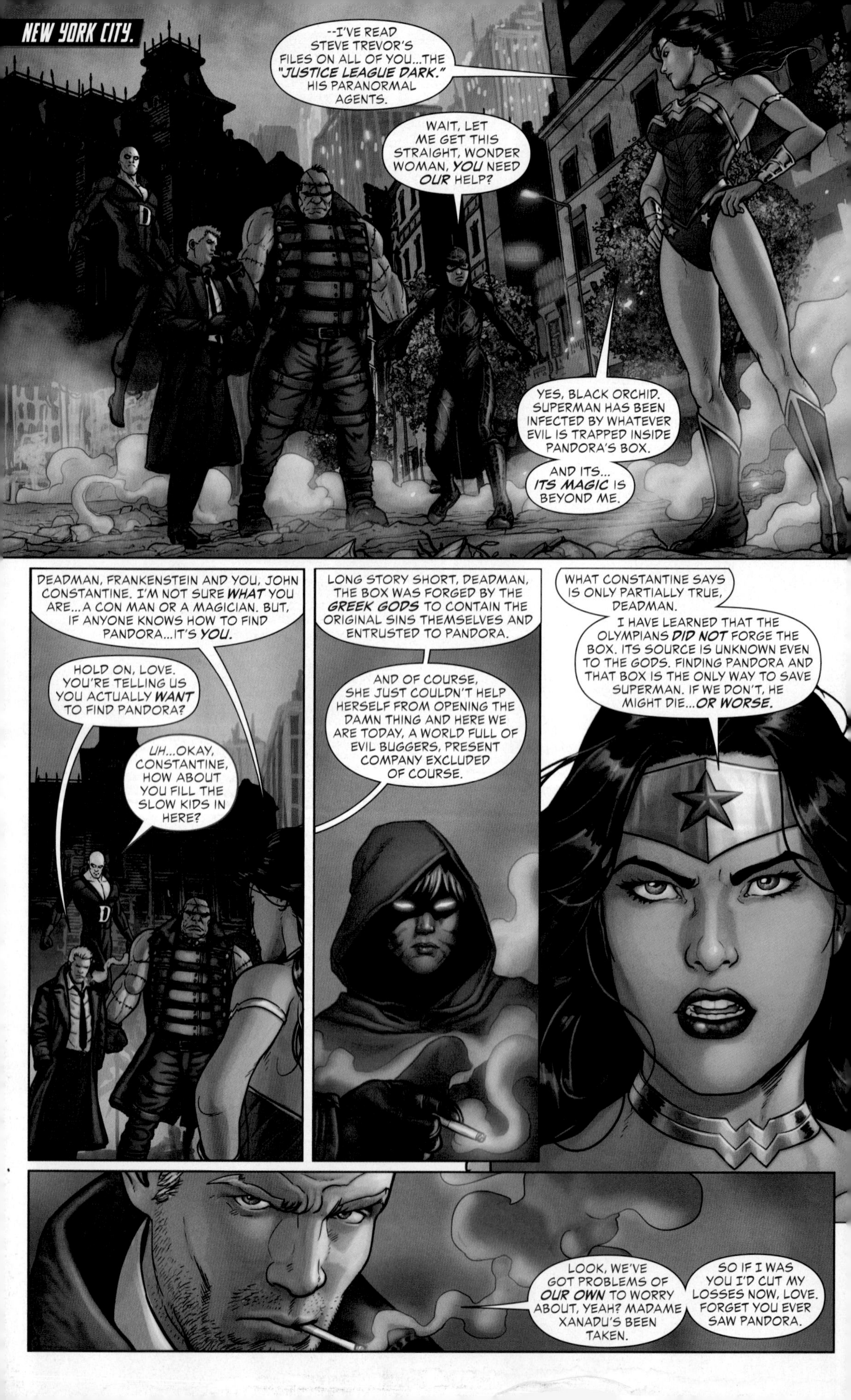
NEW YORK CITY.
--I'VE READ STEVE TREVOR'S FILES ON ALL OF YOU...THE "JUSTICE LEAGUE DARK." HIS PARANORMAL AGENTS.
WAIT, LET ME GET THIS STRAIGHT, WONDER WOMAN, YOU NEED OUR HELP?
YES, BLACK ORCHID. SUPERMAN HAS BEEN INFECTED BY WHATEVER EVIL IS TRAPPED INSIDE PANDORA'S BOX.
AND ITS... ITS MAGIC IS BEYOND ME.
DEADMAN, FRANKENSTEIN AND YOU, JOHN CONSTANTINE. I'M NOT SURE WHAT YOU ARE...A CON MAN OR A MAGICIAN. BUT, IF ANYONE KNOWS HOW TO FIND PANDORA...IT'S YOU.
HOLD ON, LOVE. YOU'RE TELLING US YOU ACTUALLY WANT TO FIND PANDORA?
UH...OKAY, CONSTANTINE, HOW ABOUT YOU FILL THE SLOW KIDS IN HERE?
LONG STORY SHORT, DEADMAN, THE BOX WAS FORGED BY THE GREEK GODS TO CONTAIN THE ORIGINAL SINS THEMSELVES AND ENTRUSTED TO PANDORA.
AND OF COURSE, SHE JUST COULDN'T HELP HERSELF FROM OPENING THE DAMN THING AND HERE WE ARE TODAY, A WORLD FULL OF EVIL BUGGERS, PRESENT COMPANY EXCLUDED OF COURSE.
WHAT CONSTANTINE SAYS IS ONLY PARTIALLY TRUE, DEADMAN.
I HAVE LEARNED THAT THE OLYMPIANS DID NOT FORGE THE BOX. ITS SOURCE IS UNKNOWN EVEN TO THE GODS. FINDING PANDORA AND THAT BOX IS THE ONLY WAY TO SAVE SUPERMAN. IF WE DON'T, HE MIGHT DIE...OR WORSE.
LOOK, WE'VE GOT PROBLEMS OF OUR OWN TO WORRY ABOUT, YEAH? MADAME XANADU'S BEEN TAKEN.
SO IF I WAS YOU I'D CUT MY LOSSES NOW, LOVE. FORGET YOU EVER SAW PANDORA.

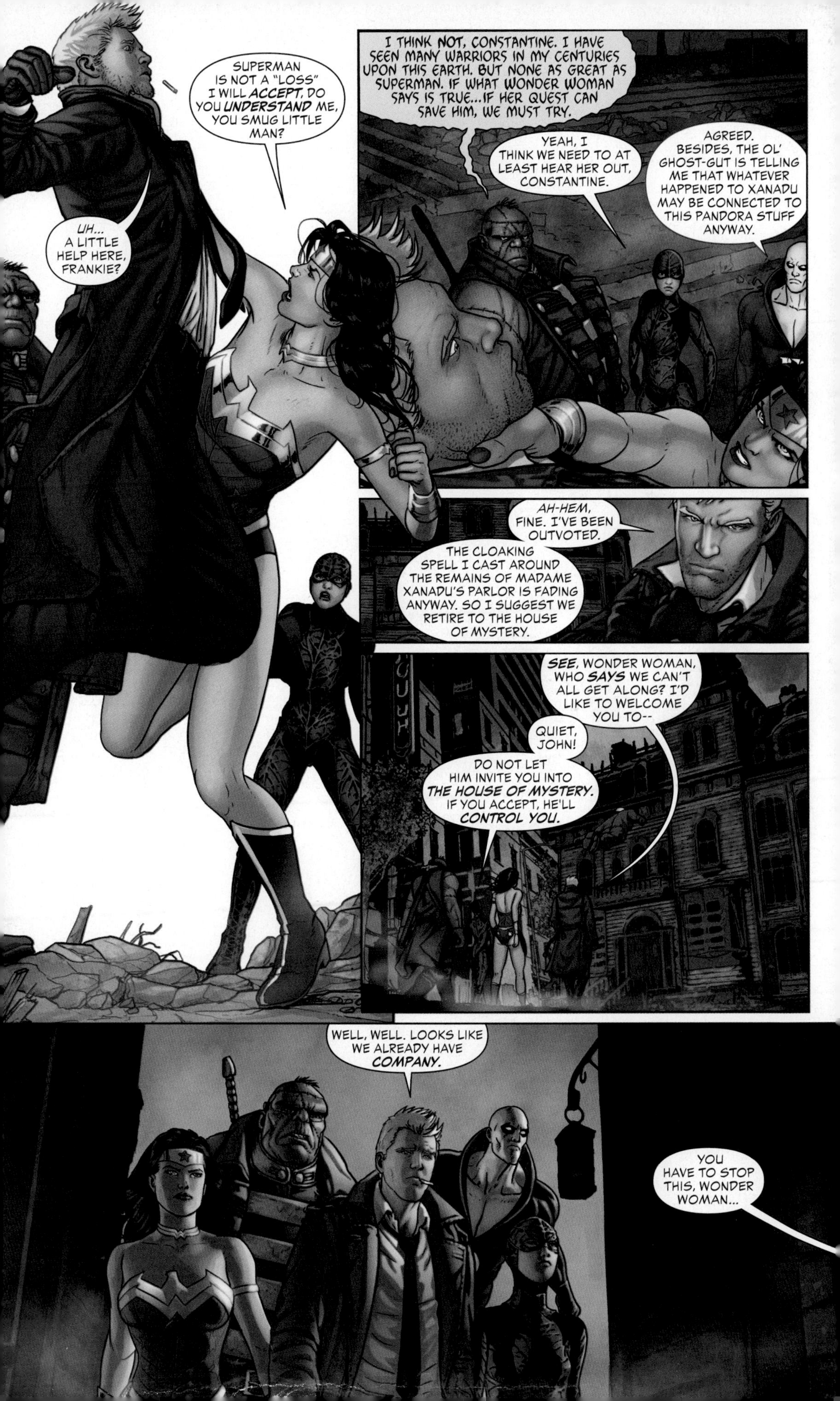
SUPERMAN IS NOT A "LOSS" I WILL ACCEPT, DO YOU UNDERSTAND ME, YOU SMUG LITTLE MAN?
UH... A LITTLE HELP HERE, FRANKIE?
I THINK NOT, CONSTANTINE. I HAVE SEEN MANY WARRIORS IN MY CENTURIES UPON THIS EARTH. BUT NONE AS GREAT AS SUPERMAN. IF WHAT WONDER WOMAN SAYS IS TRUE...IF HER QUEST CAN SAVE HIM, WE MUST TRY.
YEAH, I THINK WE NEED TO AT LEAST HEAR HER OUT, CONSTANTINE.
AGREED. BESIDES, THE OL' GHOST-GUT IS TELLING ME THAT WHATEVER HAPPENED TO XANADU MAY BE CONNECTED TO THIS PANDORA STUFF ANYWAY.
AH-HEM, FINE. I'VE BEEN OUTVOTED.
THE CLOAKING SPELL I CAST AROUND THE REMAINS OF MADAME XANADU'S PARLOR IS FADING ANYWAY. SO I SUGGEST WE RETIRE TO THE HOUSE OF MYSTERY.
SEE, WONDER WOMAN, WHO SAYS WE CAN'T ALL GET ALONG? I'D LIKE TO WELCOME YOU TO--
QUIET, JOHN!
DO NOT LET HIM INVITE YOU INTO THE HOUSE OF MYSTERY. IF YOU ACCEPT, HE'LL CONTROL YOU.
WELL, WELL. LOOKS LIKE WE ALREADY HAVE COMPANY.
YOU HAVE TO STOP THIS, WONDER WOMAN...

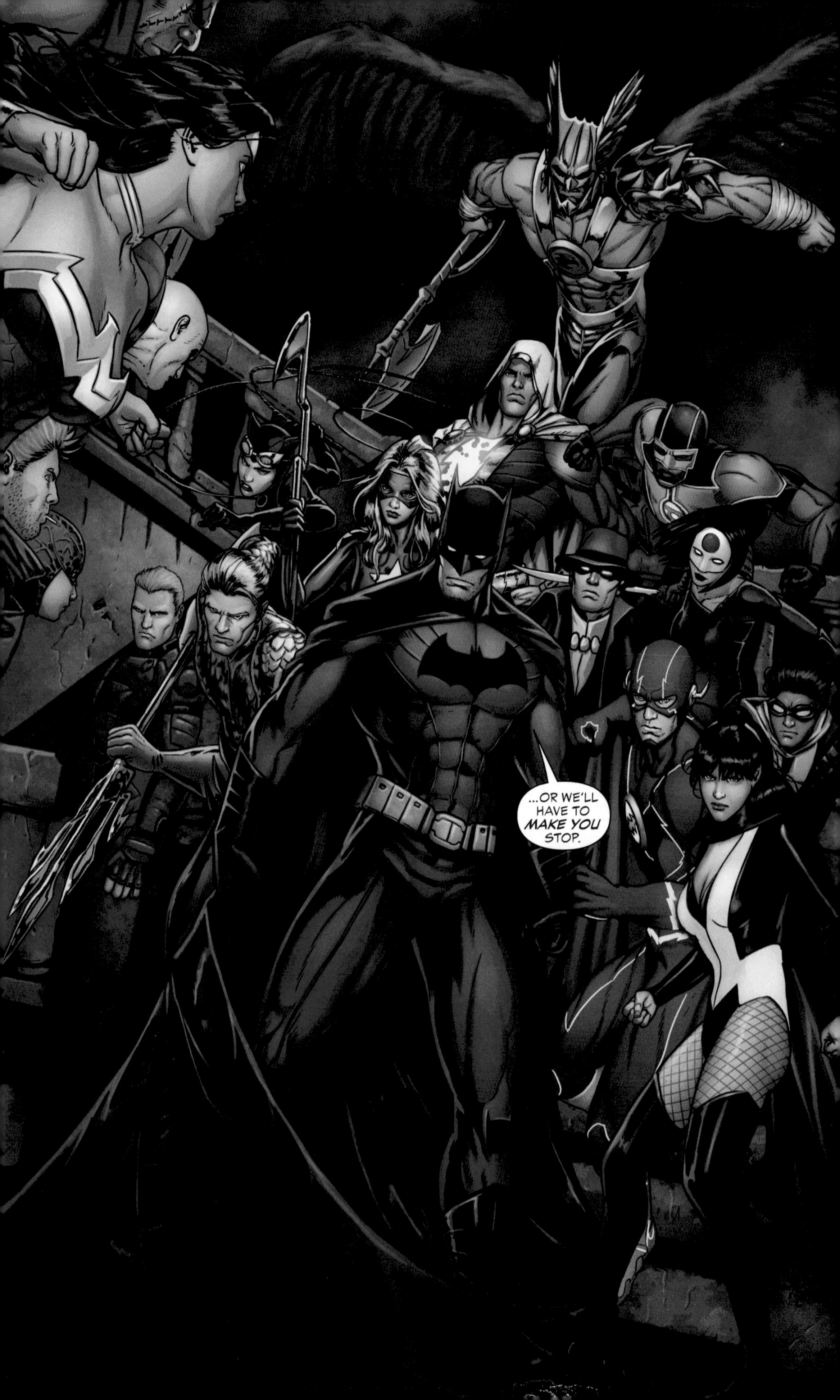
...OR WE'LL HAVE TO MAKE YOU STOP.

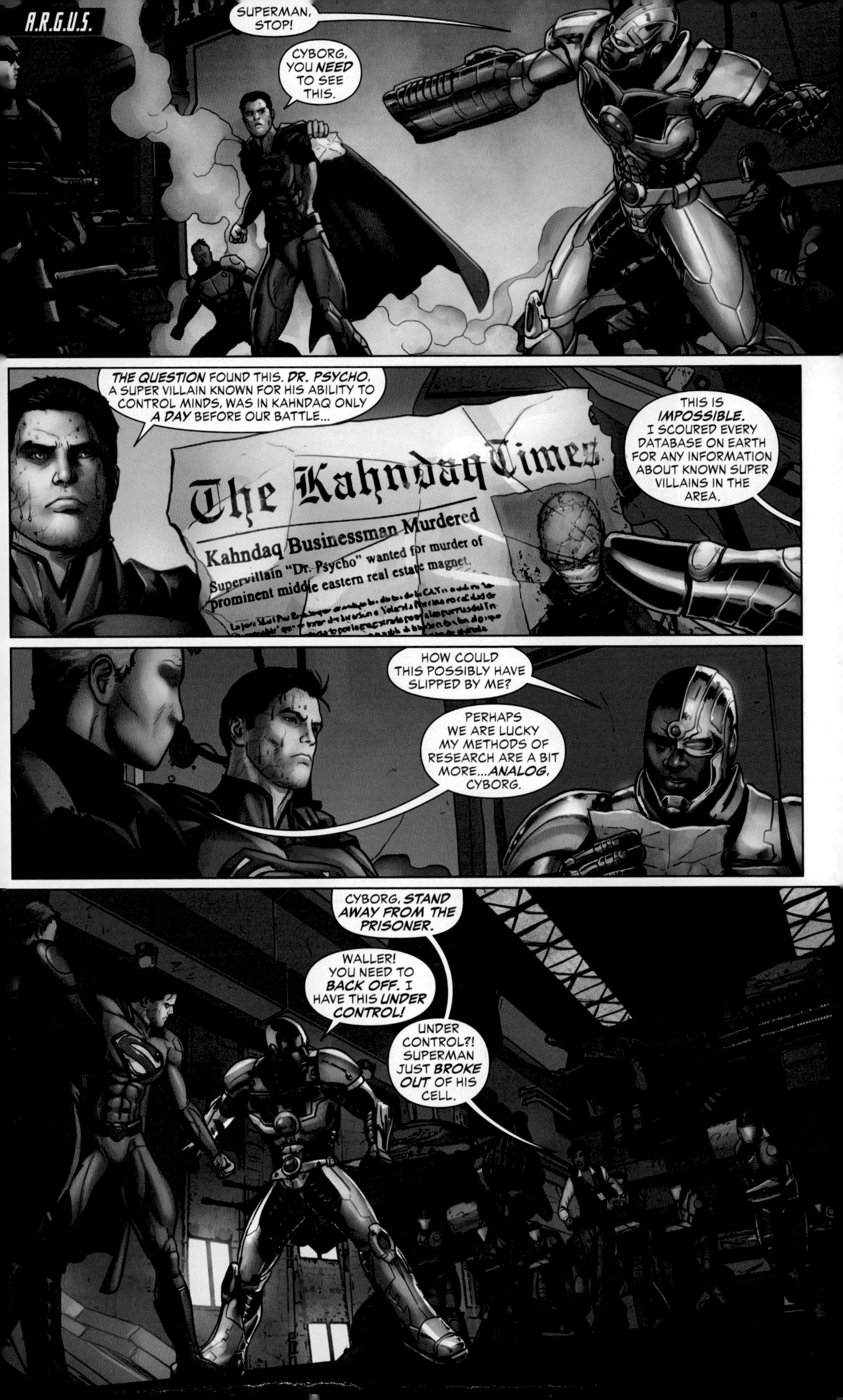
A.R.G.U.S.
SUPERMAN, STOP!
CYBORG, YOU NEED TO SEE THIS.
THE QUESTION FOUND THIS. DR. PSYCHO, A SUPER VILLAIN KNOWN FOR HIS ABILITY TO CONTROL MINDS, WAS IN KAHNDAQ ONLY A DAY BEFORE OUR BATTLE...
The Kahndaq Times
Kahndaq Businessman Murdered
Supervillain "Dr. Psycho" wanted for murder of prominent middle eastern real estate magnet.
THIS IS IMPOSSIBLE. I SCOURED EVERY DATABASE ON EARTH FOR ANY INFORMATION ABOUT KNOWN SUPER VILLAINS IN THE AREA.
HOW COULD THIS POSSIBLY HAVE SLIPPED BY ME?
PERHAPS WE ARE LUCKY MY METHODS OF RESEARCH ARE A BIT MORE...ANALOG, CYBORG.
CYBORG, STAND AWAY FROM THE PRISONER.
WALLER! YOU NEED TO BACK OFF. I HAVE THIS UNDER CONTROL!
UNDER CONTROL?! SUPERMAN JUST BROKE OUT OF HIS CELL.

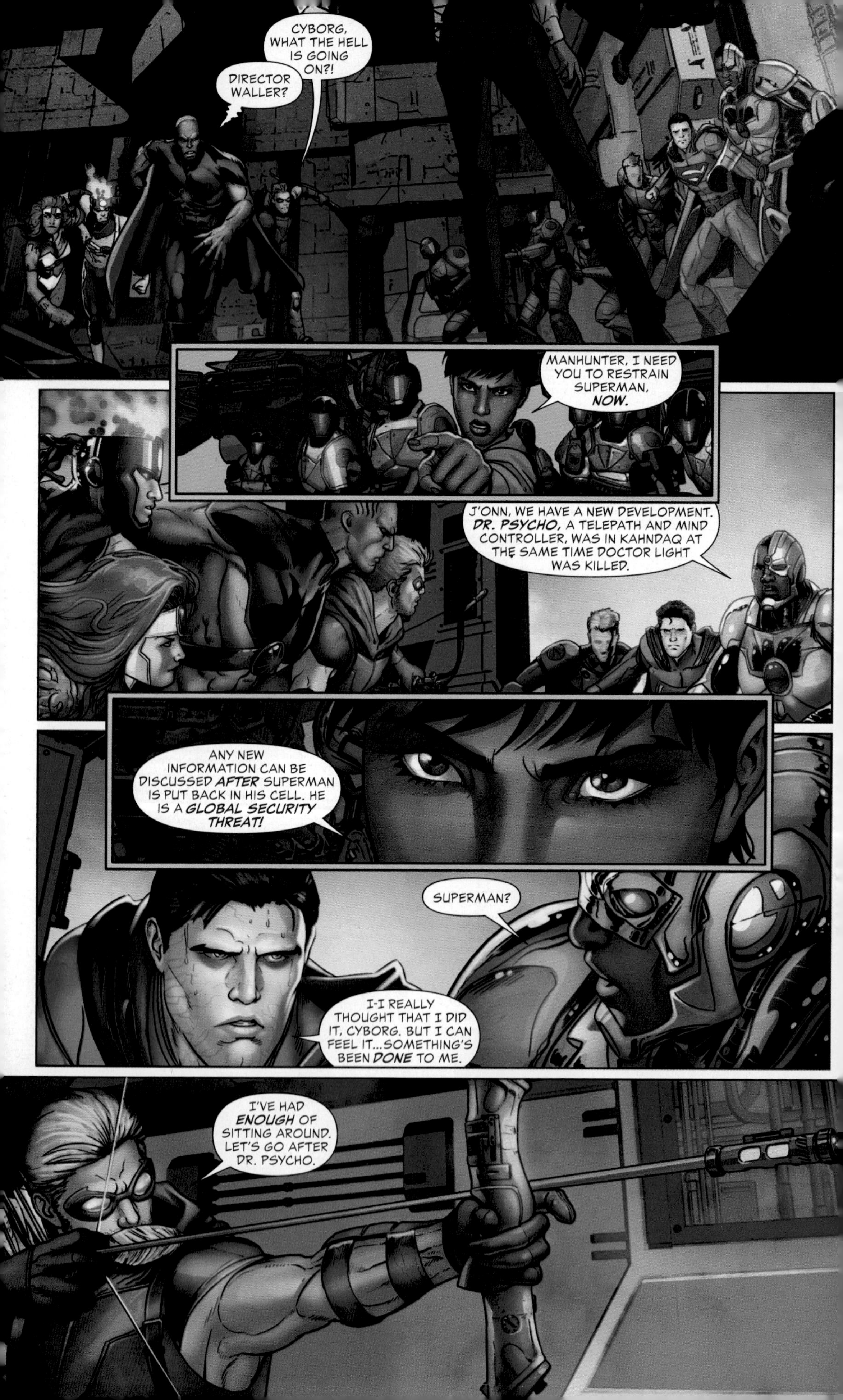
CYBORG, WHAT THE HELL IS GOING ON?!
DIRECTOR WALLER?
MANHUNTER, I NEED YOU TO RESTRAIN SUPERMAN, NOW.
J'ONN, WE HAVE A NEW DEVELOPMENT. DR. PSYCHO, A TELEPATH AND MIND CONTROLLER, WAS IN KAHNDAQ AT THE SAME TIME DOCTOR LIGHT WAS KILLED.
ANY NEW INFORMATION CAN BE DISCUSSED AFTER SUPERMAN IS PUT BACK IN HIS CELL. HE IS A GLOBAL SECURITY THREAT!
SUPERMAN?
I-I REALLY THOUGHT THAT I DID IT, CYBORG. BUT I CAN FEEL IT...SOMETHING'S BEEN DONE TO ME.
I'VE HAD ENOUGH OF SITTING AROUND. LET'S GO AFTER DR. PSYCHO.

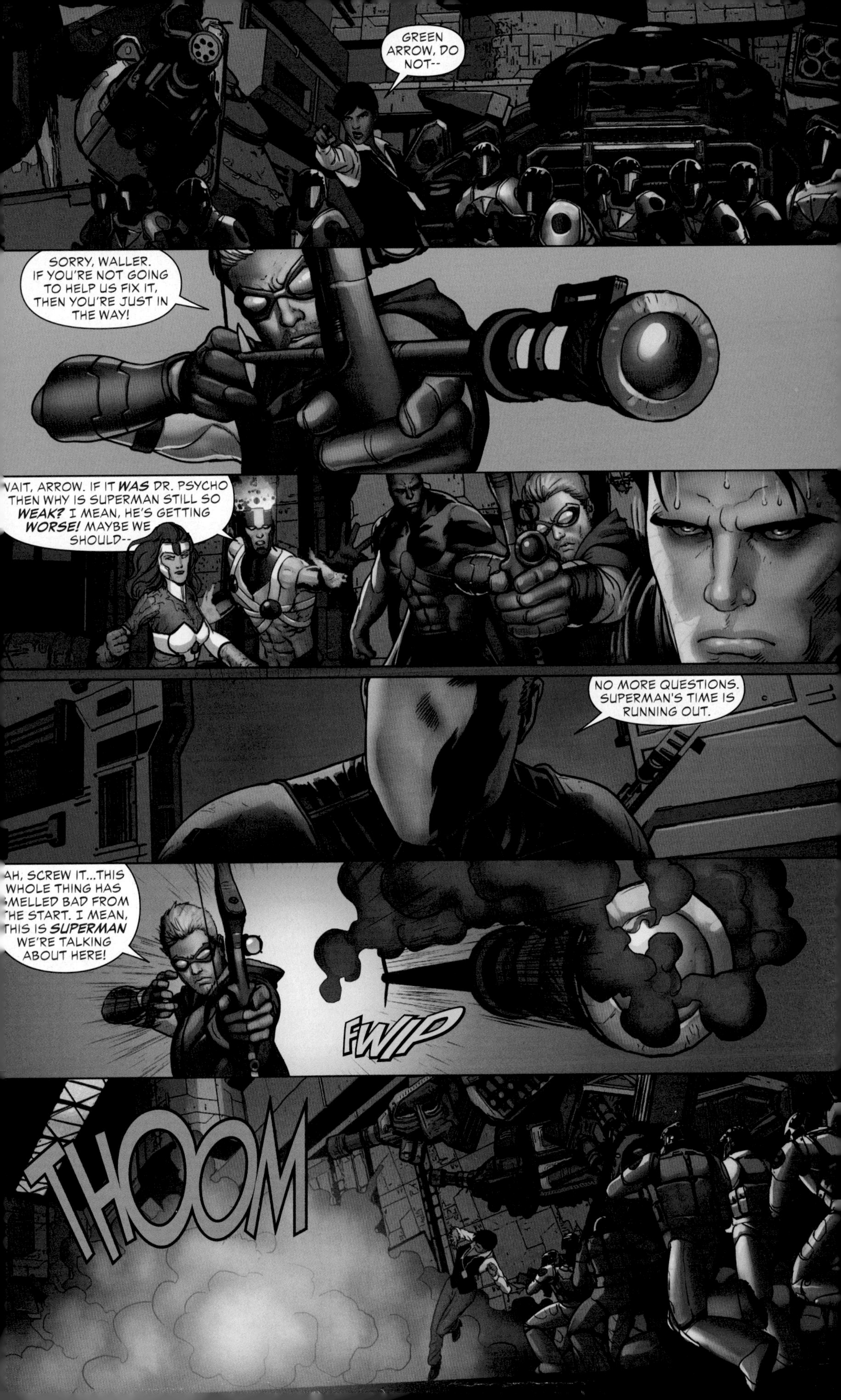
GREEN ARROW, DO NOT--
SORRY, WALLER. IF YOU'RE NOT GOING TO HELP US FIX IT, THEN YOU'RE JUST IN THE WAY!
VAIT, ARROW. IF IT WAS DR. PSYCHO THEN WHY IS SUPERMAN STILL SO WEAK? I MEAN, HE'S GETTING WORSE! MAYBE WE SHOULD--
NO MORE QUESTIONS. SUPERMAN'S TIME IS RUNNING OUT.
AH, SCREW IT...THIS WHOLE THING HAS SMELLED BAD FROM THE START. I MEAN, THIS IS SUPERMAN WE'RE TALKING ABOUT HERE!
FWIP
THOOM

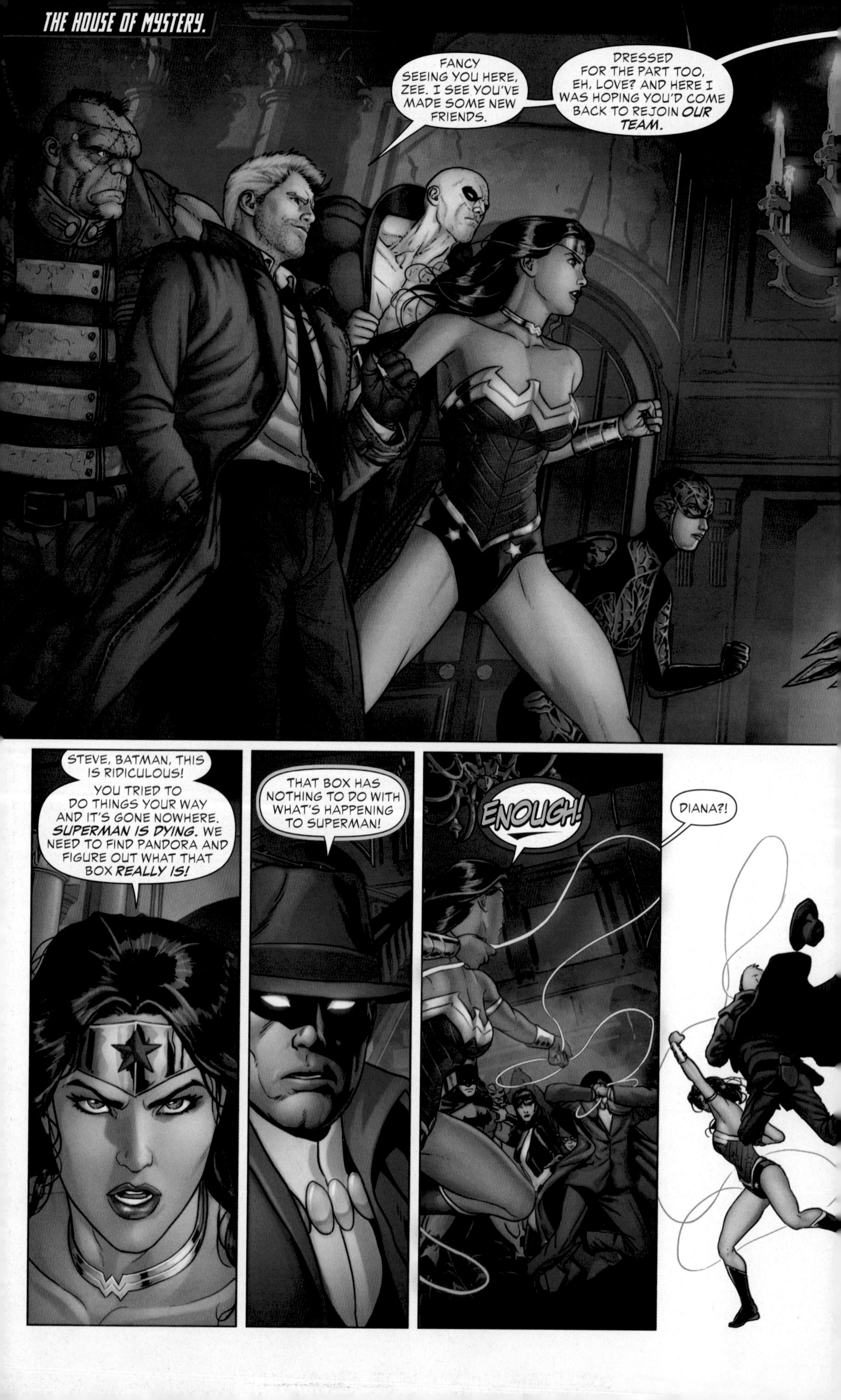
THE HOUSE OF MYSTERY.
FANCY SEEING YOU HERE, ZEE. I SEE YOU'VE MADE SOME NEW FRIENDS.
DRESSED FOR THE PART TOO, EH, LOVE? AND HERE I WAS HOPING YOU'D COME BACK TO REJOIN *OUR TEAM.*
STEVE, BATMAN, THIS IS RIDICULOUS!
YOU TRIED TO DO THINGS YOUR WAY AND IT'S GONE NOWHERE. ***SUPERMAN IS DYING.*** WE NEED TO FIND PANDORA AND FIGURE OUT WHAT THAT BOX ***REALLY IS!***
THAT BOX HAS NOTHING TO DO WITH WHAT'S HAPPENING TO SUPERMAN!
ENOUGH!
DIANA?!

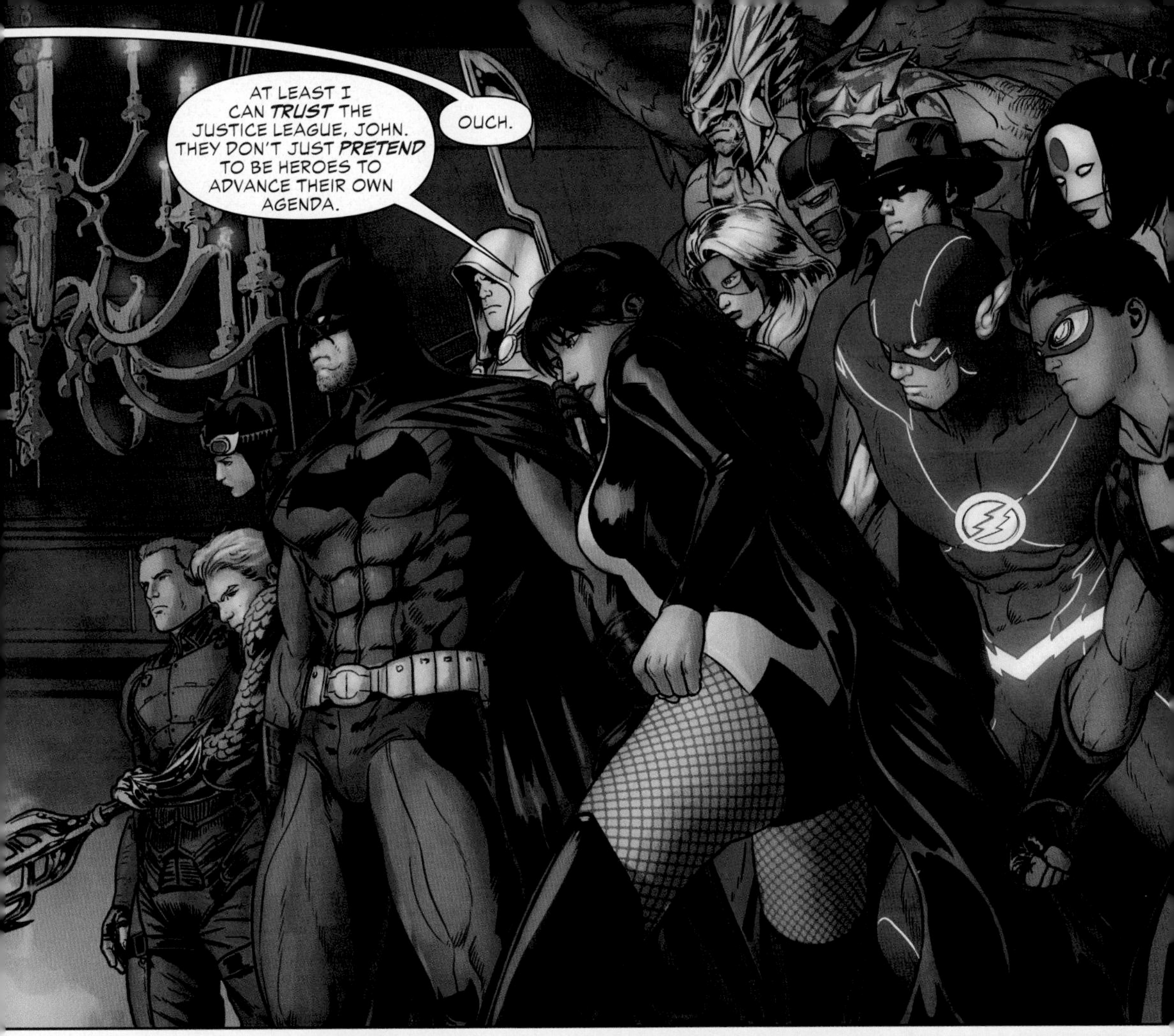
AT LEAST I CAN TRUST THE JUSTICE LEAGUE, JOHN. THEY DON'T JUST PRETEND TO BE HEROES TO ADVANCE THEIR OWN AGENDA.
OUCH.

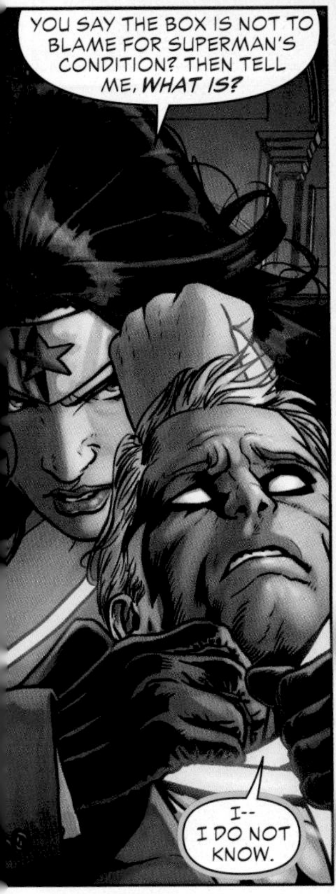
YOU SAY THE BOX IS NOT TO BLAME FOR SUPERMAN'S CONDITION? THEN TELL ME, WHAT IS?
I-- I DO NOT KNOW.

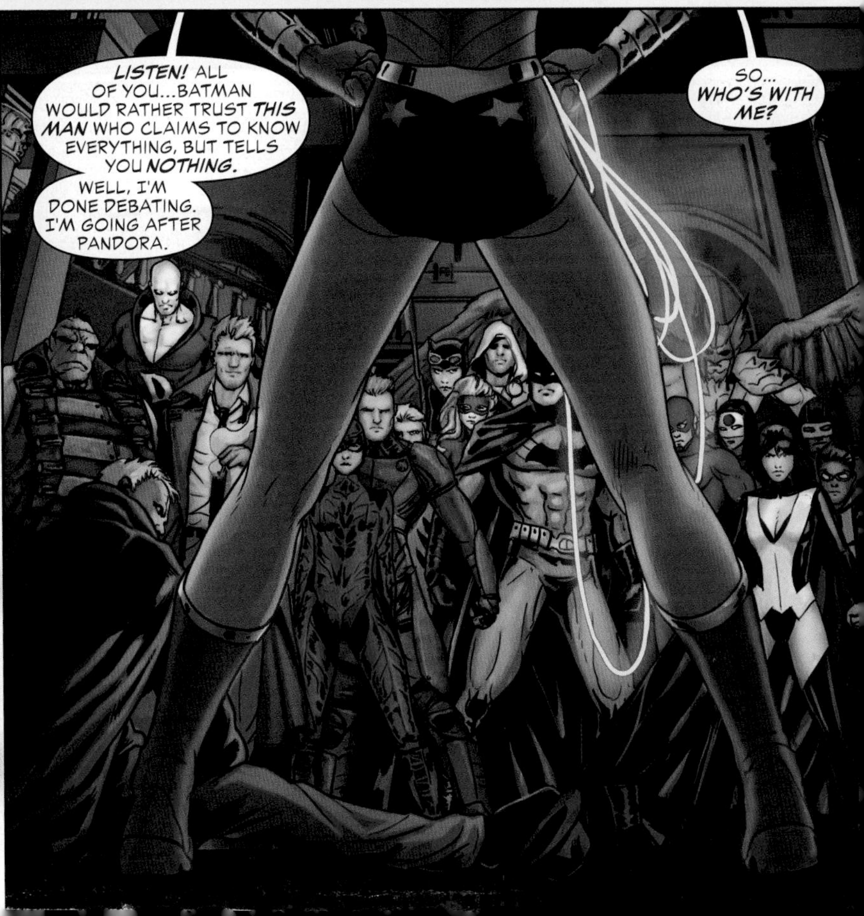
LISTEN! ALL OF YOU...BATMAN WOULD RATHER TRUST THIS MAN WHO CLAIMS TO KNOW EVERYTHING, BUT TELLS YOU NOTHING.
WELL, I'M DONE DEBATING. I'M GOING AFTER PANDORA.
SO... WHO'S WITH ME?

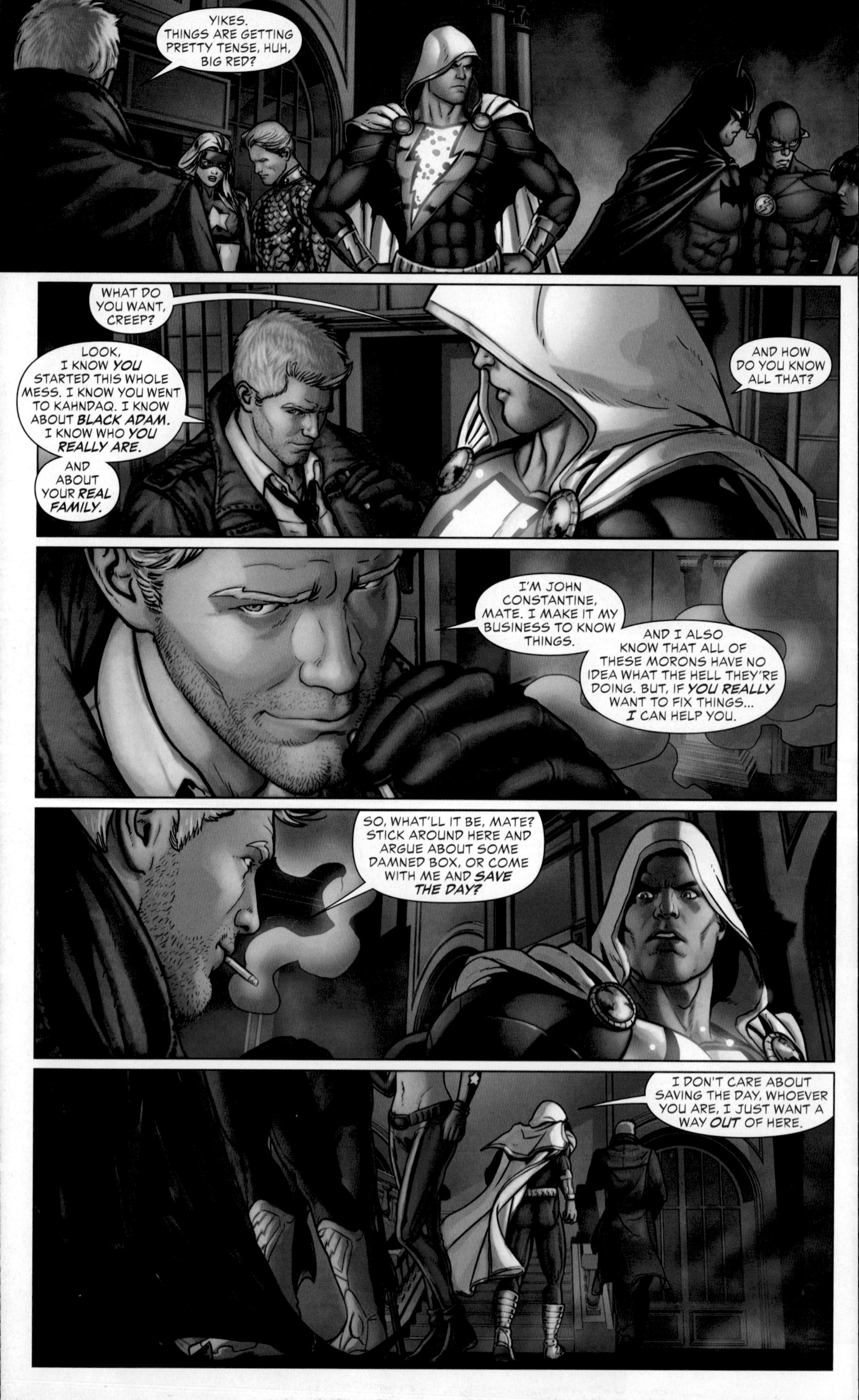
YIKES. THINGS ARE GETTING PRETTY TENSE, HUH, BIG RED?
WHAT DO YOU WANT, CREEP?
LOOK, I KNOW *YOU* STARTED THIS WHOLE MESS. I KNOW YOU WENT TO KAHNDAQ. I KNOW ABOUT *BLACK ADAM*. I KNOW WHO *YOU REALLY ARE*.
AND ABOUT YOUR *REAL FAMILY*.
AND HOW DO YOU KNOW ALL THAT?
I'M JOHN CONSTANTINE, MATE. I MAKE IT MY BUSINESS TO KNOW THINGS.
AND I ALSO KNOW THAT ALL OF THESE MORONS HAVE NO IDEA WHAT THE HELL THEY'RE DOING. BUT, IF *YOU REALLY* WANT TO FIX THINGS... *I* CAN HELP YOU.
SO, WHAT'LL IT BE, MATE? STICK AROUND HERE AND ARGUE ABOUT SOME DAMNED BOX, OR COME WITH ME AND *SAVE THE DAY?*
I DON'T CARE ABOUT SAVING THE DAY, WHOEVER YOU ARE, I JUST WANT A WAY *OUT* OF HERE.

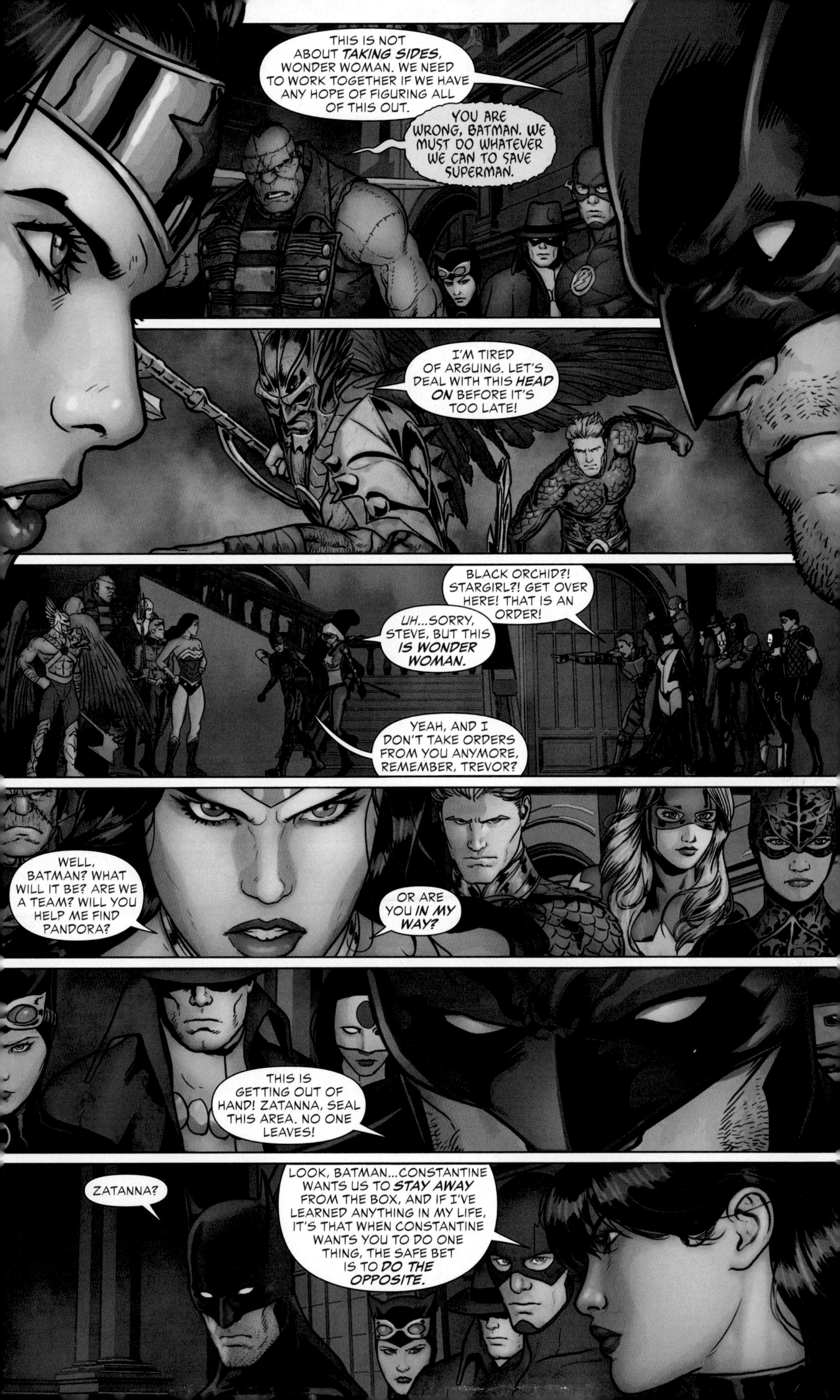

THIS IS NOT ABOUT TAKING SIDES, WONDER WOMAN. WE NEED TO WORK TOGETHER IF WE HAVE ANY HOPE OF FIGURING ALL OF THIS OUT.
YOU ARE WRONG, BATMAN. WE MUST DO WHATEVER WE CAN TO SAVE SUPERMAN.
I'M TIRED OF ARGUING. LET'S DEAL WITH THIS HEAD ON BEFORE IT'S TOO LATE!
BLACK ORCHID?! STARGIRL?! GET OVER HERE! THAT IS AN ORDER!
UH...SORRY, STEVE, BUT THIS IS WONDER WOMAN.
YEAH, AND I DON'T TAKE ORDERS FROM YOU ANYMORE, REMEMBER, TREVOR?
WELL, BATMAN? WHAT WILL IT BE? ARE WE A TEAM? WILL YOU HELP ME FIND PANDORA?
OR ARE YOU IN MY WAY?
THIS IS GETTING OUT OF HAND! ZATANNA, SEAL THIS AREA. NO ONE LEAVES!
ZATANNA?
LOOK, BATMAN...CONSTANTINE WANTS US TO STAY AWAY FROM THE BOX, AND IF I'VE LEARNED ANYTHING IN MY LIFE, IT'S THAT WHEN CONSTANTINE WANTS YOU TO DO ONE THING, THE SAFE BET IS TO DO THE OPPOSITE.

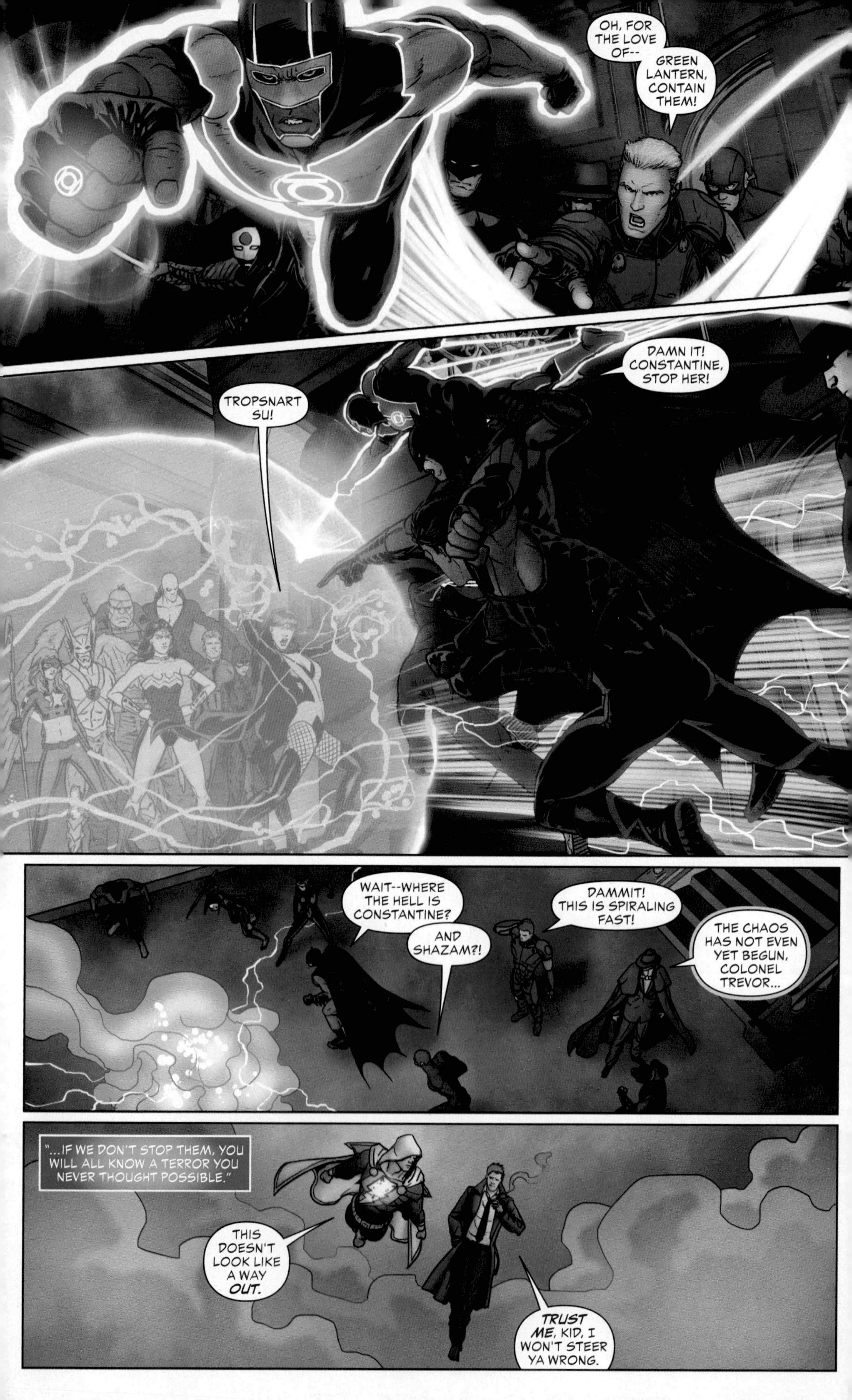
OH, FOR THE LOVE OF--
GREEN LANTERN, CONTAIN THEM!
DAMN IT! CONSTANTINE, STOP HER!
TROPSNART SU!
WAIT--WHERE THE HELL IS CONSTANTINE?
AND SHAZAM?!
DAMMIT! THIS IS SPIRALING FAST!
THE CHAOS HAS NOT EVEN YET BEGUN, COLONEL TREVOR...
"...IF WE DON'T STOP THEM, YOU WILL ALL KNOW A TERROR YOU NEVER THOUGHT POSSIBLE."
THIS DOESN'T LOOK LIKE A WAY *OUT*.
TRUST ME, KID, I WON'T STEER YA WRONG.

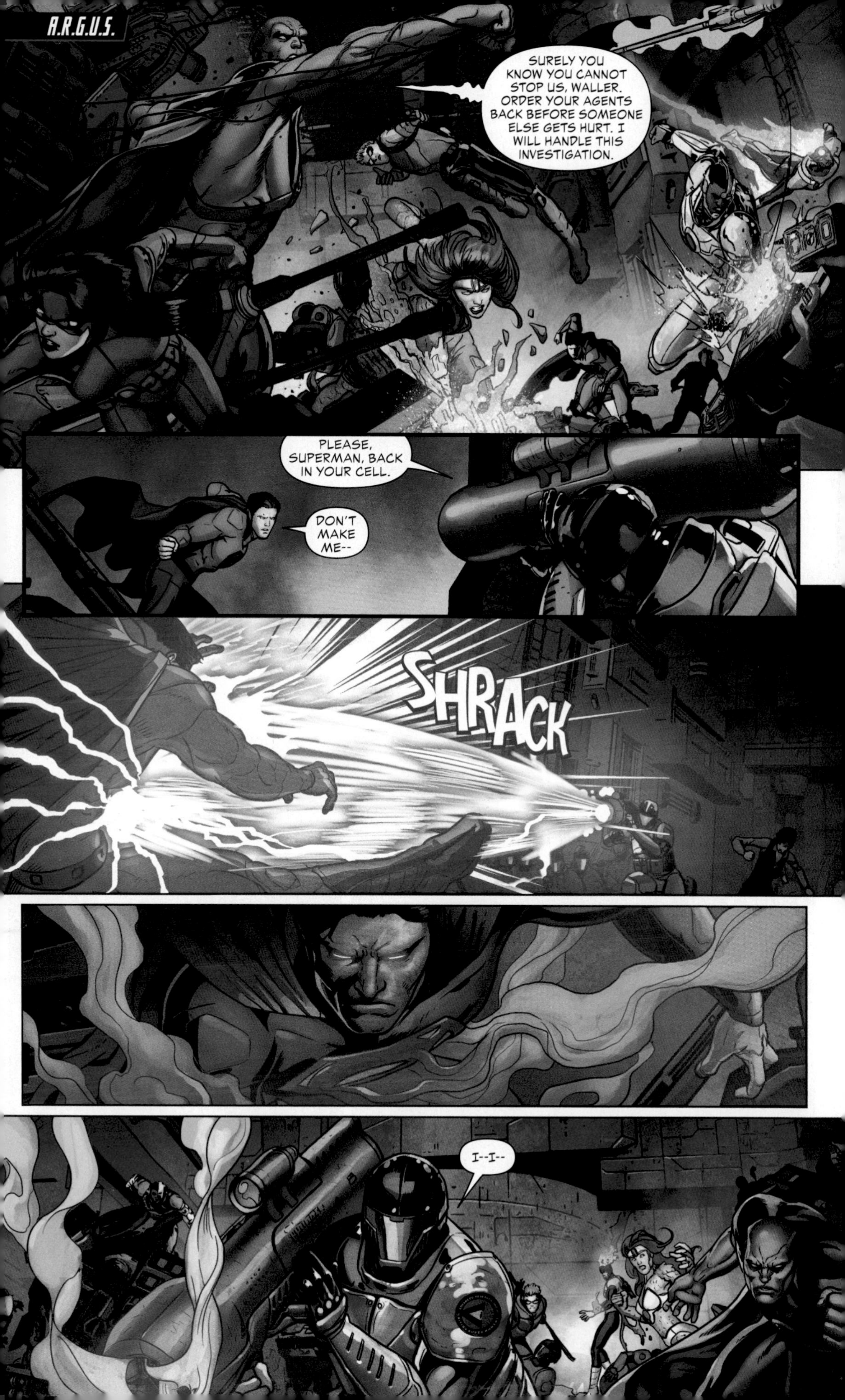
A.R.G.U.S.
SURELY YOU KNOW YOU CANNOT STOP US, WALLER. ORDER YOUR AGENTS BACK BEFORE SOMEONE ELSE GETS HURT. I WILL HANDLE THIS INVESTIGATION.
PLEASE, SUPERMAN, BACK IN YOUR CELL.
DON'T MAKE ME--
SHRACK
I--I--

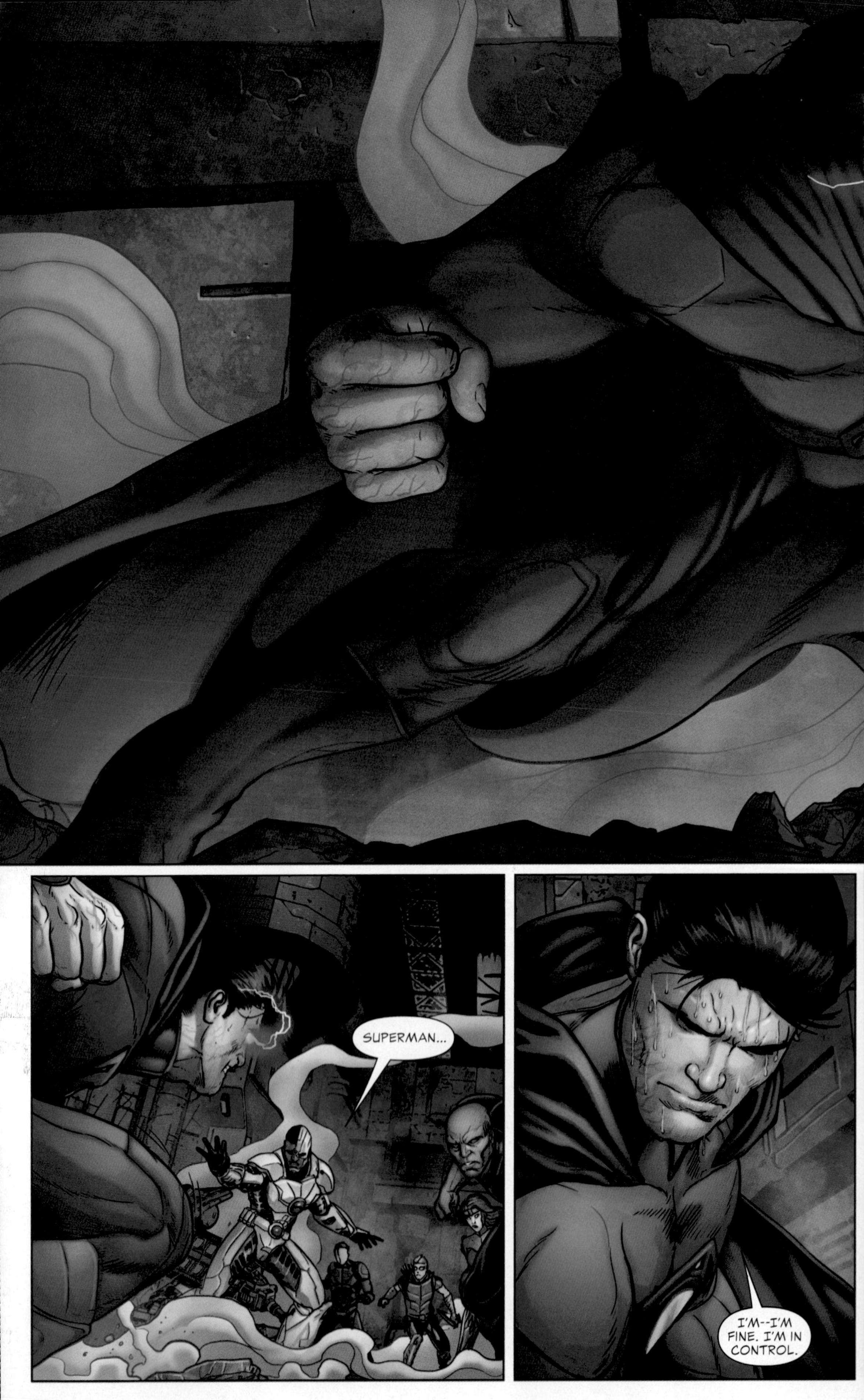
SUPERMAN...
I'M--I'M FINE. I'M IN CONTROL.

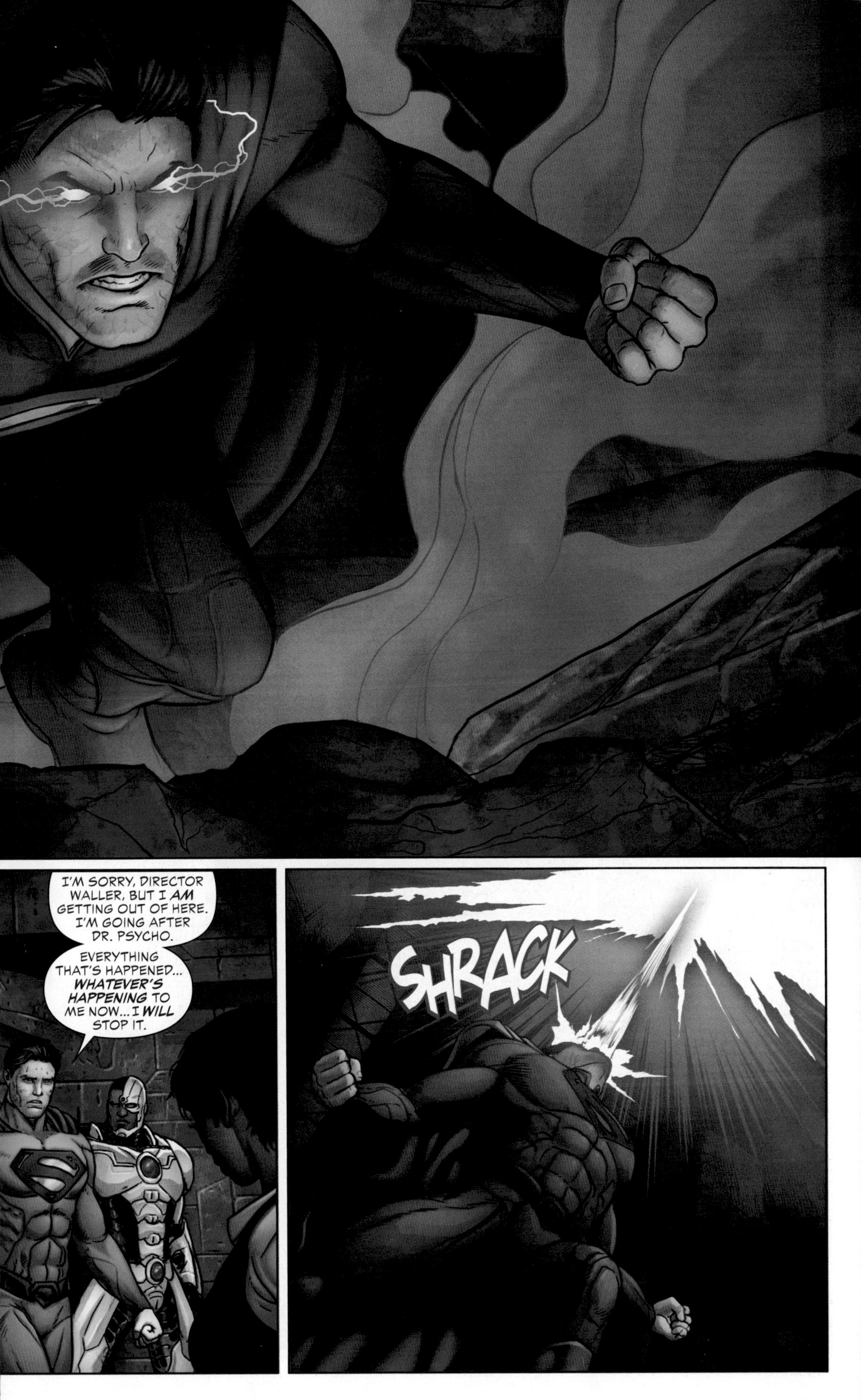
I'M SORRY, DIRECTOR WALLER, BUT I *AM* GETTING OUT OF HERE. I'M GOING AFTER DR. PSYCHO.
EVERYTHING THAT'S HAPPENED... ***WHATEVER'S HAPPENING*** TO ME NOW... I ***WILL*** STOP IT.
SHRACK

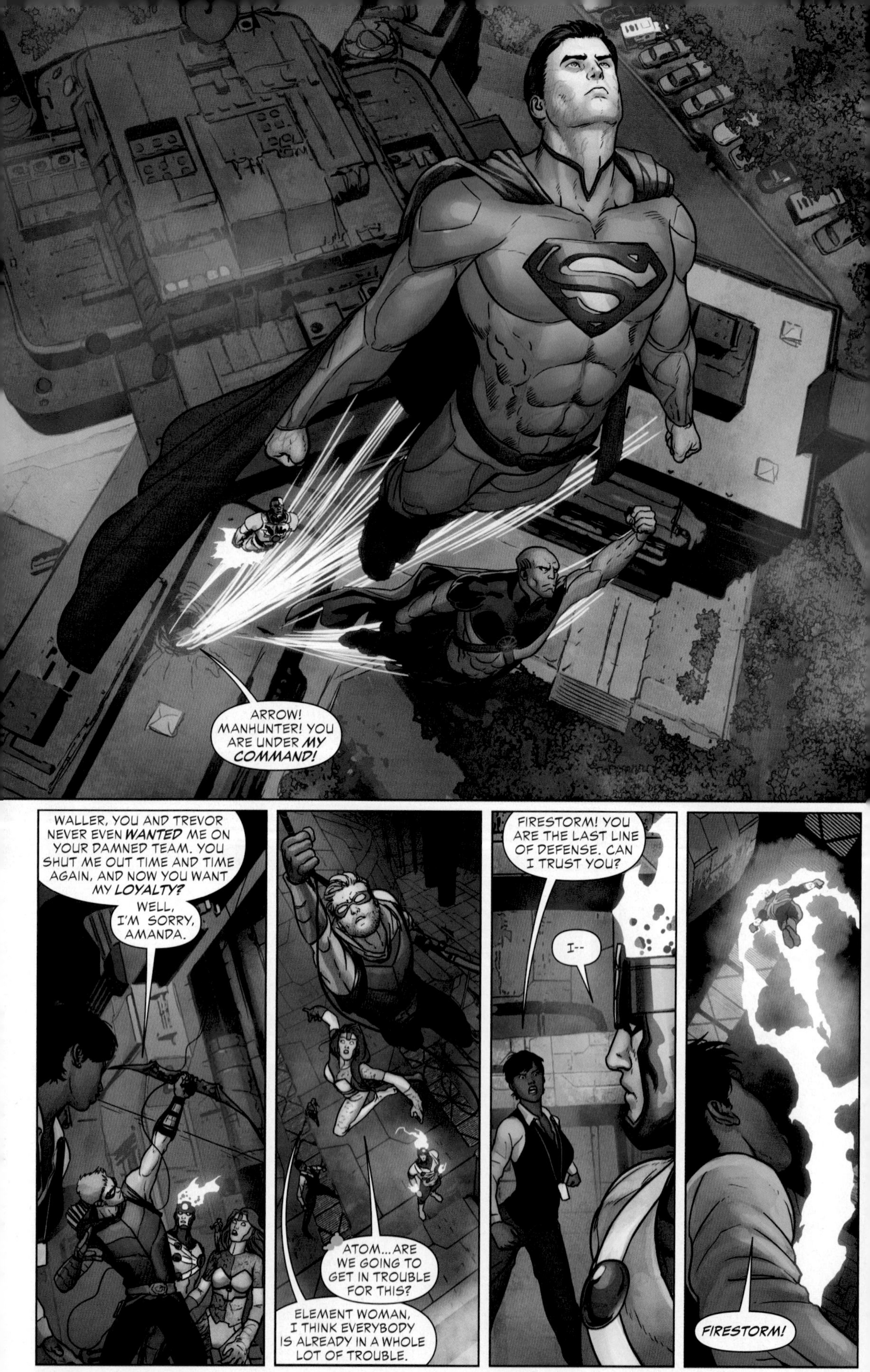
ARROW! MANHUNTER! YOU ARE UNDER MY COMMAND!
WALLER, YOU AND TREVOR NEVER EVEN WANTED ME ON YOUR DAMNED TEAM. YOU SHUT ME OUT TIME AND TIME AGAIN, AND NOW YOU WANT MY LOYALTY?
WELL, I'M SORRY, AMANDA.
ATOM...ARE WE GOING TO GET IN TROUBLE FOR THIS?
ELEMENT WOMAN, I THINK EVERYBODY IS ALREADY IN A WHOLE LOT OF TROUBLE.
FIRESTORM! YOU ARE THE LAST LINE OF DEFENSE. CAN I TRUST YOU?
I--
FIRESTORM!

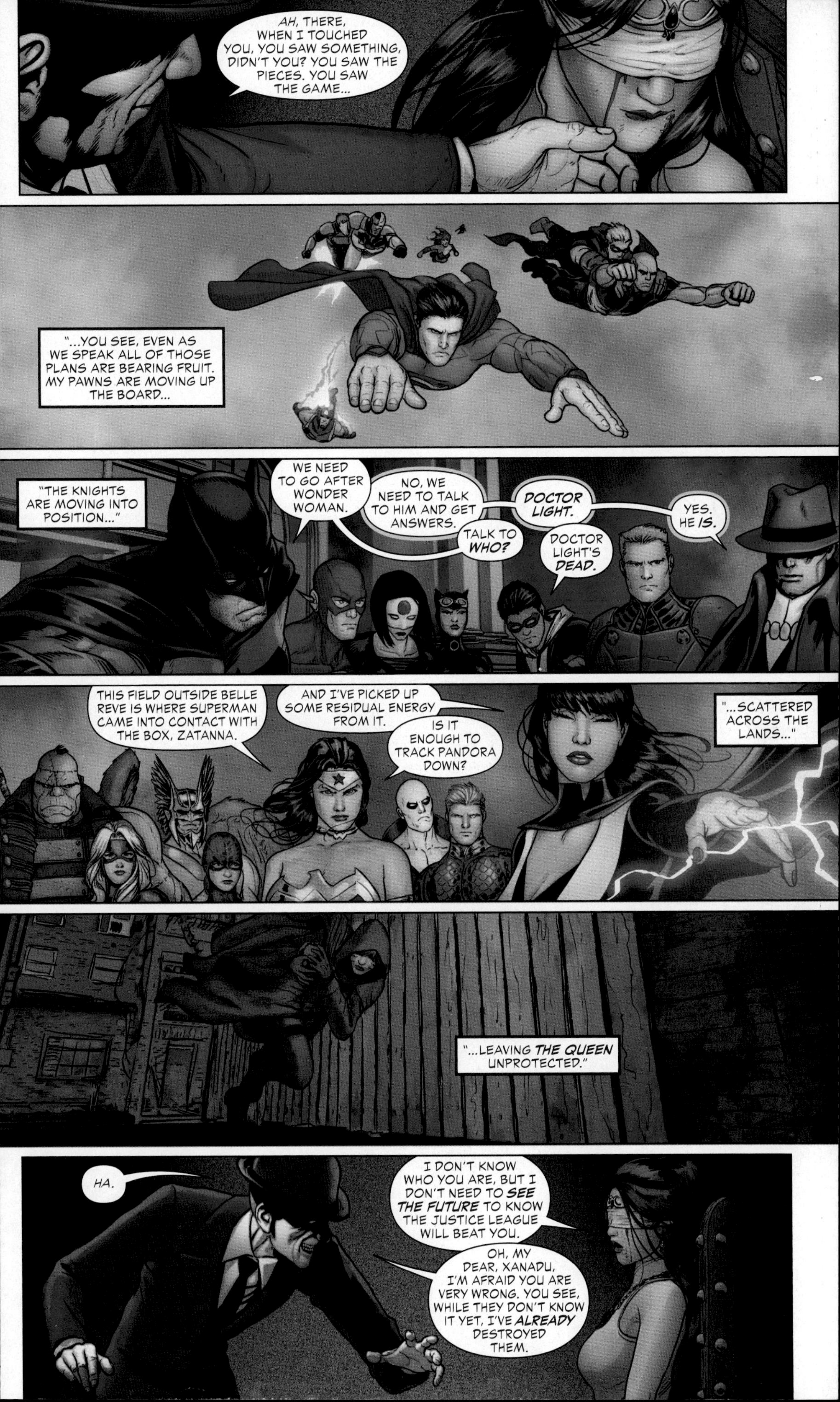
AH, THERE, WHEN I TOUCHED YOU, YOU SAW SOMETHING, DIDN'T YOU? YOU SAW THE PIECES. YOU SAW THE GAME...
"...YOU SEE, EVEN AS WE SPEAK ALL OF THOSE PLANS ARE BEARING FRUIT. MY PAWNS ARE MOVING UP THE BOARD...
"THE KNIGHTS ARE MOVING INTO POSITION..."
WE NEED TO GO AFTER WONDER WOMAN.
NO, WE NEED TO TALK TO HIM AND GET ANSWERS.
TALK TO WHO?
DOCTOR LIGHT.
DOCTOR LIGHT'S DEAD.
YES. HE IS.
THIS FIELD OUTSIDE BELLE REVE IS WHERE SUPERMAN CAME INTO CONTACT WITH THE BOX, ZATANNA.
AND I'VE PICKED UP SOME RESIDUAL ENERGY FROM IT.
IS IT ENOUGH TO TRACK PANDORA DOWN?
"...SCATTERED ACROSS THE LANDS..."
"...LEAVING THE QUEEN UNPROTECTED."
HA.
I DON'T KNOW WHO YOU ARE, BUT I DON'T NEED TO SEE THE FUTURE TO KNOW THE JUSTICE LEAGUE WILL BEAT YOU.
OH, MY DEAR, XANADU, I'M AFRAID YOU ARE VERY WRONG. YOU SEE, WHILE THEY DON'T KNOW IT YET, I'VE ALREADY DESTROYED THEM.

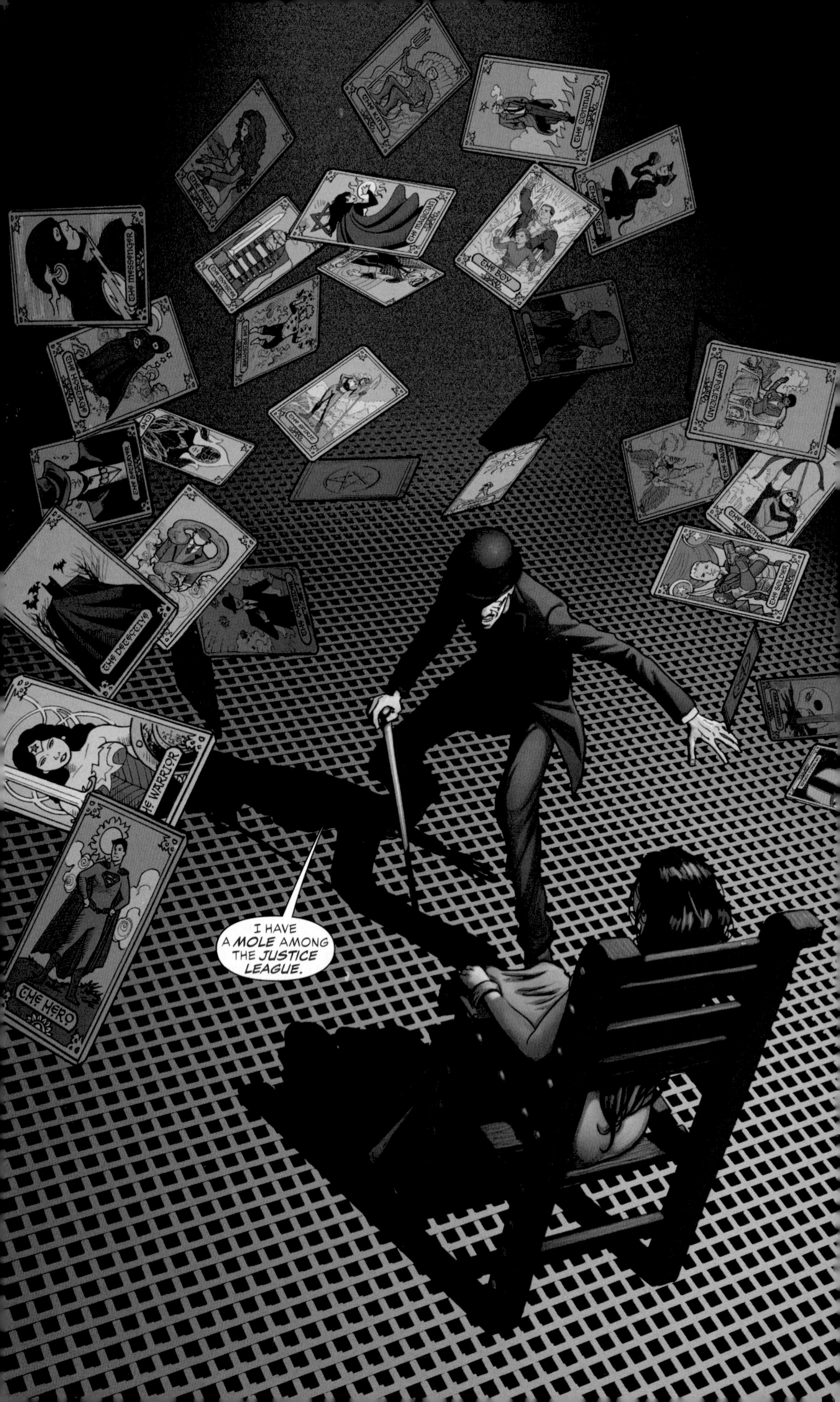
THE KING
THE CONMAN
THE MAGICIAN
THE MESSENGER
THE BOY
THE HOSTAGE
THE POLITICIAN
THE BETRAYER
THE SOLDIER
THE DETECTIVE
THE WARRIOR
THE HERO
I HAVE A MOLE AMONG THE JUSTICE LEAGUE.

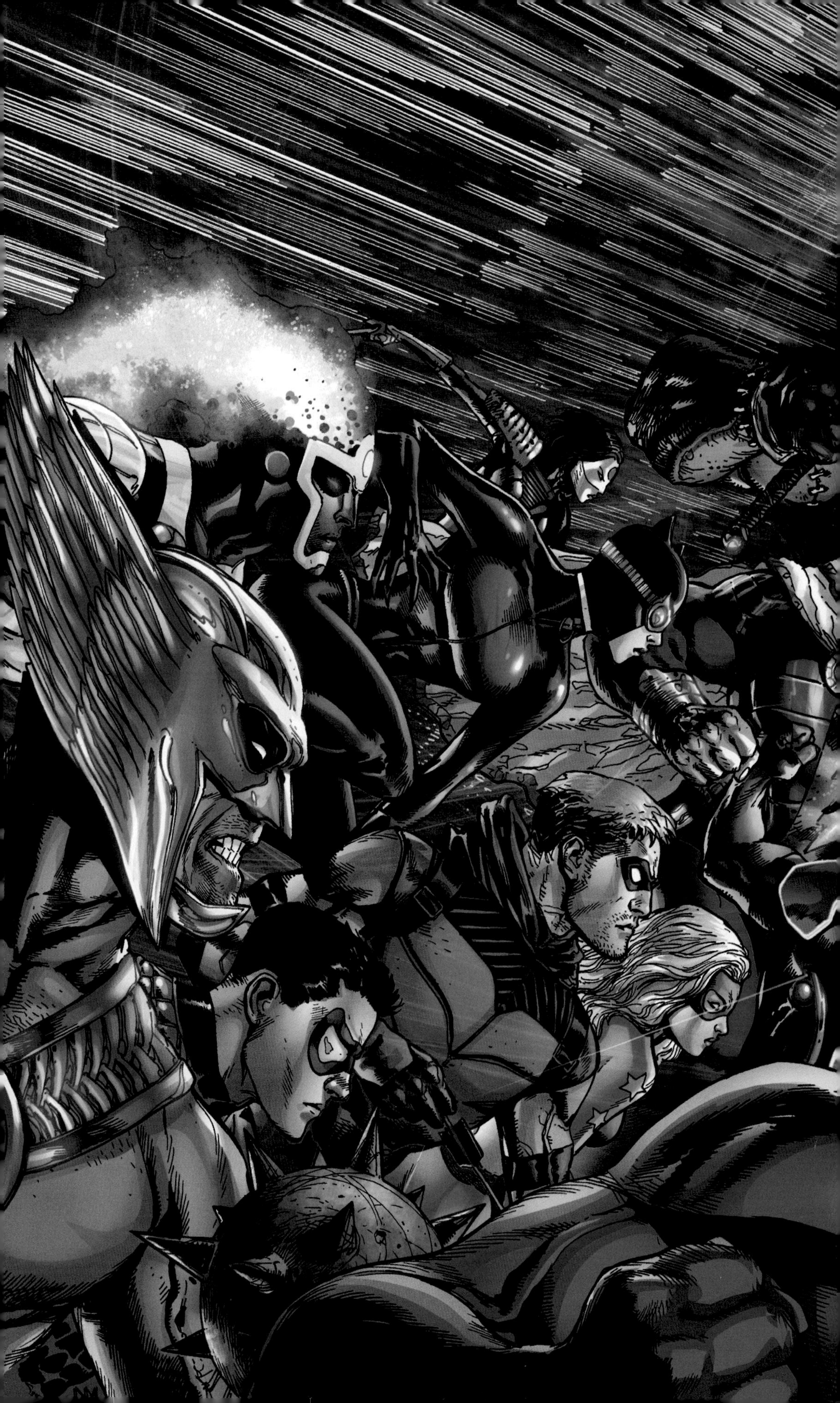

JEFF LEMIRE
writer

MIKEL JANIN
artist

DOUG MAHNKE & ALEX SINCLAIR
cover artists

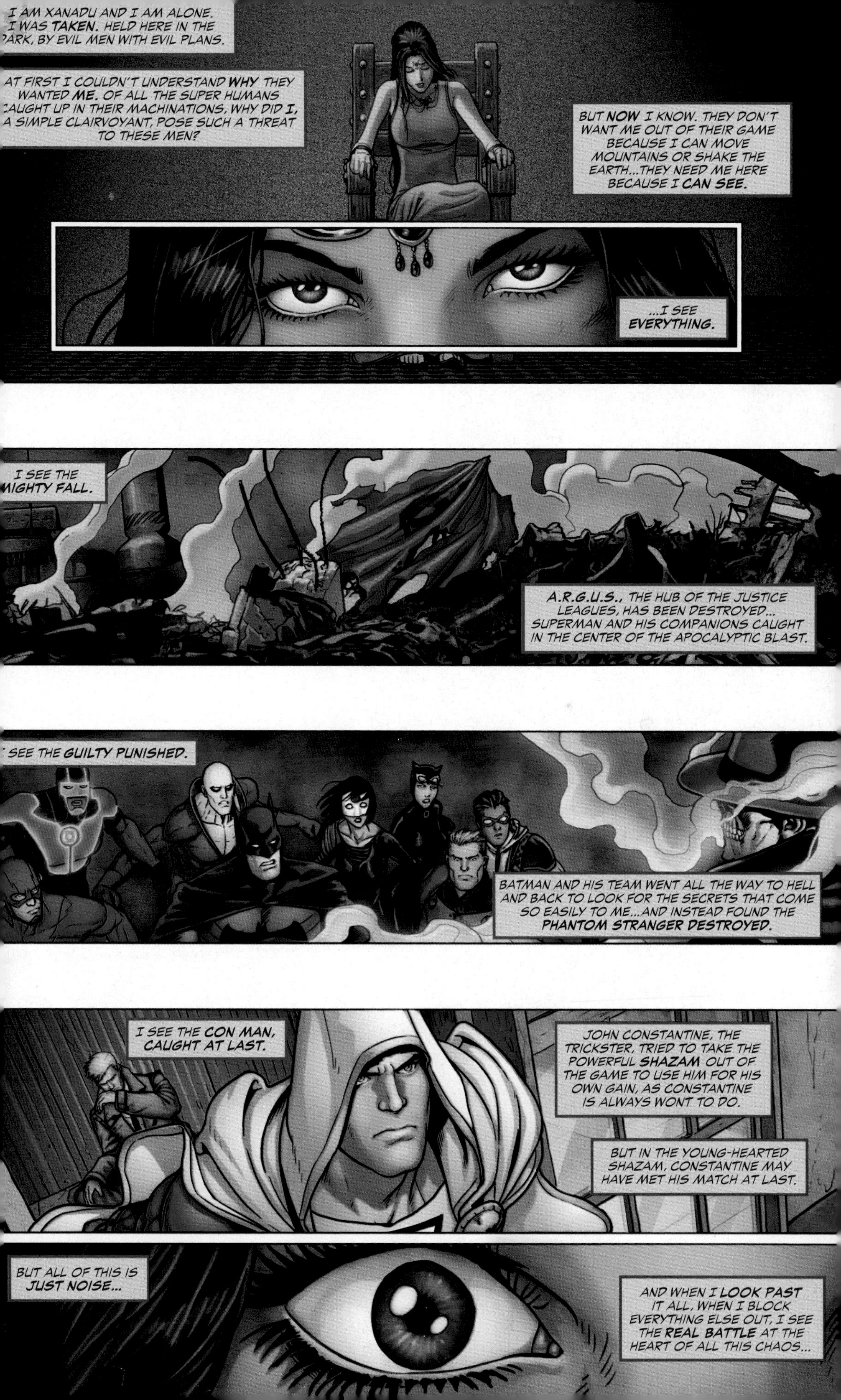

I AM XANADU AND I AM ALONE. I WAS TAKEN. HELD HERE IN THE DARK, BY EVIL MEN WITH EVIL PLANS.
AT FIRST I COULDN'T UNDERSTAND WHY THEY WANTED ME. OF ALL THE SUPER HUMANS CAUGHT UP IN THEIR MACHINATIONS, WHY DID I, A SIMPLE CLAIRVOYANT, POSE SUCH A THREAT TO THESE MEN?
BUT NOW I KNOW. THEY DON'T WANT ME OUT OF THEIR GAME BECAUSE I CAN MOVE MOUNTAINS OR SHAKE THE EARTH...THEY NEED ME HERE BECAUSE I CAN SEE.
...I SEE EVERYTHING.
I SEE THE MIGHTY FALL.
A.R.G.U.S., THE HUB OF THE JUSTICE LEAGUES, HAS BEEN DESTROYED... SUPERMAN AND HIS COMPANIONS CAUGHT IN THE CENTER OF THE APOCALYPTIC BLAST.
I SEE THE GUILTY PUNISHED.
BATMAN AND HIS TEAM WENT ALL THE WAY TO HELL AND BACK TO LOOK FOR THE SECRETS THAT COME SO EASILY TO ME...AND INSTEAD FOUND THE PHANTOM STRANGER DESTROYED.
I SEE THE CON MAN, CAUGHT AT LAST.
JOHN CONSTANTINE, THE TRICKSTER, TRIED TO TAKE THE POWERFUL SHAZAM OUT OF THE GAME TO USE HIM FOR HIS OWN GAIN, AS CONSTANTINE IS ALWAYS WONT TO DO.
BUT IN THE YOUNG-HEARTED SHAZAM, CONSTANTINE MAY HAVE MET HIS MATCH AT LAST.
BUT ALL OF THIS IS JUST NOISE...
AND WHEN I LOOK PAST IT ALL, WHEN I BLOCK EVERYTHING ELSE OUT, I SEE THE REAL BATTLE AT THE HEART OF ALL THIS CHAOS...

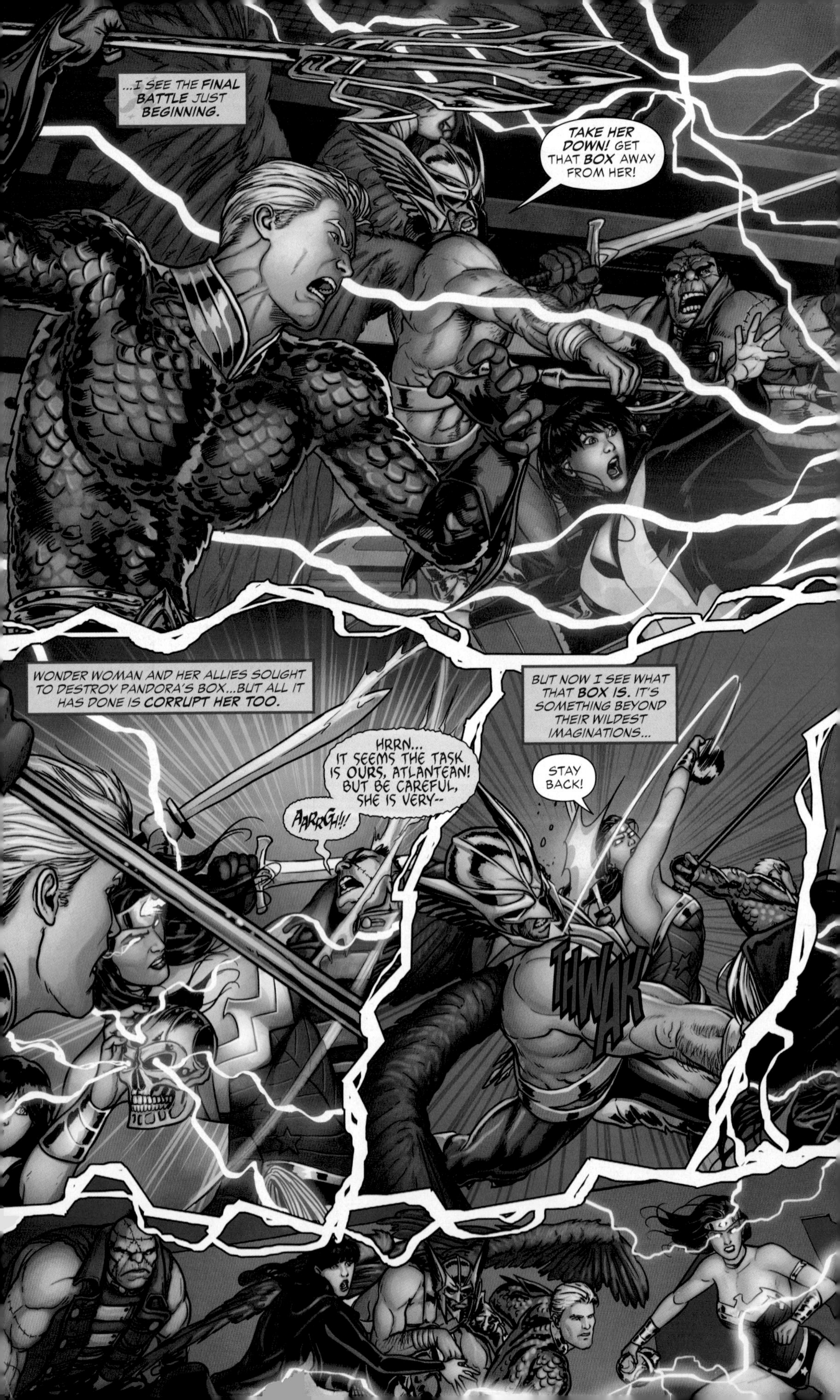
...I SEE THE FINAL BATTLE JUST BEGINNING.
TAKE HER DOWN! GET THAT BOX AWAY FROM HER!
WONDER WOMAN AND HER ALLIES SOUGHT TO DESTROY PANDORA'S BOX...BUT ALL IT HAS DONE IS CORRUPT HER TOO.
HRRN... IT SEEMS THE TASK IS OURS, ATLANTEAN! BUT BE CAREFUL, SHE IS VERY--
AARRGH!!!
BUT NOW I SEE WHAT THAT BOX IS. IT'S SOMETHING BEYOND THEIR WILDEST IMAGINATIONS...
STAY BACK!
THWAK

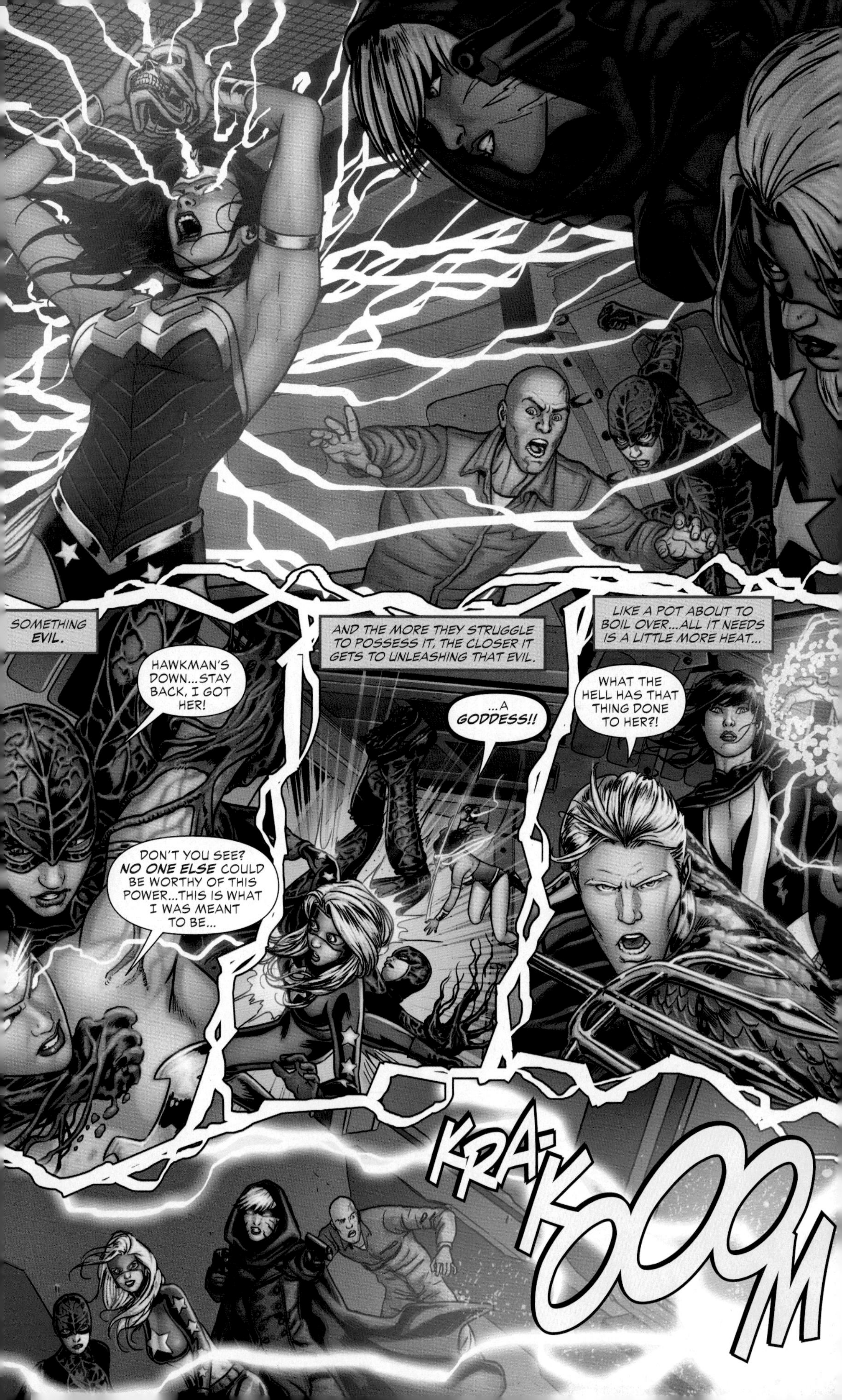
SOMETHING EVIL.
HAWKMAN'S DOWN...STAY BACK, I GOT HER!
DON'T YOU SEE? NO ONE ELSE COULD BE WORTHY OF THIS POWER...THIS IS WHAT I WAS MEANT TO BE...
AND THE MORE THEY STRUGGLE TO POSSESS IT, THE CLOSER IT GETS TO UNLEASHING THAT EVIL.
...A GODDESS!!
LIKE A POT ABOUT TO BOIL OVER...ALL IT NEEDS IS A LITTLE MORE HEAT...
WHAT THE HELL HAS THAT THING DONE TO HER?!
KRA-KOOOM

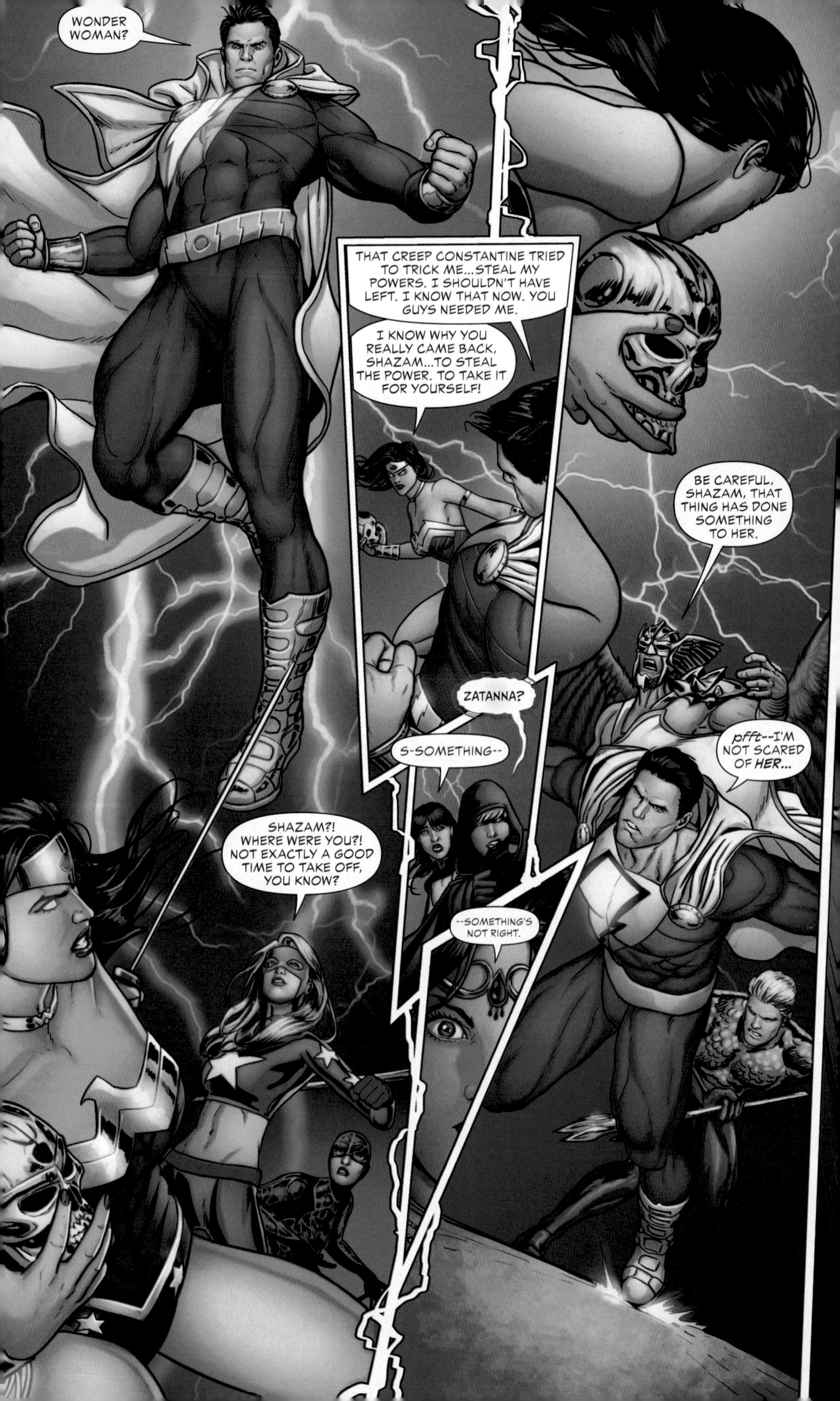
WONDER WOMAN?
THAT CREEP CONSTANTINE TRIED TO TRICK ME...STEAL MY POWERS. I SHOULDN'T HAVE LEFT. I KNOW THAT NOW. YOU GUYS NEEDED ME.
I KNOW WHY YOU REALLY CAME BACK, SHAZAM...TO STEAL THE POWER. TO TAKE IT FOR YOURSELF!
BE CAREFUL, SHAZAM, THAT THING HAS DONE SOMETHING TO HER.
SHAZAM?! WHERE WERE YOU?! NOT EXACTLY A GOOD TIME TO TAKE OFF, YOU KNOW?
ZATANNA?
S-SOMETHING--
--SOMETHING'S NOT RIGHT.
pfft--I'M NOT SCARED OF HER...

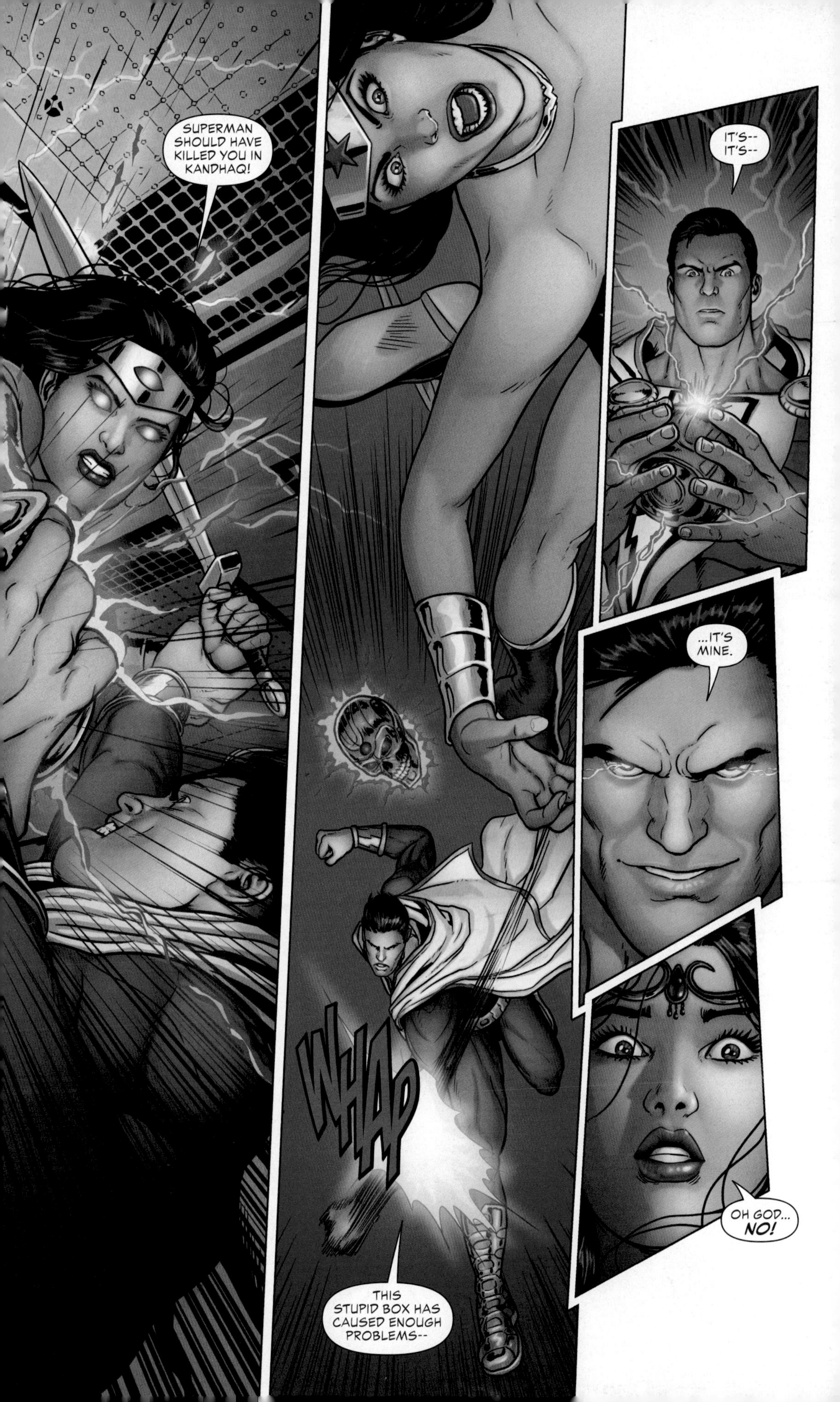
SUPERMAN SHOULD HAVE KILLED YOU IN KANDHAQ!
WHAP
THIS STUPID BOX HAS CAUSED ENOUGH PROBLEMS--
IT'S-- IT'S--
...IT'S MINE.
OH GOD... NO!

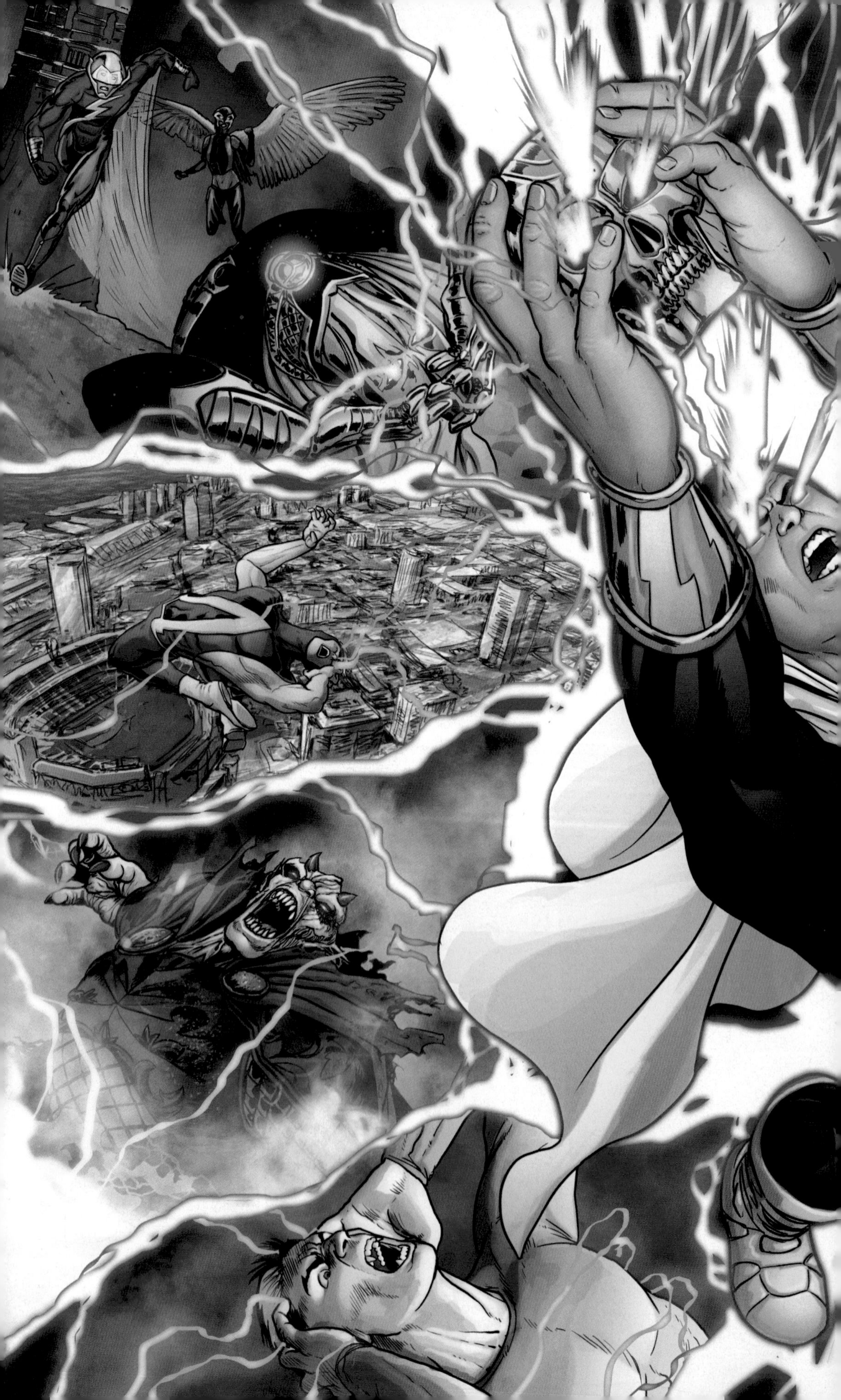

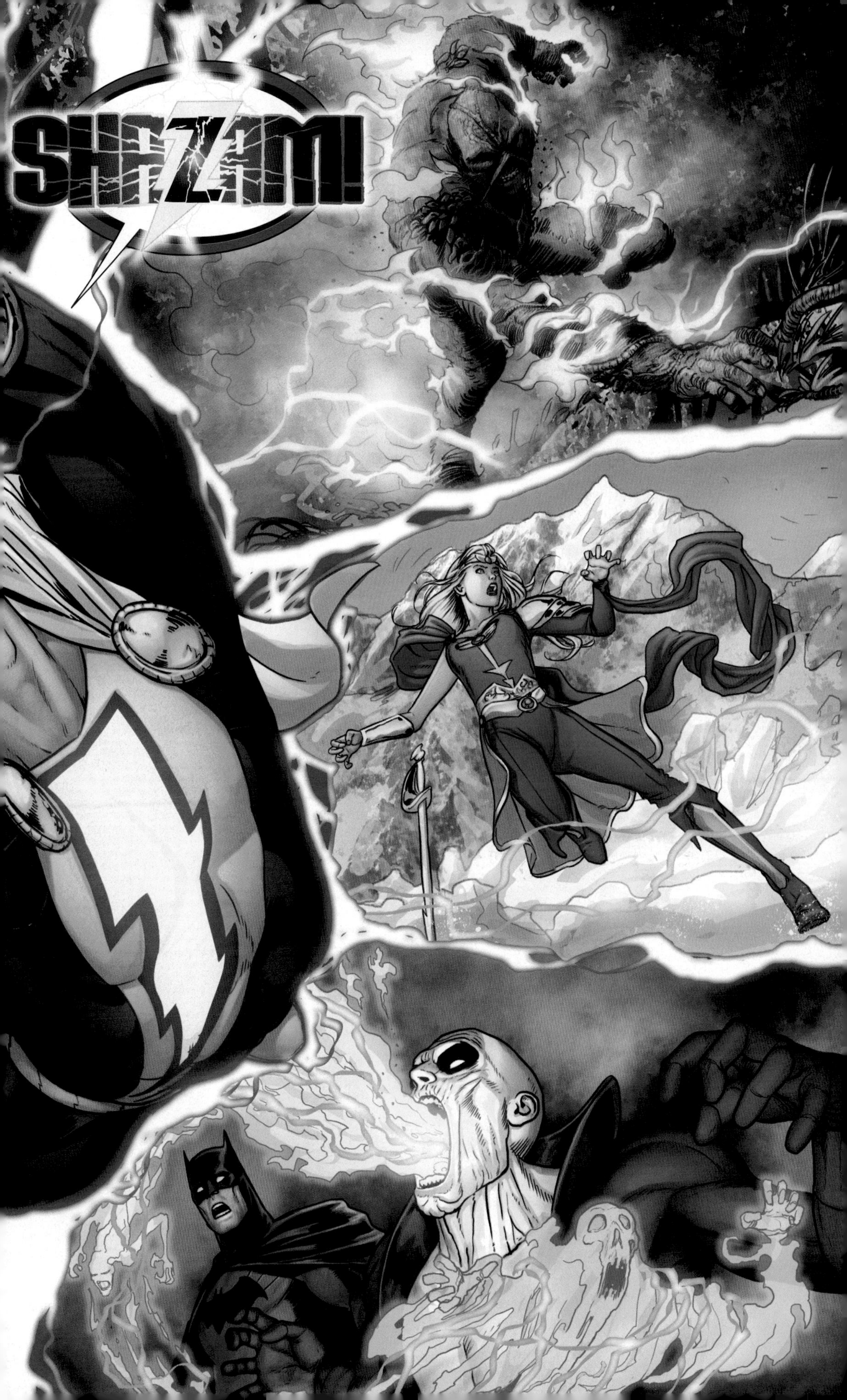
SHAZAM!

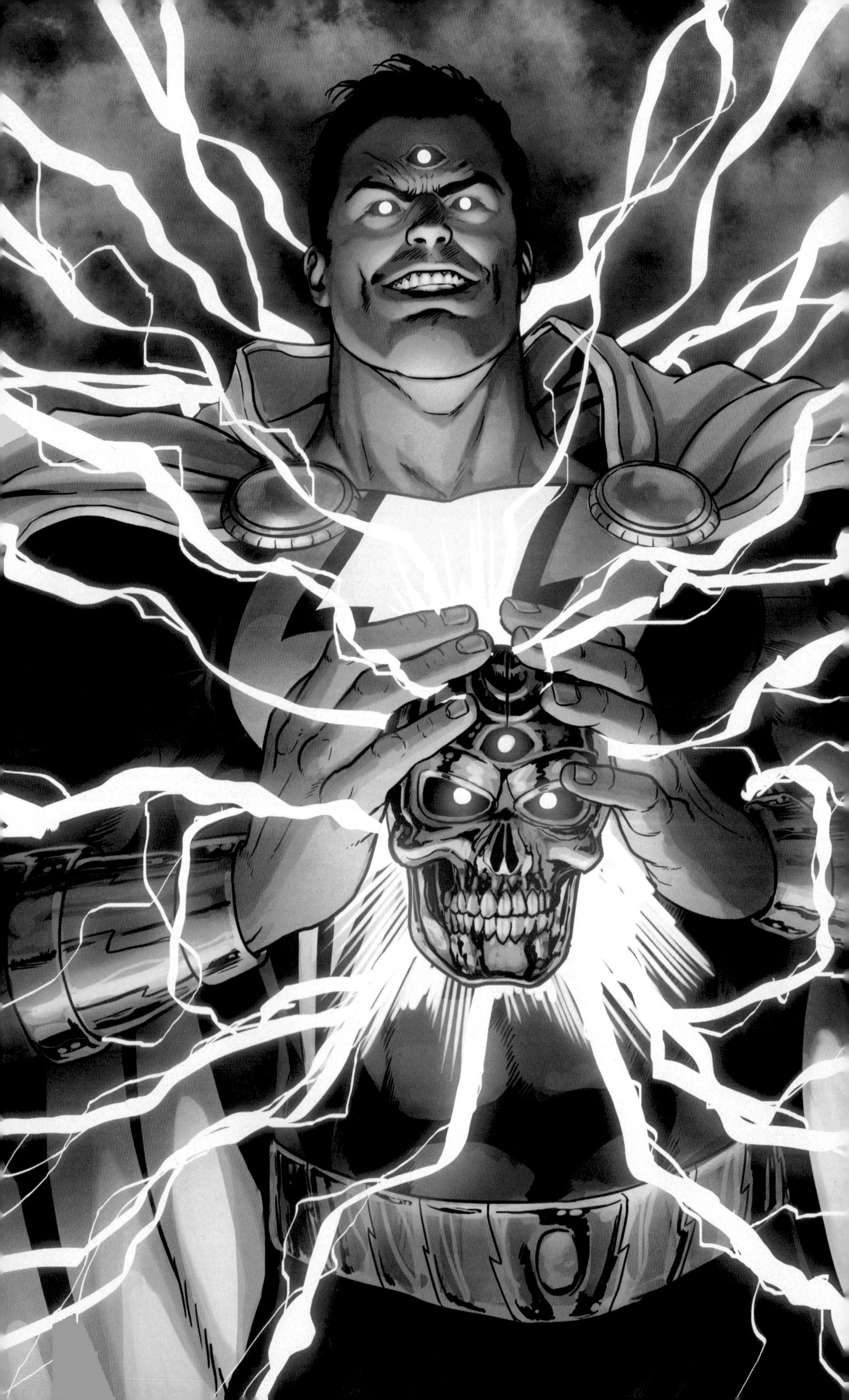

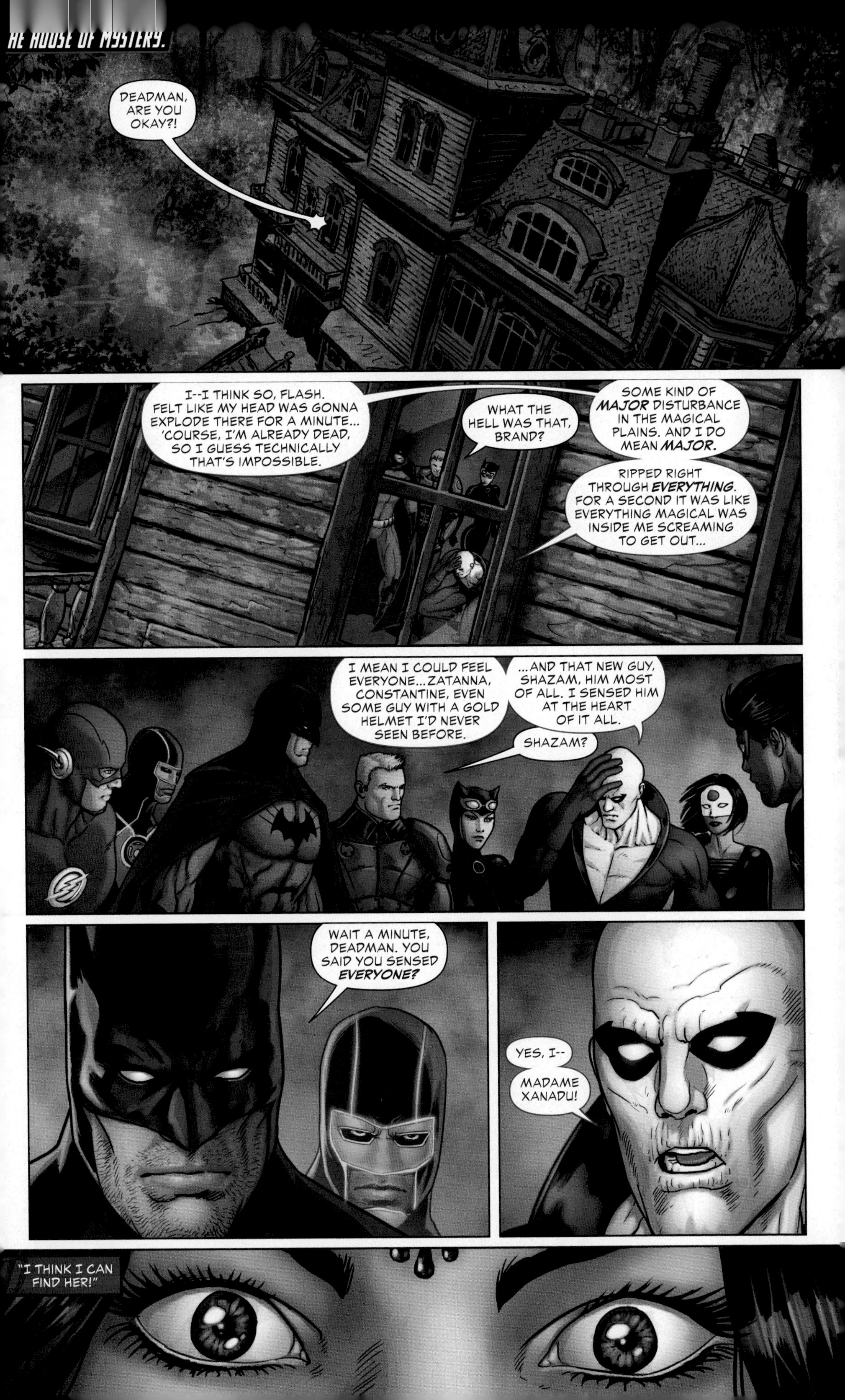
HE HOUSE OF MYSTERY.
DEADMAN, ARE YOU OKAY?!
I--I THINK SO, FLASH. FELT LIKE MY HEAD WAS GONNA EXPLODE THERE FOR A MINUTE... 'COURSE, I'M ALREADY DEAD, SO I GUESS TECHNICALLY THAT'S IMPOSSIBLE.
WHAT THE HELL WAS THAT, BRAND?
SOME KIND OF MAJOR DISTURBANCE IN THE MAGICAL PLAINS. AND I DO MEAN MAJOR.
RIPPED RIGHT THROUGH EVERYTHING. FOR A SECOND IT WAS LIKE EVERYTHING MAGICAL WAS INSIDE ME SCREAMING TO GET OUT...
I MEAN I COULD FEEL EVERYONE... ZATANNA, CONSTANTINE, EVEN SOME GUY WITH A GOLD HELMET I'D NEVER SEEN BEFORE.
...AND THAT NEW GUY, SHAZAM, HIM MOST OF ALL. I SENSED HIM AT THE HEART OF IT ALL.
SHAZAM?
WAIT A MINUTE, DEADMAN. YOU SAID YOU SENSED EVERYONE?
YES, I--
MADAME XANADU!
"I THINK I CAN FIND HER!"

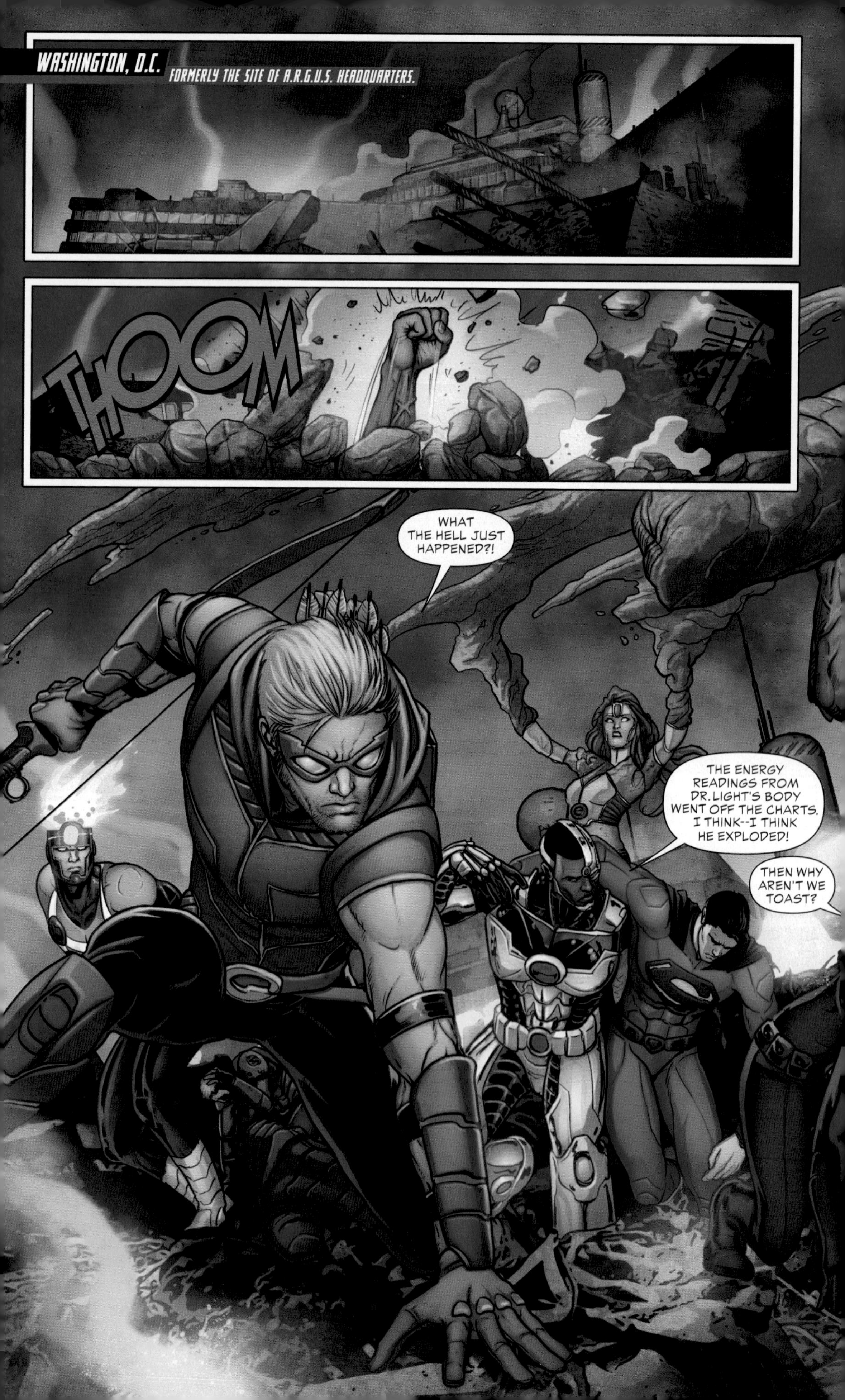
WASHINGTON, D.C.
FORMERLY THE SITE OF A.R.G.U.S. HEADQUARTERS.
THOOM
WHAT THE HELL JUST HAPPENED?!
THE ENERGY READINGS FROM DR. LIGHT'S BODY WENT OFF THE CHARTS. I THINK--I THINK HE EXPLODED!
THEN WHY AREN'T WE TOAST?

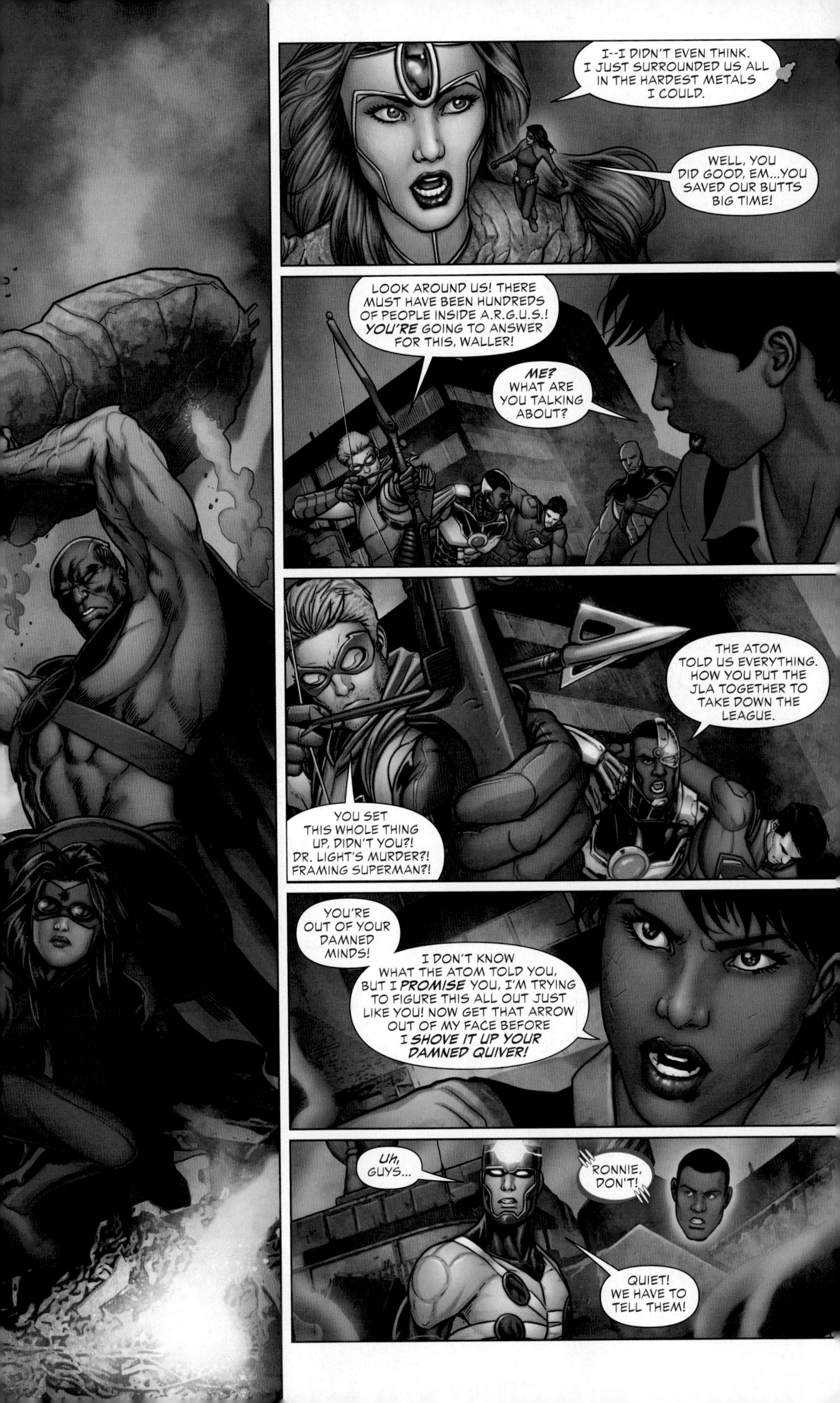
I--I DIDN'T EVEN THINK. I JUST SURROUNDED US ALL IN THE HARDEST METALS I COULD.
WELL, YOU DID GOOD, EM...YOU SAVED OUR BUTTS BIG TIME!
LOOK AROUND US! THERE MUST HAVE BEEN HUNDREDS OF PEOPLE INSIDE A.R.G.U.S.! YOU'RE GOING TO ANSWER FOR THIS, WALLER!
ME? WHAT ARE YOU TALKING ABOUT?
THE ATOM TOLD US EVERYTHING. HOW YOU PUT THE JLA TOGETHER TO TAKE DOWN THE LEAGUE.
YOU SET THIS WHOLE THING UP, DIDN'T YOU?! DR. LIGHT'S MURDER?! FRAMING SUPERMAN?!
YOU'RE OUT OF YOUR DAMNED MINDS!
I DON'T KNOW WHAT THE ATOM TOLD YOU, BUT I PROMISE YOU, I'M TRYING TO FIGURE THIS ALL OUT JUST LIKE YOU! NOW GET THAT ARROW OUT OF MY FACE BEFORE I SHOVE IT UP YOUR DAMNED QUIVER!
Uh, GUYS...
RONNIE, DON'T!
QUIET! WE HAVE TO TELL THEM!

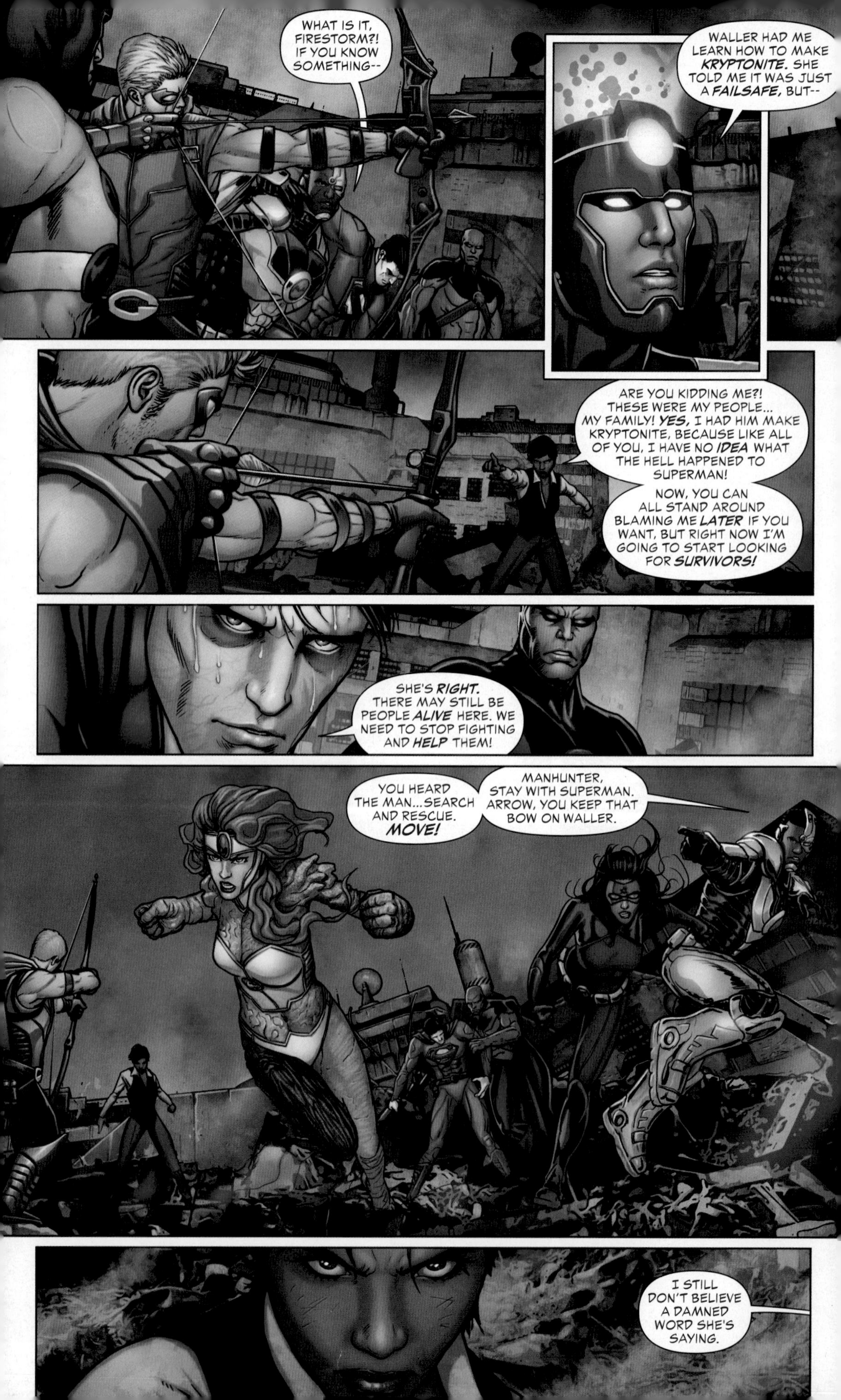

WHAT IS IT, FIRESTORM?! IF YOU KNOW SOMETHING--
WALLER HAD ME LEARN HOW TO MAKE KRYPTONITE. SHE TOLD ME IT WAS JUST A FAILSAFE, BUT--
ARE YOU KIDDING ME?! THESE WERE MY PEOPLE... MY FAMILY! YES, I HAD HIM MAKE KRYPTONITE, BECAUSE LIKE ALL OF YOU, I HAVE NO IDEA WHAT THE HELL HAPPENED TO SUPERMAN!
NOW, YOU CAN ALL STAND AROUND BLAMING ME LATER IF YOU WANT, BUT RIGHT NOW I'M GOING TO START LOOKING FOR SURVIVORS!
SHE'S RIGHT. THERE MAY STILL BE PEOPLE ALIVE HERE. WE NEED TO STOP FIGHTING AND HELP THEM!
YOU HEARD THE MAN...SEARCH AND RESCUE. MOVE!
MANHUNTER, STAY WITH SUPERMAN. ARROW, YOU KEEP THAT BOW ON WALLER.
I STILL DON'T BELIEVE A DAMNED WORD SHE'S SAYING.

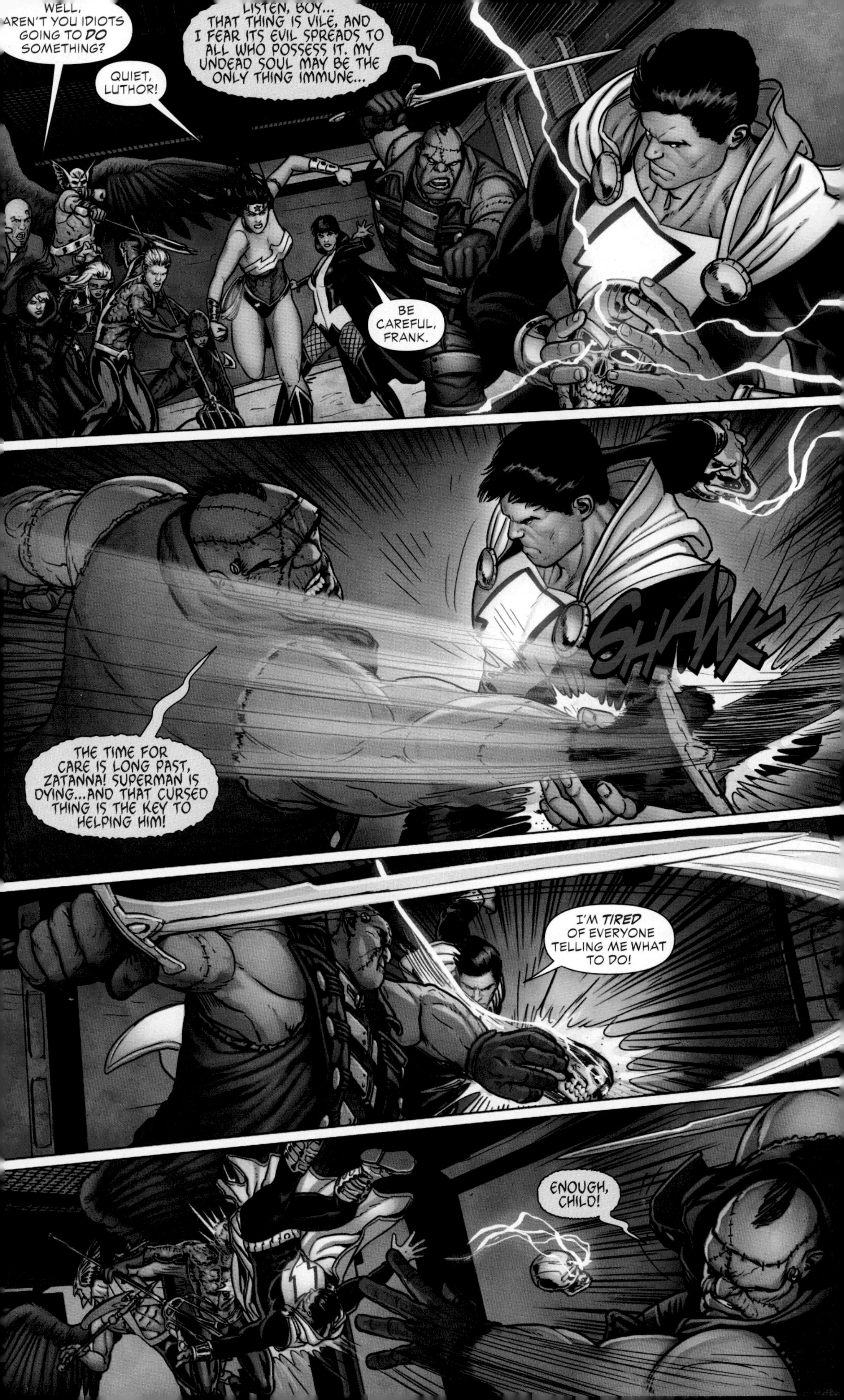

WELL, AREN'T YOU IDIOTS GOING TO DO SOMETHING?
QUIET, LUTHOR!
LISTEN, BOY... THAT THING IS VILE, AND I FEAR ITS EVIL SPREADS TO ALL WHO POSSESS IT. MY UNDEAD SOUL MAY BE THE ONLY THING IMMUNE...
BE CAREFUL, FRANK.
SHANK
THE TIME FOR CARE IS LONG PAST, ZATANNA! SUPERMAN IS DYING...AND THAT CURSED THING IS THE KEY TO HELPING HIM!
I'M TIRED OF EVERYONE TELLING ME WHAT TO DO!
ENOUGH, CHILD!

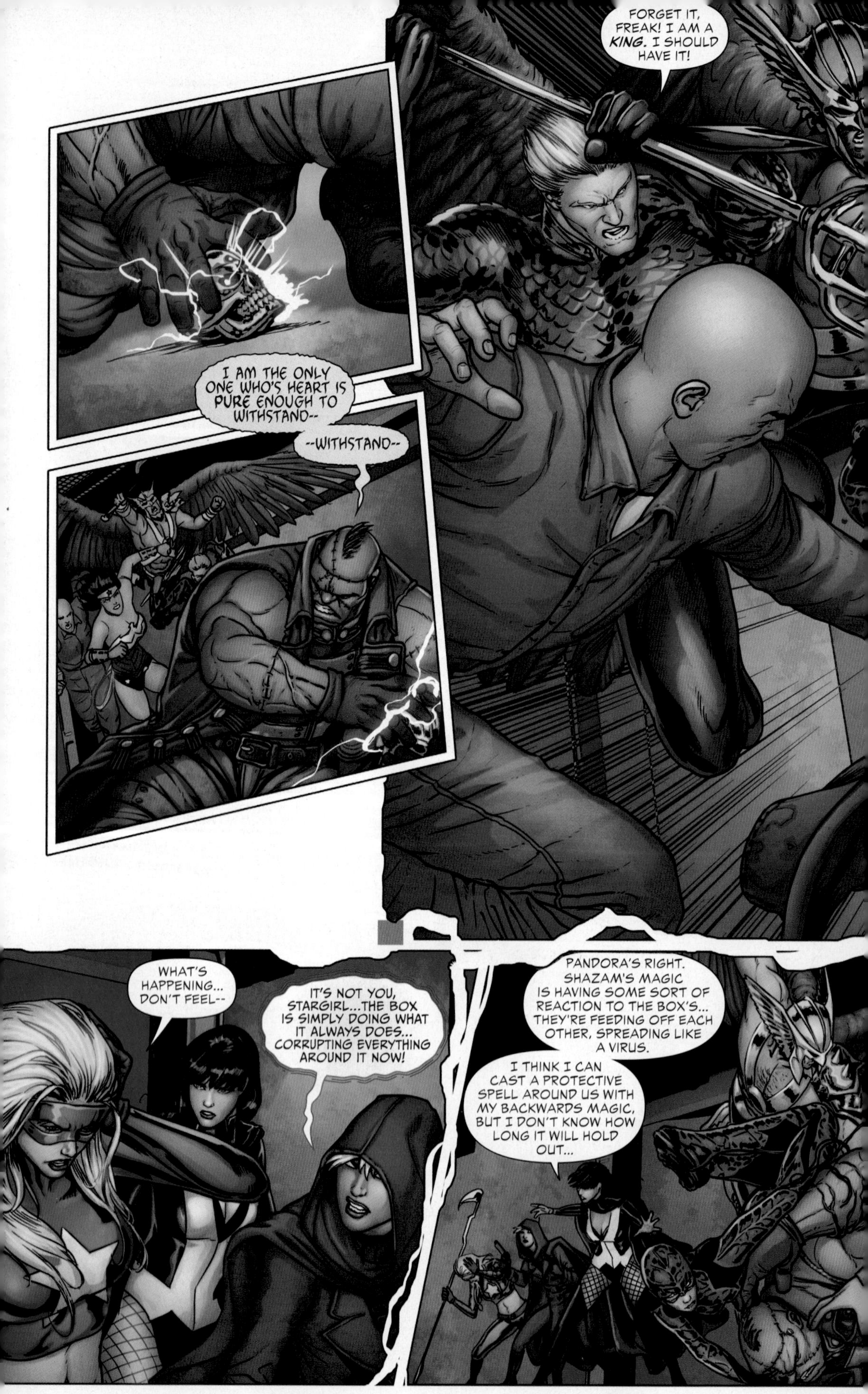

FORGET IT, FREAK! I AM A KING. I SHOULD HAVE IT!
I AM THE ONLY ONE WHO'S HEART IS PURE ENOUGH TO WITHSTAND--
--WITHSTAND--
WHAT'S HAPPENING... DON'T FEEL--
IT'S NOT YOU, STARGIRL...THE BOX IS SIMPLY DOING WHAT IT ALWAYS DOES... CORRUPTING EVERYTHING AROUND IT NOW!
PANDORA'S RIGHT. SHAZAM'S MAGIC IS HAVING SOME SORT OF REACTION TO THE BOX'S... THEY'RE FEEDING OFF EACH OTHER, SPREADING LIKE A VIRUS.
I THINK I CAN CAST A PROTECTIVE SPELL AROUND US WITH MY BACKWARDS MAGIC, BUT I DON'T KNOW HOW LONG IT WILL HOLD OUT...

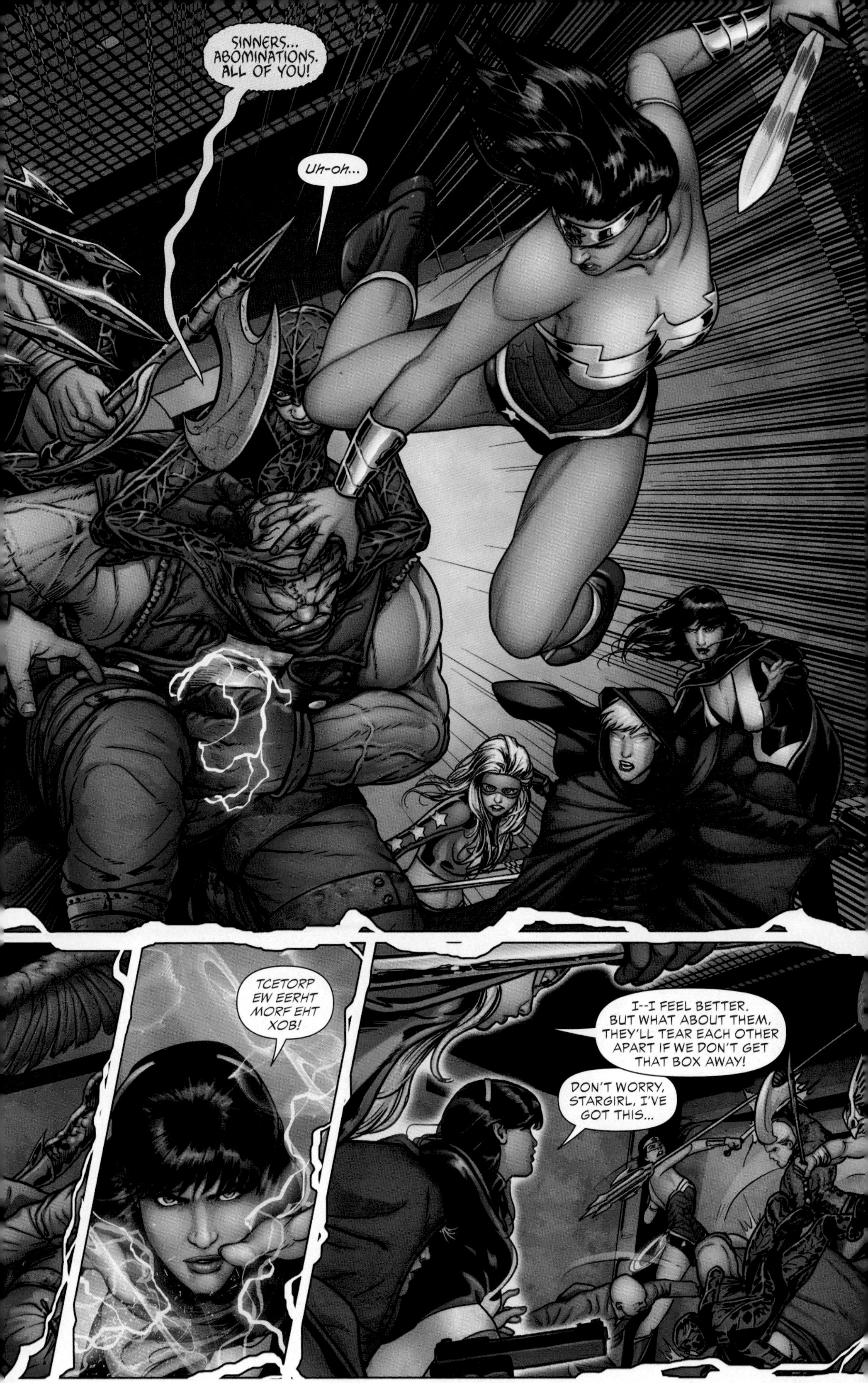
SINNERS... ABOMINATIONS. ALL OF YOU!
Uh-oh...
TCETORP EW EERHT MORF EHT XOB!
I--I FEEL BETTER. BUT WHAT ABOUT THEM, THEY'LL TEAR EACH OTHER APART IF WE DON'T GET THAT BOX AWAY!
DON'T WORRY, STARGIRL, I'VE GOT THIS...

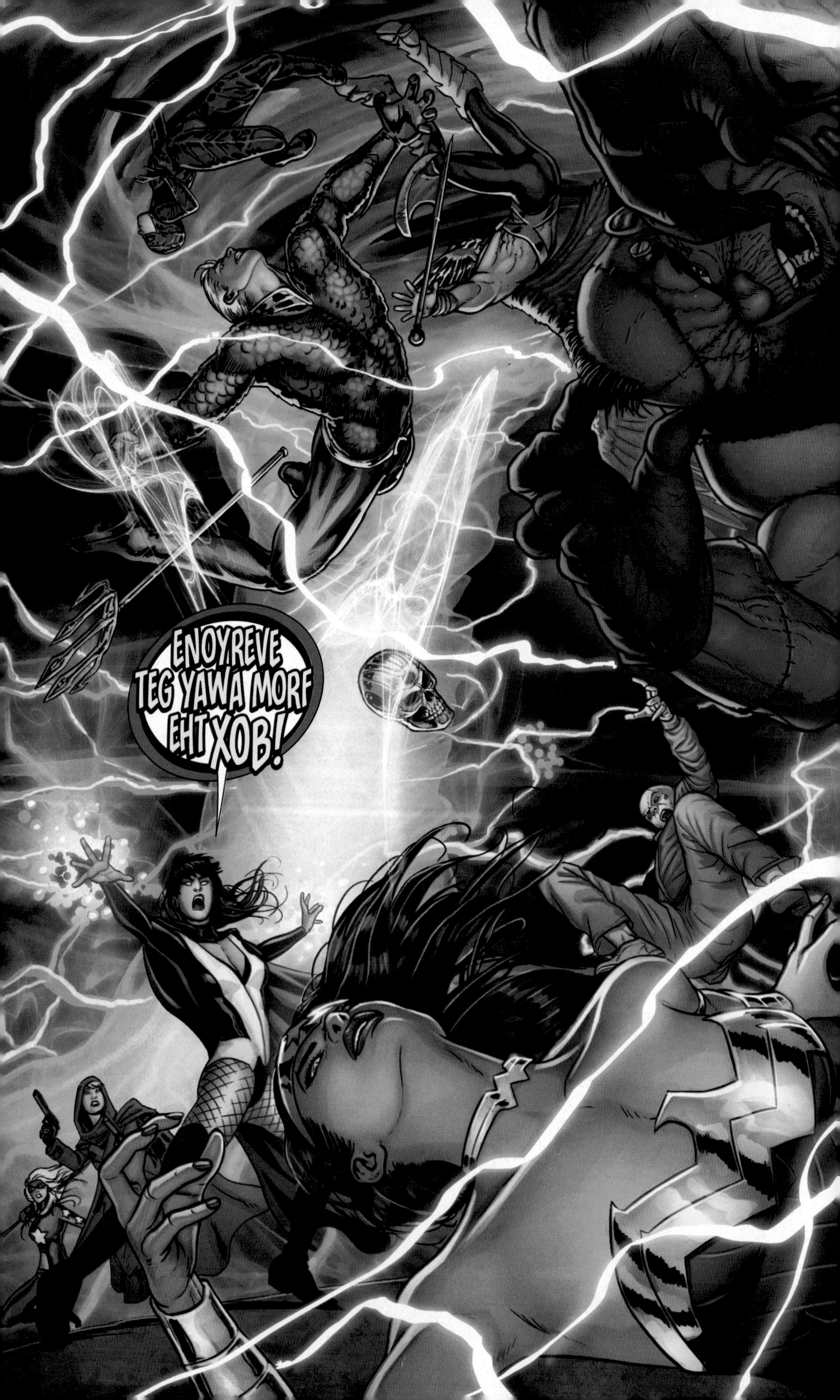
ENOYREVE TEG YAWA MORF EHT XOB!

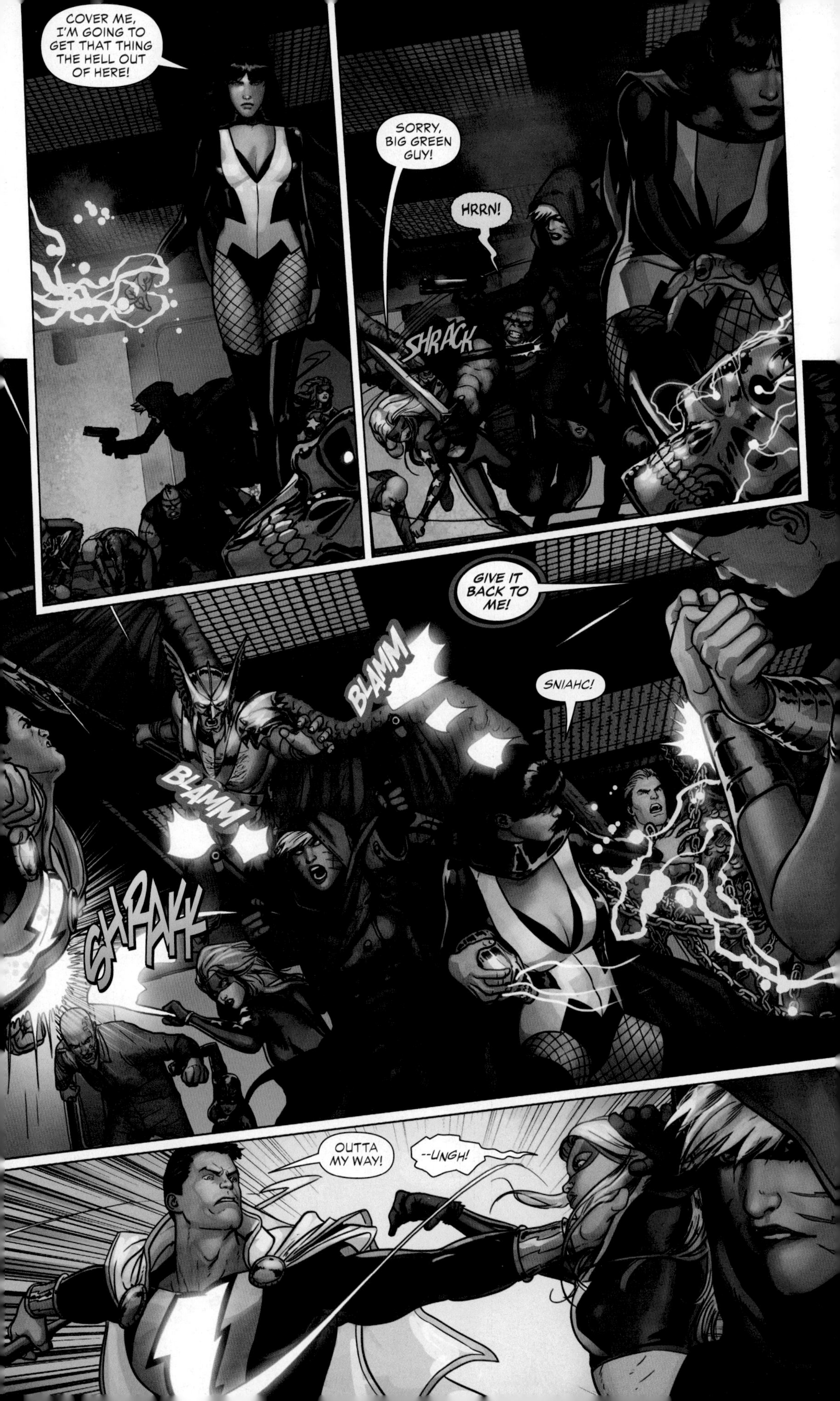
COVER ME, I'M GOING TO GET THAT THING THE HELL OUT OF HERE!
SORRY, BIG GREEN GUY!
HRRN!
SHRACK
GIVE IT BACK TO ME!
BLAMM
SNIAHC!
BLAMM
SHRAKK
OUTTA MY WAY!
--UNGH!

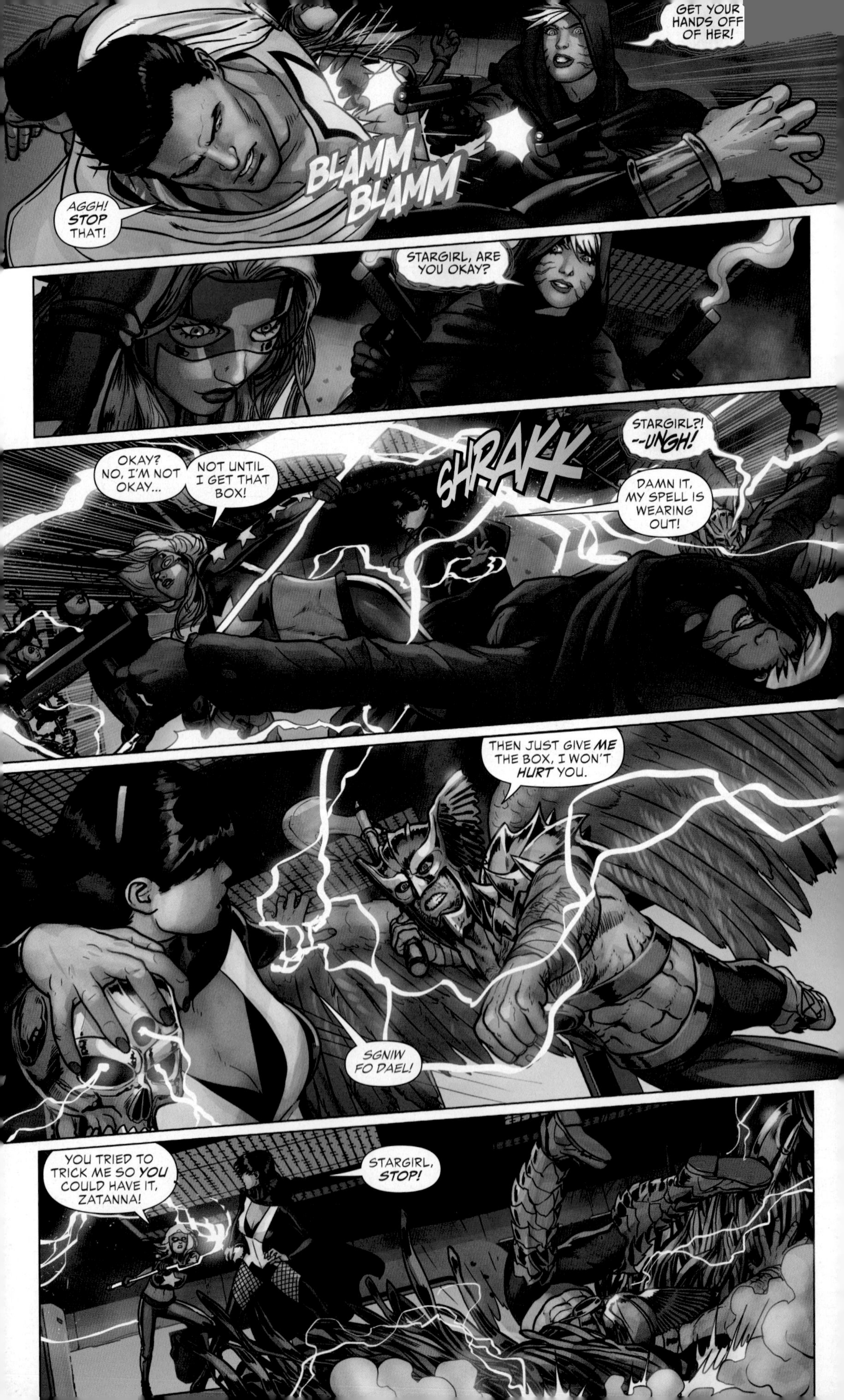
GET YOUR HANDS OFF OF HER!
BLAMM BLAMM
AGGH! STOP THAT!
STARGIRL, ARE YOU OKAY?
OKAY? NO, I'M NOT OKAY...
NOT UNTIL I GET THAT BOX!
SHRAKK
STARGIRL?! --UNGH!
DAMN IT, MY SPELL IS WEARING OUT!
THEN JUST GIVE ME THE BOX, I WON'T HURT YOU.
SGNIW FO DAEL!
YOU TRIED TO TRICK ME SO YOU COULD HAVE IT, ZATANNA!
STARGIRL, STOP!

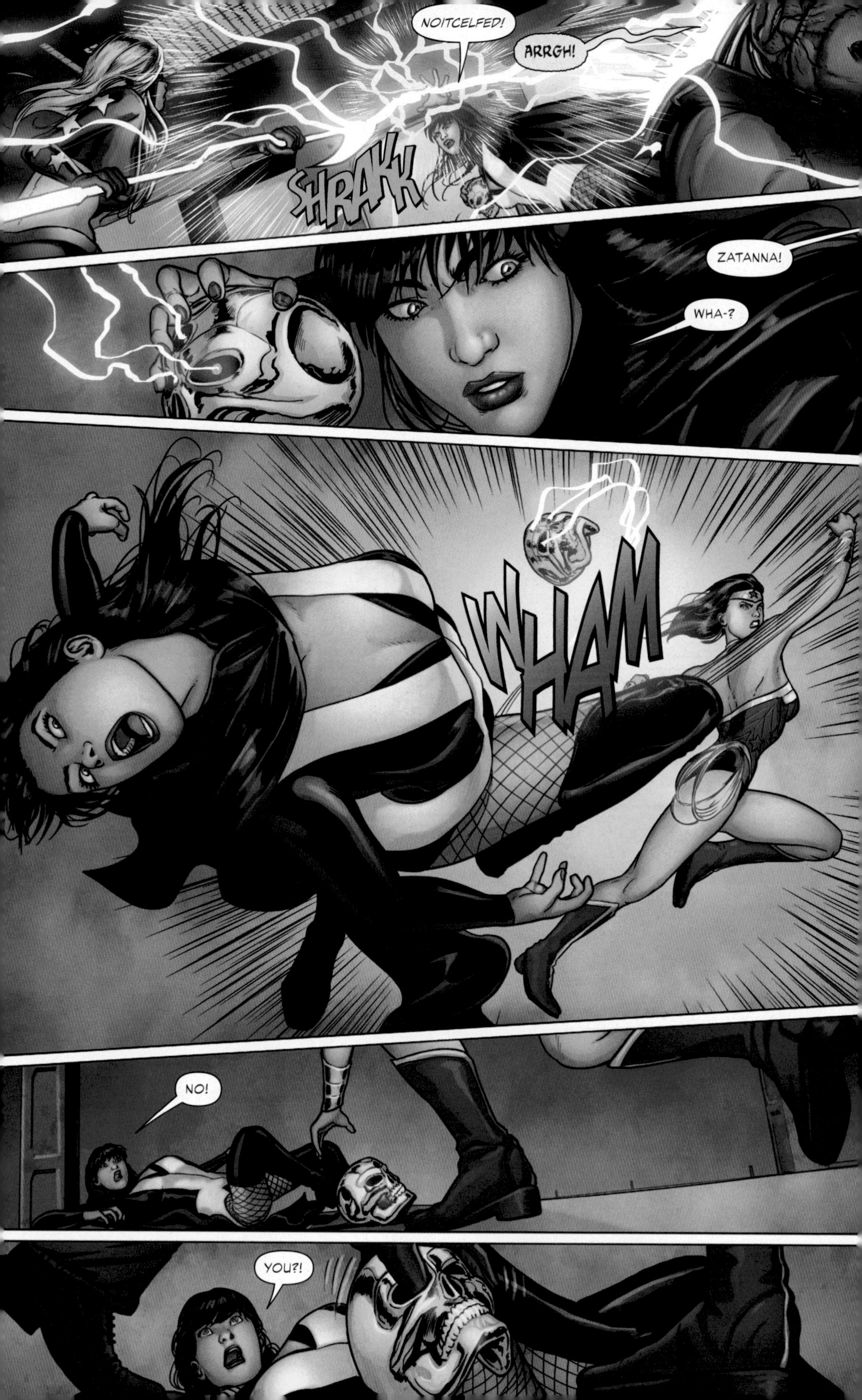
NOITCELFED!
ARRGH!
SHRAKK
ZATANNA!
WHA-?
WHAM
NO!
YOU?!

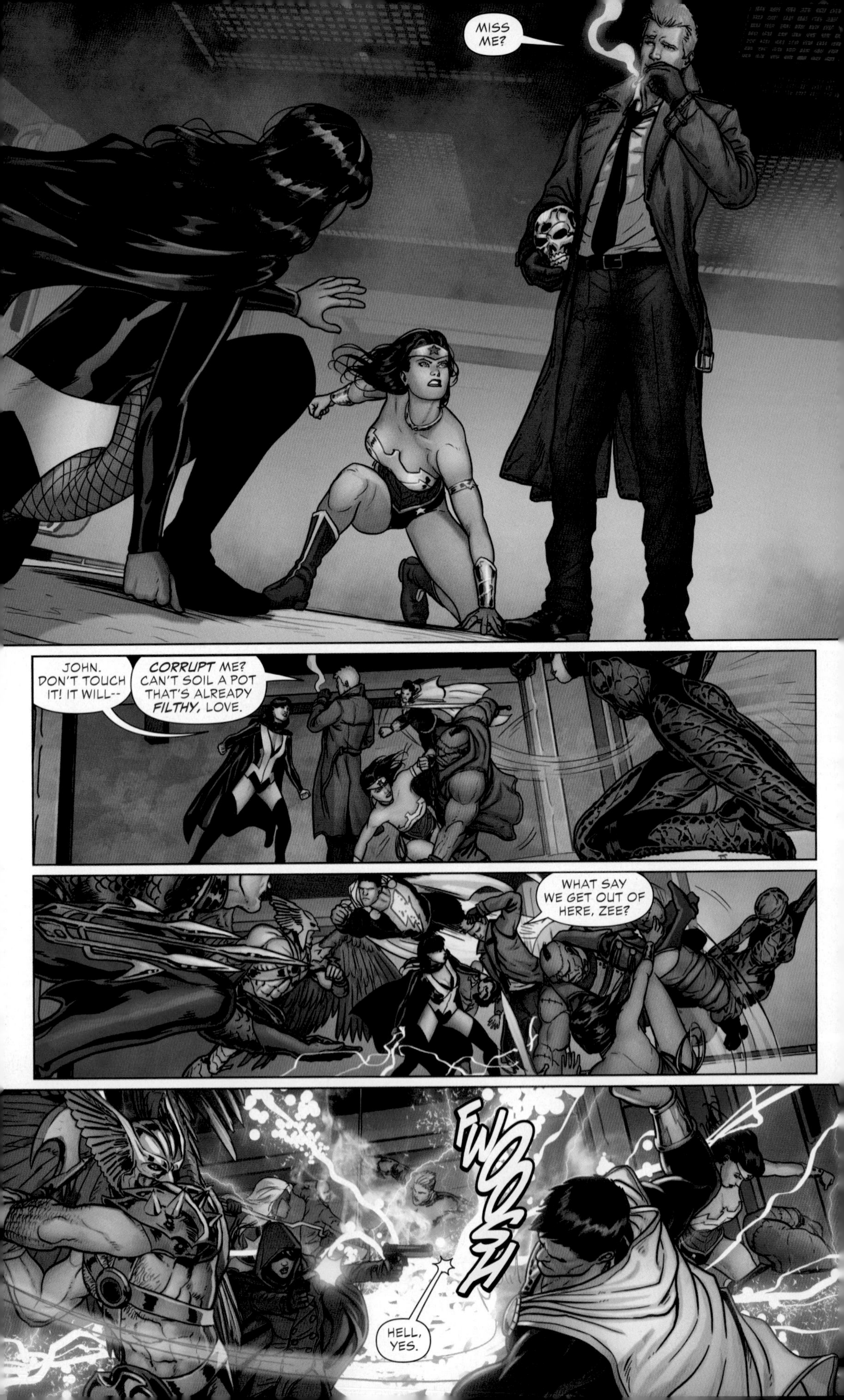
MISS ME?
JOHN. DON'T TOUCH IT! IT WILL--
CORRUPT ME? CAN'T SOIL A POT THAT'S ALREADY FILTHY, LOVE.
WHAT SAY WE GET OUT OF HERE, ZEE?
FWOOSH
HELL, YES.

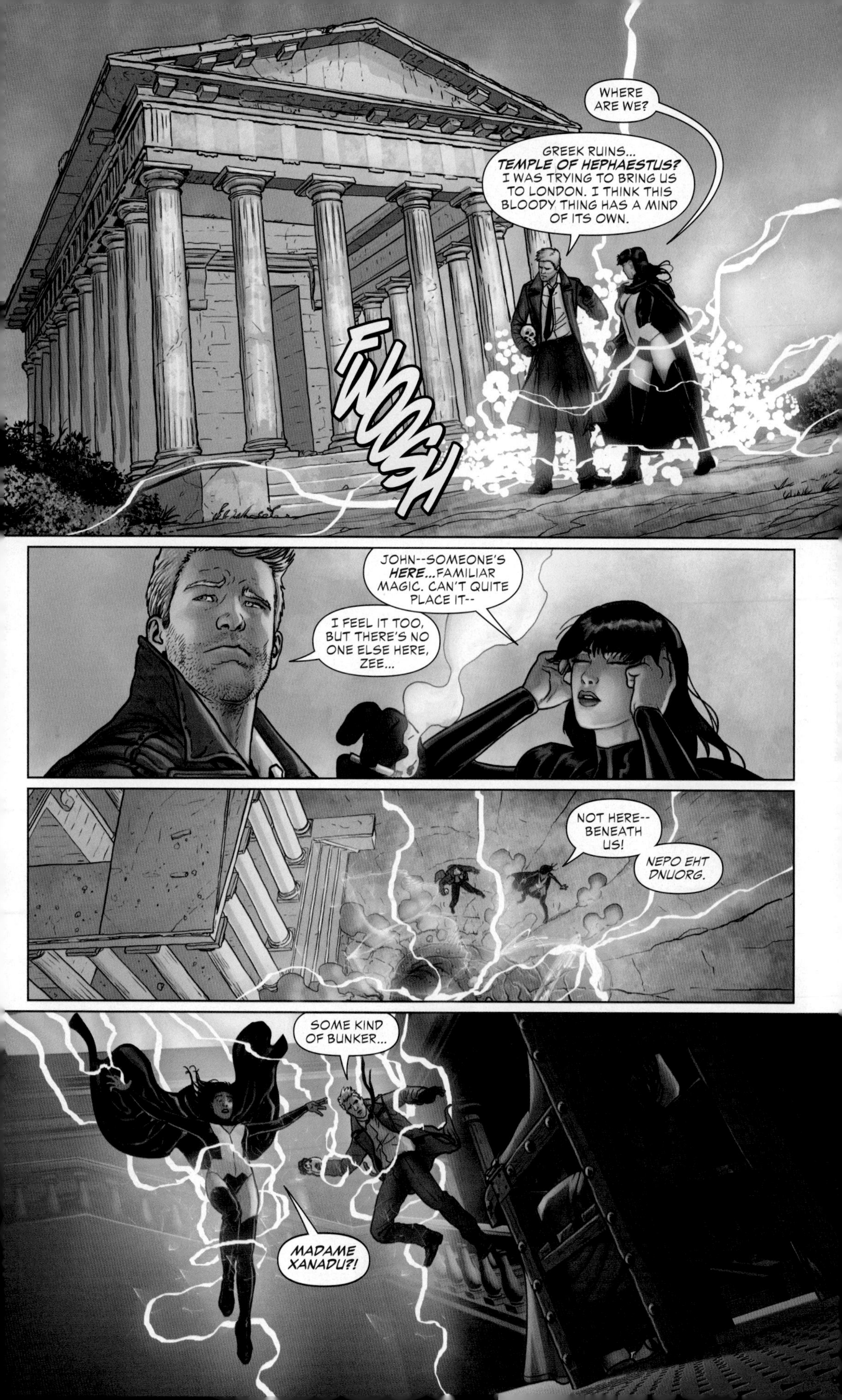
WHERE ARE WE?
GREEK RUINS... TEMPLE OF HEPHAESTUS? I WAS TRYING TO BRING US TO LONDON. I THINK THIS BLOODY THING HAS A MIND OF ITS OWN.
FWOOSH
JOHN--SOMEONE'S HERE...FAMILIAR MAGIC. CAN'T QUITE PLACE IT--
I FEEL IT TOO, BUT THERE'S NO ONE ELSE HERE, ZEE...
NOT HERE-- BENEATH US!
NEPO EHT DNUORG.
SOME KIND OF BUNKER...
MADAME XANADU?!

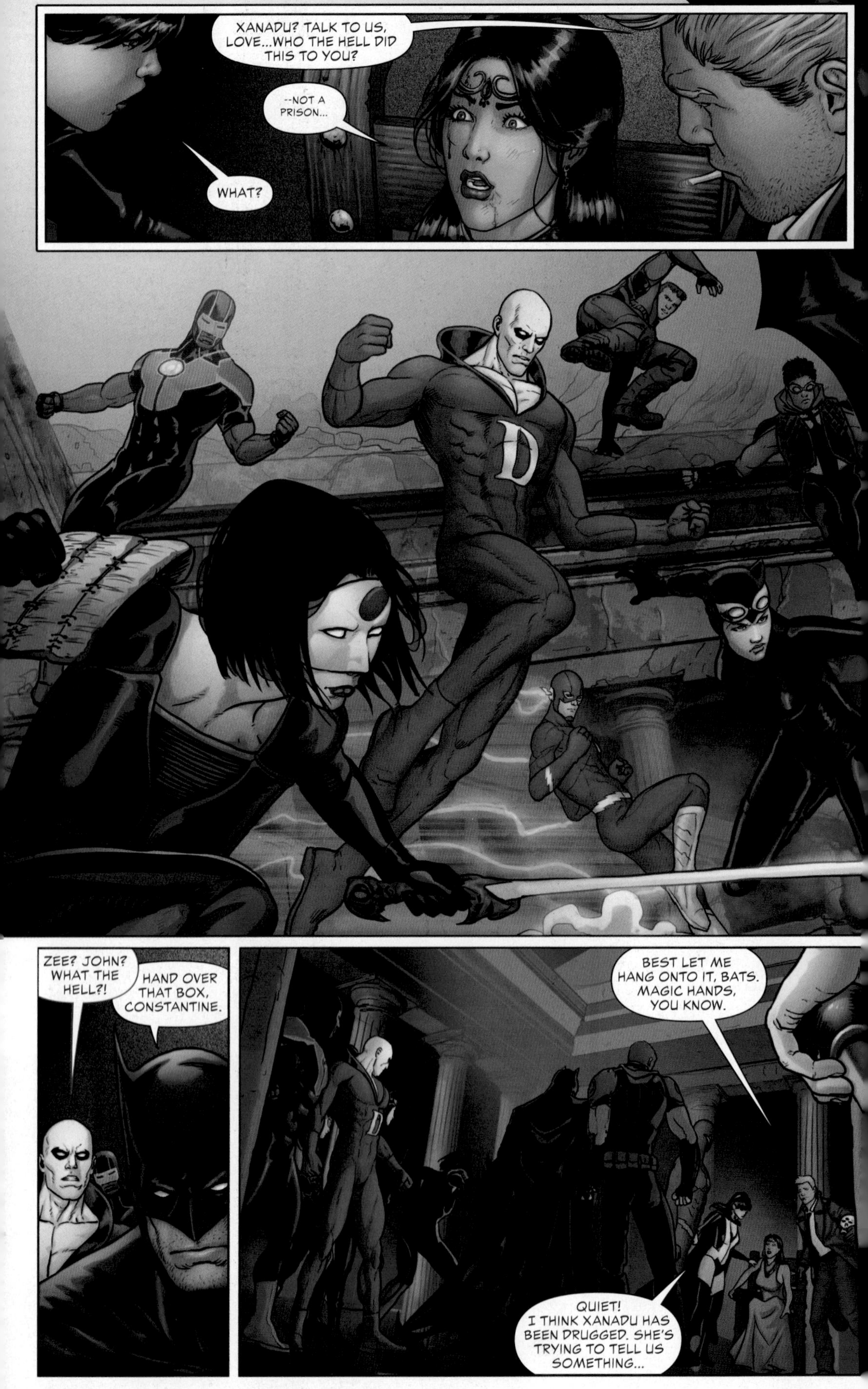
XANADU? TALK TO US, LOVE...WHO THE HELL DID THIS TO YOU?
--NOT A PRISON...
WHAT?
ZEE? JOHN? WHAT THE HELL?!
HAND OVER THAT BOX, CONSTANTINE.
BEST LET ME HANG ONTO IT, BATS. MAGIC HANDS, YOU KNOW.
QUIET! I THINK XANADU HAS BEEN DRUGGED. SHE'S TRYING TO TELL US SOMETHING...

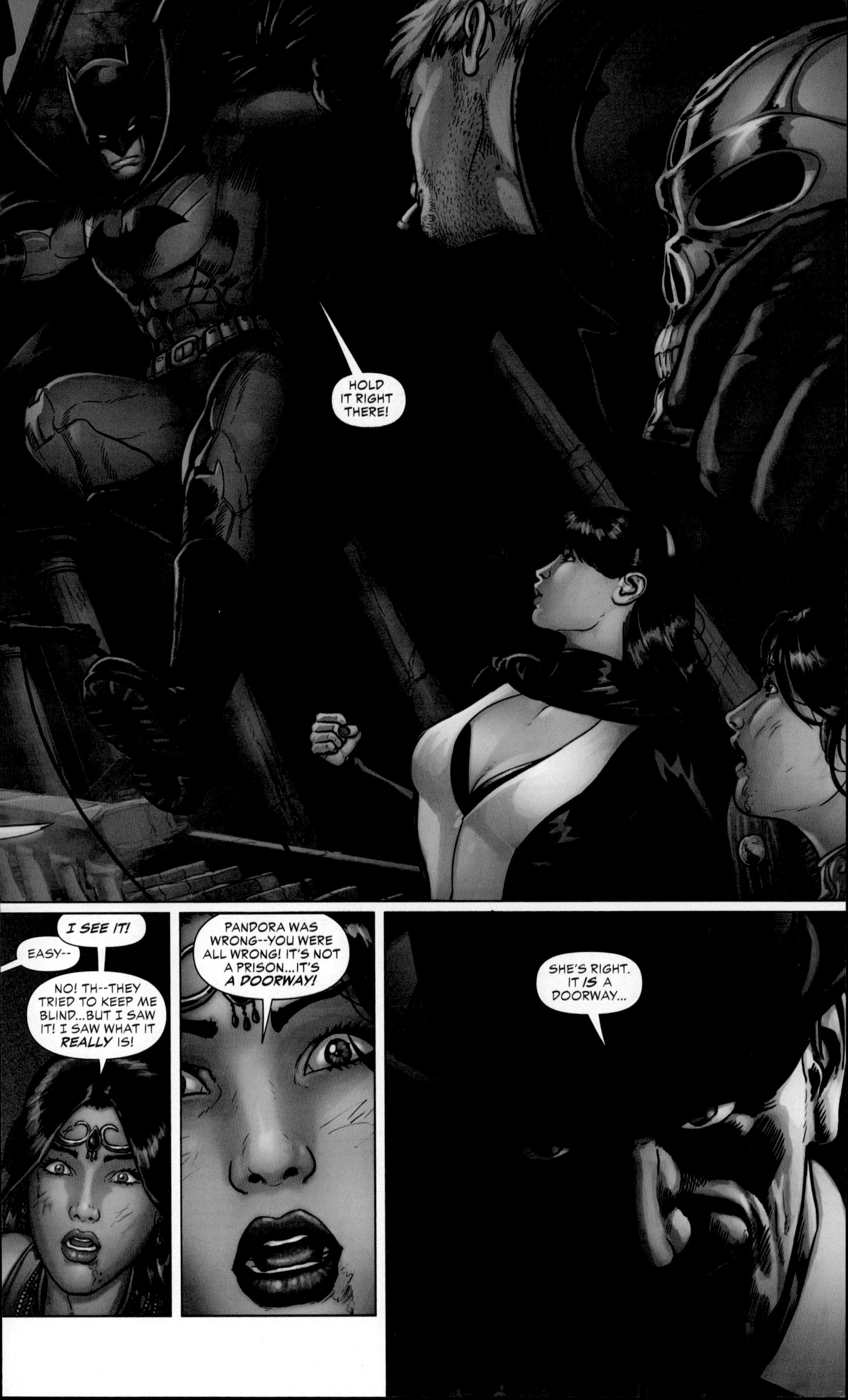
HOLD IT RIGHT THERE!
I SEE IT!
EASY--
NO! TH--THEY TRIED TO KEEP ME BLIND...BUT I SAW IT! I SAW WHAT IT REALLY IS!
PANDORA WAS WRONG--YOU WERE ALL WRONG! IT'S NOT A PRISON...IT'S A DOORWAY!
SHE'S RIGHT. IT IS A DOORWAY...

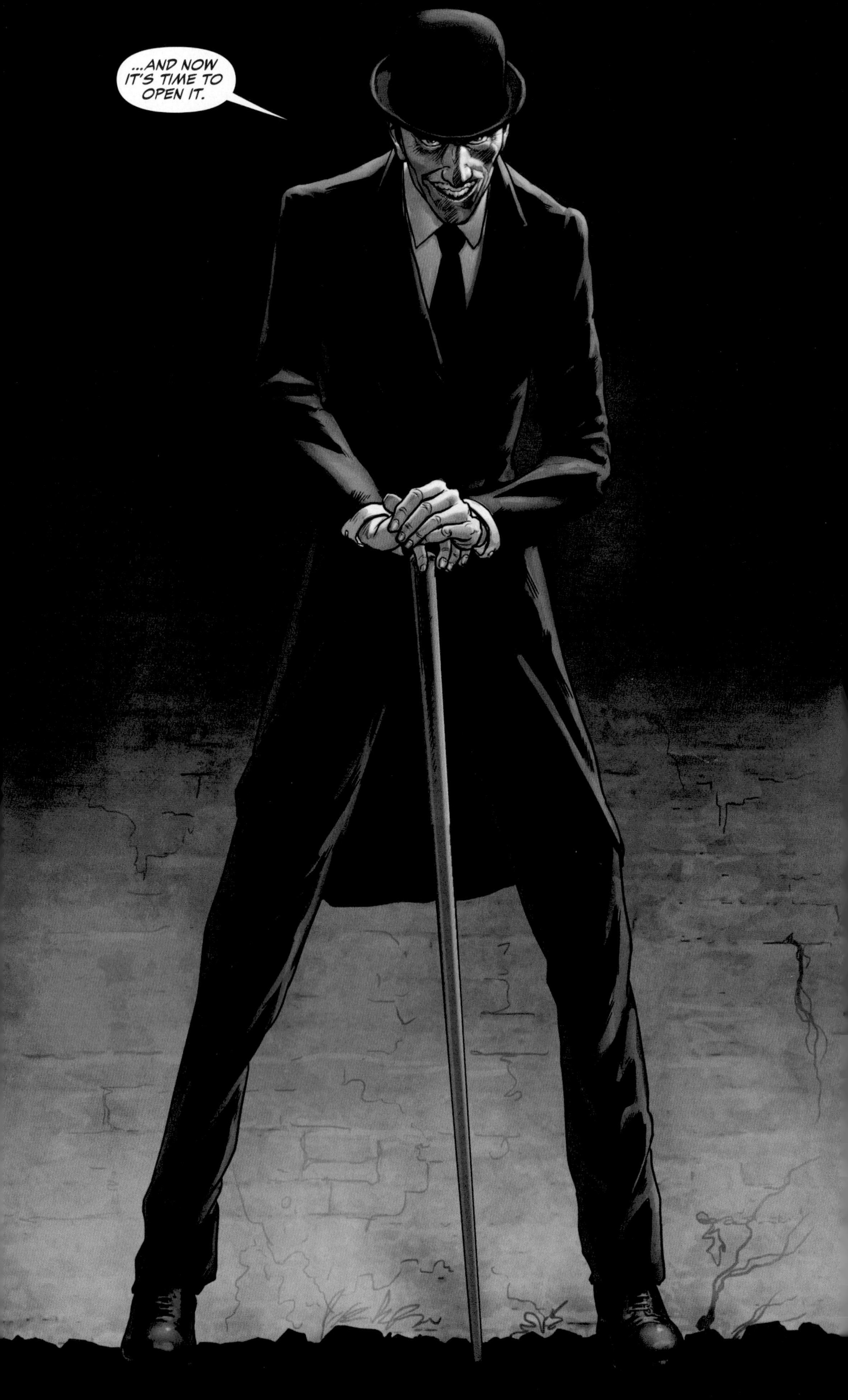
...AND NOW IT'S TIME TO OPEN IT.

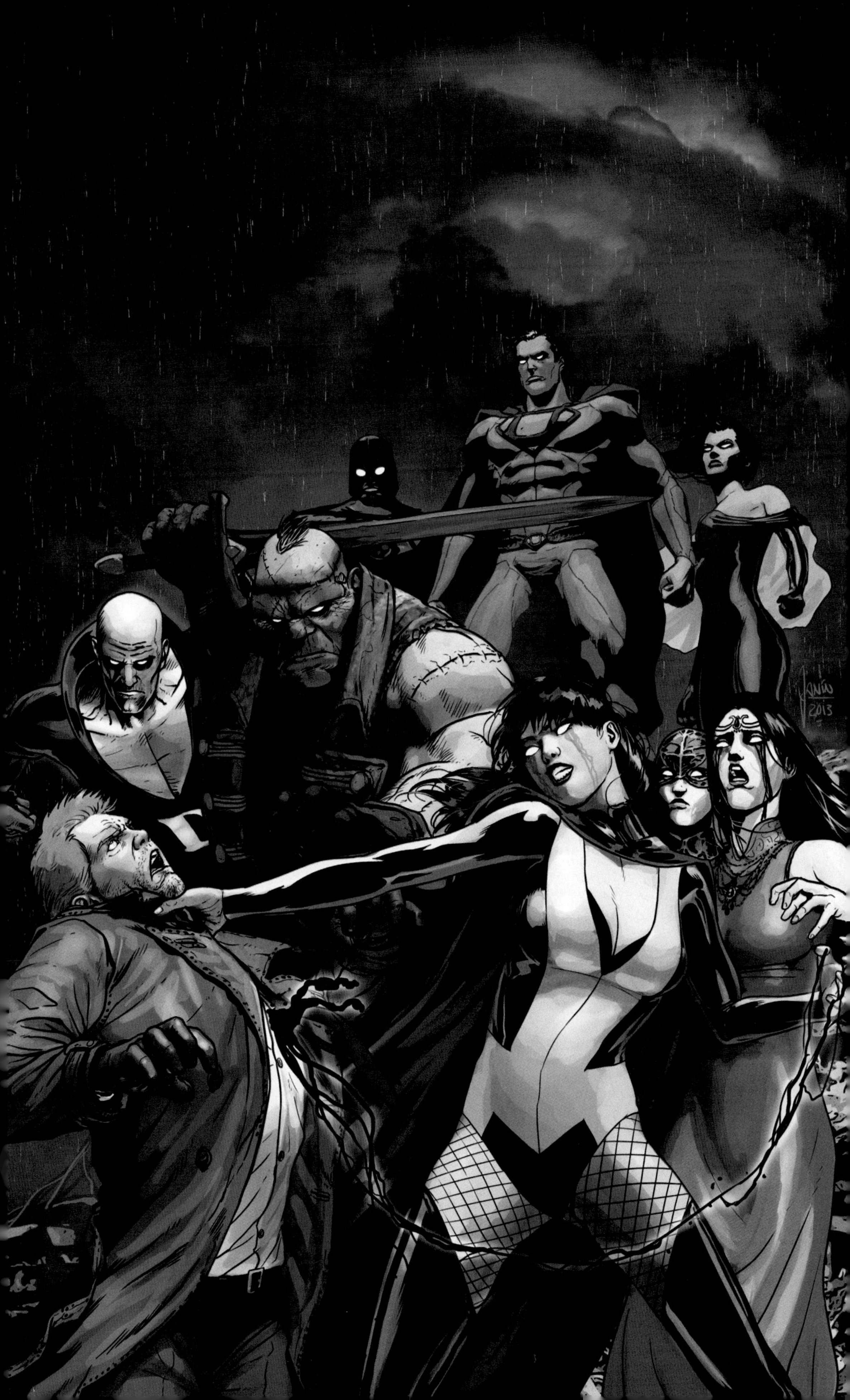

J. M. DeMATTEIS
writer

MIKEL JANIN
artist

MIKEL JANIN
cover artist

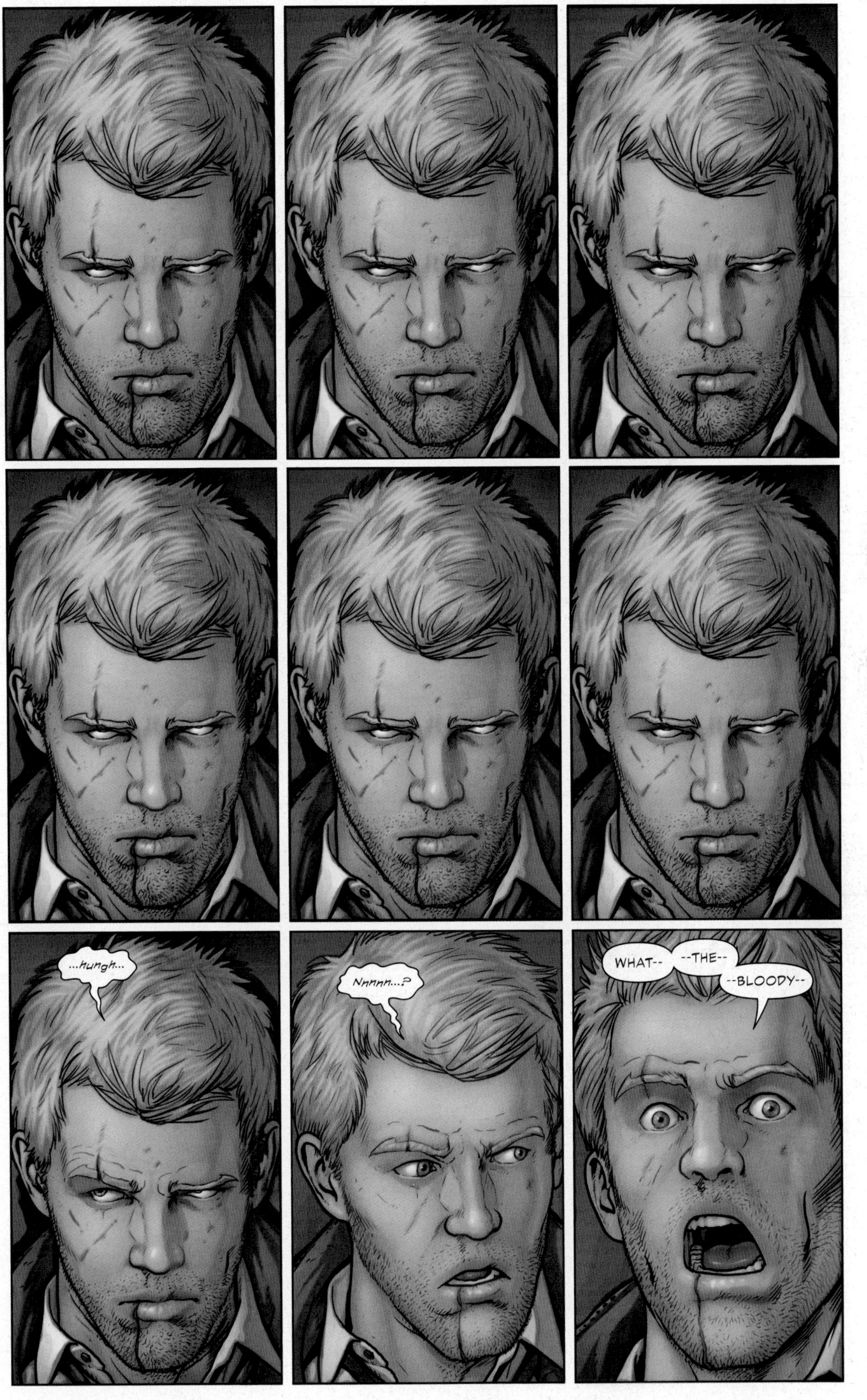
...hungh...
Nnnnn...?
WHAT--
--THE--
--BLOODY--

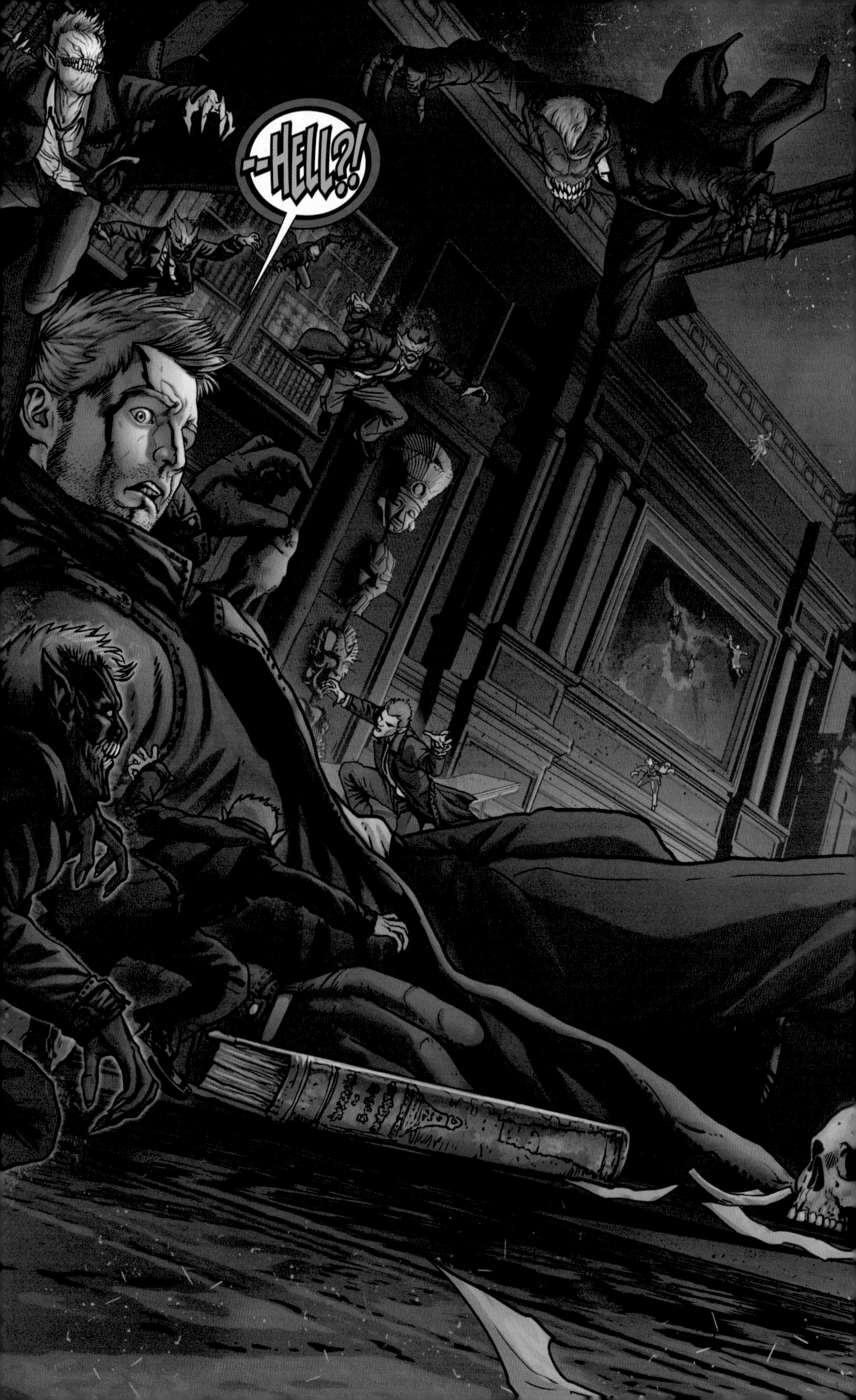
--HELL?!

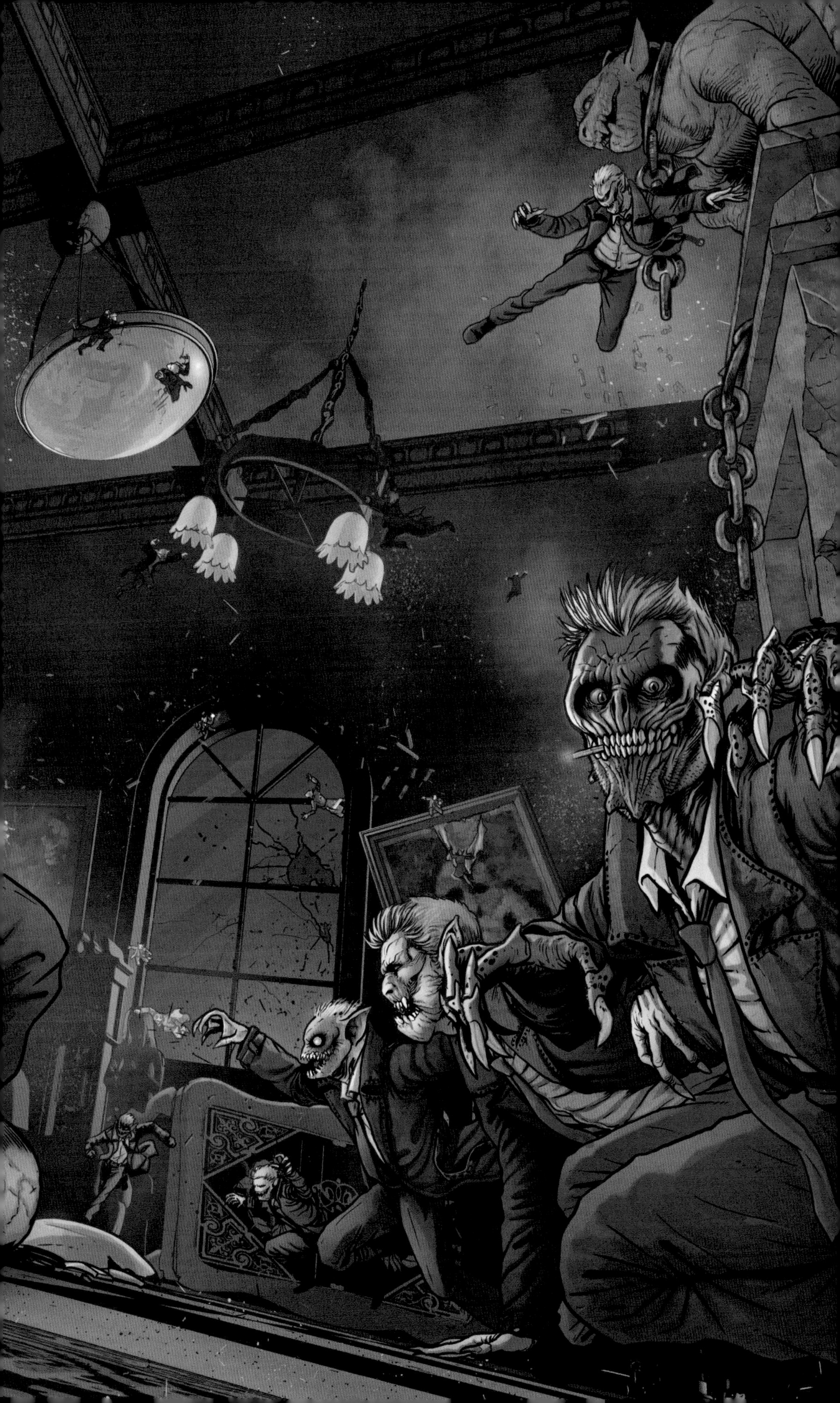

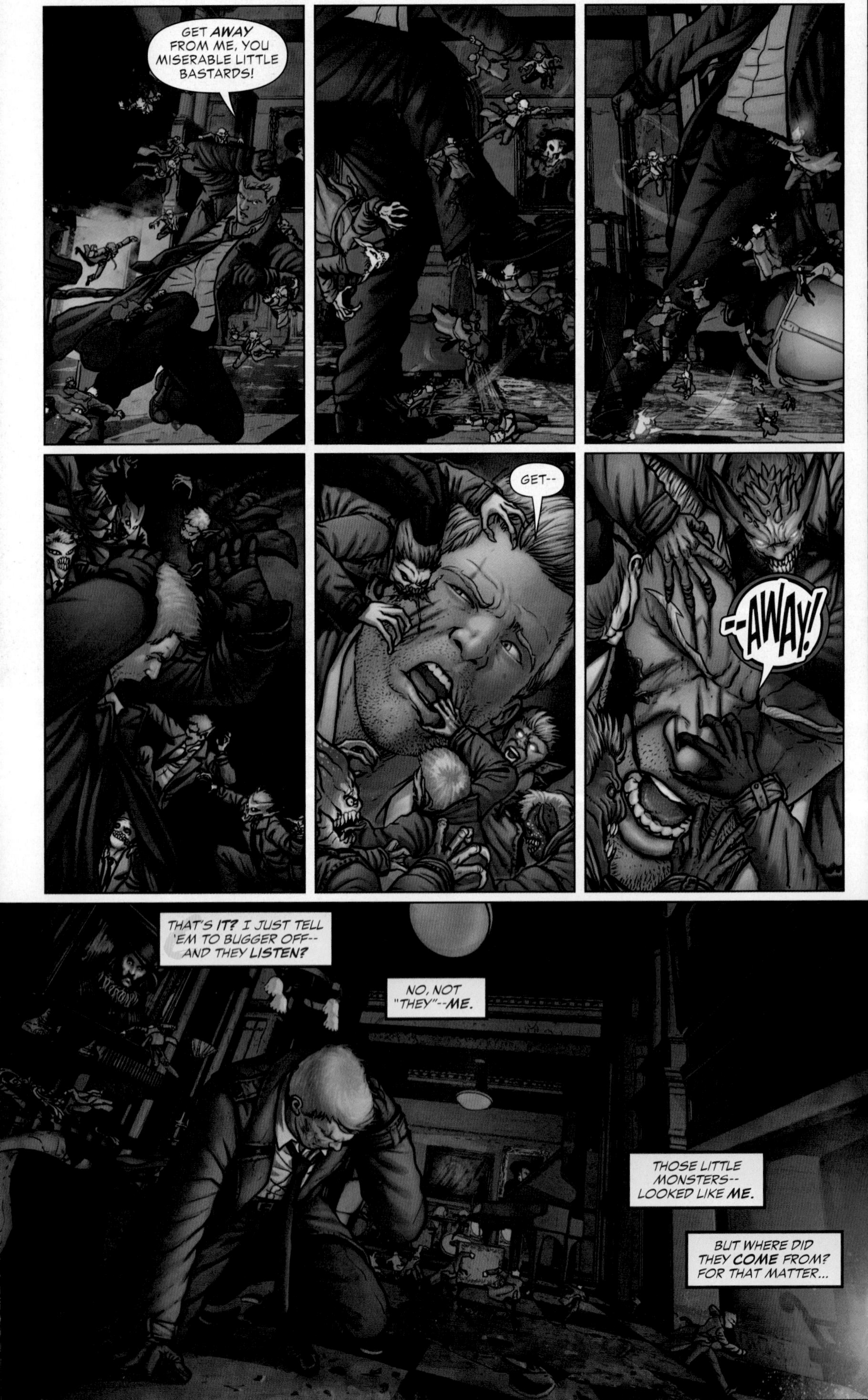
GET AWAY FROM ME, YOU MISERABLE LITTLE BASTARDS!
GET--
--AWAY!
THAT'S IT? I JUST TELL 'EM TO BUGGER OFF-- AND THEY LISTEN?
NO, NOT "THEY"--ME.
THOSE LITTLE MONSTERS-- LOOKED LIKE ME.
BUT WHERE DID THEY COME FROM? FOR THAT MATTER...

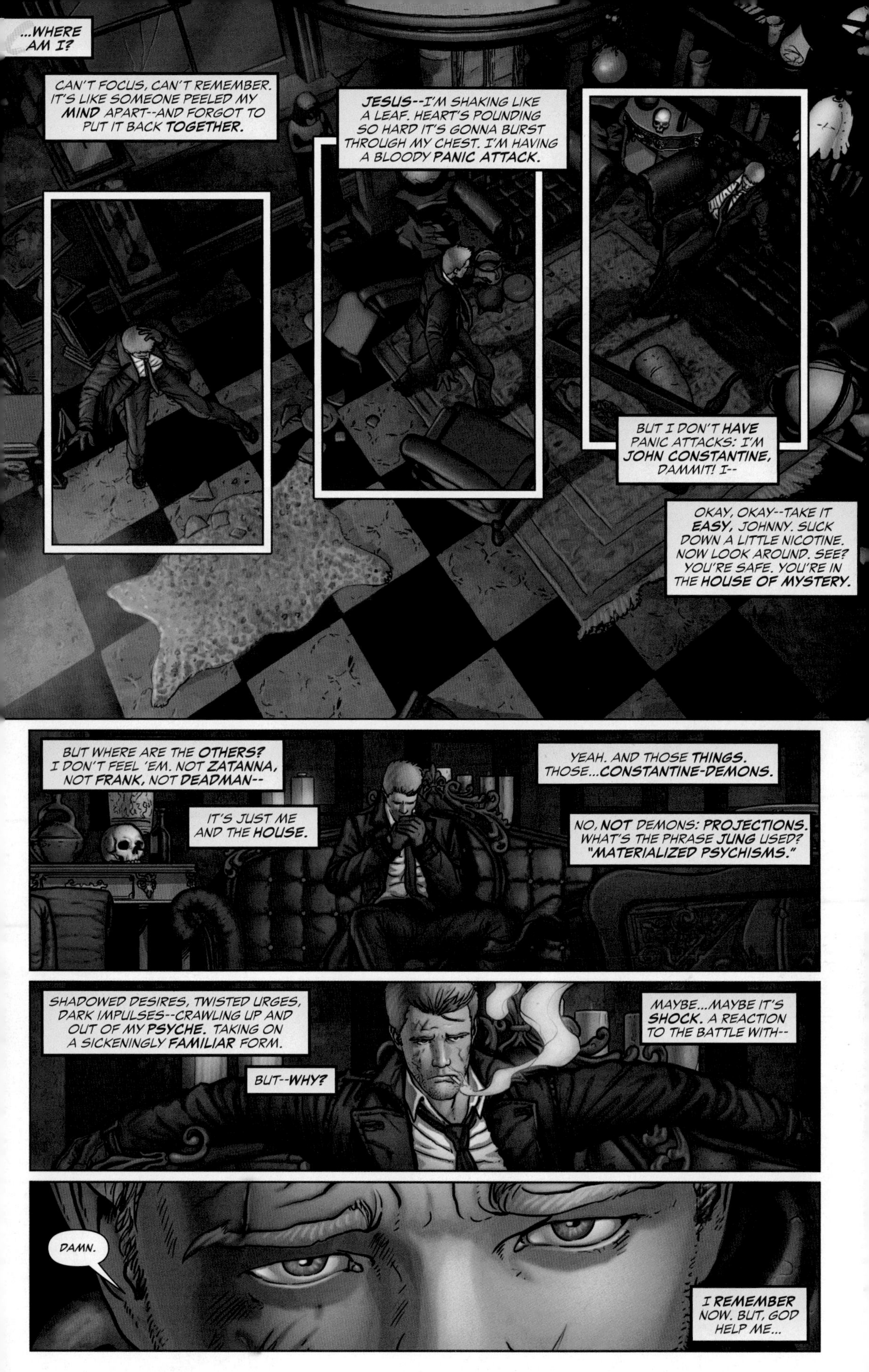
...WHERE AM I?
CAN'T FOCUS, CAN'T REMEMBER. IT'S LIKE SOMEONE PEELED MY MIND APART--AND FORGOT TO PUT IT BACK TOGETHER.
JESUS--I'M SHAKING LIKE A LEAF. HEART'S POUNDING SO HARD IT'S GONNA BURST THROUGH MY CHEST. I'M HAVING A BLOODY PANIC ATTACK.
BUT I DON'T HAVE PANIC ATTACKS: I'M JOHN CONSTANTINE, DAMMIT! I--
OKAY, OKAY--TAKE IT EASY, JOHNNY. SUCK DOWN A LITTLE NICOTINE. NOW LOOK AROUND. SEE? YOU'RE SAFE. YOU'RE IN THE HOUSE OF MYSTERY.
BUT WHERE ARE THE OTHERS? I DON'T FEEL 'EM. NOT ZATANNA, NOT FRANK, NOT DEADMAN--
IT'S JUST ME AND THE HOUSE.
YEAH. AND THOSE THINGS. THOSE...CONSTANTINE-DEMONS.
NO, NOT DEMONS: PROJECTIONS. WHAT'S THE PHRASE JUNG USED? "MATERIALIZED PSYCHISMS."
SHADOWED DESIRES, TWISTED URGES, DARK IMPULSES--CRAWLING UP AND OUT OF MY PSYCHE. TAKING ON A SICKENINGLY FAMILIAR FORM.
BUT--WHY?
MAYBE...MAYBE IT'S SHOCK. A REACTION TO THE BATTLE WITH--
DAMN.
I REMEMBER NOW. BUT, GOD HELP ME...

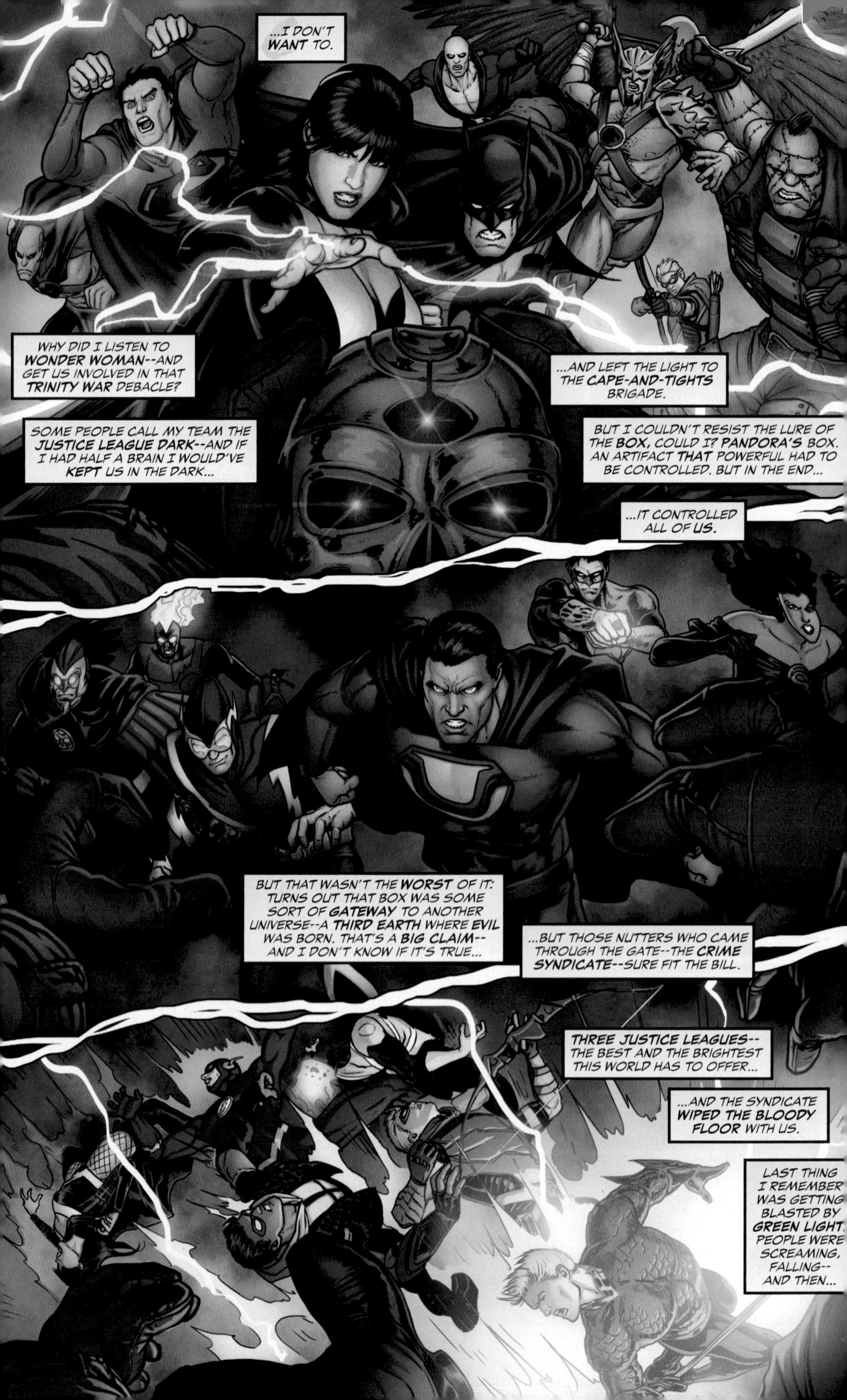
...I DON'T WANT TO.
WHY DID I LISTEN TO WONDER WOMAN--AND GET US INVOLVED IN THAT TRINITY WAR DEBACLE?
...AND LEFT THE LIGHT TO THE CAPE-AND-TIGHTS BRIGADE.
SOME PEOPLE CALL MY TEAM THE JUSTICE LEAGUE DARK--AND IF I HAD HALF A BRAIN I WOULD'VE KEPT US IN THE DARK...
BUT I COULDN'T RESIST THE LURE OF THE BOX, COULD I? PANDORA'S BOX. AN ARTIFACT THAT POWERFUL HAD TO BE CONTROLLED. BUT IN THE END...
...IT CONTROLLED ALL OF US.
BUT THAT WASN'T THE WORST OF IT: TURNS OUT THAT BOX WAS SOME SORT OF GATEWAY TO ANOTHER UNIVERSE--A THIRD EARTH WHERE EVIL WAS BORN. THAT'S A BIG CLAIM--AND I DON'T KNOW IF IT'S TRUE...
...BUT THOSE NUTTERS WHO CAME THROUGH THE GATE--THE CRIME SYNDICATE--SURE FIT THE BILL.
THREE JUSTICE LEAGUES--THE BEST AND THE BRIGHTEST THIS WORLD HAS TO OFFER...
...AND THE SYNDICATE WIPED THE BLOODY FLOOR WITH US.
LAST THING I REMEMBER WAS GETTING BLASTED BY GREEN LIGHT. PEOPLE WERE SCREAMING, FALLING--AND THEN...

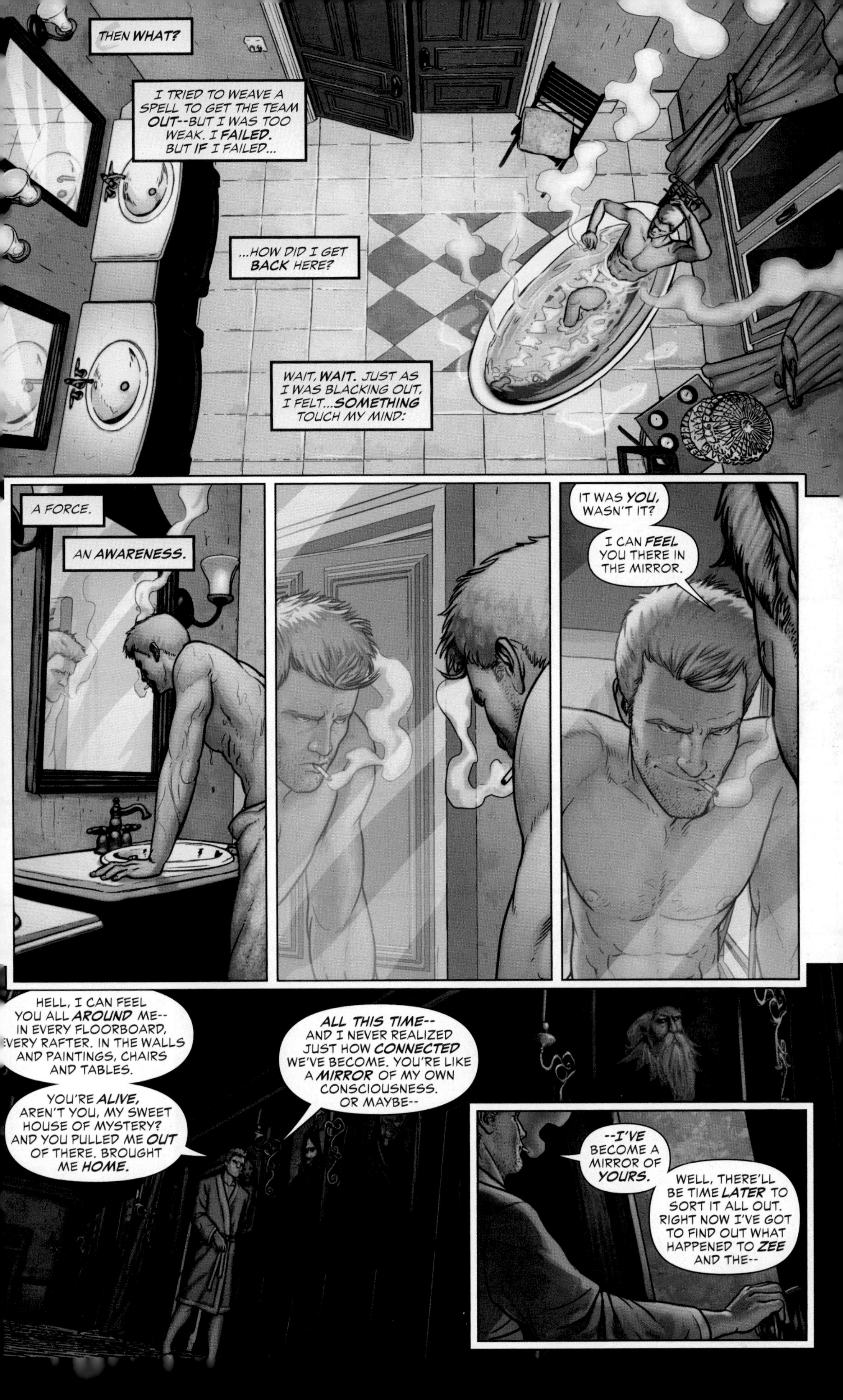
THEN WHAT?
I TRIED TO WEAVE A SPELL TO GET THE TEAM OUT--BUT I WAS TOO WEAK. I FAILED. BUT IF I FAILED...
...HOW DID I GET BACK HERE?
WAIT, WAIT. JUST AS I WAS BLACKING OUT, I FELT...SOMETHING TOUCH MY MIND:
A FORCE.
AN AWARENESS.
IT WAS YOU, WASN'T IT?
I CAN FEEL YOU THERE IN THE MIRROR.
HELL, I CAN FEEL YOU ALL AROUND ME-- IN EVERY FLOORBOARD, EVERY RAFTER. IN THE WALLS AND PAINTINGS, CHAIRS AND TABLES.
YOU'RE ALIVE, AREN'T YOU, MY SWEET HOUSE OF MYSTERY? AND YOU PULLED ME OUT OF THERE. BROUGHT ME HOME.
ALL THIS TIME-- AND I NEVER REALIZED JUST HOW CONNECTED WE'VE BECOME. YOU'RE LIKE A MIRROR OF MY OWN CONSCIOUSNESS. OR MAYBE--
--I'VE BECOME A MIRROR OF YOURS.
WELL, THERE'LL BE TIME LATER TO SORT IT ALL OUT. RIGHT NOW I'VE GOT TO FIND OUT WHAT HAPPENED TO ZEE AND THE--

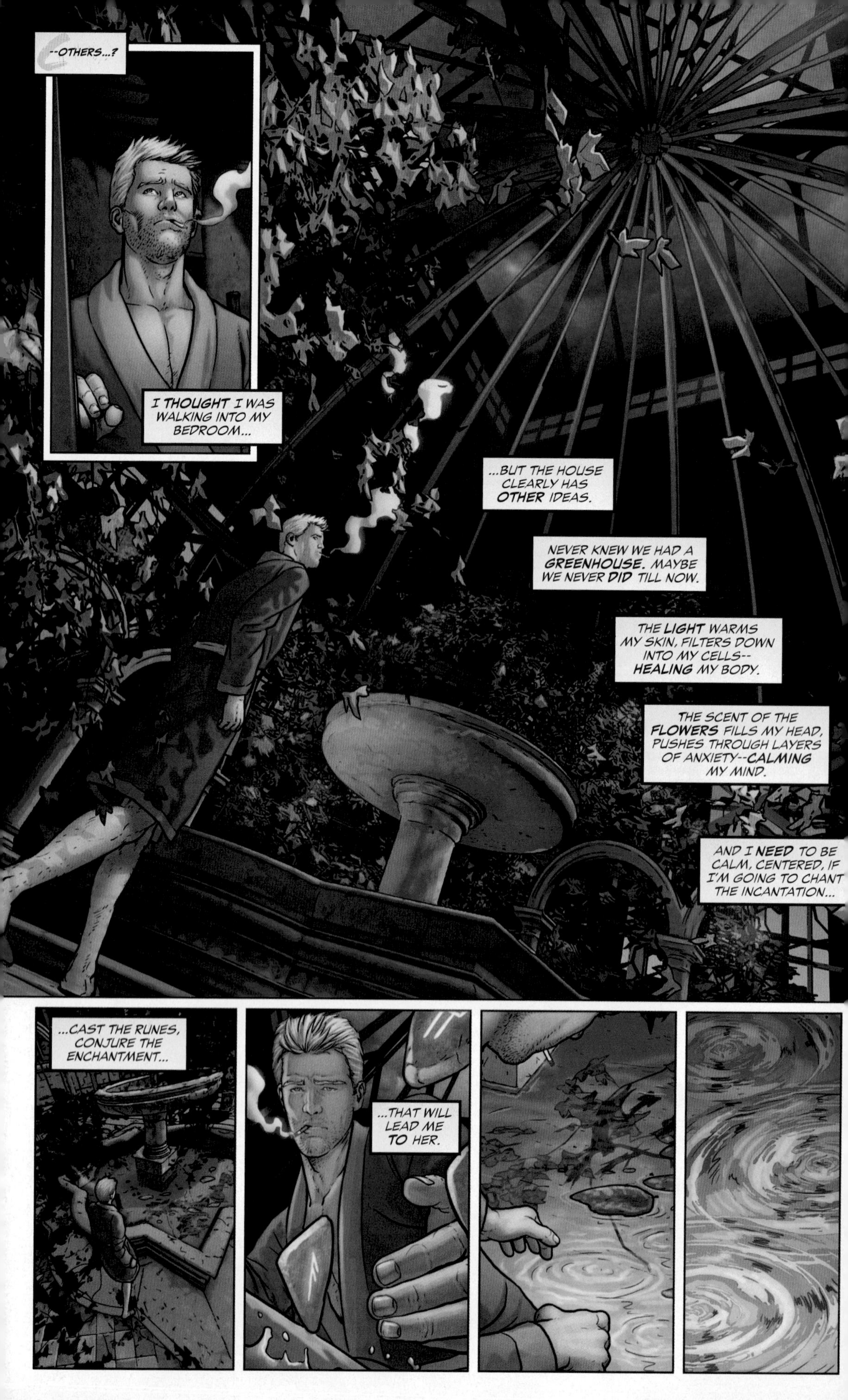
--OTHERS...?
I THOUGHT I WAS WALKING INTO MY BEDROOM...
...BUT THE HOUSE CLEARLY HAS OTHER IDEAS.
NEVER KNEW WE HAD A GREENHOUSE. MAYBE WE NEVER DID TILL NOW.
THE LIGHT WARMS MY SKIN, FILTERS DOWN INTO MY CELLS--HEALING MY BODY.
THE SCENT OF THE FLOWERS FILLS MY HEAD, PUSHES THROUGH LAYERS OF ANXIETY--CALMING MY MIND.
AND I NEED TO BE CALM, CENTERED, IF I'M GOING TO CHANT THE INCANTATION...
...CAST THE RUNES, CONJURE THE ENCHANTMENT...
...THAT WILL LEAD ME TO HER.

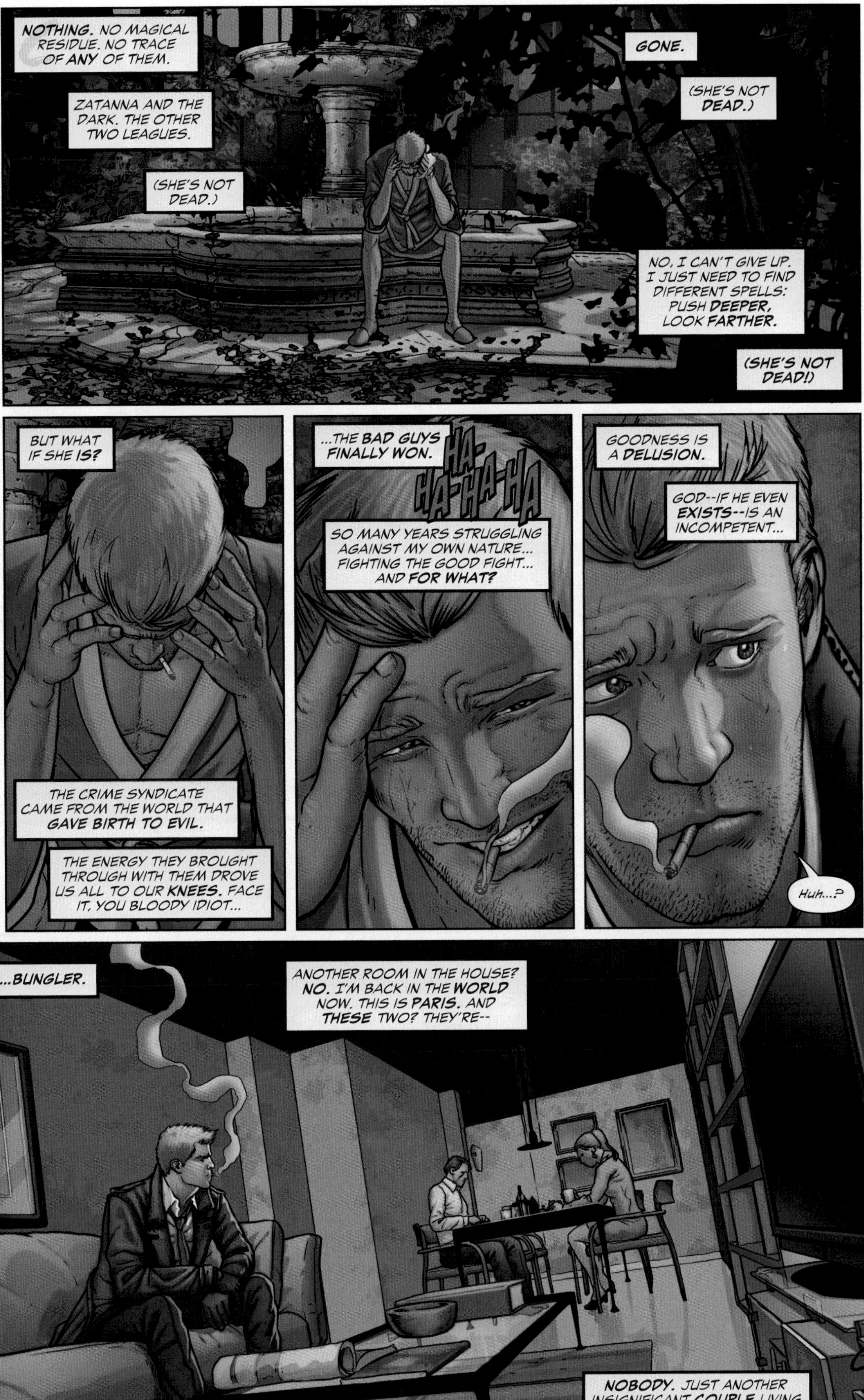
NOTHING. NO MAGICAL RESIDUE. NO TRACE OF ANY OF THEM.
ZATANNA AND THE DARK. THE OTHER TWO LEAGUES.
(SHE'S NOT DEAD.)
GONE.
(SHE'S NOT DEAD.)
NO, I CAN'T GIVE UP. I JUST NEED TO FIND DIFFERENT SPELLS: PUSH DEEPER, LOOK FARTHER.
(SHE'S NOT DEAD!)
BUT WHAT IF SHE IS?
THE CRIME SYNDICATE CAME FROM THE WORLD THAT GAVE BIRTH TO EVIL.
THE ENERGY THEY BROUGHT THROUGH WITH THEM DROVE US ALL TO OUR KNEES. FACE IT, YOU BLOODY IDIOT...
...THE BAD GUYS FINALLY WON.
HA-HA-HA-HA
SO MANY YEARS STRUGGLING AGAINST MY OWN NATURE... FIGHTING THE GOOD FIGHT... AND FOR WHAT?
GOODNESS IS A DELUSION.
GOD--IF HE EVEN EXISTS--IS AN INCOMPETENT...
Huh...?
...BUNGLER.
ANOTHER ROOM IN THE HOUSE? NO. I'M BACK IN THE WORLD NOW. THIS IS PARIS. AND THESE TWO? THEY'RE--
NOBODY. JUST ANOTHER INSIGNIFICANT COUPLE LIVING IN AN INSIGNIFICANT FLAT ON AN INSIGNIFICANT STREET.

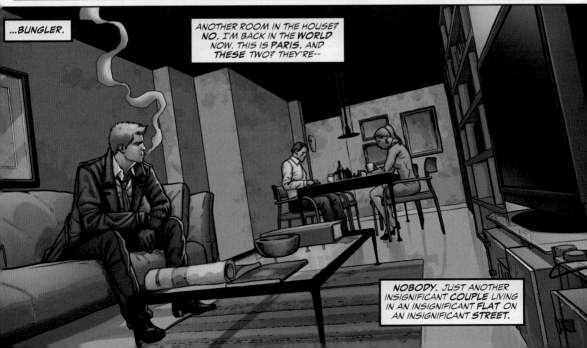

DON'T NEED TO BE A PSYCHIC TO FEEL THE *TENSION* BETWEEN THEM. THE ANGER, THE STUBBORNNESS, THE REFUSAL TO *COMMUNICATE.*

A STUPID, TRIVIAL ARGUMENT. PROBABLY HAVE 'EM TWICE A *WEEK.*

THEY'LL PATCH IT UP *LATER*--IN THE *BEDROOM*, NO DOUBT. BUT FOR NOW IT'S LIKE A LITTLE *WAR* AND--

WHAT THE HELL *IS* THAT?

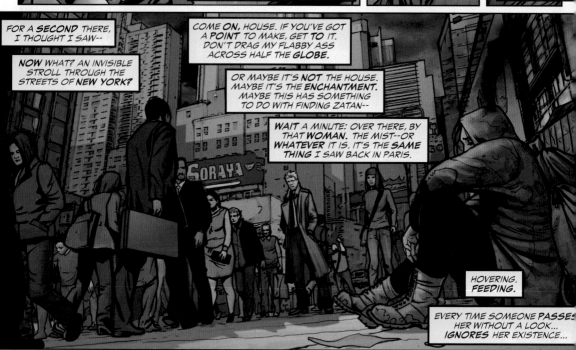

FOR A *SECOND* THERE, I THOUGHT I SAW--

NOW WHAT? AN INVISIBLE STROLL THROUGH THE STREETS OF *NEW YORK?*

COME *ON*, HOUSE. IF YOU'VE GOT A *POINT* TO MAKE, GET *TO* IT. DON'T DRAG MY FLABBY ASS ACROSS HALF THE *GLOBE.*

OR MAYBE IT'S *NOT* THE HOUSE. MAYBE IT'S THE *ENCHANTMENT.* MAYBE THIS HAS SOMETHING TO DO WITH FINDING ZATAN--

WAIT A MINUTE: OVER THERE, BY THAT *WOMAN.* THE MIST--OR *WHATEVER* IT IS. IT'S THE *SAME* THING I SAW BACK IN PARIS.

SORAYA

HOVERING. FEEDING.

EVERY TIME SOMEONE *PASSES* HER WITHOUT A LOOK... *IGNORES* HER EXISTENCE...

AND HOW MANY TIMES HAVE *YOU* FED IT? SAVED THE *WORLD*...BUT CLOSED YOUR *HEART?*

...THAT THING *GROWS* IN STRENGTH.

YOU CAN *SEE* ME?

I'M MAD AS A *HATTER*--

TEWWW

--YOU'D BE *SURPRISED* WHAT I CAN SEE.

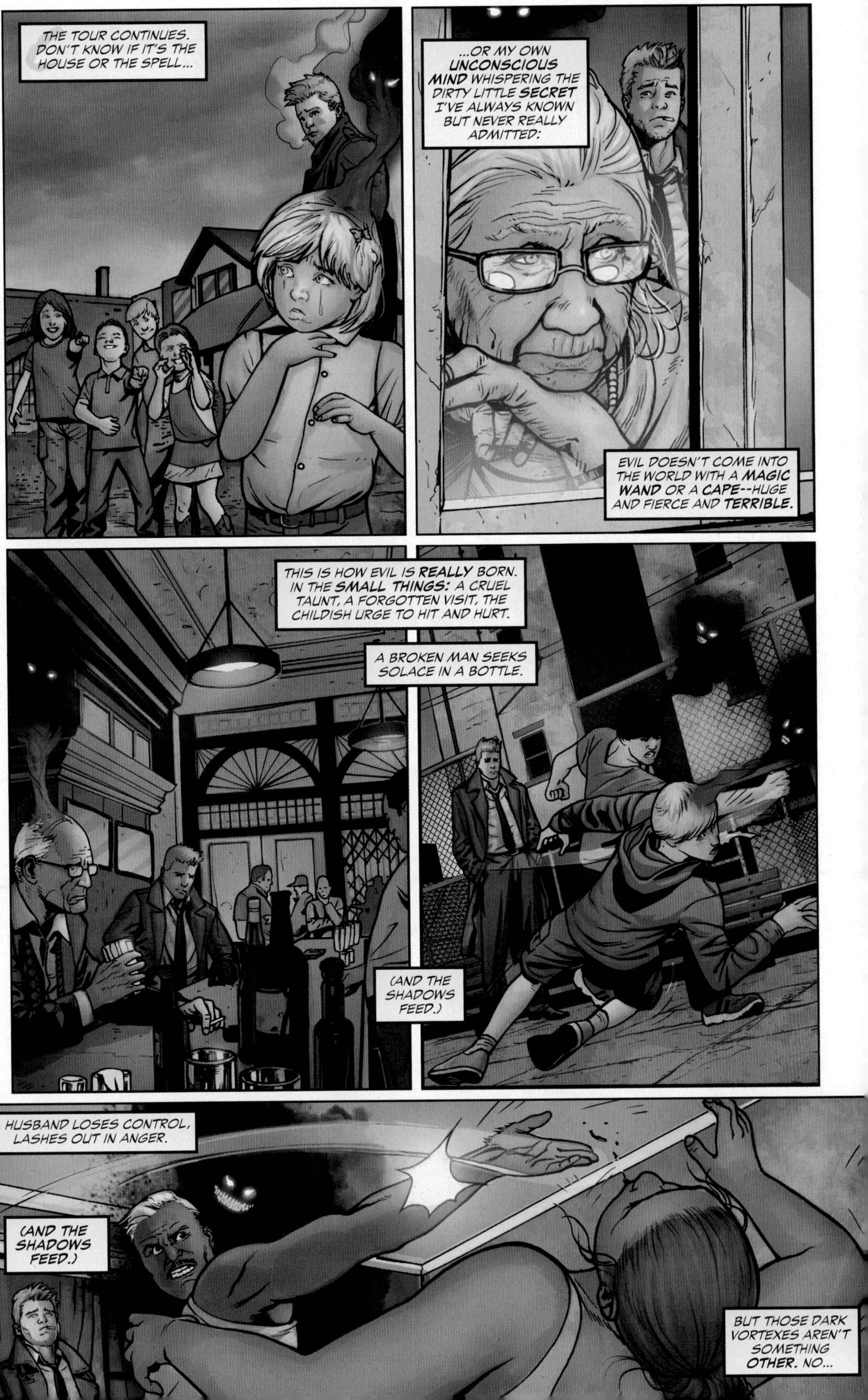

THE TOUR CONTINUES. DON'T KNOW IF IT'S THE HOUSE OR THE SPELL...
...OR MY OWN UNCONSCIOUS MIND WHISPERING THE DIRTY LITTLE SECRET I'VE ALWAYS KNOWN BUT NEVER REALLY ADMITTED:
EVIL DOESN'T COME INTO THE WORLD WITH A MAGIC WAND OR A CAPE--HUGE AND FIERCE AND TERRIBLE.
THIS IS HOW EVIL IS REALLY BORN. IN THE SMALL THINGS: A CRUEL TAUNT, A FORGOTTEN VISIT, THE CHILDISH URGE TO HIT AND HURT.
A BROKEN MAN SEEKS SOLACE IN A BOTTLE.
(AND THE SHADOWS FEED.)
A HUSBAND LOSES CONTROL, LASHES OUT IN ANGER.
(AND THE SHADOWS FEED.)
BUT THOSE DARK VORTEXES AREN'T SOMETHING OTHER. NO...

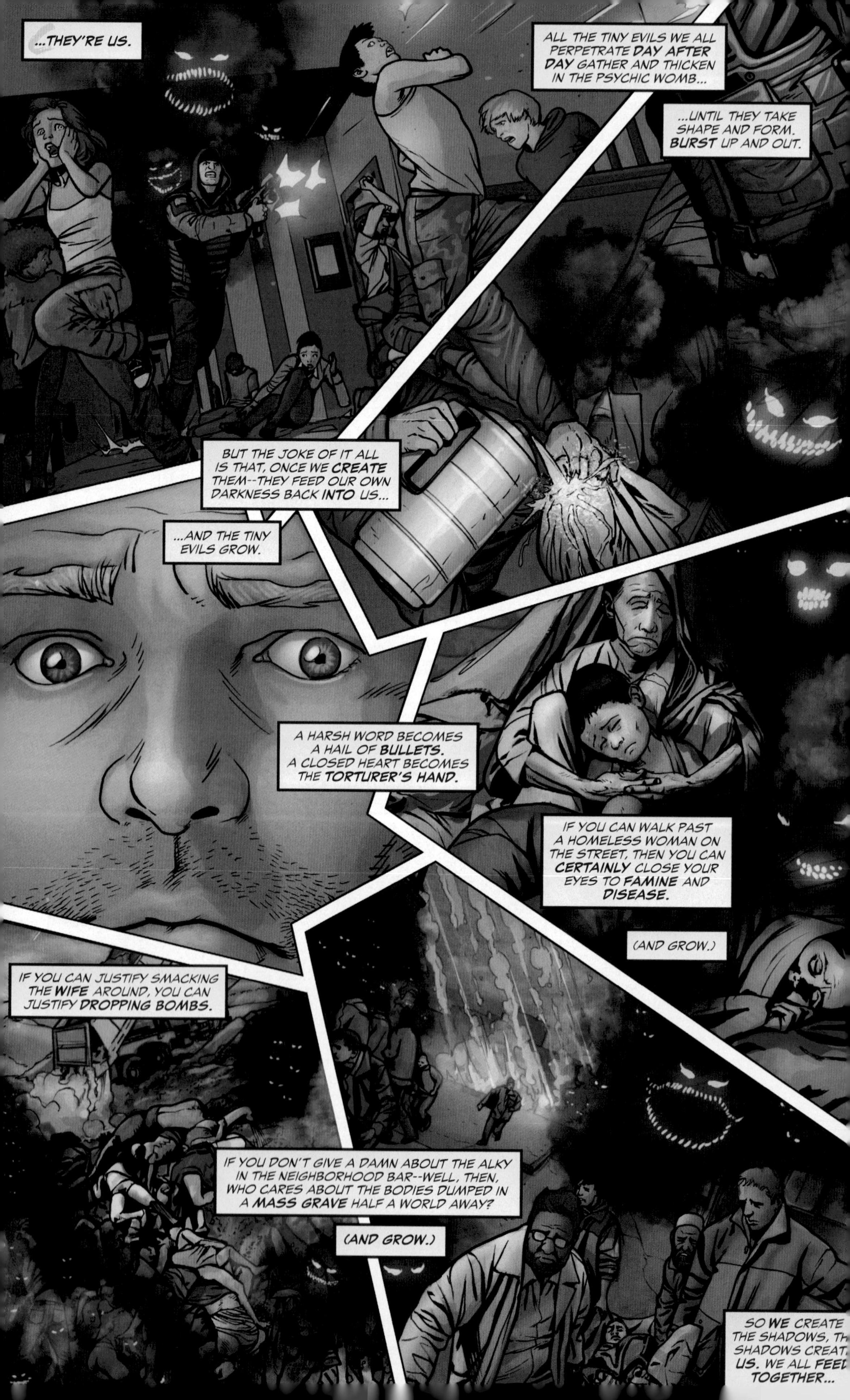
...THEY'RE US.
ALL THE TINY EVILS WE ALL PERPETRATE DAY AFTER DAY GATHER AND THICKEN IN THE PSYCHIC WOMB...
...UNTIL THEY TAKE SHAPE AND FORM. BURST UP AND OUT.
BUT THE JOKE OF IT ALL IS THAT, ONCE WE CREATE THEM--THEY FEED OUR OWN DARKNESS BACK INTO US...
...AND THE TINY EVILS GROW.
A HARSH WORD BECOMES A HAIL OF BULLETS. A CLOSED HEART BECOMES THE TORTURER'S HAND.
IF YOU CAN WALK PAST A HOMELESS WOMAN ON THE STREET, THEN YOU CAN CERTAINLY CLOSE YOUR EYES TO FAMINE AND DISEASE.
(AND GROW.)
IF YOU CAN JUSTIFY SMACKING THE WIFE AROUND, YOU CAN JUSTIFY DROPPING BOMBS.
IF YOU DON'T GIVE A DAMN ABOUT THE ALKY IN THE NEIGHBORHOOD BAR--WELL, THEN, WHO CARES ABOUT THE BODIES DUMPED IN A MASS GRAVE HALF A WORLD AWAY?
(AND GROW.)
SO WE CREATE THE SHADOWS, TH SHADOWS CREAT US. WE ALL FEED TOGETHER...

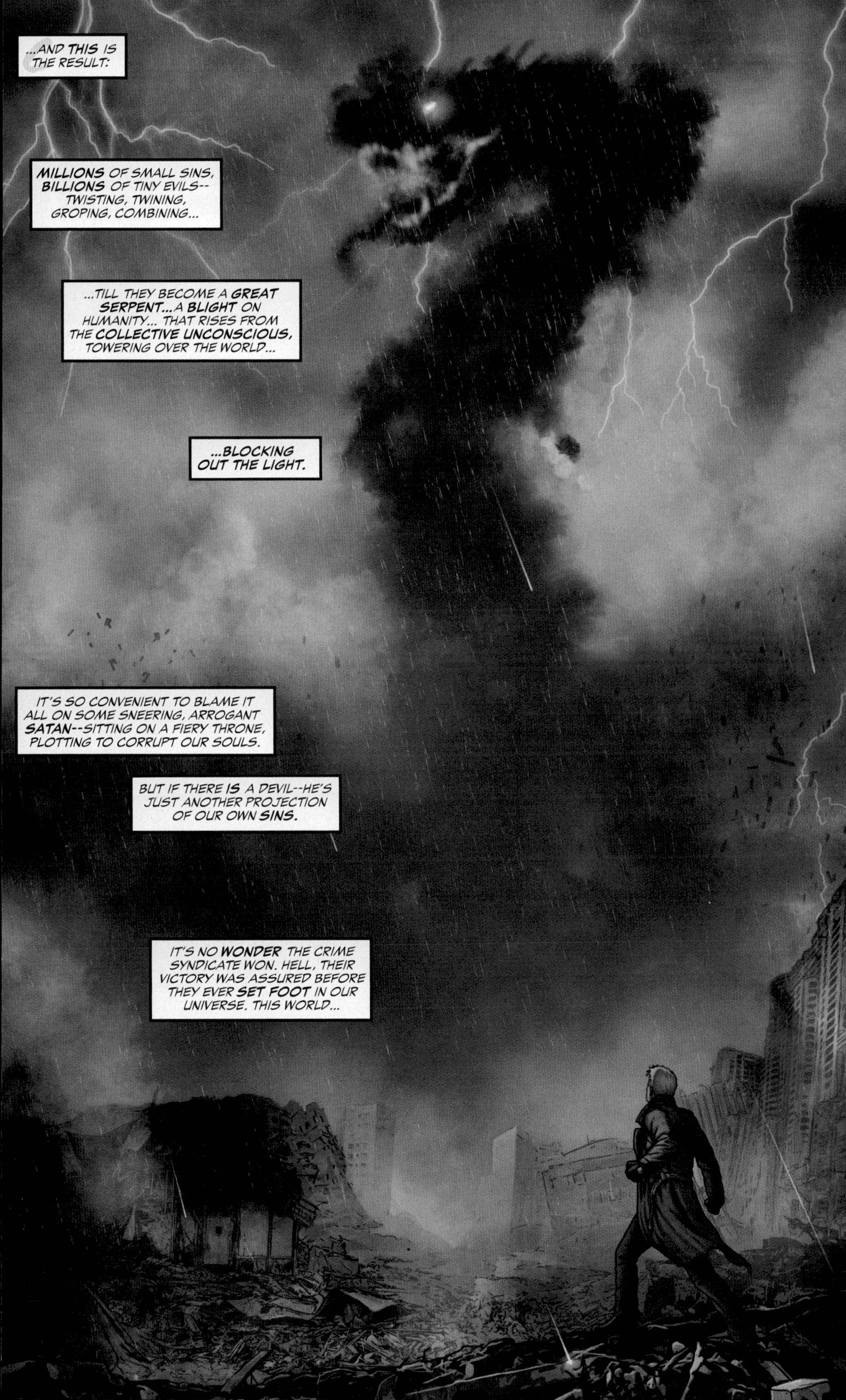

...AND THIS IS THE RESULT:
MILLIONS OF SMALL SINS, BILLIONS OF TINY EVILS-- TWISTING, TWINING, GROPING, COMBINING...
...TILL THEY BECOME A GREAT SERPENT...A BLIGHT ON HUMANITY... THAT RISES FROM THE COLLECTIVE UNCONSCIOUS, TOWERING OVER THE WORLD...
...BLOCKING OUT THE LIGHT.
IT'S SO CONVENIENT TO BLAME IT ALL ON SOME SNEERING, ARROGANT SATAN--SITTING ON A FIERY THRONE, PLOTTING TO CORRUPT OUR SOULS.
BUT IF THERE IS A DEVIL--HE'S JUST ANOTHER PROJECTION OF OUR OWN SINS.
IT'S NO WONDER THE CRIME SYNDICATE WON. HELL, THEIR VICTORY WAS ASSURED BEFORE THEY EVER SET FOOT IN OUR UNIVERSE. THIS WORLD...

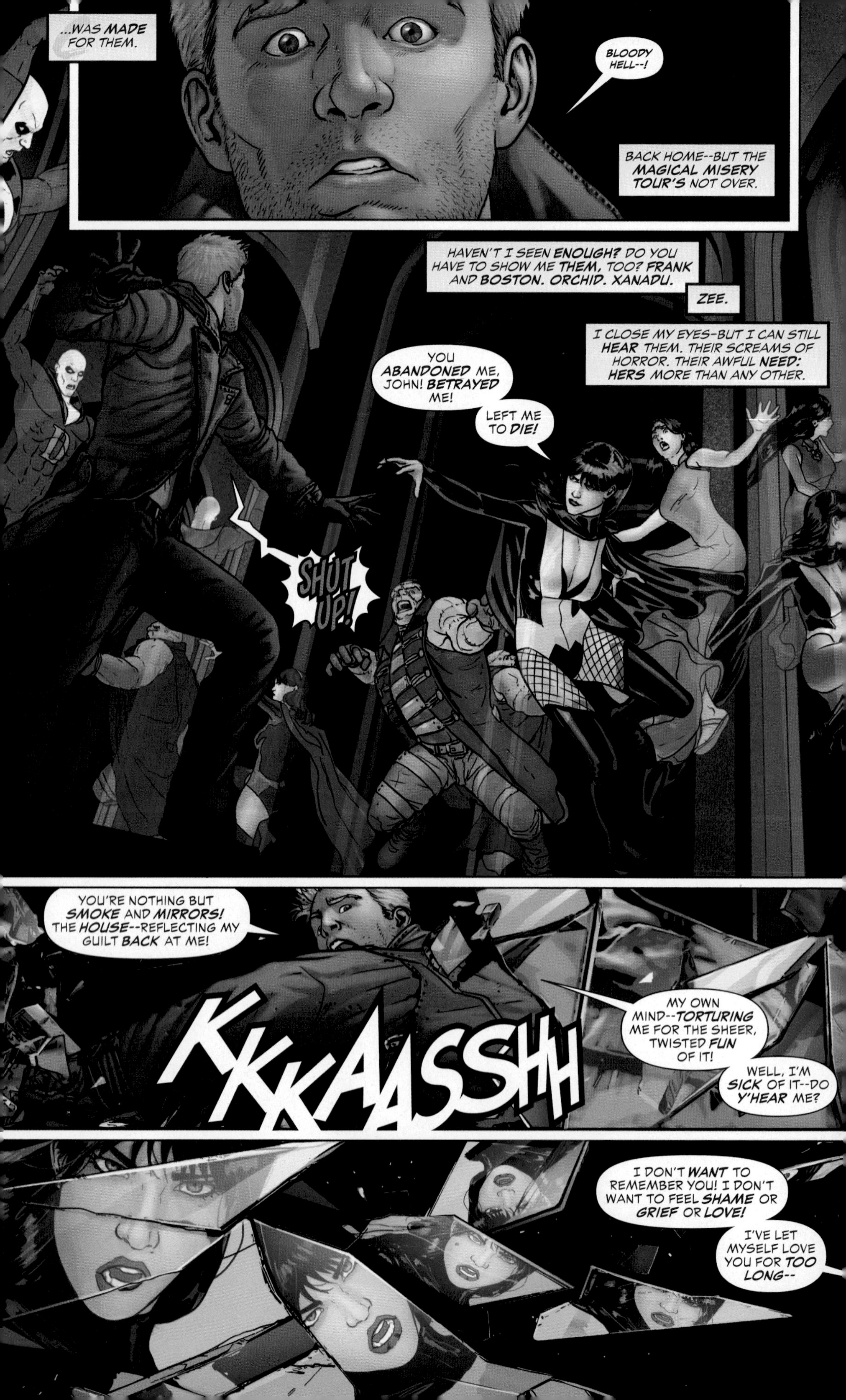
...WAS MADE FOR THEM.
BLOODY HELL--!
BACK HOME--BUT THE MAGICAL MISERY TOUR'S NOT OVER.
HAVEN'T I SEEN ENOUGH? DO YOU HAVE TO SHOW ME THEM, TOO? FRANK AND BOSTON. ORCHID. XANADU.
ZEE.
I CLOSE MY EYES--BUT I CAN STILL HEAR THEM. THEIR SCREAMS OF HORROR. THEIR AWFUL NEED: HERS MORE THAN ANY OTHER.
YOU ABANDONED ME, JOHN! BETRAYED ME!
LEFT ME TO DIE!
SHUT UP!
YOU'RE NOTHING BUT SMOKE AND MIRRORS! THE HOUSE--REFLECTING MY GUILT BACK AT ME!
KKKAASSHH
MY OWN MIND--TORTURING ME FOR THE SHEER, TWISTED FUN OF IT!
WELL, I'M SICK OF IT--DO Y'HEAR ME?
I DON'T WANT TO REMEMBER YOU! I DON'T WANT TO FEEL SHAME OR GRIEF OR LOVE!
I'VE LET MYSELF LOVE YOU FOR TOO LONG--

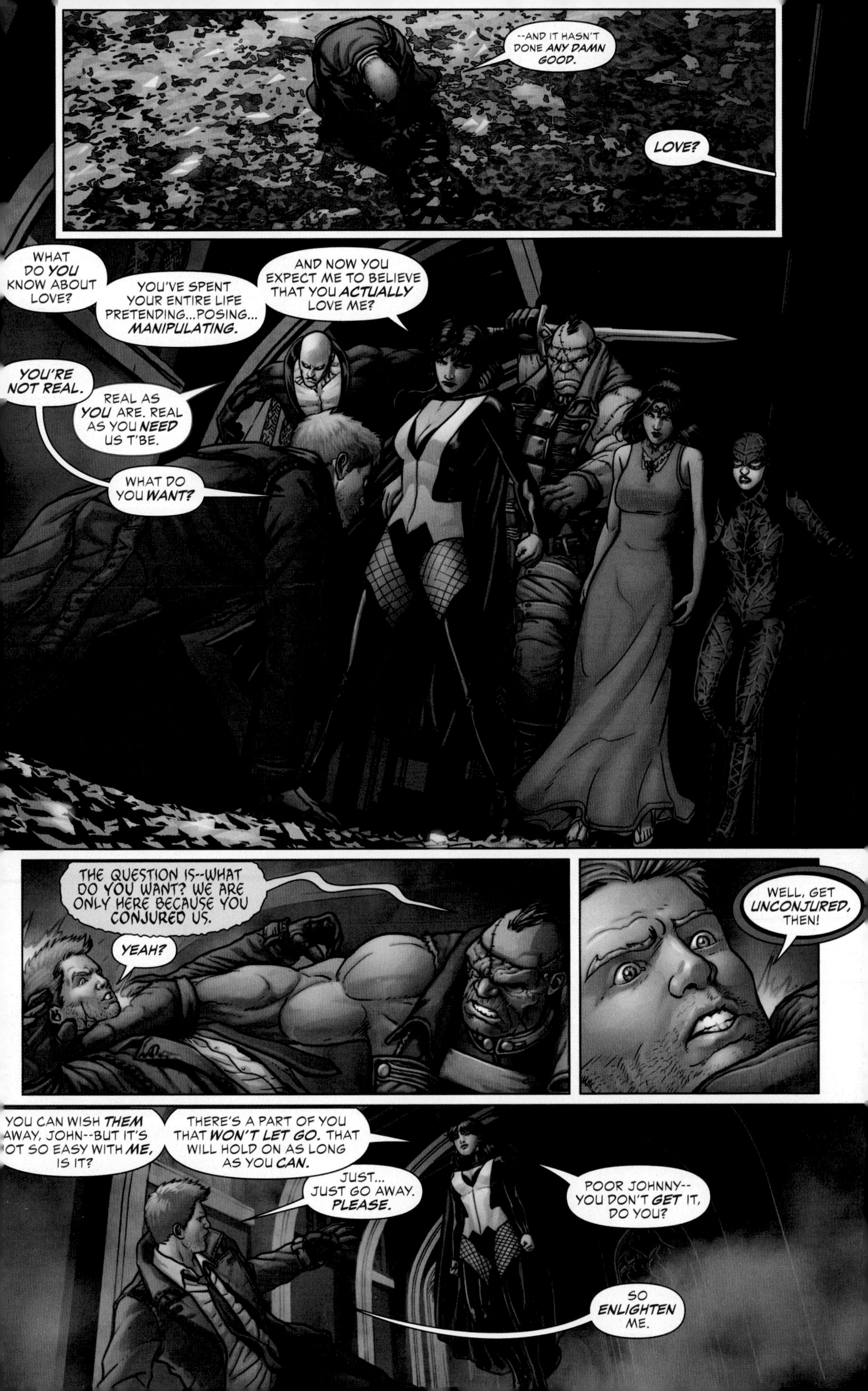
--AND IT HASN'T DONE ANY DAMN GOOD.
LOVE?
WHAT DO YOU KNOW ABOUT LOVE?
YOU'VE SPENT YOUR ENTIRE LIFE PRETENDING...POSING... MANIPULATING.
AND NOW YOU EXPECT ME TO BELIEVE THAT YOU ACTUALLY LOVE ME?
YOU'RE NOT REAL.
REAL AS YOU ARE. REAL AS YOU NEED US T'BE.
WHAT DO YOU WANT?
THE QUESTION IS--WHAT DO YOU WANT? WE ARE ONLY HERE BECAUSE YOU CONJURED US.
YEAH?
WELL, GET UNCONJURED, THEN!
YOU CAN WISH THEM AWAY, JOHN--BUT IT'S OT SO EASY WITH ME, IS IT?
THERE'S A PART OF YOU THAT WON'T LET GO. THAT WILL HOLD ON AS LONG AS YOU CAN.
JUST... JUST GO AWAY. PLEASE.
POOR JOHNNY-- YOU DON'T GET IT, DO YOU?
SO ENLIGHTEN ME.

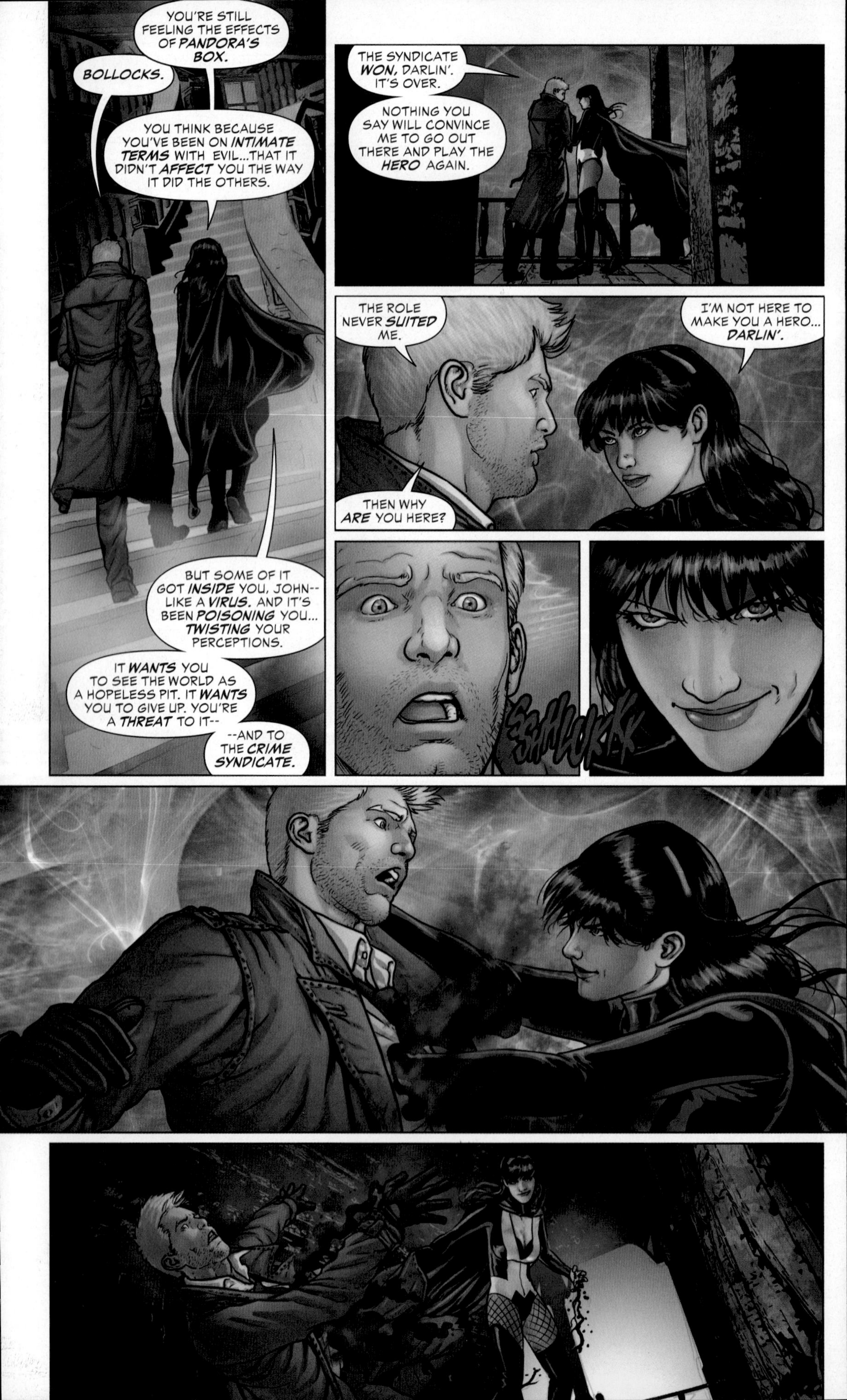

YOU'RE STILL FEELING THE EFFECTS OF PANDORA'S BOX.
BOLLOCKS.
YOU THINK BECAUSE YOU'VE BEEN ON INTIMATE TERMS WITH EVIL...THAT IT DIDN'T AFFECT YOU THE WAY IT DID THE OTHERS.
BUT SOME OF IT GOT INSIDE YOU, JOHN-- LIKE A VIRUS. AND IT'S BEEN POISONING YOU... TWISTING YOUR PERCEPTIONS.
IT WANTS YOU TO SEE THE WORLD AS A HOPELESS PIT. IT WANTS YOU TO GIVE UP. YOU'RE A THREAT TO IT--
--AND TO THE CRIME SYNDICATE.
THE SYNDICATE WON, DARLIN'. IT'S OVER.
NOTHING YOU SAY WILL CONVINCE ME TO GO OUT THERE AND PLAY THE HERO AGAIN.
THE ROLE NEVER SUITED ME.
I'M NOT HERE TO MAKE YOU A HERO... DARLIN'.
THEN WHY ARE YOU HERE?
SSHLUKKK

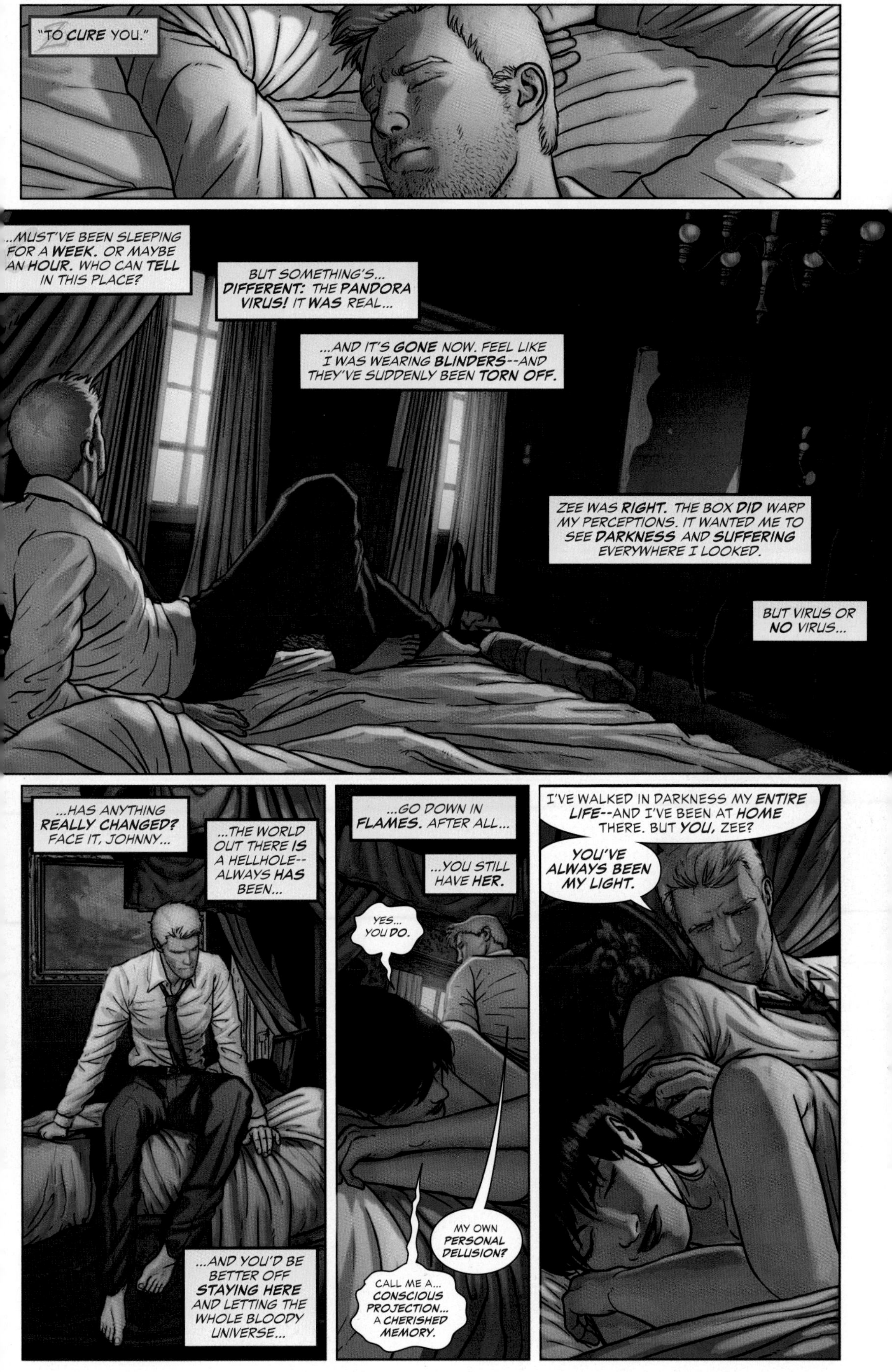

"TO CURE YOU."
...MUST'VE BEEN SLEEPING FOR A WEEK. OR MAYBE AN HOUR. WHO CAN TELL IN THIS PLACE?
BUT SOMETHING'S... DIFFERENT: THE PANDORA VIRUS! IT WAS REAL...
...AND IT'S GONE NOW. FEEL LIKE I WAS WEARING BLINDERS--AND THEY'VE SUDDENLY BEEN TORN OFF.
ZEE WAS RIGHT. THE BOX DID WARP MY PERCEPTIONS. IT WANTED ME TO SEE DARKNESS AND SUFFERING EVERYWHERE I LOOKED.
BUT VIRUS OR NO VIRUS...
...HAS ANYTHING REALLY CHANGED? FACE IT, JOHNNY...
...THE WORLD OUT THERE IS A HELLHOLE--ALWAYS HAS BEEN...
...AND YOU'D BE BETTER OFF STAYING HERE AND LETTING THE WHOLE BLOODY UNIVERSE...
...GO DOWN IN FLAMES. AFTER ALL...
...YOU STILL HAVE HER.
YES... YOU DO.
MY OWN PERSONAL DELUSION?
CALL ME A... CONSCIOUS PROJECTION... A CHERISHED MEMORY.
I'VE WALKED IN DARKNESS MY ENTIRE LIFE--AND I'VE BEEN AT HOME THERE. BUT YOU, ZEE?
YOU'VE ALWAYS BEEN MY LIGHT.

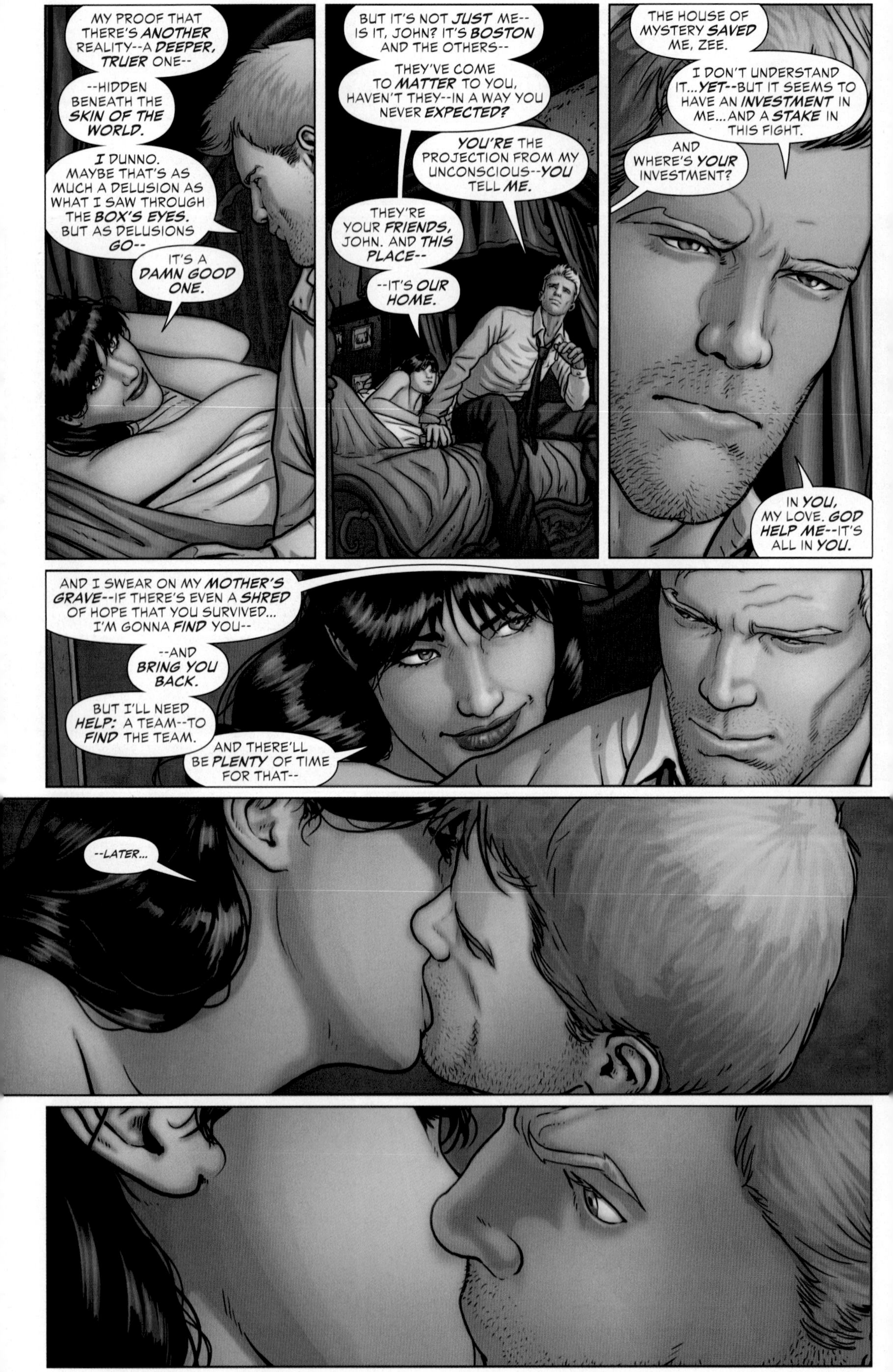

MY PROOF THAT THERE'S ANOTHER REALITY--A DEEPER, TRUER ONE--
--HIDDEN BENEATH THE SKIN OF THE WORLD.
I DUNNO. MAYBE THAT'S AS MUCH A DELUSION AS WHAT I SAW THROUGH THE BOX'S EYES. BUT AS DELUSIONS GO--
IT'S A DAMN GOOD ONE.
BUT IT'S NOT JUST ME-- IS IT, JOHN? IT'S BOSTON AND THE OTHERS--
THEY'VE COME TO MATTER TO YOU, HAVEN'T THEY--IN A WAY YOU NEVER EXPECTED?
YOU'RE THE PROJECTION FROM MY UNCONSCIOUS--YOU TELL ME.
THEY'RE YOUR FRIENDS, JOHN. AND THIS PLACE--
--IT'S OUR HOME.
THE HOUSE OF MYSTERY SAVED ME, ZEE.
I DON'T UNDERSTAND IT...YET--BUT IT SEEMS TO HAVE AN INVESTMENT IN ME...AND A STAKE IN THIS FIGHT.
AND WHERE'S YOUR INVESTMENT?
IN YOU, MY LOVE. GOD HELP ME--IT'S ALL IN YOU.
AND I SWEAR ON MY MOTHER'S GRAVE--IF THERE'S EVEN A SHRED OF HOPE THAT YOU SURVIVED... I'M GONNA FIND YOU--
--AND BRING YOU BACK.
BUT I'LL NEED HELP: A TEAM--TO FIND THE TEAM.
AND THERE'LL BE PLENTY OF TIME FOR THAT--
--LATER...

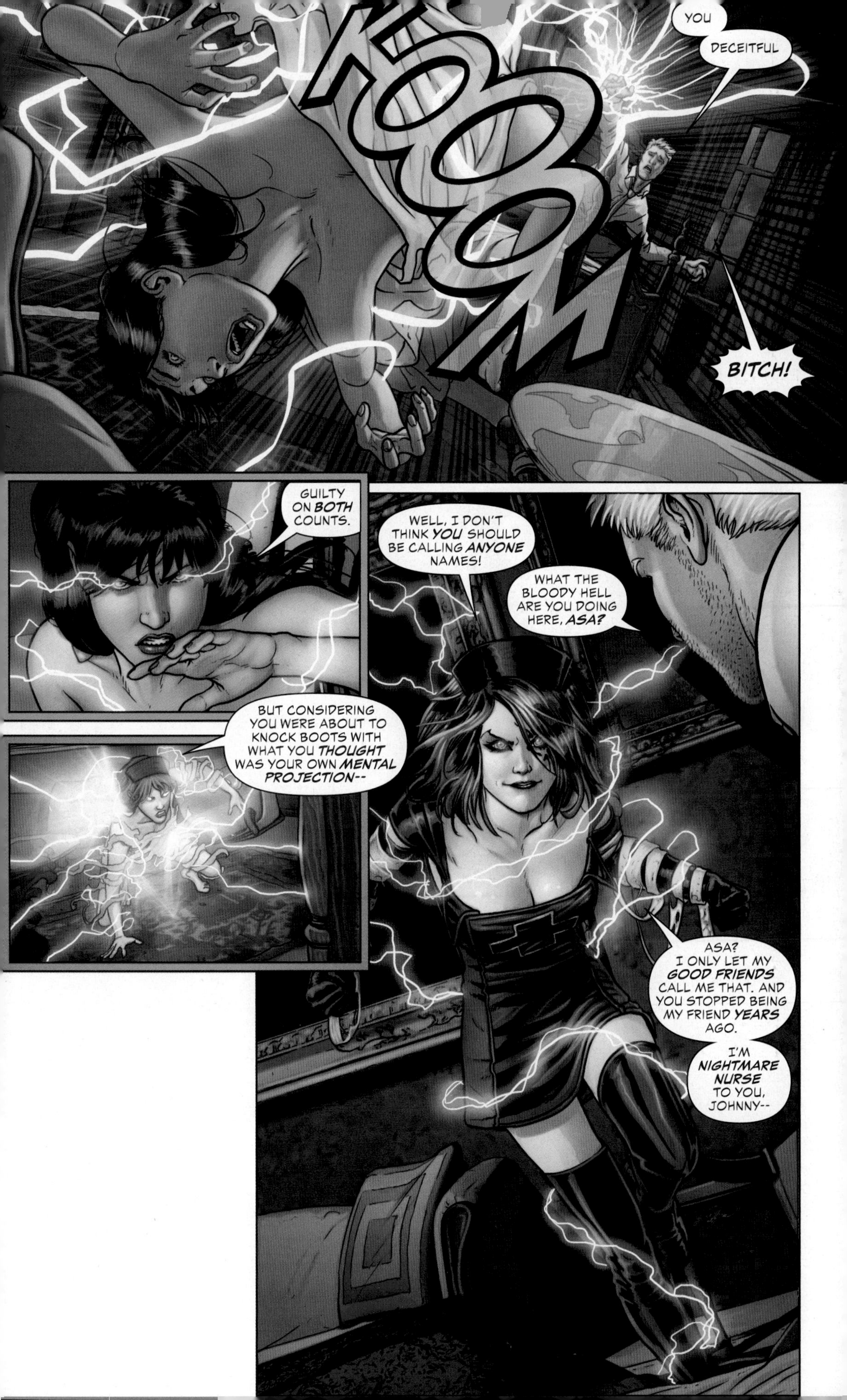
KROOOM
YOU
DECEITFUL
BITCH!
GUILTY ON BOTH COUNTS.
WELL, I DON'T THINK YOU SHOULD BE CALLING ANYONE NAMES!
WHAT THE BLOODY HELL ARE YOU DOING HERE, ASA?
BUT CONSIDERING YOU WERE ABOUT TO KNOCK BOOTS WITH WHAT YOU THOUGHT WAS YOUR OWN MENTAL PROJECTION--
ASA? I ONLY LET MY GOOD FRIENDS CALL ME THAT. AND YOU STOPPED BEING MY FRIEND YEARS AGO.
I'M NIGHTMARE NURSE TO YOU, JOHNNY--

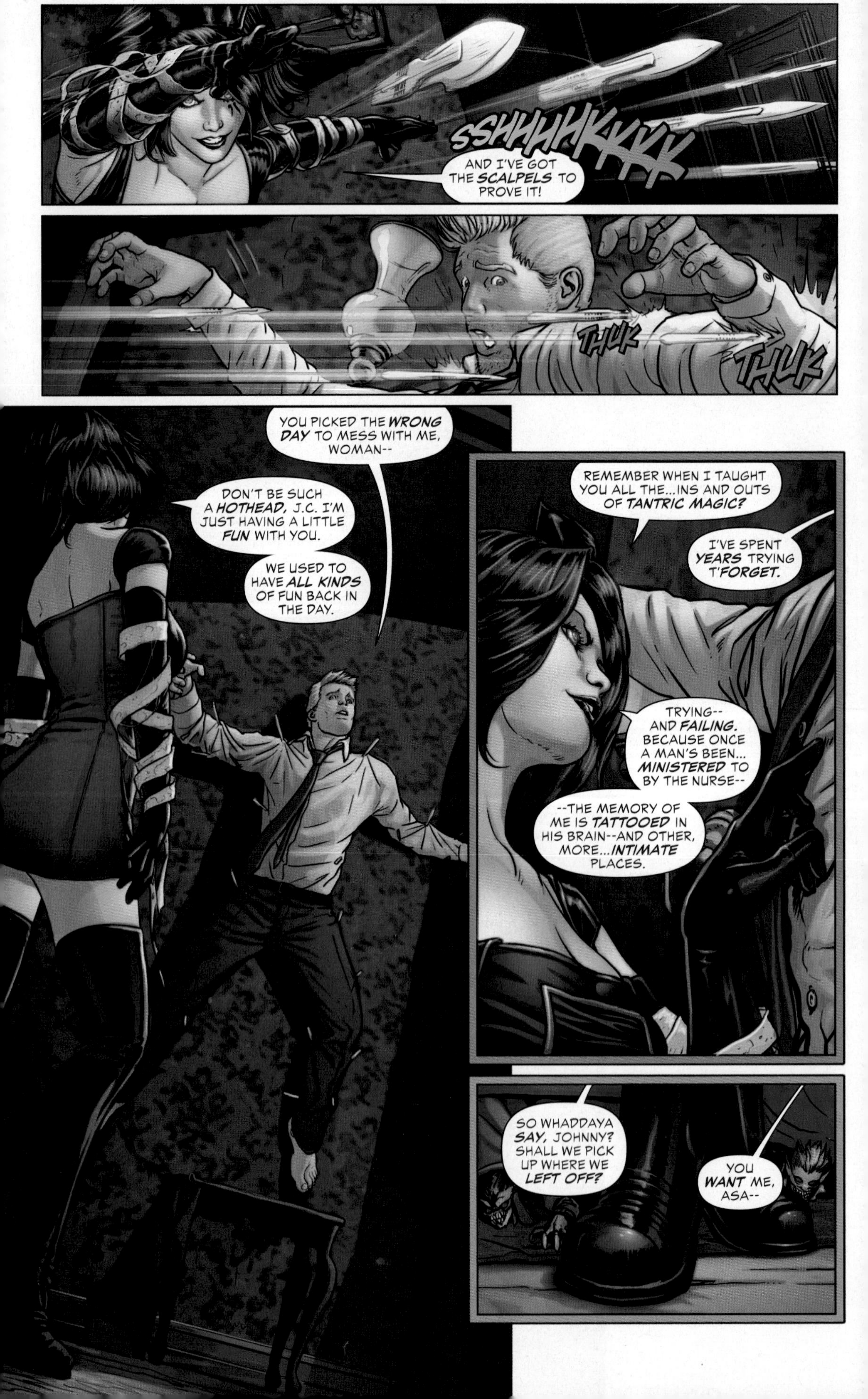
SSHHHKKKKK
AND I'VE GOT THE SCALPELS TO PROVE IT!
THUK
THUK
YOU PICKED THE WRONG DAY TO MESS WITH ME, WOMAN--
DON'T BE SUCH A HOTHEAD, J.C. I'M JUST HAVING A LITTLE FUN WITH YOU.
WE USED TO HAVE ALL KINDS OF FUN BACK IN THE DAY.
REMEMBER WHEN I TAUGHT YOU ALL THE...INS AND OUTS OF TANTRIC MAGIC?
I'VE SPENT YEARS TRYING T'FORGET.
TRYING-- AND FAILING. BECAUSE ONCE A MAN'S BEEN... MINISTERED TO BY THE NURSE--
--THE MEMORY OF ME IS TATTOOED IN HIS BRAIN--AND OTHER, MORE...INTIMATE PLACES.
SO WHADDAYA SAY, JOHNNY? SHALL WE PICK UP WHERE WE LEFT OFF?
YOU WANT ME, ASA--

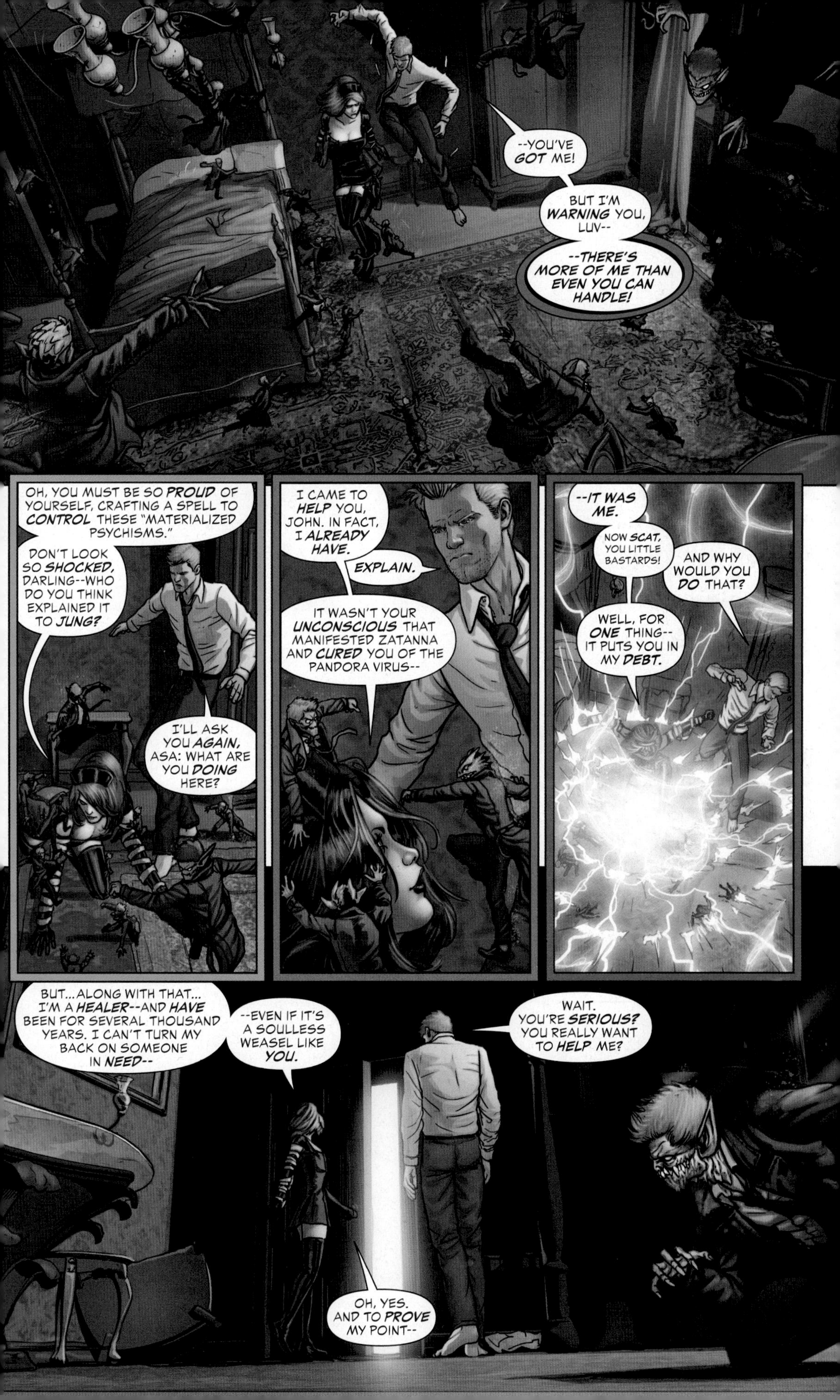
--YOU'VE GOT ME!
BUT I'M WARNING YOU, LUV--
--THERE'S MORE OF ME THAN EVEN YOU CAN HANDLE!
OH, YOU MUST BE SO PROUD OF YOURSELF, CRAFTING A SPELL TO CONTROL THESE "MATERIALIZED PSYCHISMS."
DON'T LOOK SO SHOCKED, DARLING--WHO DO YOU THINK EXPLAINED IT TO JUNG?
I'LL ASK YOU AGAIN, ASA: WHAT ARE YOU DOING HERE?
I CAME TO HELP YOU, JOHN. IN FACT, I ALREADY HAVE.
EXPLAIN.
IT WASN'T YOUR UNCONSCIOUS THAT MANIFESTED ZATANNA AND CURED YOU OF THE PANDORA VIRUS--
--IT WAS ME.
NOW SCAT, YOU LITTLE BASTARDS!
AND WHY WOULD YOU DO THAT?
WELL, FOR ONE THING--IT PUTS YOU IN MY DEBT.
BUT...ALONG WITH THAT... I'M A HEALER--AND HAVE BEEN FOR SEVERAL THOUSAND YEARS. I CAN'T TURN MY BACK ON SOMEONE IN NEED--
--EVEN IF IT'S A SOULLESS WEASEL LIKE YOU.
WAIT. YOU'RE SERIOUS? YOU REALLY WANT TO HELP ME?
OH, YES. AND TO PROVE MY POINT--

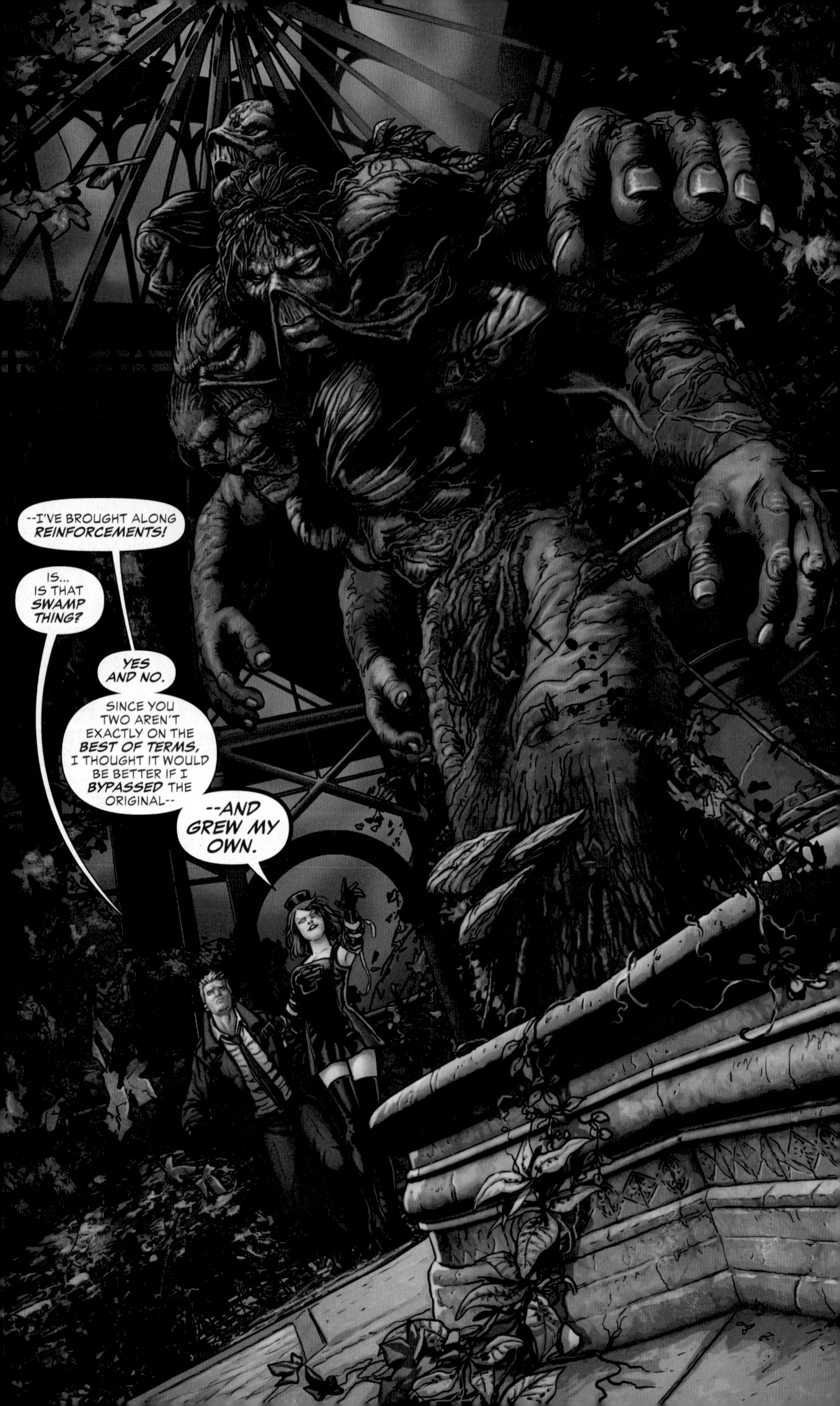

--I'VE BROUGHT ALONG REINFORCEMENTS!
IS... IS THAT SWAMP THING?
YES AND NO.
SINCE YOU TWO AREN'T EXACTLY ON THE BEST OF TERMS, I THOUGHT IT WOULD BE BETTER IF I BYPASSED THE ORIGINAL--
--AND GREW MY OWN.

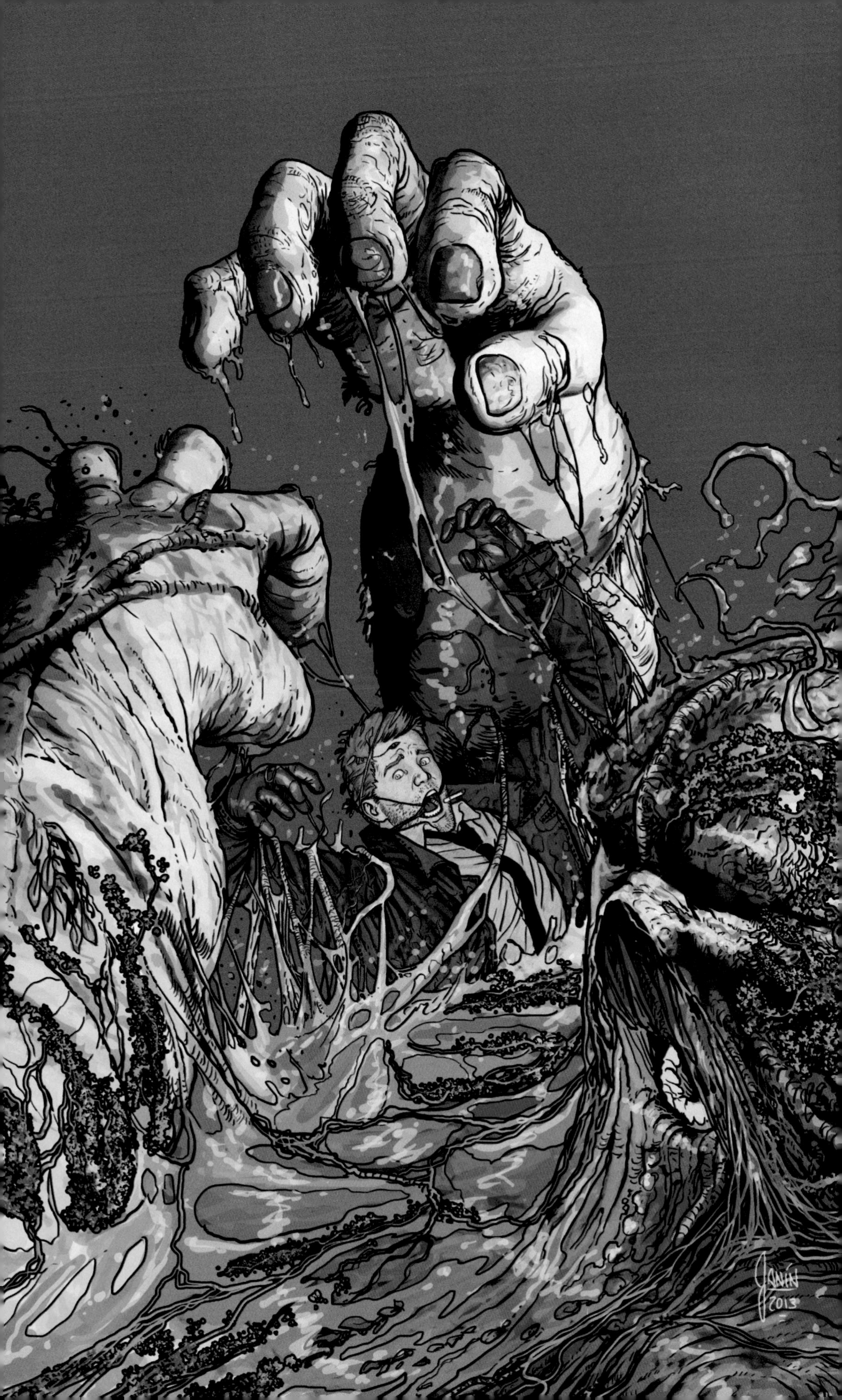

J. M. DeMATTEIS
writer

MIKEL JANIN
penciller & graytone artist

VICENTE CIFUENTES & GUILLERMO ORTEGO
inkers

MIKEL JANIN
cover artist

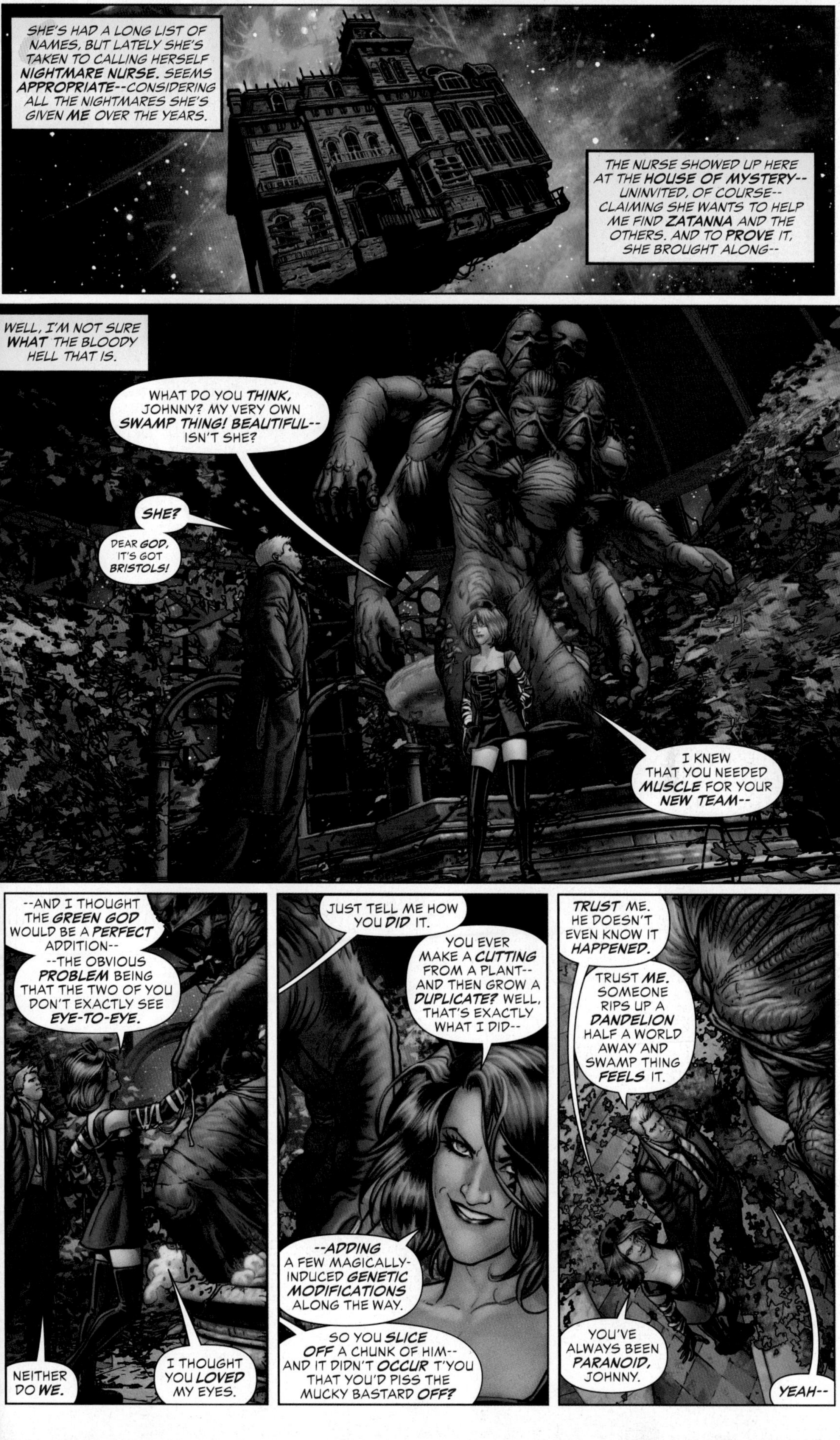
SHE'S HAD A LONG LIST OF NAMES, BUT LATELY SHE'S TAKEN TO CALLING HERSELF NIGHTMARE NURSE. SEEMS APPROPRIATE--CONSIDERING ALL THE NIGHTMARES SHE'S GIVEN ME OVER THE YEARS.
THE NURSE SHOWED UP HERE AT THE HOUSE OF MYSTERY--UNINVITED, OF COURSE--CLAIMING SHE WANTS TO HELP ME FIND ZATANNA AND THE OTHERS. AND TO PROVE IT, SHE BROUGHT ALONG--
WELL, I'M NOT SURE WHAT THE BLOODY HELL THAT IS.
WHAT DO YOU THINK, JOHNNY? MY VERY OWN SWAMP THING! BEAUTIFUL--ISN'T SHE?
SHE?
DEAR GOD, IT'S GOT BRISTOLS!
I KNEW THAT YOU NEEDED MUSCLE FOR YOUR NEW TEAM--
--AND I THOUGHT THE GREEN GOD WOULD BE A PERFECT ADDITION--
--THE OBVIOUS PROBLEM BEING THAT THE TWO OF YOU DON'T EXACTLY SEE EYE-TO-EYE.
NEITHER DO WE.
I THOUGHT YOU LOVED MY EYES.
JUST TELL ME HOW YOU DID IT.
YOU EVER MAKE A CUTTING FROM A PLANT--AND THEN GROW A DUPLICATE? WELL, THAT'S EXACTLY WHAT I DID--
--ADDING A FEW MAGICALLY-INDUCED GENETIC MODIFICATIONS ALONG THE WAY.
SO YOU SLICE OFF A CHUNK OF HIM--AND IT DIDN'T OCCUR T'YOU THAT YOU'D PISS THE MUCKY BASTARD OFF?
TRUST ME. HE DOESN'T EVEN KNOW IT HAPPENED.
TRUST ME. SOMEONE RIPS UP A DANDELION HALF A WORLD AWAY AND SWAMP THING FEELS IT.
YOU'VE ALWAYS BEEN PARANOID, JOHNNY.
YEAH--

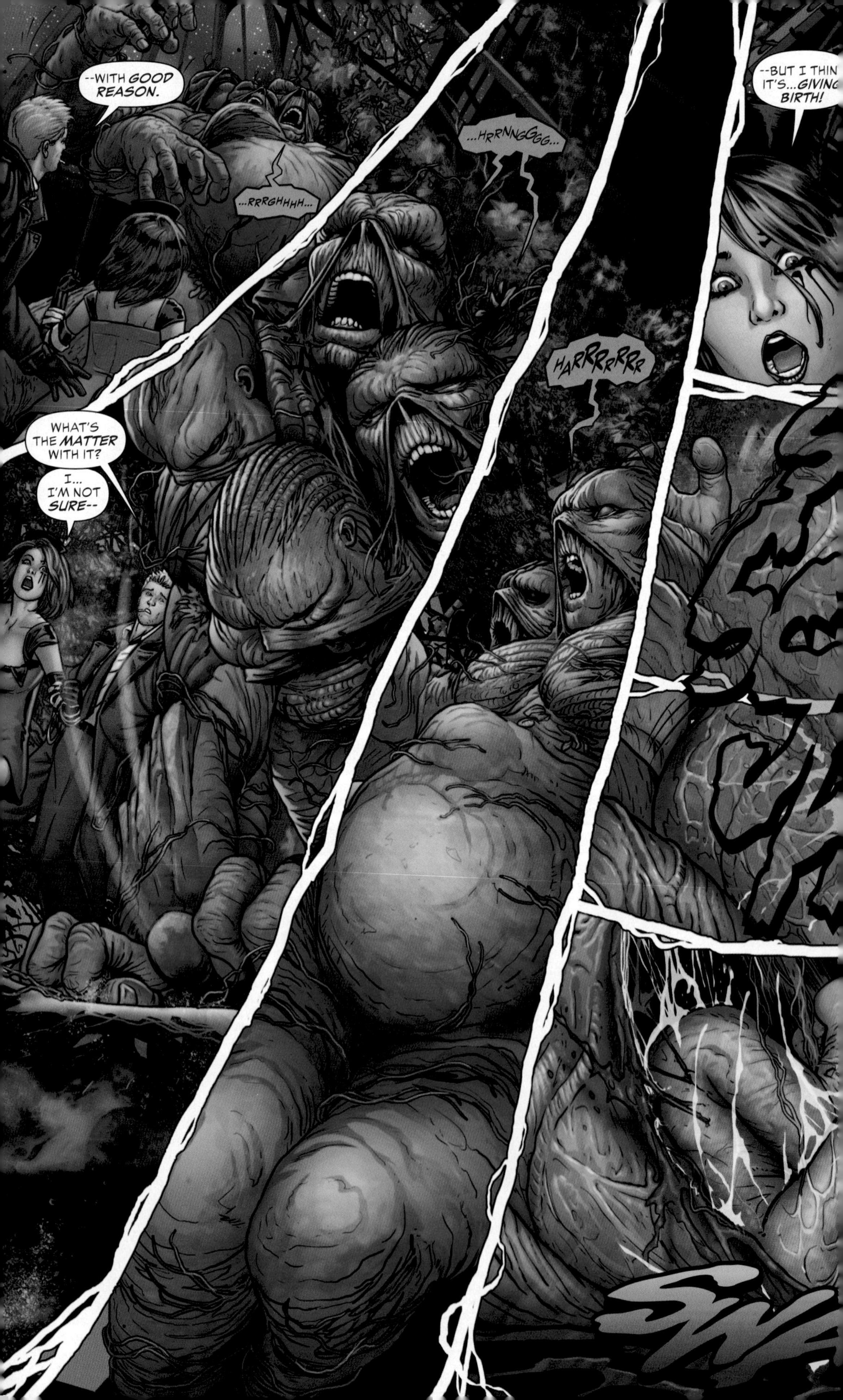
--WITH GOOD REASON.
...RRRGHHHH...
...HRRNNGGGG...
--BUT I THIN
IT'S...GIVING
BIRTH!
WHAT'S THE MATTER WITH IT?
I... I'M NOT SURE--
HARRRRRRR

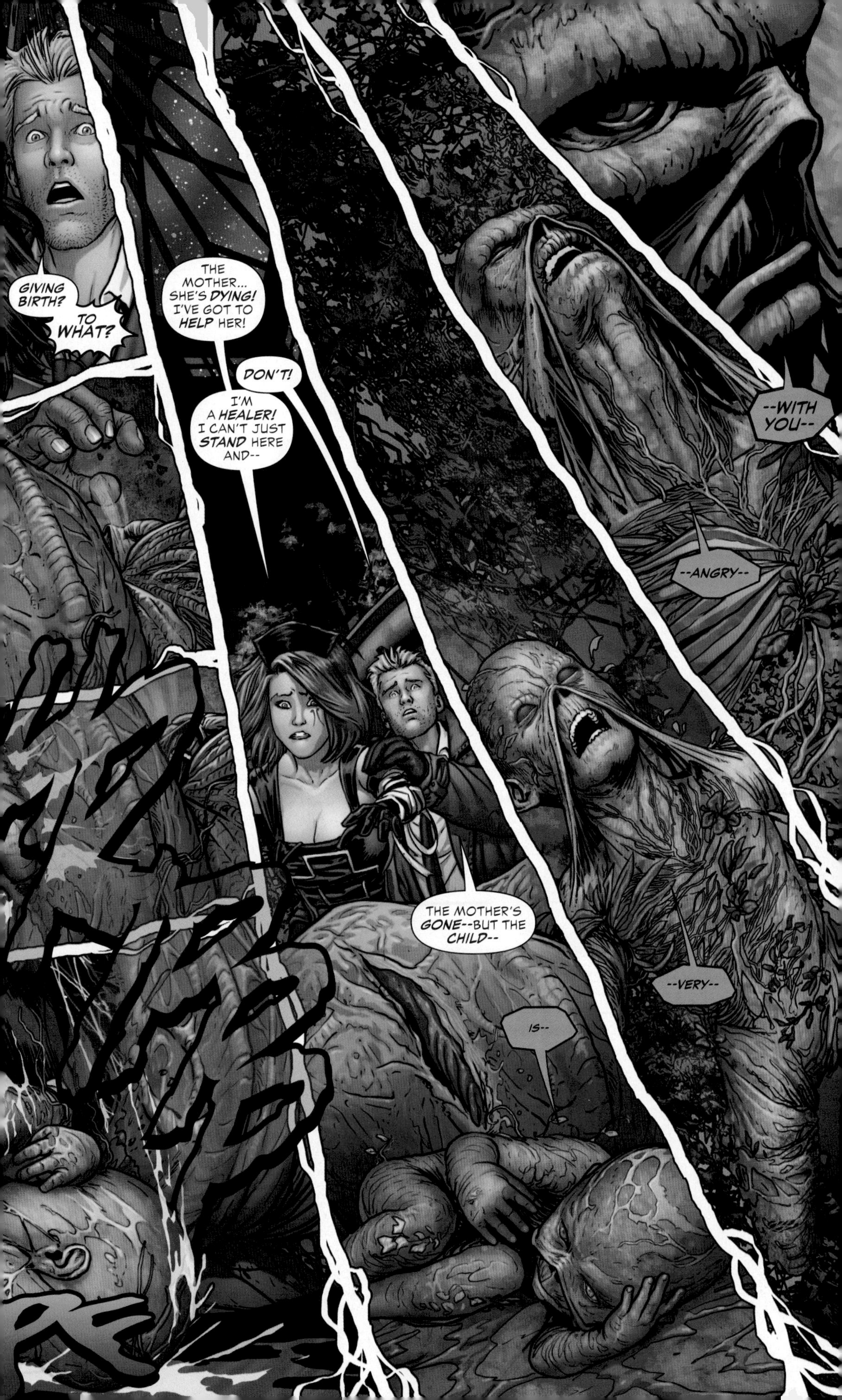
GIVING BIRTH? TO WHAT?
THE MOTHER... SHE'S DYING! I'VE GOT TO HELP HER!
DON'T!
I'M A HEALER! I CAN'T JUST STAND HERE AND--
--WITH YOU--
--ANGRY--
THE MOTHER'S GONE--BUT THE CHILD--
--VERY--
IS--

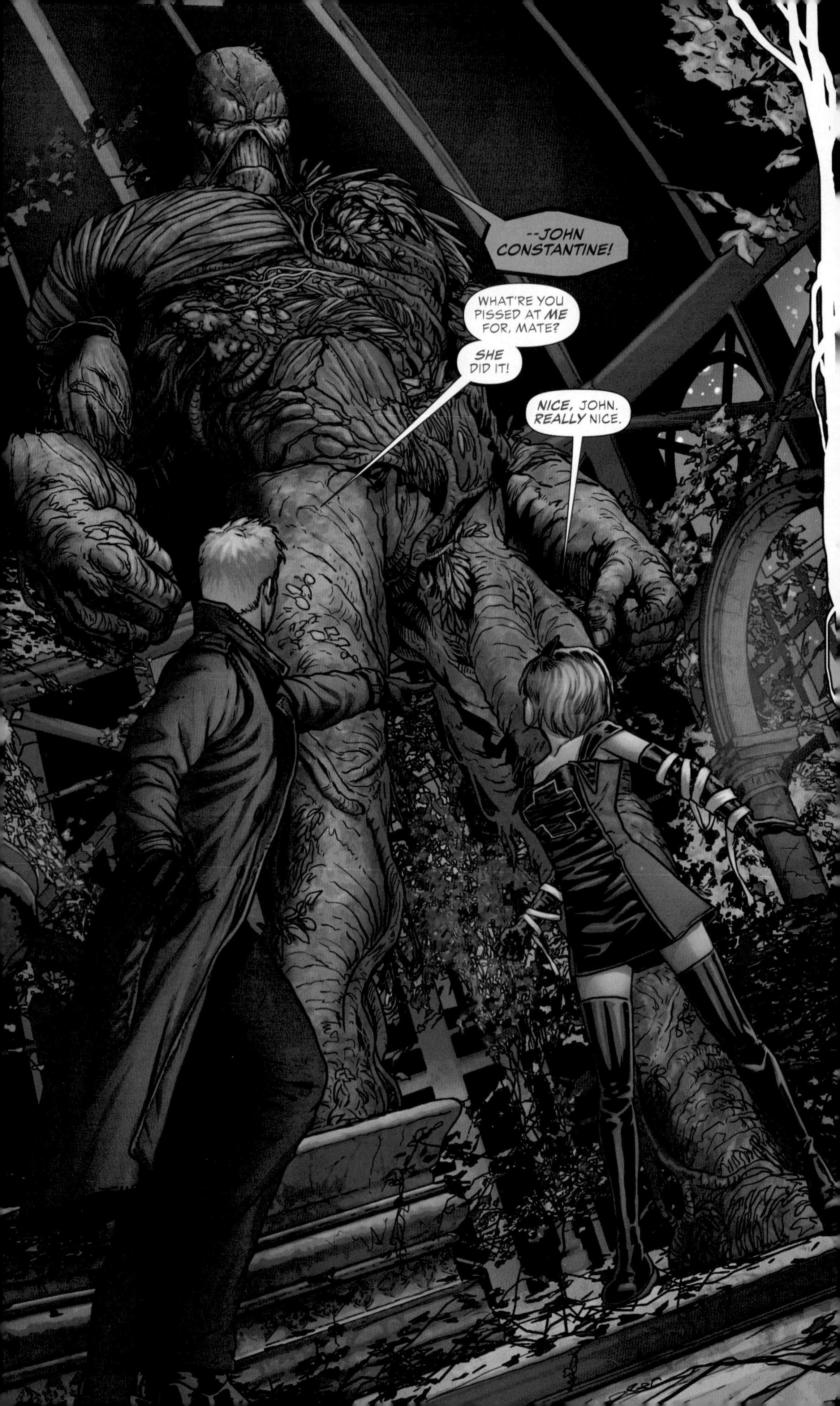
--JOHN CONSTANTINE!
WHAT'RE YOU PISSED AT ME FOR, MATE?
SHE DID IT!
NICE, JOHN. REALLY NICE.

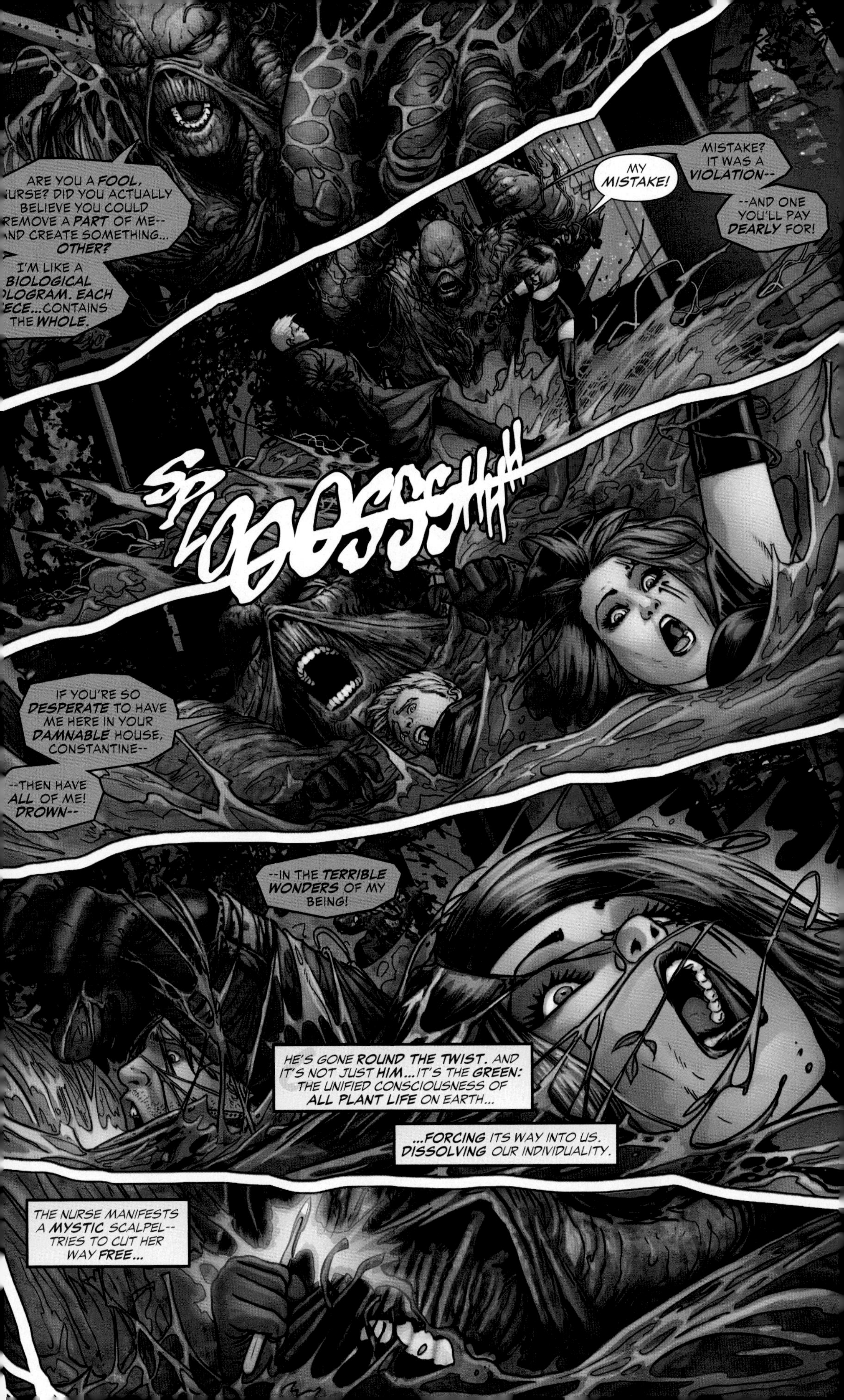
ARE YOU A FOOL, NURSE? DID YOU ACTUALLY BELIEVE YOU COULD REMOVE A PART OF ME-- AND CREATE SOMETHING... OTHER?
I'M LIKE A BIOLOGICAL HOLOGRAM. EACH PIECE...CONTAINS THE WHOLE.
MY MISTAKE!
MISTAKE? IT WAS A VIOLATION--
--AND ONE YOU'LL PAY DEARLY FOR!
SPLOOOSSSHHH
IF YOU'RE SO DESPERATE TO HAVE ME HERE IN YOUR DAMNABLE HOUSE, CONSTANTINE--
--THEN HAVE ALL OF ME! DROWN--
--IN THE TERRIBLE WONDERS OF MY BEING!
HE'S GONE ROUND THE TWIST. AND IT'S NOT JUST HIM...IT'S THE GREEN: THE UNIFIED CONSCIOUSNESS OF ALL PLANT LIFE ON EARTH...
...FORCING ITS WAY INTO US. DISSOLVING OUR INDIVIDUALITY.
THE NURSE MANIFESTS A MYSTIC SCALPEL-- TRIES TO CUT HER WAY FREE...

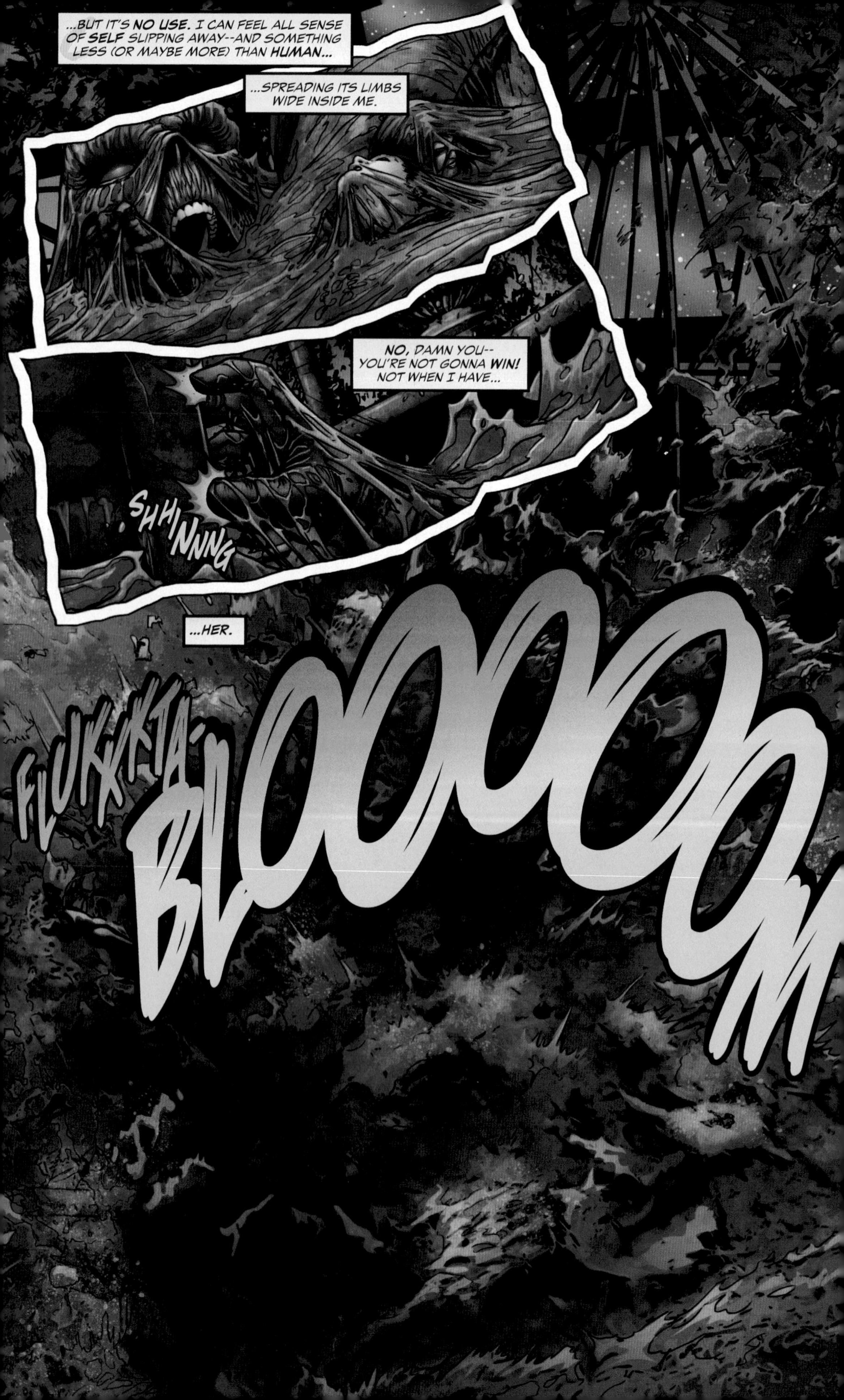
...BUT IT'S NO USE. I CAN FEEL ALL SENSE OF SELF SLIPPING AWAY--AND SOMETHING LESS (OR MAYBE MORE) THAN HUMAN...
...SPREADING ITS LIMBS WIDE INSIDE ME.
NO, DAMN YOU-- YOU'RE NOT GONNA WIN! NOT WHEN I HAVE...
SHHINNNG
...HER.
FLUKKTA-
BLOOOOOM

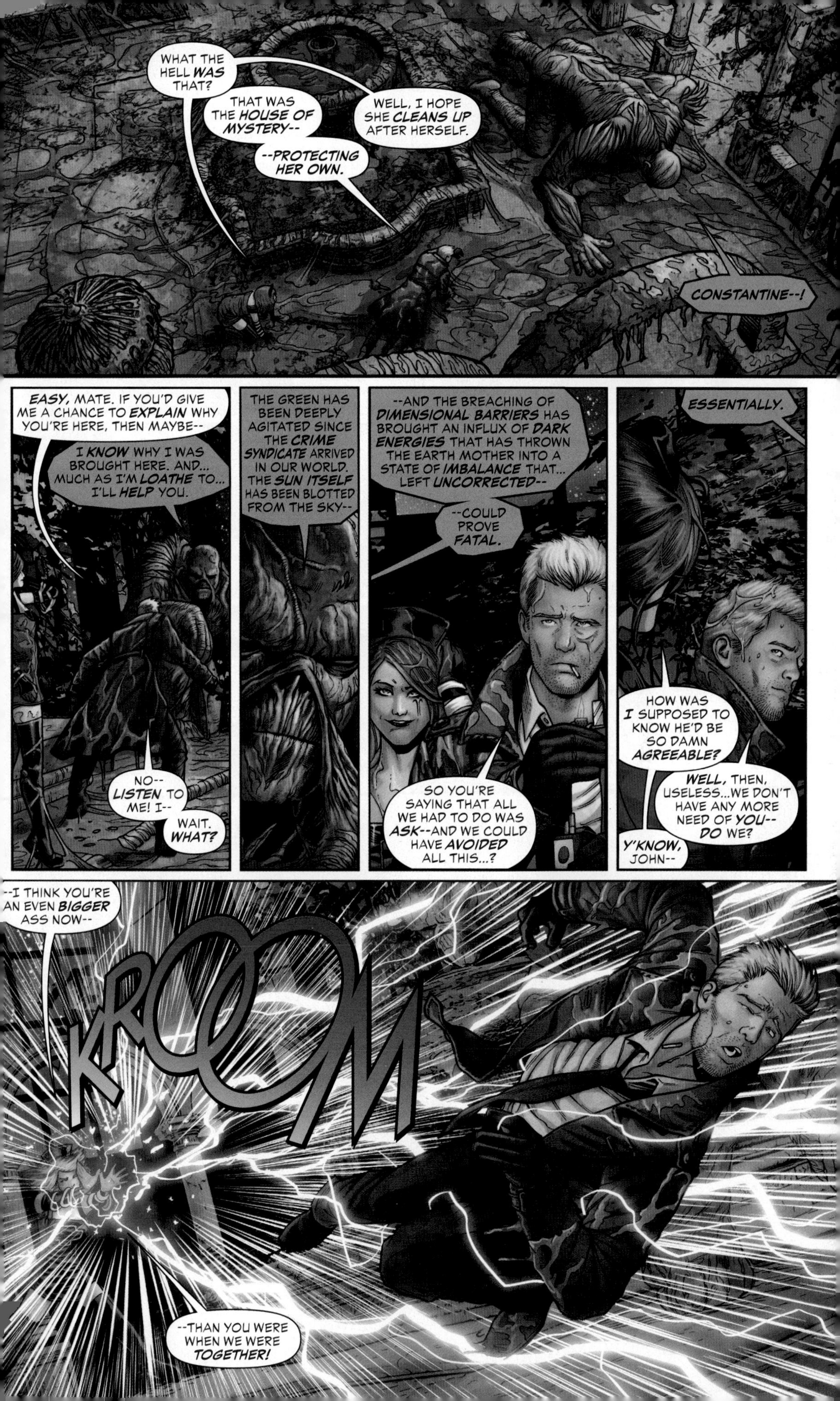

WHAT THE HELL **WAS** THAT?
THAT WAS THE ***HOUSE OF MYSTERY***--
--***PROTECTING HER OWN.***
WELL, I HOPE SHE ***CLEANS UP*** AFTER HERSELF.
CONSTANTINE--!
EASY, MATE. IF YOU'D GIVE ME A CHANCE TO ***EXPLAIN*** WHY YOU'RE HERE, THEN MAYBE--
I ***KNOW*** WHY I WAS BROUGHT HERE. AND... MUCH AS I'M ***LOATHE*** TO... I'LL ***HELP*** YOU.
NO-- ***LISTEN*** TO ME! I--
WAIT. ***WHAT?***
THE GREEN HAS BEEN DEEPLY AGITATED SINCE THE ***CRIME SYNDICATE*** ARRIVED IN OUR WORLD. THE ***SUN ITSELF*** HAS BEEN BLOTTED FROM THE SKY--
--AND THE BREACHING OF ***DIMENSIONAL BARRIERS*** HAS BROUGHT AN INFLUX OF ***DARK ENERGIES*** THAT HAS THROWN THE EARTH MOTHER INTO A STATE OF ***IMBALANCE*** THAT... LEFT ***UNCORRECTED***--
--COULD PROVE ***FATAL.***
SO YOU'RE SAYING THAT ALL WE HAD TO DO WAS ***ASK***--AND WE COULD HAVE ***AVOIDED*** ALL THIS...?
ESSENTIALLY.
HOW WAS ***I*** SUPPOSED TO KNOW HE'D BE SO DAMN ***AGREEABLE?***
WELL, THEN, USELESS...WE DON'T HAVE ANY MORE NEED OF ***YOU***-- ***DO*** WE?
Y'KNOW, JOHN--
--I THINK YOU'RE AN EVEN ***BIGGER*** ASS NOW--
KROOM
--THAN YOU WERE WHEN WE WERE ***TOGETHER!***

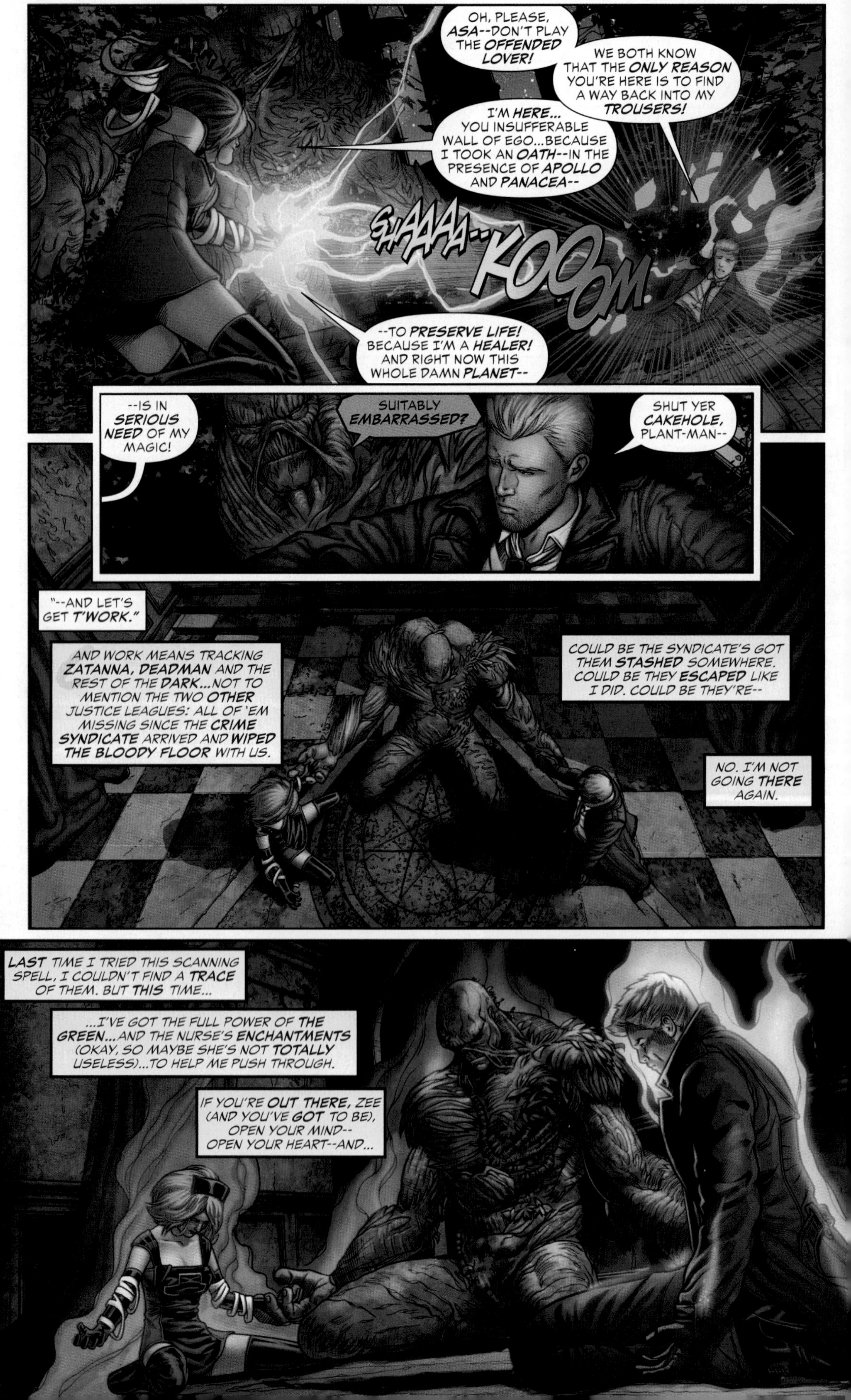

OH, PLEASE, ASA--DON'T PLAY THE OFFENDED LOVER!
WE BOTH KNOW THAT THE ONLY REASON YOU'RE HERE IS TO FIND A WAY BACK INTO MY TROUSERS!
I'M HERE... YOU INSUFFERABLE WALL OF EGO...BECAUSE I TOOK AN OATH--IN THE PRESENCE OF APOLLO AND PANACEA--
SHAAAA--KOOOOM
--TO PRESERVE LIFE! BECAUSE I'M A HEALER! AND RIGHT NOW THIS WHOLE DAMN PLANET--
--IS IN SERIOUS NEED OF MY MAGIC!
SUITABLY EMBARRASSED?
SHUT YER CAKEHOLE, PLANT-MAN--
"--AND LET'S GET T'WORK."
AND WORK MEANS TRACKING ZATANNA, DEADMAN AND THE REST OF THE DARK...NOT TO MENTION THE TWO OTHER JUSTICE LEAGUES: ALL OF 'EM MISSING SINCE THE CRIME SYNDICATE ARRIVED AND WIPED THE BLOODY FLOOR WITH US.
COULD BE THE SYNDICATE'S GOT THEM STASHED SOMEWHERE. COULD BE THEY ESCAPED LIKE I DID. COULD BE THEY'RE--
NO. I'M NOT GOING THERE AGAIN.
LAST TIME I TRIED THIS SCANNING SPELL, I COULDN'T FIND A TRACE OF THEM. BUT THIS TIME...
...I'VE GOT THE FULL POWER OF THE GREEN...AND THE NURSE'S ENCHANTMENTS (OKAY, SO MAYBE SHE'S NOT TOTALLY USELESS)...TO HELP ME PUSH THROUGH.
IF YOU'RE OUT THERE, ZEE (AND YOU'VE GOT TO BE), OPEN YOUR MIND-- OPEN YOUR HEART--AND...

AND

SOMETHING'S

BLOCKING

US!

IT'S LIKE THE MAGICAL PLANE'S BEEN ENCIRCLED BY A *RING OF PSYCHIC STATIC*...

...AND ANY SPELLS RELEASED INTO THE ETHERS ARE *CONTAMINATED*-- AND THEN *BOUNCED BACK* TO THE SENDERS.

THAT'S WHAT THOSE *MONSTROSITIES* ARE: *MUTATED SPELLS*. AND IF WE DON'T CLEAR THEM *OUT* OF HERE...

WE'RE ALL GONNA GET *INFECTED*.

SNIXOT ESREPSID!

WHAT'D YOU SAY?

HEY--YOUR GIRLFRIEND'S NOT THE *ONLY* ONE WHO KNOWS *BACKWARDS MAGIC*!

MAY BE TOO LATE. *LUNGS* ARE ON *FIRE*. *HEAD* FEELS LIKE SOMEONE JAMMED A *SPIKE* THROUGH IT.

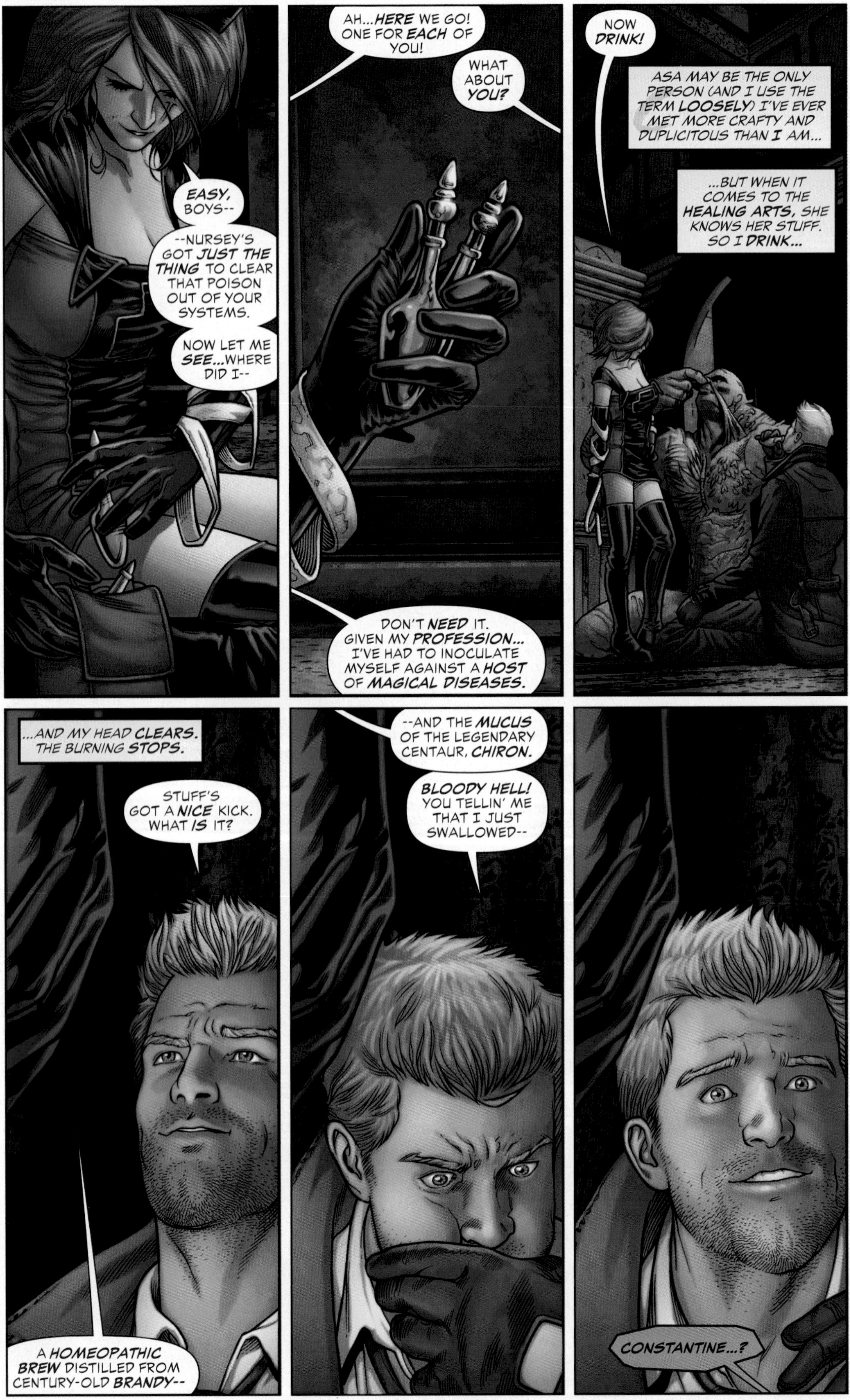
EASY, BOYS--
--NURSEY'S GOT JUST THE THING TO CLEAR THAT POISON OUT OF YOUR SYSTEMS.
NOW LET ME SEE...WHERE DID I--
AH...HERE WE GO! ONE FOR EACH OF YOU!
WHAT ABOUT YOU?
DON'T NEED IT. GIVEN MY PROFESSION... I'VE HAD TO INOCULATE MYSELF AGAINST A HOST OF MAGICAL DISEASES.
NOW DRINK!
ASA MAY BE THE ONLY PERSON (AND I USE THE TERM LOOSELY) I'VE EVER MET MORE CRAFTY AND DUPLICITOUS THAN I AM...
...BUT WHEN IT COMES TO THE HEALING ARTS, SHE KNOWS HER STUFF. SO I DRINK...
...AND MY HEAD CLEARS. THE BURNING STOPS.
STUFF'S GOT A NICE KICK. WHAT IS IT?
A HOMEOPATHIC BREW DISTILLED FROM CENTURY-OLD BRANDY--
--AND THE MUCUS OF THE LEGENDARY CENTAUR, CHIRON.
BLOODY HELL! YOU TELLIN' ME THAT I JUST SWALLOWED--
CONSTANTINE...?

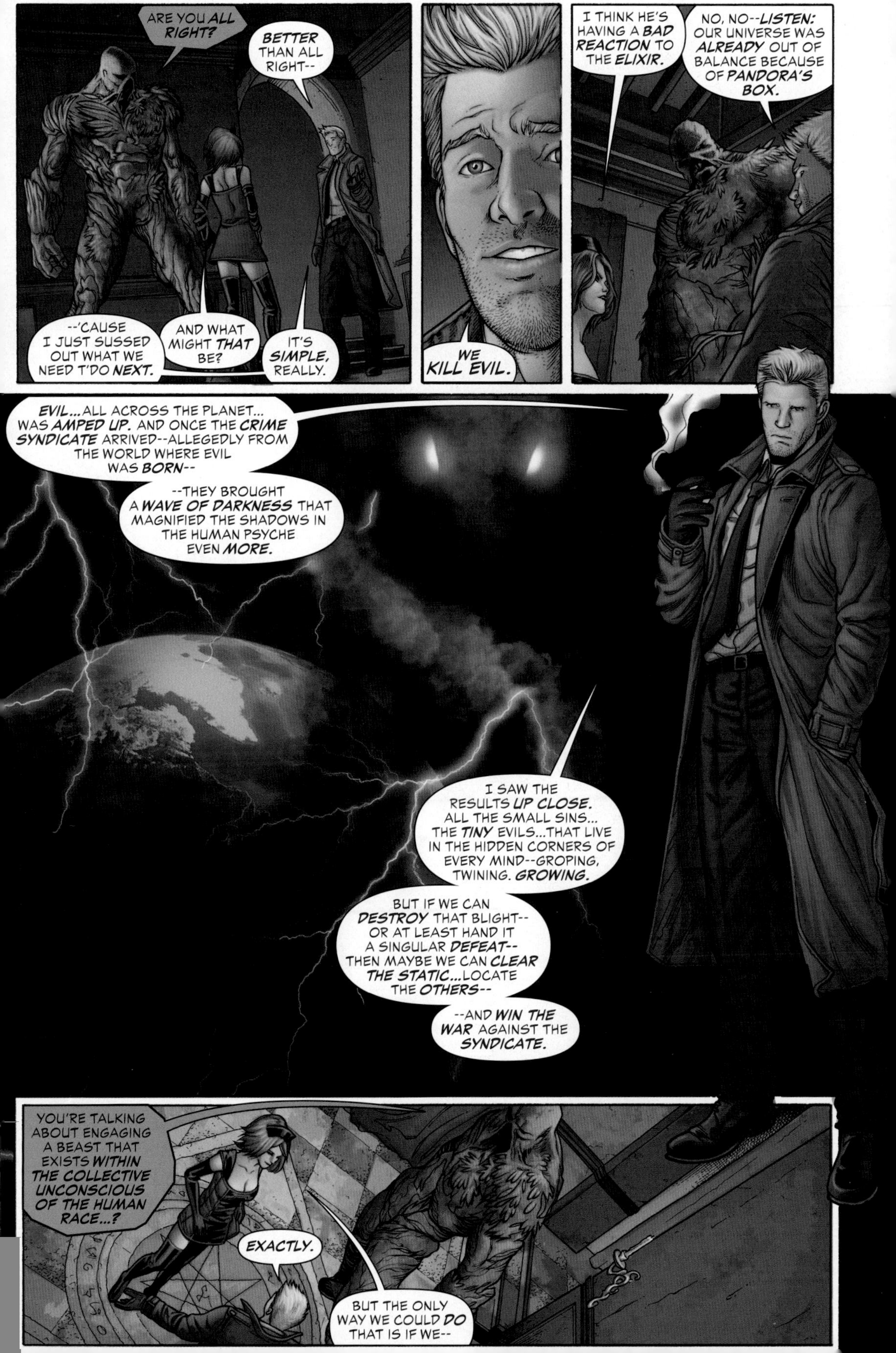
ARE YOU ALL RIGHT?
BETTER THAN ALL RIGHT--
--'CAUSE I JUST SUSSED OUT WHAT WE NEED T'DO NEXT.
AND WHAT MIGHT THAT BE?
IT'S SIMPLE, REALLY.
WE KILL EVIL.
I THINK HE'S HAVING A BAD REACTION TO THE ELIXIR.
NO, NO--LISTEN: OUR UNIVERSE WAS ALREADY OUT OF BALANCE BECAUSE OF PANDORA'S BOX.
EVIL...ALL ACROSS THE PLANET... WAS AMPED UP. AND ONCE THE CRIME SYNDICATE ARRIVED--ALLEGEDLY FROM THE WORLD WHERE EVIL WAS BORN--
--THEY BROUGHT A WAVE OF DARKNESS THAT MAGNIFIED THE SHADOWS IN THE HUMAN PSYCHE EVEN MORE.
I SAW THE RESULTS UP CLOSE. ALL THE SMALL SINS... THE TINY EVILS...THAT LIVE IN THE HIDDEN CORNERS OF EVERY MIND--GROPING, TWINING. GROWING.
BUT IF WE CAN DESTROY THAT BLIGHT-- OR AT LEAST HAND IT A SINGULAR DEFEAT-- THEN MAYBE WE CAN CLEAR THE STATIC...LOCATE THE OTHERS--
--AND WIN THE WAR AGAINST THE SYNDICATE.
YOU'RE TALKING ABOUT ENGAGING A BEAST THAT EXISTS WITHIN THE COLLECTIVE UNCONSCIOUS OF THE HUMAN RACE...?
EXACTLY.
BUT THE ONLY WAY WE COULD DO THAT IS IF WE--

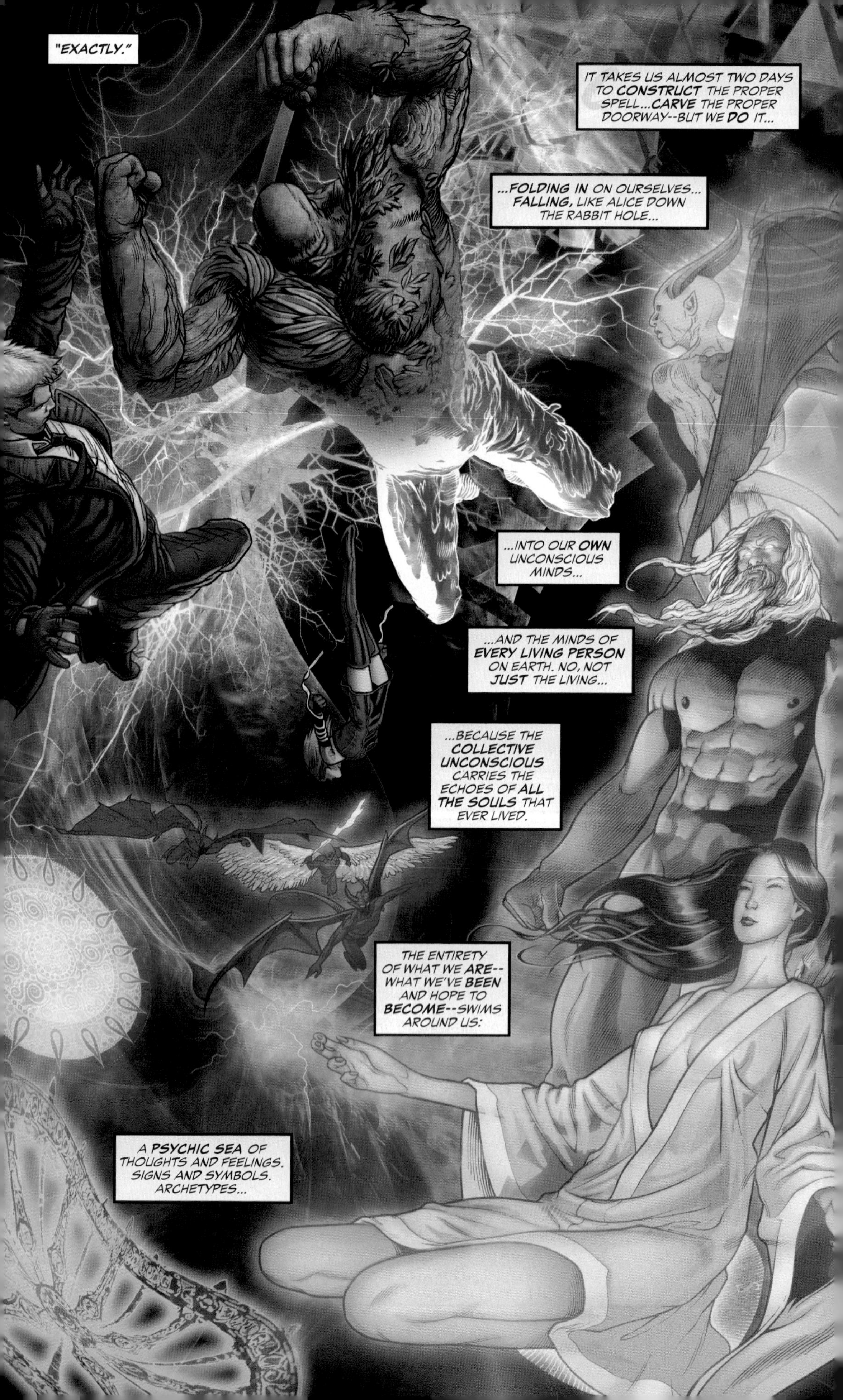

"EXACTLY."
IT TAKES US ALMOST TWO DAYS TO CONSTRUCT THE PROPER SPELL...CARVE THE PROPER DOORWAY--BUT WE DO IT...
...FOLDING IN ON OURSELVES... FALLING, LIKE ALICE DOWN THE RABBIT HOLE...
...INTO OUR OWN UNCONSCIOUS MINDS...
...AND THE MINDS OF EVERY LIVING PERSON ON EARTH. NO, NOT JUST THE LIVING...
...BECAUSE THE COLLECTIVE UNCONSCIOUS CARRIES THE ECHOES OF ALL THE SOULS THAT EVER LIVED.
THE ENTIRETY OF WHAT WE ARE--WHAT WE'VE BEEN AND HOPE TO BECOME--SWIMS AROUND US:
A PSYCHIC SEA OF THOUGHTS AND FEELINGS. SIGNS AND SYMBOLS. ARCHETYPES...

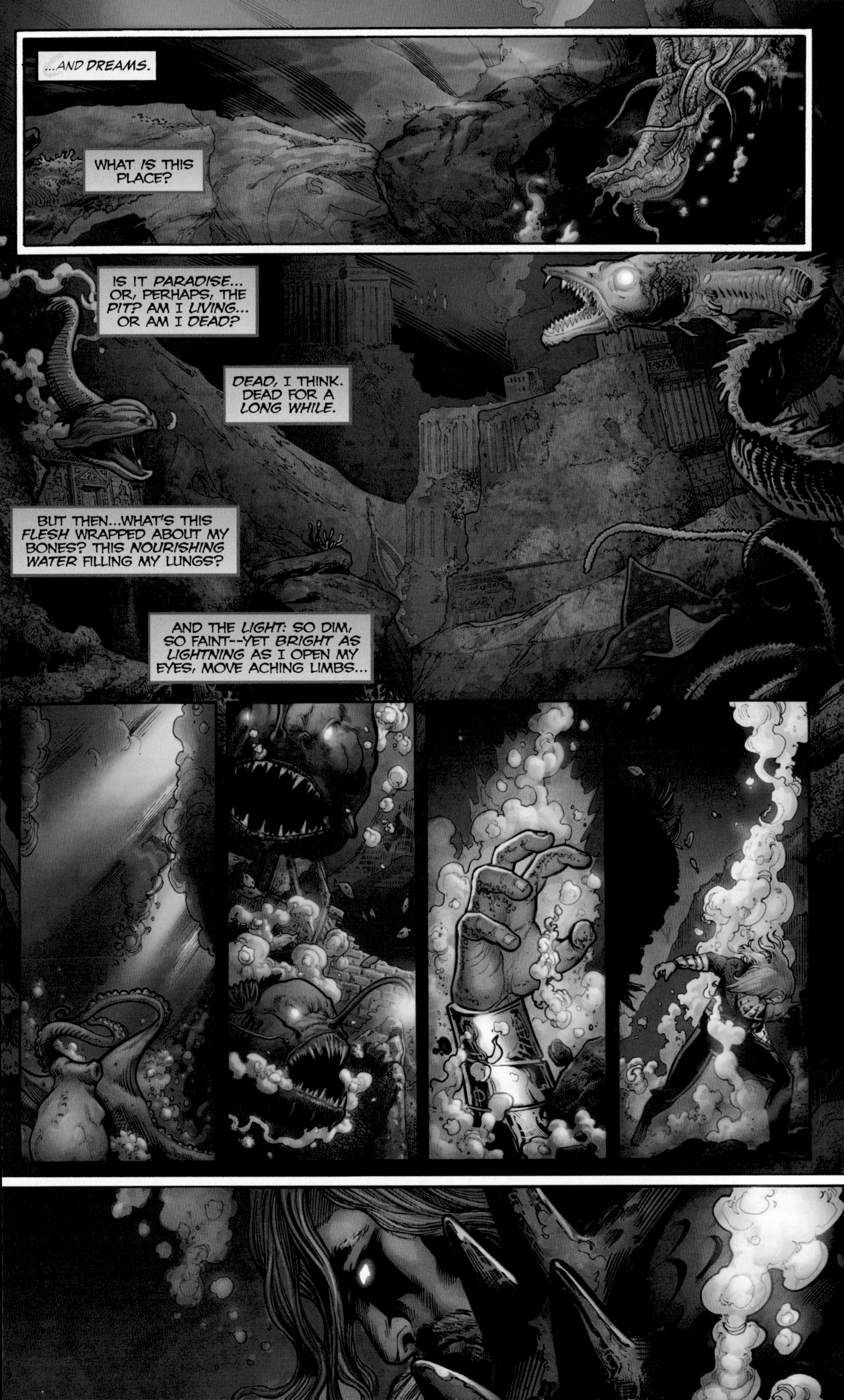
...AND DREAMS.
WHAT IS THIS PLACE?
IS IT PARADISE... OR, PERHAPS, THE PIT? AM I LIVING... OR AM I DEAD?
DEAD, I THINK. DEAD FOR A LONG WHILE.
BUT THEN...WHAT'S THIS FLESH WRAPPED ABOUT MY BONES? THIS NOURISHING WATER FILLING MY LUNGS?
AND THE LIGHT: SO DIM, SO FAINT--YET BRIGHT AS LIGHTNING AS I OPEN MY EYES, MOVE ACHING LIMBS...

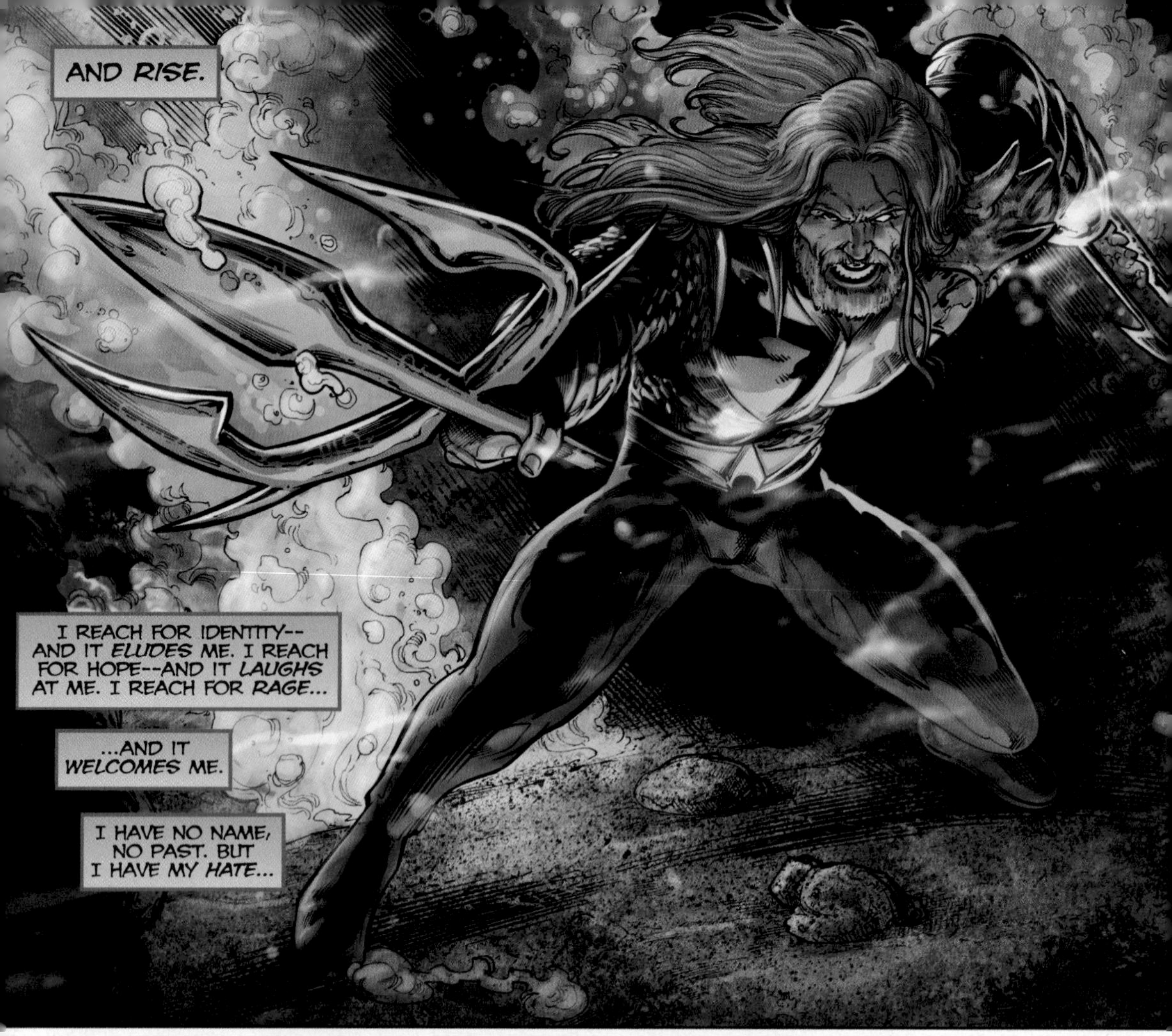
AND RISE.
I REACH FOR IDENTITY-- AND IT ELUDES ME. I REACH FOR HOPE--AND IT LAUGHS AT ME. I REACH FOR RAGE...
...AND IT WELCOMES ME.
I HAVE NO NAME, NO PAST. BUT I HAVE MY HATE...

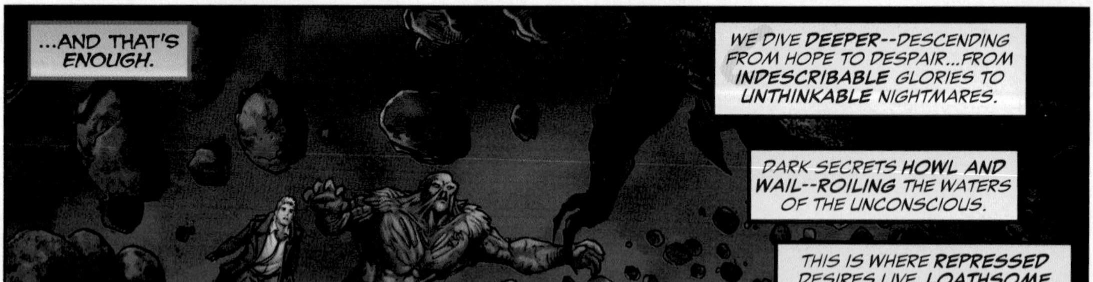
...AND THAT'S ENOUGH.
WE DIVE DEEPER--DESCENDING FROM HOPE TO DESPAIR...FROM INDESCRIBABLE GLORIES TO UNTHINKABLE NIGHTMARES.
DARK SECRETS HOWL AND WAIL--ROILING THE WATERS OF THE UNCONSCIOUS.
THIS IS WHERE REPRESSED DESIRES LIVE. LOATHSOME URGES. UNCHECKED VIOLENCE. UNFILTERED LUST.

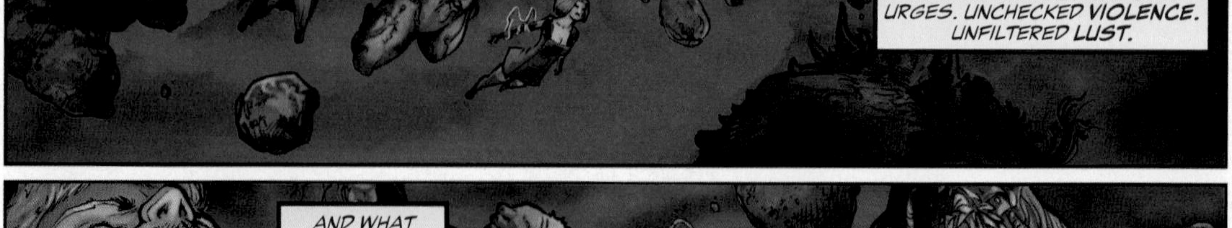
AND WHAT SWIMS AROUND US...
...ECHOES INSIDE US...

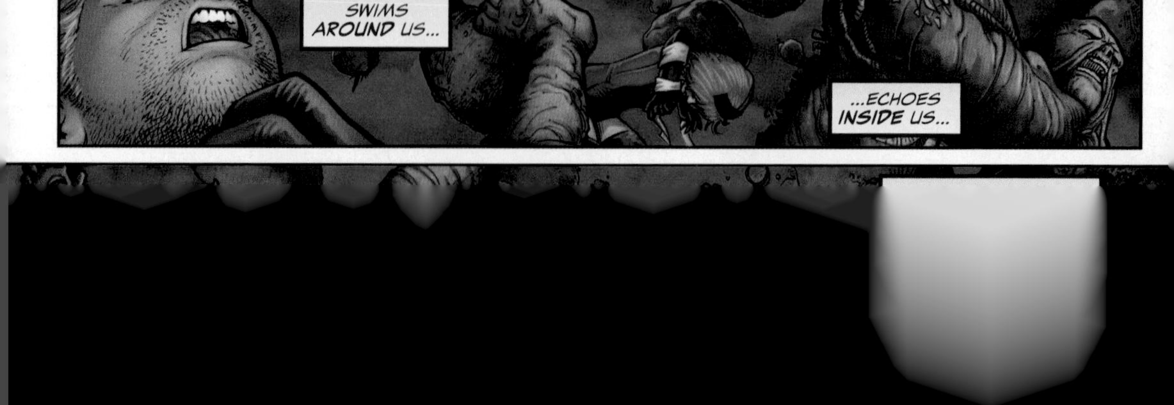

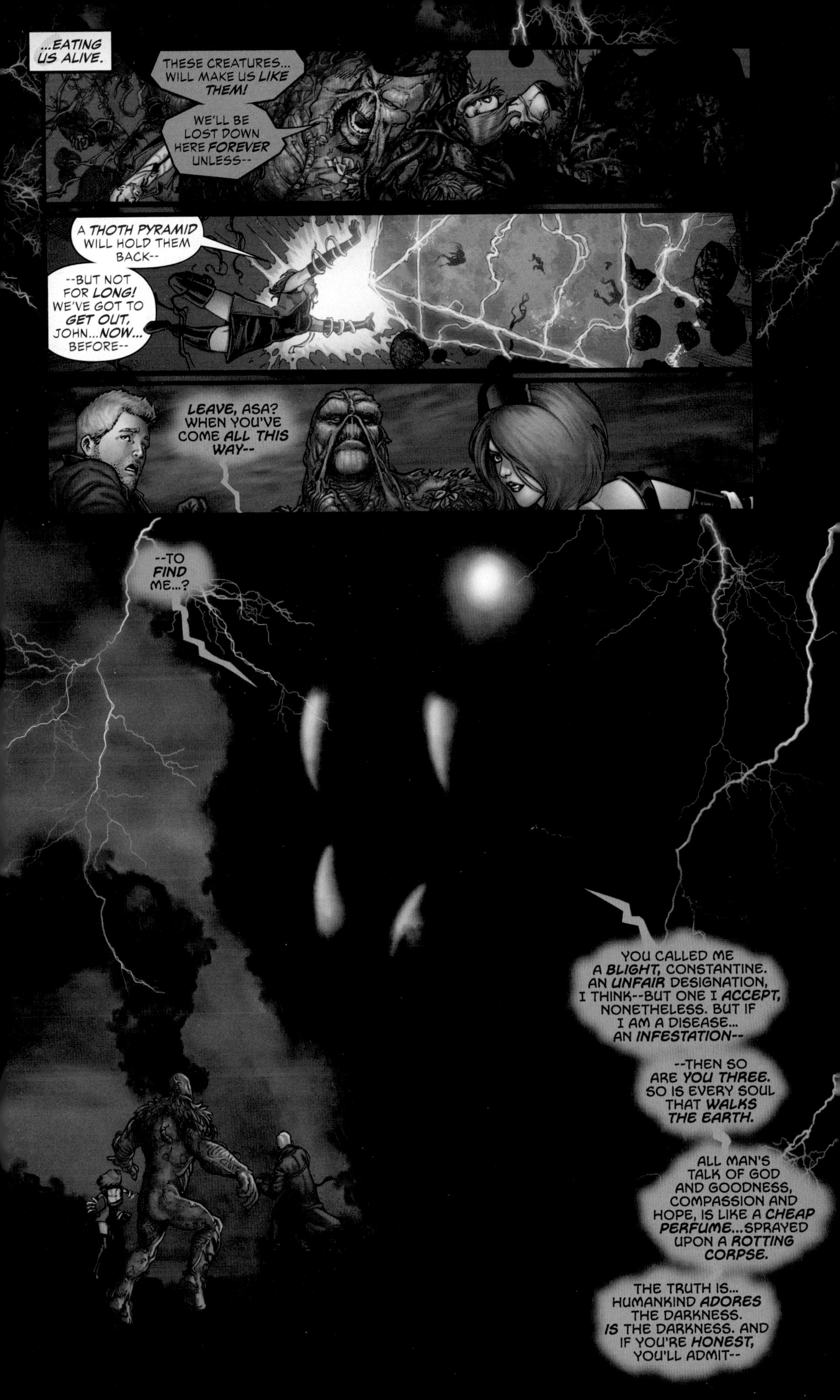
...EATING US ALIVE.
THESE CREATURES... WILL MAKE US LIKE THEM!
WE'LL BE LOST DOWN HERE FOREVER UNLESS--
A THOTH PYRAMID WILL HOLD THEM BACK--
--BUT NOT FOR LONG! WE'VE GOT TO GET OUT, JOHN...NOW... BEFORE--
LEAVE, ASA? WHEN YOU'VE COME ALL THIS WAY--
--TO FIND ME...?
YOU CALLED ME A BLIGHT, CONSTANTINE. AN UNFAIR DESIGNATION, I THINK--BUT ONE I ACCEPT, NONETHELESS. BUT IF I AM A DISEASE... AN INFESTATION--
--THEN SO ARE YOU THREE. SO IS EVERY SOUL THAT WALKS THE EARTH.
ALL MAN'S TALK OF GOD AND GOODNESS, COMPASSION AND HOPE, IS LIKE A CHEAP PERFUME...SPRAYED UPON A ROTTING CORPSE.
THE TRUTH IS... HUMANKIND ADORES THE DARKNESS. IS THE DARKNESS. AND IF YOU'RE HONEST, YOU'LL ADMIT--

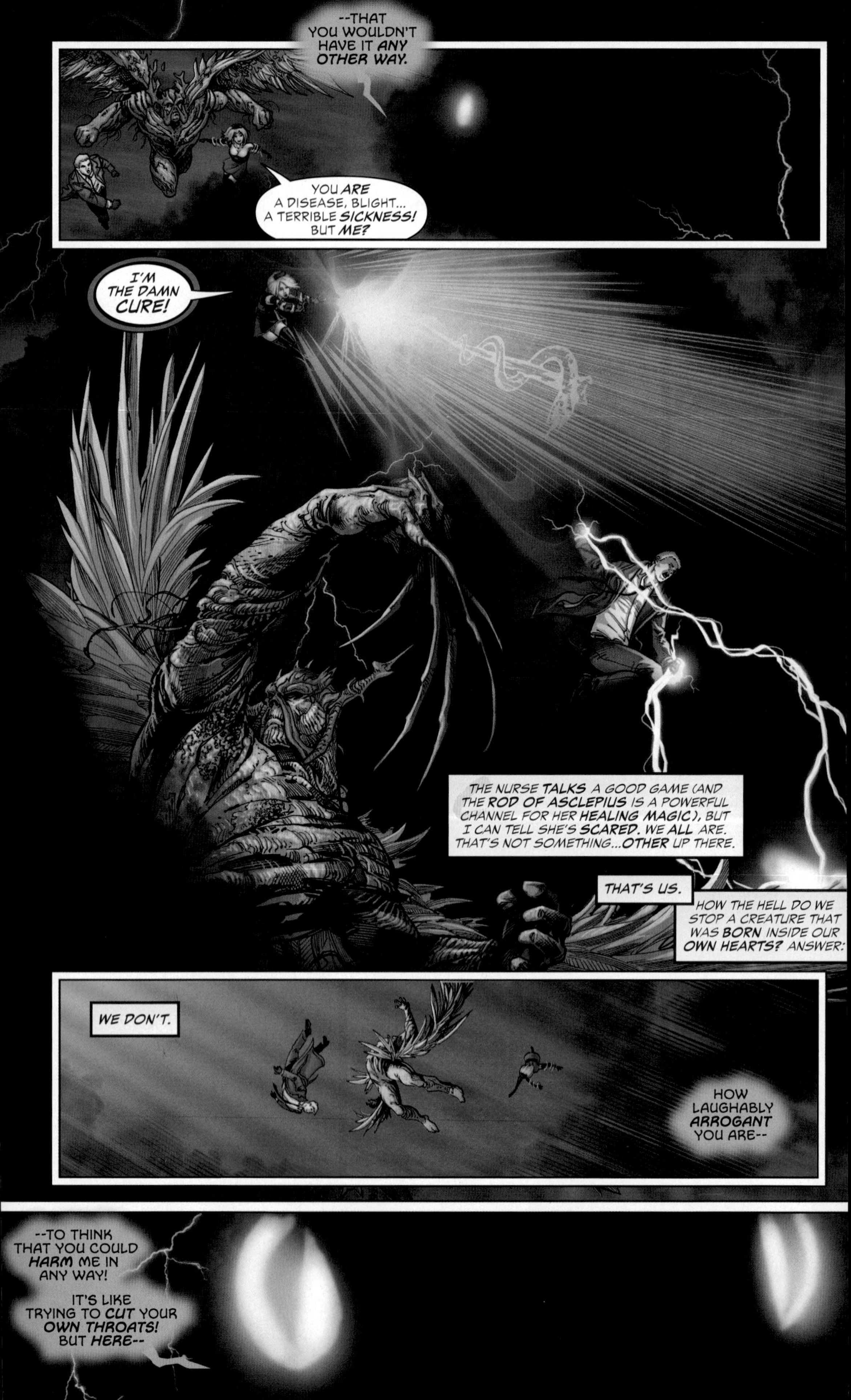
--THAT YOU WOULDN'T HAVE IT ANY OTHER WAY.
YOU ARE A DISEASE, BLIGHT... A TERRIBLE SICKNESS! BUT ME?
I'M THE DAMN CURE!
THE NURSE TALKS A GOOD GAME (AND THE ROD OF ASCLEPIUS IS A POWERFUL CHANNEL FOR HER HEALING MAGIC), BUT I CAN TELL SHE'S SCARED. WE ALL ARE. THAT'S NOT SOMETHING...OTHER UP THERE.
THAT'S US.
HOW THE HELL DO WE STOP A CREATURE THAT WAS BORN INSIDE OUR OWN HEARTS? ANSWER:
WE DON'T.
HOW LAUGHABLY ARROGANT YOU ARE--
--TO THINK THAT YOU COULD HARM ME IN ANY WAY!
IT'S LIKE TRYING TO CUT YOUR OWN THROATS! BUT HERE--

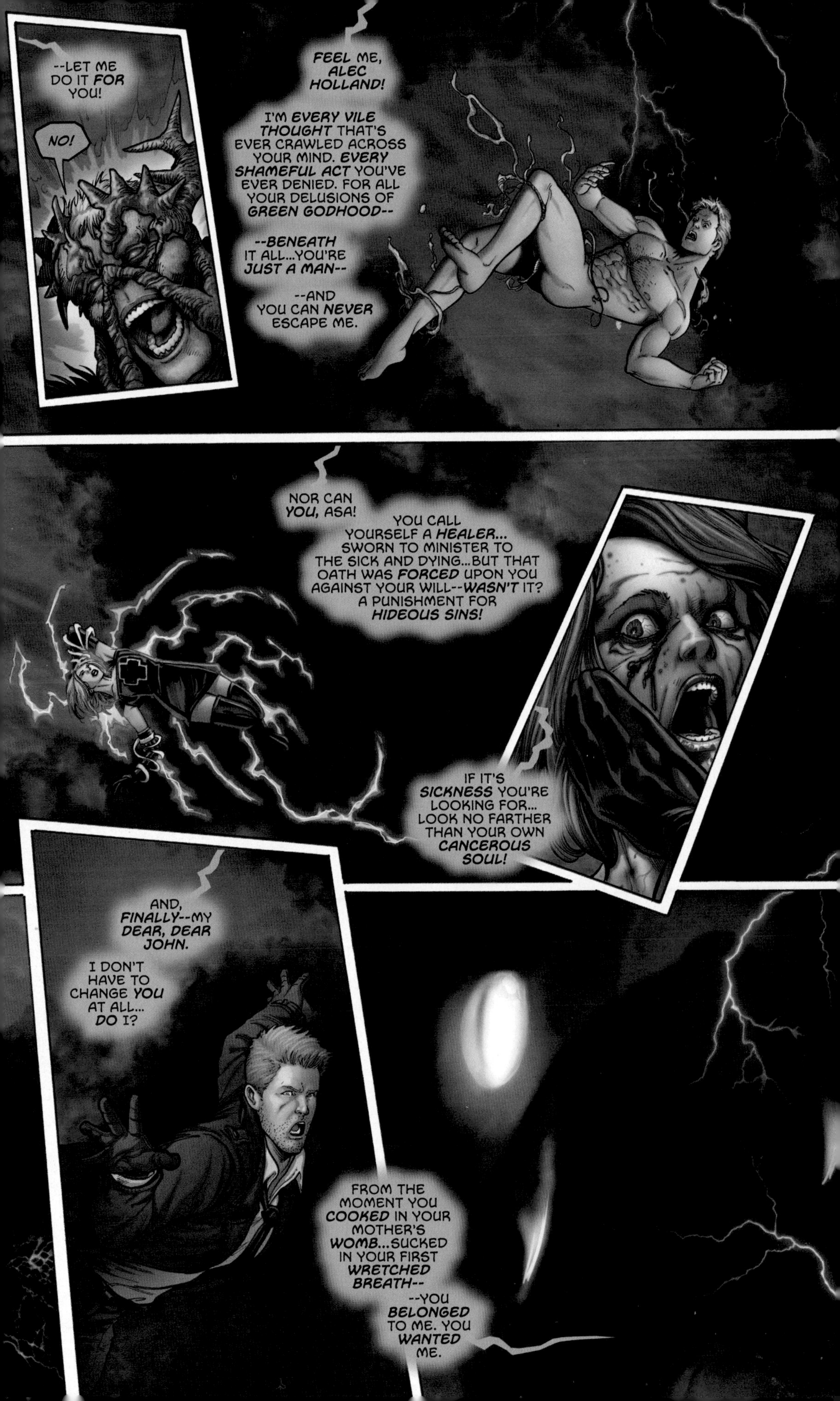

--LET ME DO IT FOR YOU!
NO!
FEEL ME, ALEC HOLLAND!
I'M EVERY VILE THOUGHT THAT'S EVER CRAWLED ACROSS YOUR MIND. EVERY SHAMEFUL ACT YOU'VE EVER DENIED. FOR ALL YOUR DELUSIONS OF GREEN GODHOOD--
--BENEATH IT ALL...YOU'RE JUST A MAN--
--AND YOU CAN NEVER ESCAPE ME.
NOR CAN YOU, ASA!
YOU CALL YOURSELF A HEALER... SWORN TO MINISTER TO THE SICK AND DYING...BUT THAT OATH WAS FORCED UPON YOU AGAINST YOUR WILL--WASN'T IT? A PUNISHMENT FOR HIDEOUS SINS!
IF IT'S SICKNESS YOU'RE LOOKING FOR... LOOK NO FARTHER THAN YOUR OWN CANCEROUS SOUL!
AND, FINALLY--MY DEAR, DEAR JOHN.
I DON'T HAVE TO CHANGE YOU AT ALL... DO I?
FROM THE MOMENT YOU COOKED IN YOUR MOTHER'S WOMB...SUCKED IN YOUR FIRST WRETCHED BREATH--
--YOU BELONGED TO ME. YOU WANTED ME.

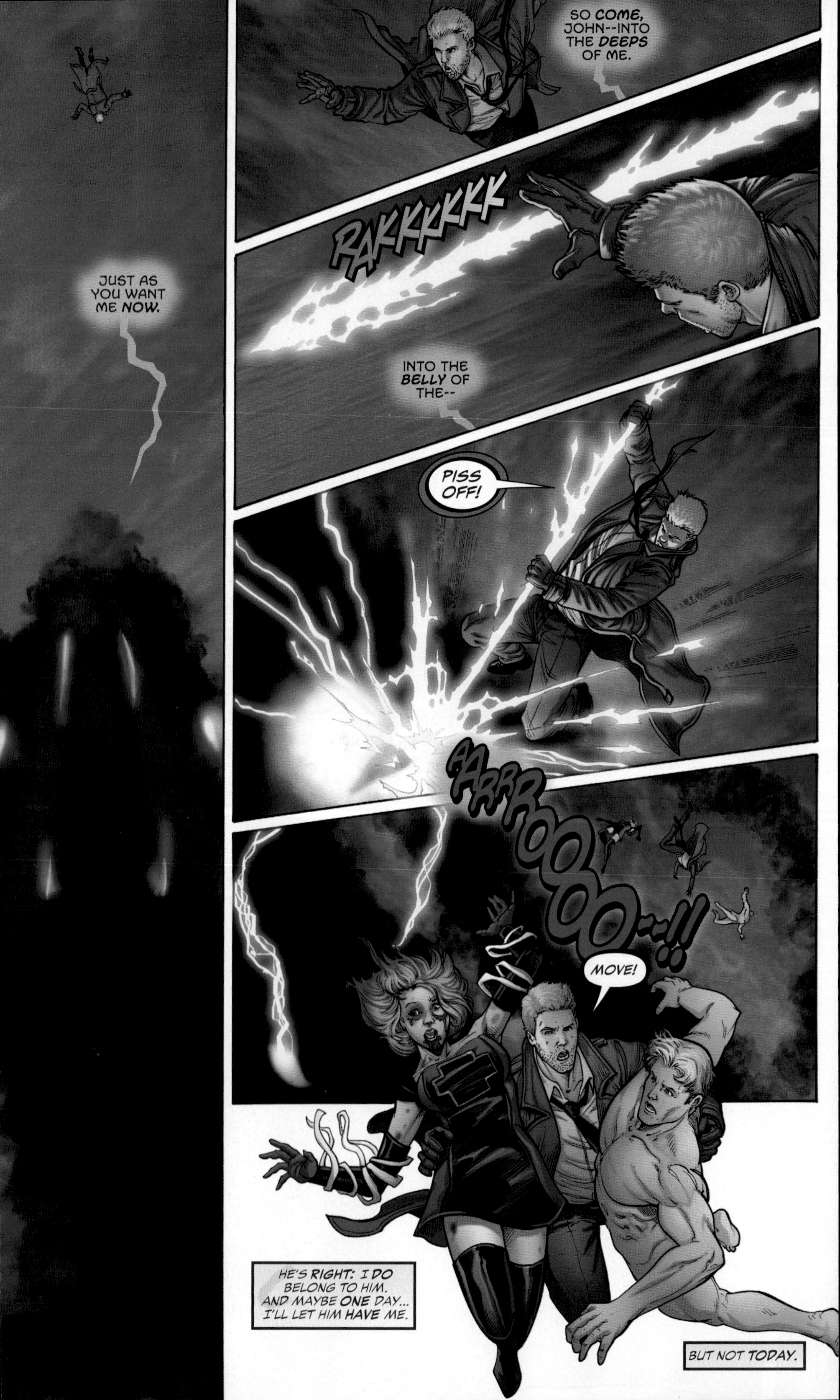

JUST AS YOU WANT ME NOW.
SO COME, JOHN--INTO THE DEEPS OF ME.
RAKKKKKK
INTO THE BELLY OF THE--
PISS OFF!
AARRROOOOO--!!
MOVE!
HE'S RIGHT: I DO BELONG TO HIM. AND MAYBE ONE DAY... I'LL LET HIM HAVE ME.
BUT NOT TODAY.

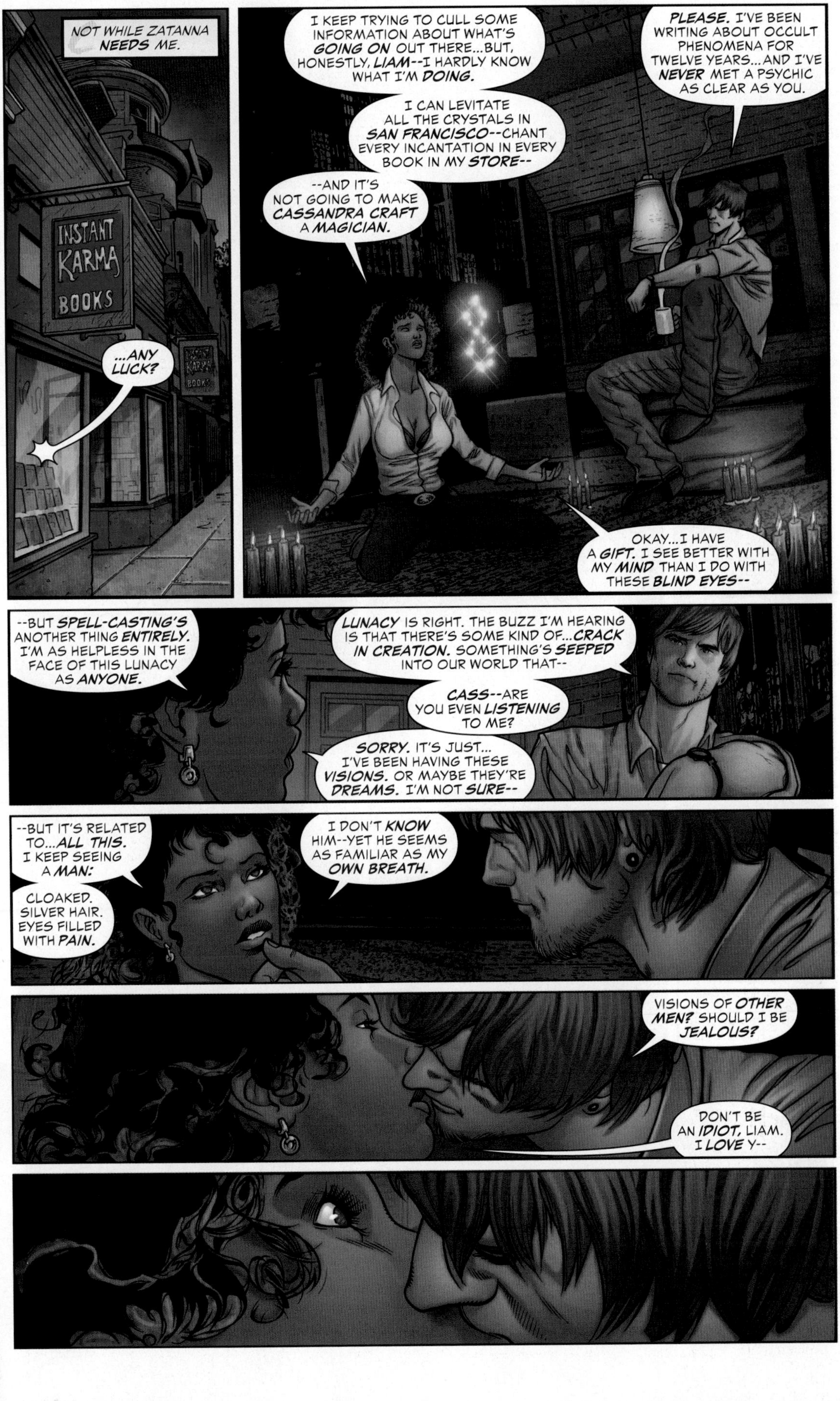
NOT WHILE ZATANNA NEEDS ME.
INSTANT KARMA BOOKS
...ANY LUCK?
I KEEP TRYING TO CULL SOME INFORMATION ABOUT WHAT'S GOING ON OUT THERE...BUT, HONESTLY, LIAM--I HARDLY KNOW WHAT I'M DOING.
I CAN LEVITATE ALL THE CRYSTALS IN SAN FRANCISCO--CHANT EVERY INCANTATION IN EVERY BOOK IN MY STORE--
--AND IT'S NOT GOING TO MAKE CASSANDRA CRAFT A MAGICIAN.
PLEASE. I'VE BEEN WRITING ABOUT OCCULT PHENOMENA FOR TWELVE YEARS...AND I'VE NEVER MET A PSYCHIC AS CLEAR AS YOU.
OKAY...I HAVE A GIFT. I SEE BETTER WITH MY MIND THAN I DO WITH THESE BLIND EYES--
--BUT SPELL-CASTING'S ANOTHER THING ENTIRELY. I'M AS HELPLESS IN THE FACE OF THIS LUNACY AS ANYONE.
LUNACY IS RIGHT. THE BUZZ I'M HEARING IS THAT THERE'S SOME KIND OF...CRACK IN CREATION. SOMETHING'S SEEPED INTO OUR WORLD THAT--
CASS--ARE YOU EVEN LISTENING TO ME?
SORRY. IT'S JUST... I'VE BEEN HAVING THESE VISIONS. OR MAYBE THEY'RE DREAMS. I'M NOT SURE--
--BUT IT'S RELATED TO...ALL THIS. I KEEP SEEING A MAN:
CLOAKED. SILVER HAIR. EYES FILLED WITH PAIN.
I DON'T KNOW HIM--YET HE SEEMS AS FAMILIAR AS MY OWN BREATH.
VISIONS OF OTHER MEN? SHOULD I BE JEALOUS?
DON'T BE AN IDIOT, LIAM. I LOVE Y--

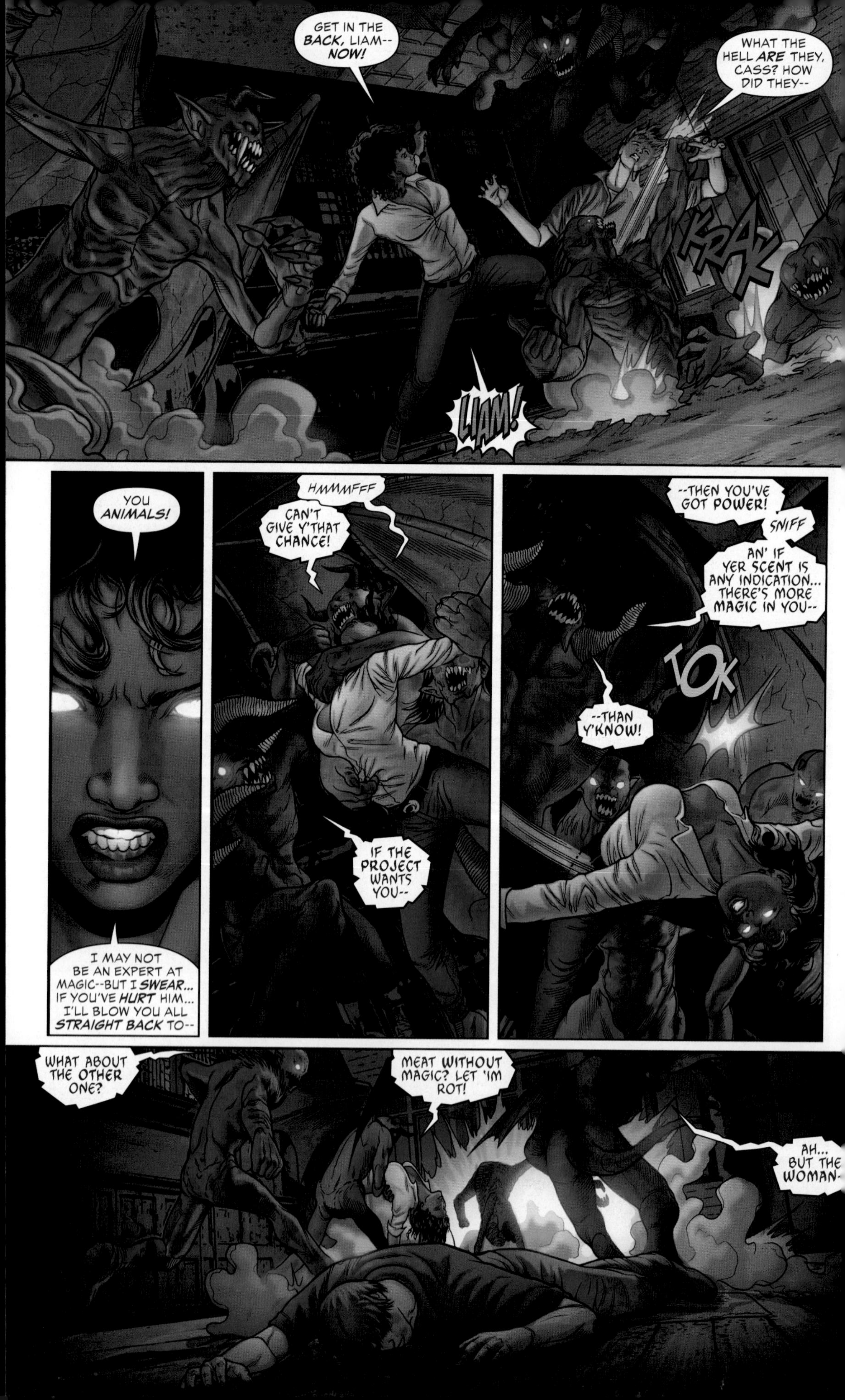
GET IN THE BACK, LIAM-- NOW!
WHAT THE HELL ARE THEY, CASS? HOW DID THEY--
KRAK
LIAM!
YOU ANIMALS!
I MAY NOT BE AN EXPERT AT MAGIC--BUT I SWEAR... IF YOU'VE HURT HIM... I'LL BLOW YOU ALL STRAIGHT BACK TO--
HMMMFFF
CAN'T GIVE Y'THAT CHANCE!
IF THE PROJECT WANTS YOU--
--THEN YOU'VE GOT POWER!
SNIFF
AN' IF YER SCENT IS ANY INDICATION... THERE'S MORE MAGIC IN YOU--
TOK
--THAN Y'KNOW!
WHAT ABOUT THE OTHER ONE?
MEAT WITHOUT MAGIC? LET 'IM ROT!
AH... BUT THE WOMAN-

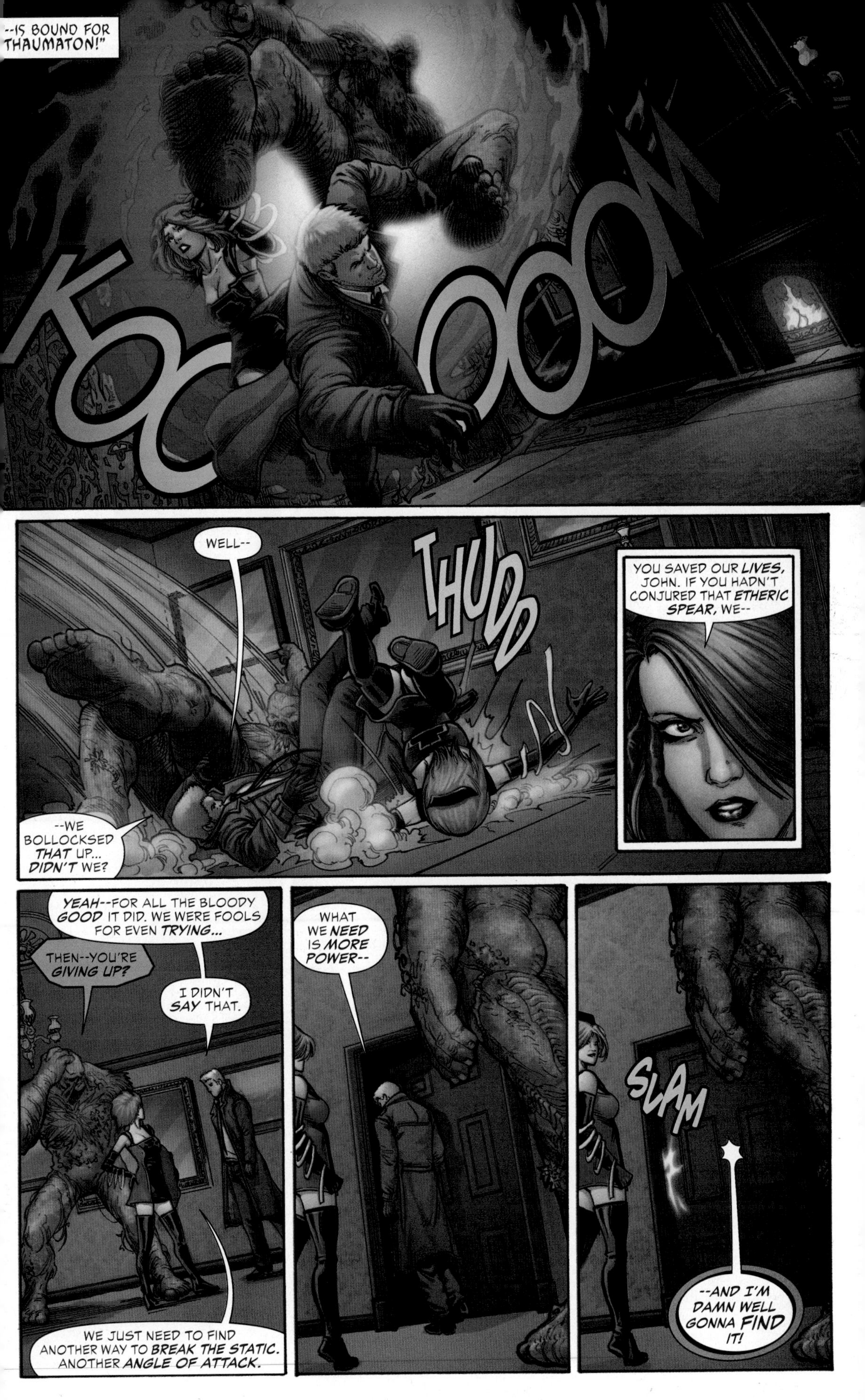
--IS BOUND FOR THAUMATON!"
KOOOOOOM
WELL--
THUDD
--WE BOLLOCKSED THAT UP... DIDN'T WE?
YOU SAVED OUR LIVES, JOHN. IF YOU HADN'T CONJURED THAT ETHERIC SPEAR, WE--
YEAH--FOR ALL THE BLOODY GOOD IT DID. WE WERE FOOLS FOR EVEN TRYING...
THEN--YOU'RE GIVING UP?
I DIDN'T SAY THAT.
WE JUST NEED TO FIND ANOTHER WAY TO BREAK THE STATIC. ANOTHER ANGLE OF ATTACK.
WHAT WE NEED IS MORE POWER--
SLAM
--AND I'M DAMN WELL GONNA FIND IT!

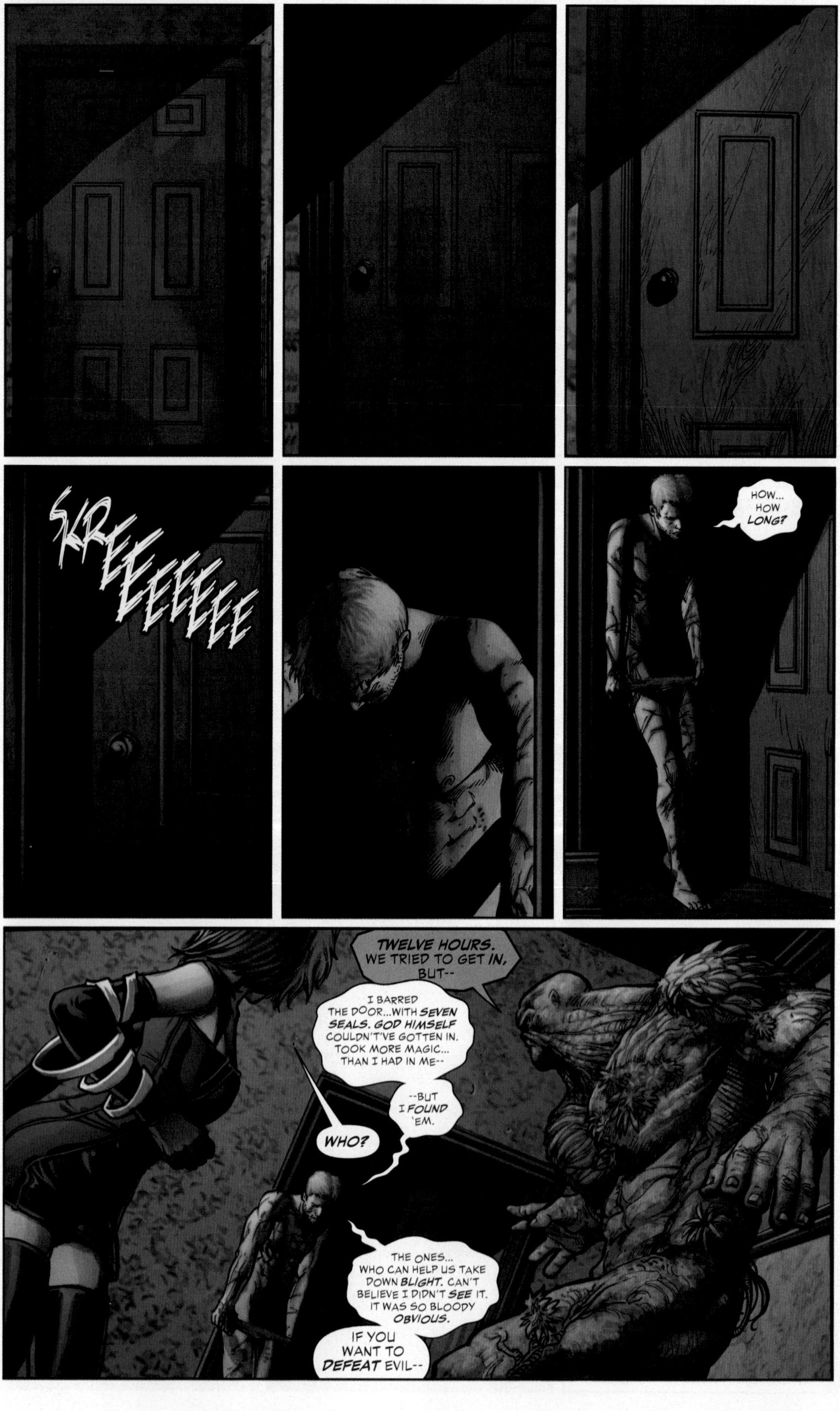
SKREEEEEEEE
HOW... HOW LONG?
TWELVE HOURS. WE TRIED TO GET IN, BUT--
I BARRED THE DOOR...WITH SEVEN SEALS. GOD HIMSELF COULDN'T'VE GOTTEN IN. TOOK MORE MAGIC... THAN I HAD IN ME--
--BUT I FOUND 'EM.
WHO?
THE ONES... WHO CAN HELP US TAKE DOWN BLIGHT. CAN'T BELIEVE I DIDN'T SEE IT. IT WAS SO BLOODY OBVIOUS.
IF YOU WANT TO DEFEAT EVIL--

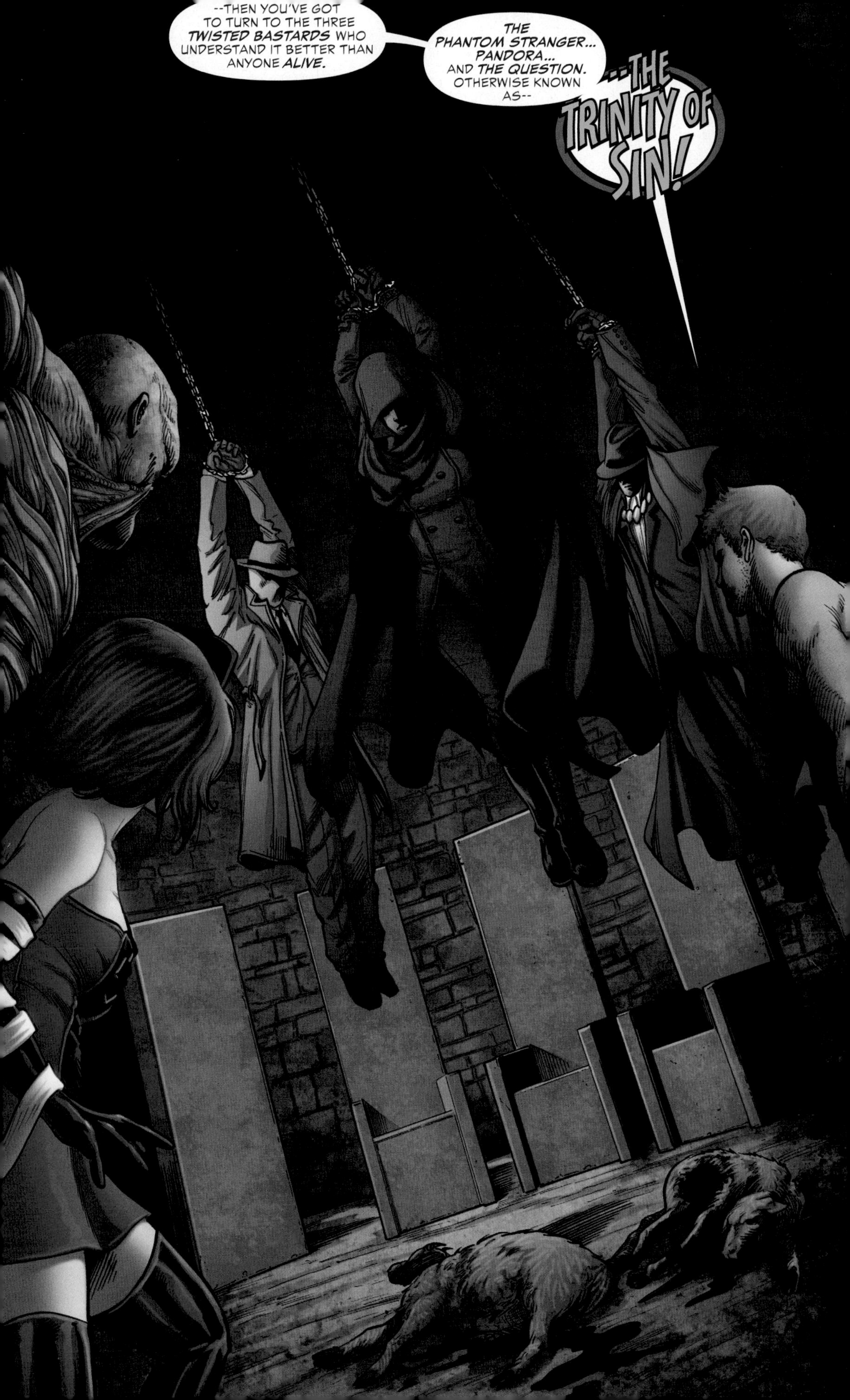
--THEN YOU'VE GOT TO TURN TO THE THREE TWISTED BASTARDS WHO UNDERSTAND IT BETTER THAN ANYONE ALIVE.
THE PHANTOM STRANGER... PANDORA... AND THE QUESTION. OTHERWISE KNOWN AS--
--THE TRINITY OF SIN!

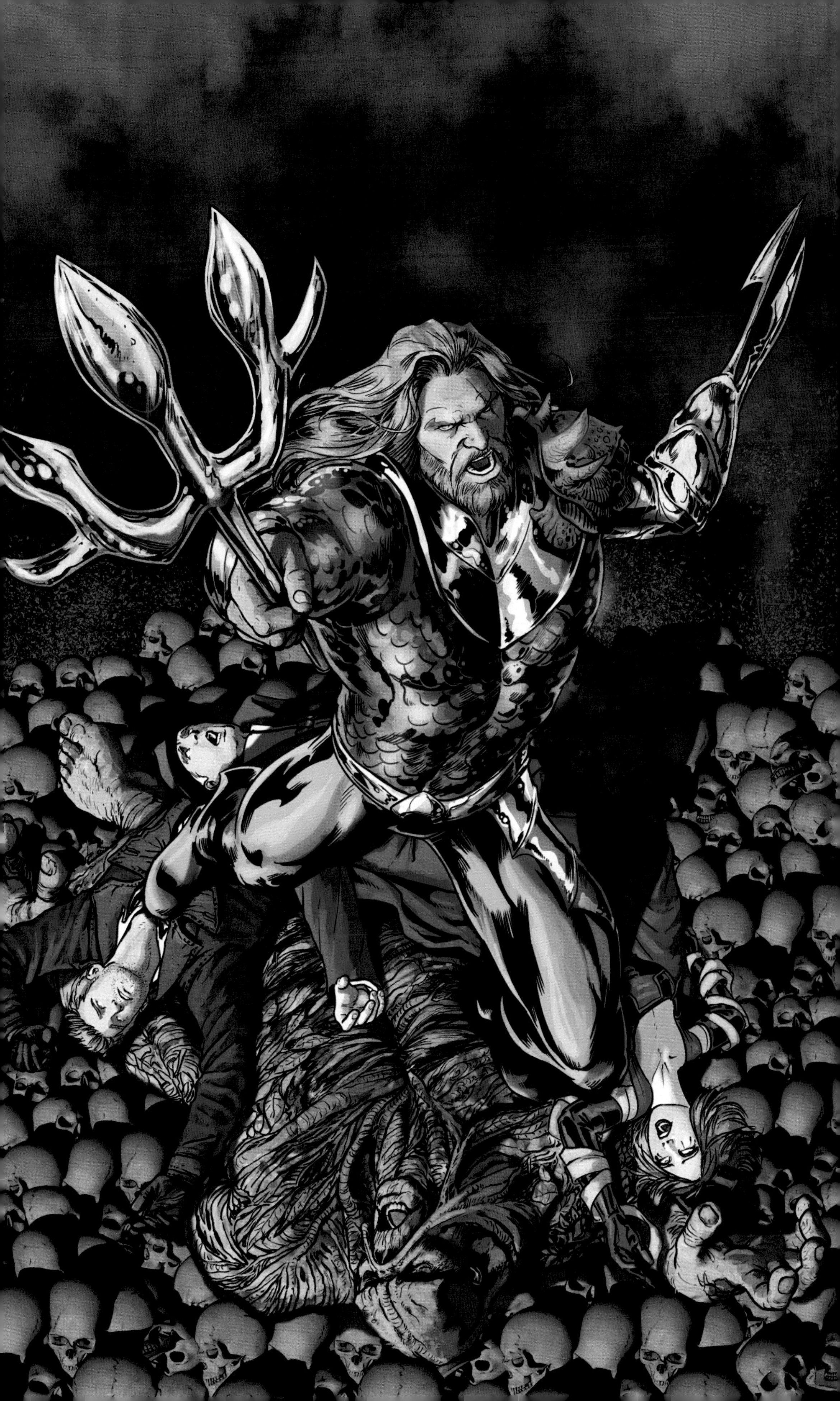

J. M. DeMATTEIS
writer

MIKEL JANIN
penciller & graytone artist

VICENTE CIFUENTES, GUILLERMO ORTEGO & JORDI TARRAGONA
inkers

MIKEL JANIN
cover artist

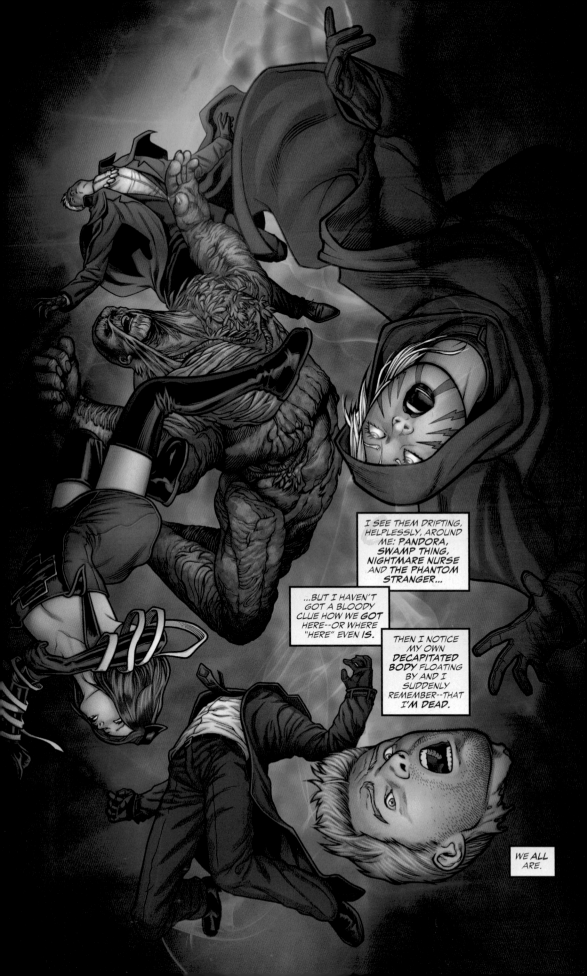

I SEE THEM DRIFTING, HELPLESSLY, AROUND ME: PANDORA, SWAMP THING, NIGHTMARE NURSE AND THE PHANTOM STRANGER...

...BUT I HAVEN'T GOT A BLOODY CLUE HOW WE GOT HERE--OR WHERE "HERE" EVEN IS.

THEN I NOTICE MY OWN DECAPITATED BODY FLOATING BY AND I SUDDENLY REMEMBER--THAT I'M DEAD.

WE ALL ARE.

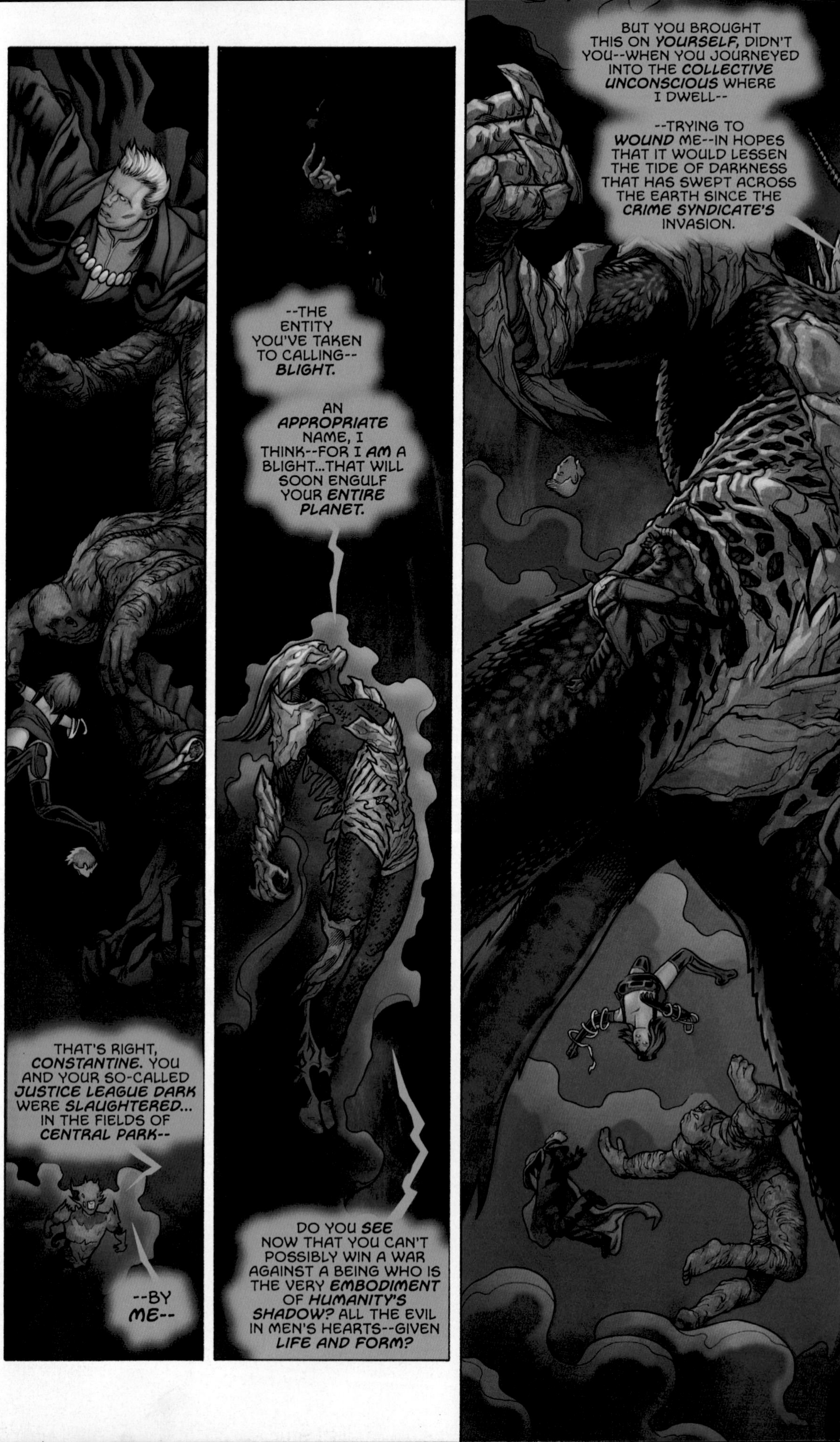
THAT'S RIGHT, CONSTANTINE. YOU AND YOUR SO-CALLED JUSTICE LEAGUE DARK WERE SLAUGHTERED... IN THE FIELDS OF CENTRAL PARK--
--BY ME--
--THE ENTITY YOU'VE TAKEN TO CALLING-- BLIGHT.
AN APPROPRIATE NAME, I THINK--FOR I AM A BLIGHT...THAT WILL SOON ENGULF YOUR ENTIRE PLANET.
DO YOU SEE NOW THAT YOU CAN'T POSSIBLY WIN A WAR AGAINST A BEING WHO IS THE VERY EMBODIMENT OF HUMANITY'S SHADOW? ALL THE EVIL IN MEN'S HEARTS--GIVEN LIFE AND FORM?
BUT YOU BROUGHT THIS ON YOURSELF, DIDN'T YOU--WHEN YOU JOURNEYED INTO THE COLLECTIVE UNCONSCIOUS WHERE I DWELL--
--TRYING TO WOUND ME--IN HOPES THAT IT WOULD LESSEN THE TIDE OF DARKNESS THAT HAS SWEPT ACROSS THE EARTH SINCE THE CRIME SYNDICATE'S INVASION.

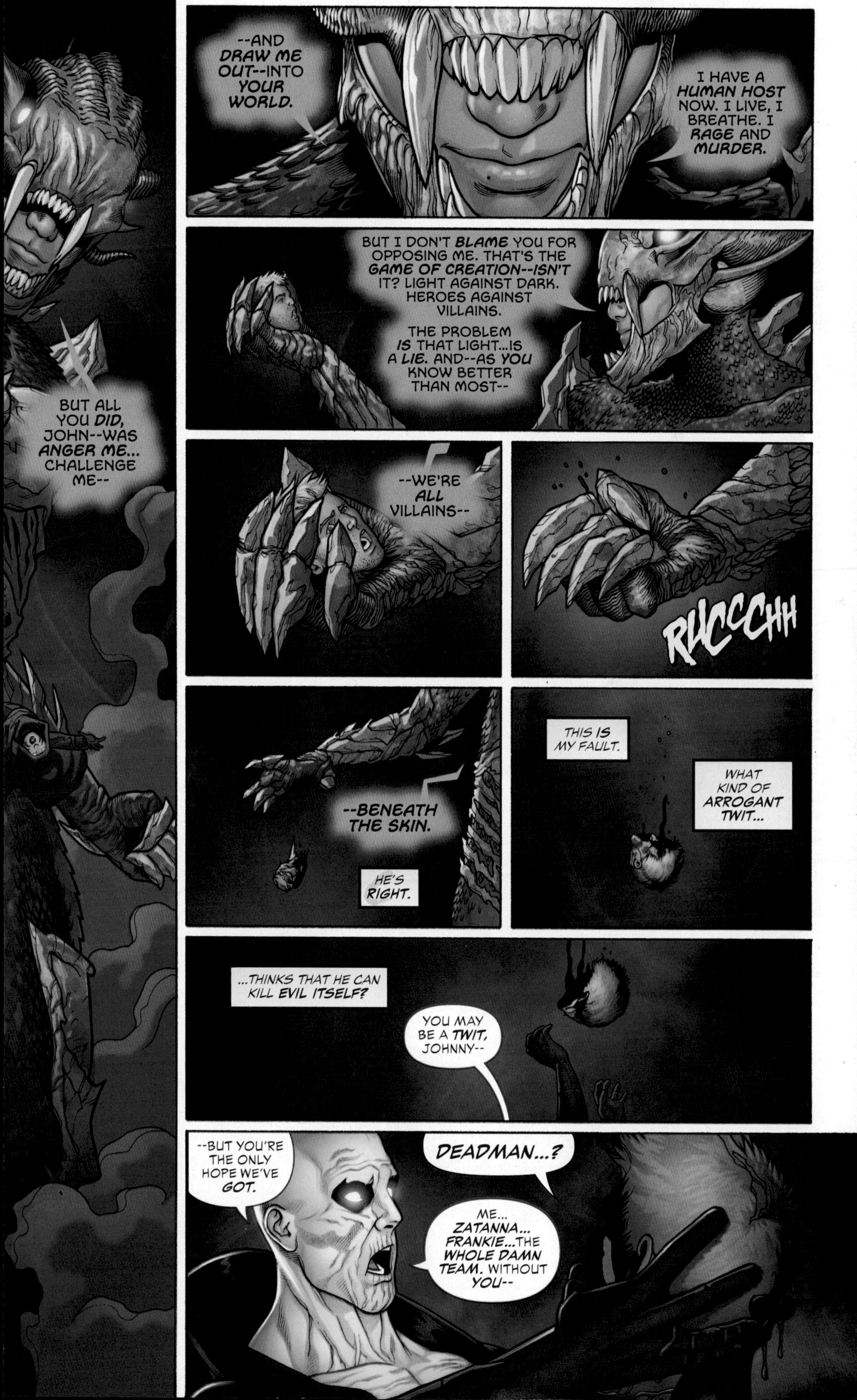
--AND DRAW ME OUT--INTO YOUR WORLD.
I HAVE A HUMAN HOST NOW. I LIVE, I BREATHE. I RAGE AND MURDER.
BUT ALL YOU DID, JOHN--WAS ANGER ME... CHALLENGE ME--
BUT I DON'T BLAME YOU FOR OPPOSING ME. THAT'S THE GAME OF CREATION--ISN'T IT? LIGHT AGAINST DARK. HEROES AGAINST VILLAINS.
THE PROBLEM IS THAT LIGHT...IS A LIE. AND--AS YOU KNOW BETTER THAN MOST--
--WE'RE ALL VILLAINS--
RUCCCHH
--BENEATH THE SKIN.
HE'S RIGHT.
THIS IS MY FAULT.
WHAT KIND OF ARROGANT TWIT...
...THINKS THAT HE CAN KILL EVIL ITSELF?
YOU MAY BE A TWIT, JOHNNY--
--BUT YOU'RE THE ONLY HOPE WE'VE GOT.
DEADMAN...?
ME... ZATANNA... FRANKIE...THE WHOLE DAMN TEAM. WITHOUT YOU--

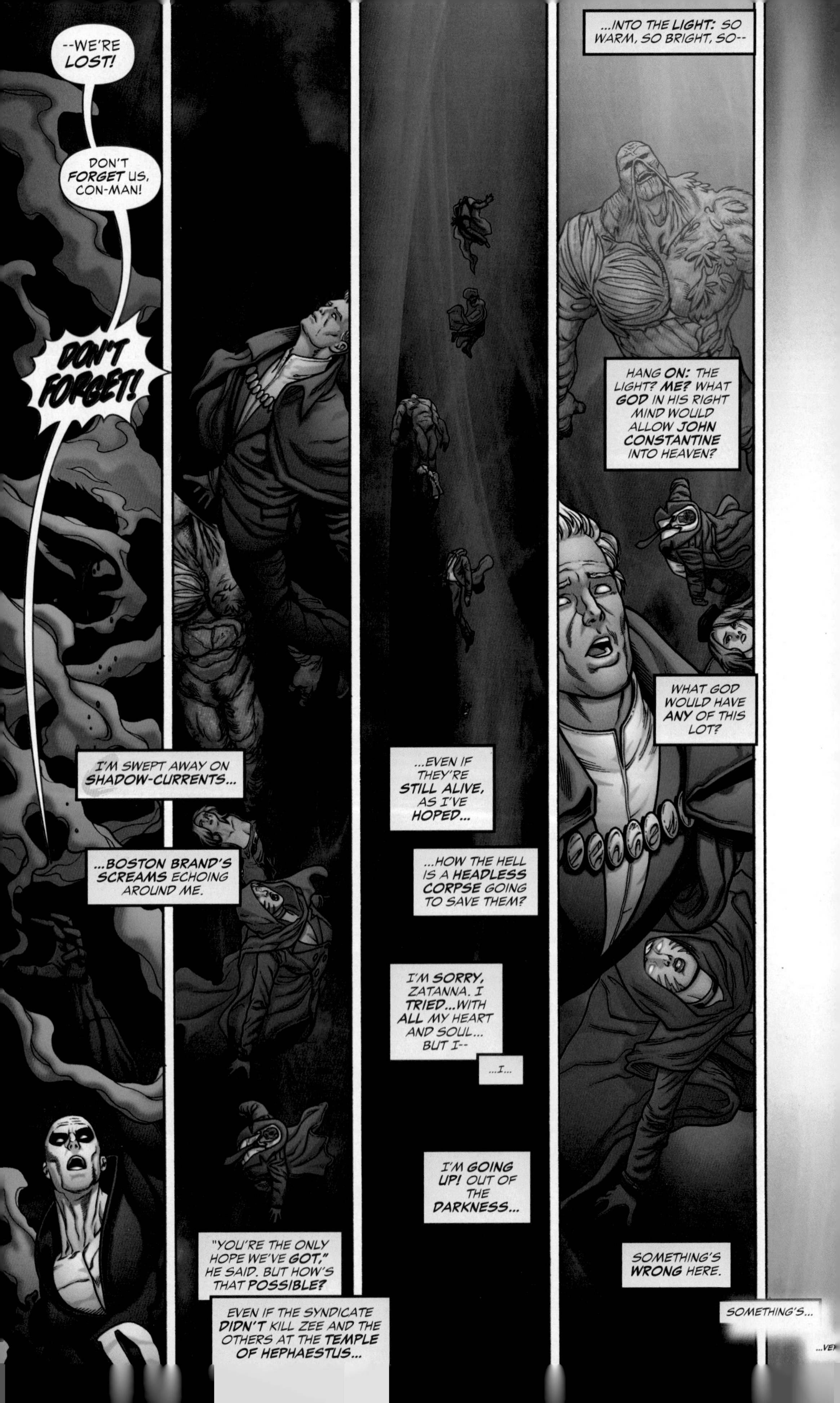

--WE'RE LOST!
DON'T FORGET US, CON-MAN!
DON'T FORGET!
I'M SWEPT AWAY ON SHADOW-CURRENTS...
...BOSTON BRAND'S SCREAMS ECHOING AROUND ME.
"YOU'RE THE ONLY HOPE WE'VE GOT," HE SAID. BUT HOW'S THAT POSSIBLE?
EVEN IF THE SYNDICATE DIDN'T KILL ZEE AND THE OTHERS AT THE TEMPLE OF HEPHAESTUS...
...EVEN IF THEY'RE STILL ALIVE, AS I'VE HOPED...
...HOW THE HELL IS A HEADLESS CORPSE GOING TO SAVE THEM?
I'M SORRY, ZATANNA. I TRIED...WITH ALL MY HEART AND SOUL... BUT I--
...I...
I'M GOING UP! OUT OF THE DARKNESS...
...INTO THE LIGHT: SO WARM, SO BRIGHT, SO--
HANG ON: THE LIGHT? ME? WHAT GOD IN HIS RIGHT MIND WOULD ALLOW JOHN CONSTANTINE INTO HEAVEN?
WHAT GOD WOULD HAVE ANY OF THIS LOT?
SOMETHING'S WRONG HERE.
SOMETHING'S...
...VE

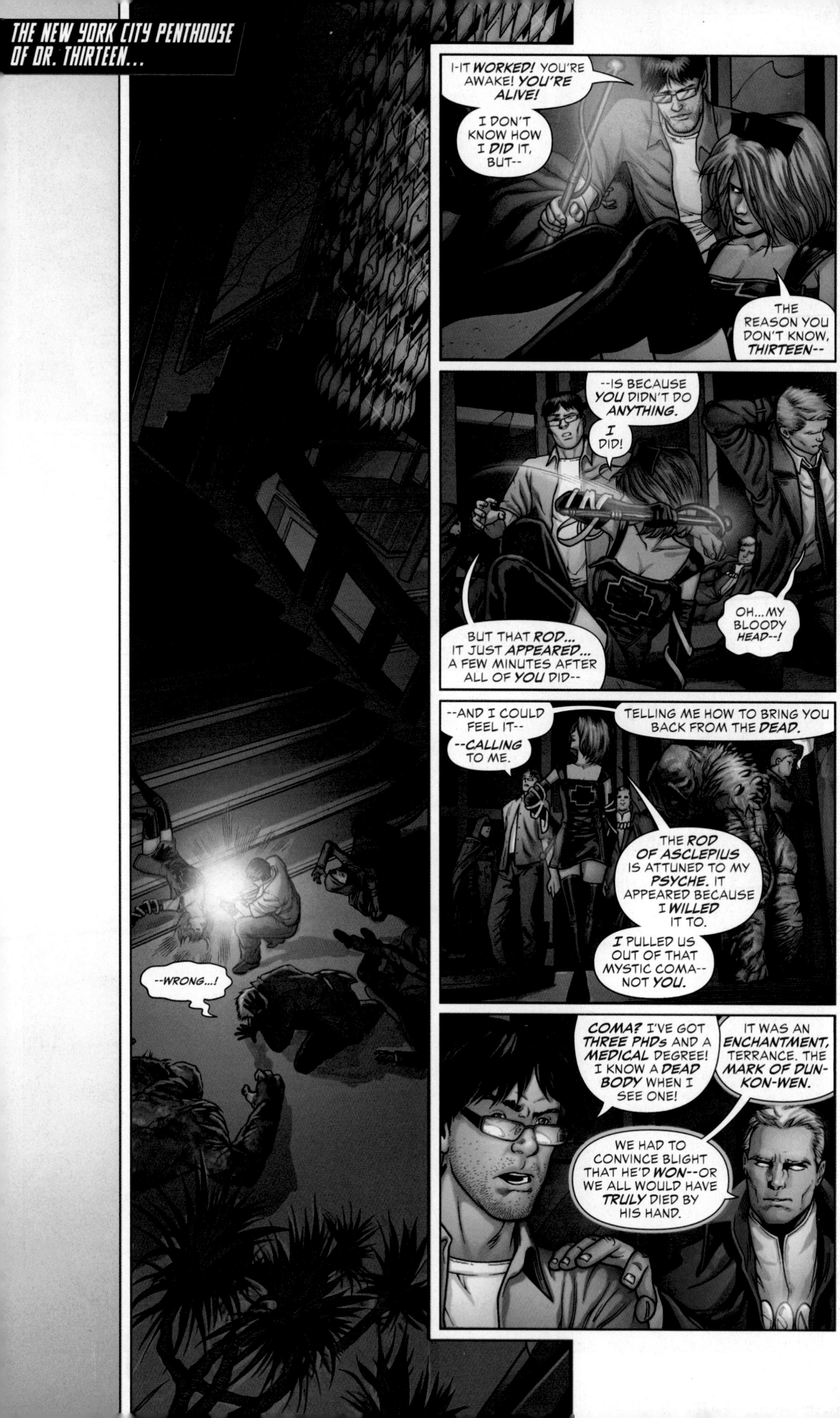
THE NEW YORK CITY PENTHOUSE OF DR. THIRTEEN...
--WRONG...!
I-IT WORKED! YOU'RE AWAKE! YOU'RE ALIVE!
I DON'T KNOW HOW I DID IT, BUT--
THE REASON YOU DON'T KNOW, THIRTEEN--
--IS BECAUSE YOU DIDN'T DO ANYTHING.
I DID!
BUT THAT ROD... IT JUST APPEARED... A FEW MINUTES AFTER ALL OF YOU DID--
OH... MY BLOODY HEAD--!
--AND I COULD FEEL IT--
--CALLING TO ME.
TELLING ME HOW TO BRING YOU BACK FROM THE DEAD.
THE ROD OF ASCLEPIUS IS ATTUNED TO MY PSYCHE. IT APPEARED BECAUSE I WILLED IT TO.
I PULLED US OUT OF THAT MYSTIC COMA-- NOT YOU.
COMA? I'VE GOT THREE PHDs AND A MEDICAL DEGREE! I KNOW A DEAD BODY WHEN I SEE ONE!
IT WAS AN ENCHANTMENT, TERRANCE. THE MARK OF DUN-KON-WEN.
WE HAD TO CONVINCE BLIGHT THAT HE'D WON--OR WE ALL WOULD HAVE TRULY DIED BY HIS HAND.

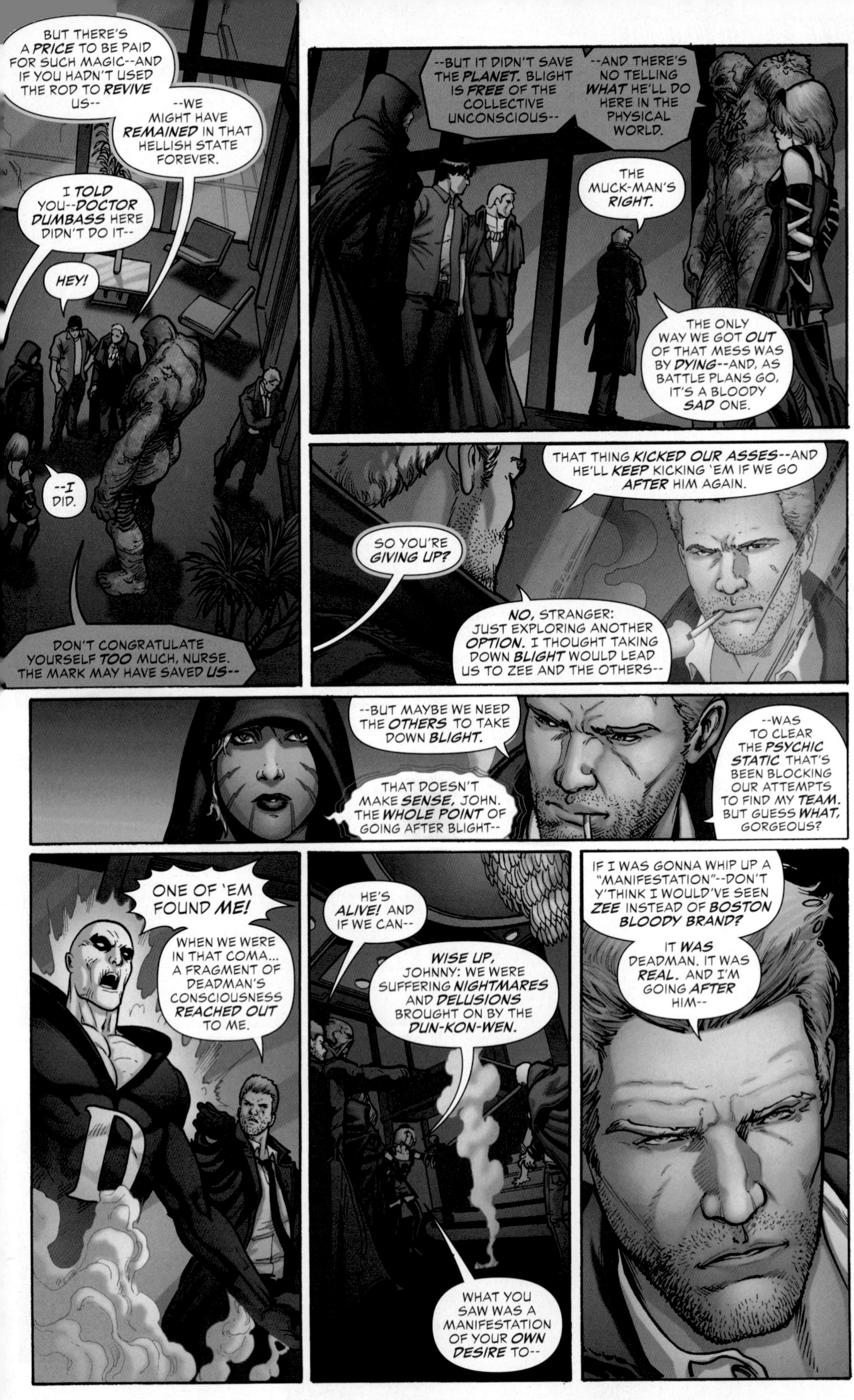

BUT THERE'S A PRICE TO BE PAID FOR SUCH MAGIC--AND IF YOU HADN'T USED THE ROD TO REVIVE US--
--WE MIGHT HAVE REMAINED IN THAT HELLISH STATE FOREVER.
I TOLD YOU--DOCTOR DUMBASS HERE DIDN'T DO IT--
HEY!
--I DID.
DON'T CONGRATULATE YOURSELF TOO MUCH, NURSE. THE MARK MAY HAVE SAVED US--
--BUT IT DIDN'T SAVE THE PLANET. BLIGHT IS FREE OF THE COLLECTIVE UNCONSCIOUS--
--AND THERE'S NO TELLING WHAT HE'LL DO HERE IN THE PHYSICAL WORLD.
THE MUCK-MAN'S RIGHT.
THE ONLY WAY WE GOT OUT OF THAT MESS WAS BY DYING--AND, AS BATTLE PLANS GO, IT'S A BLOODY SAD ONE.
THAT THING KICKED OUR ASSES--AND HE'LL KEEP KICKING 'EM IF WE GO AFTER HIM AGAIN.
SO YOU'RE GIVING UP?
NO, STRANGER: JUST EXPLORING ANOTHER OPTION. I THOUGHT TAKING DOWN BLIGHT WOULD LEAD US TO ZEE AND THE OTHERS--
--BUT MAYBE WE NEED THE OTHERS TO TAKE DOWN BLIGHT.
THAT DOESN'T MAKE SENSE, JOHN. THE WHOLE POINT OF GOING AFTER BLIGHT--
--WAS TO CLEAR THE PSYCHIC STATIC THAT'S BEEN BLOCKING OUR ATTEMPTS TO FIND MY TEAM. BUT GUESS WHAT, GORGEOUS?
ONE OF 'EM FOUND ME!
WHEN WE WERE IN THAT COMA... A FRAGMENT OF DEADMAN'S CONSCIOUSNESS REACHED OUT TO ME.
HE'S ALIVE! AND IF WE CAN--
WISE UP, JOHNNY: WE WERE SUFFERING NIGHTMARES AND DELUSIONS BROUGHT ON BY THE DUN-KON-WEN.
WHAT YOU SAW WAS A MANIFESTATION OF YOUR OWN DESIRE TO--
IF I WAS GONNA WHIP UP A "MANIFESTATION"--DON'T Y'THINK I WOULD'VE SEEN ZEE INSTEAD OF BOSTON BLOODY BRAND?
IT WAS DEADMAN. IT WAS REAL. AND I'M GOING AFTER HIM--

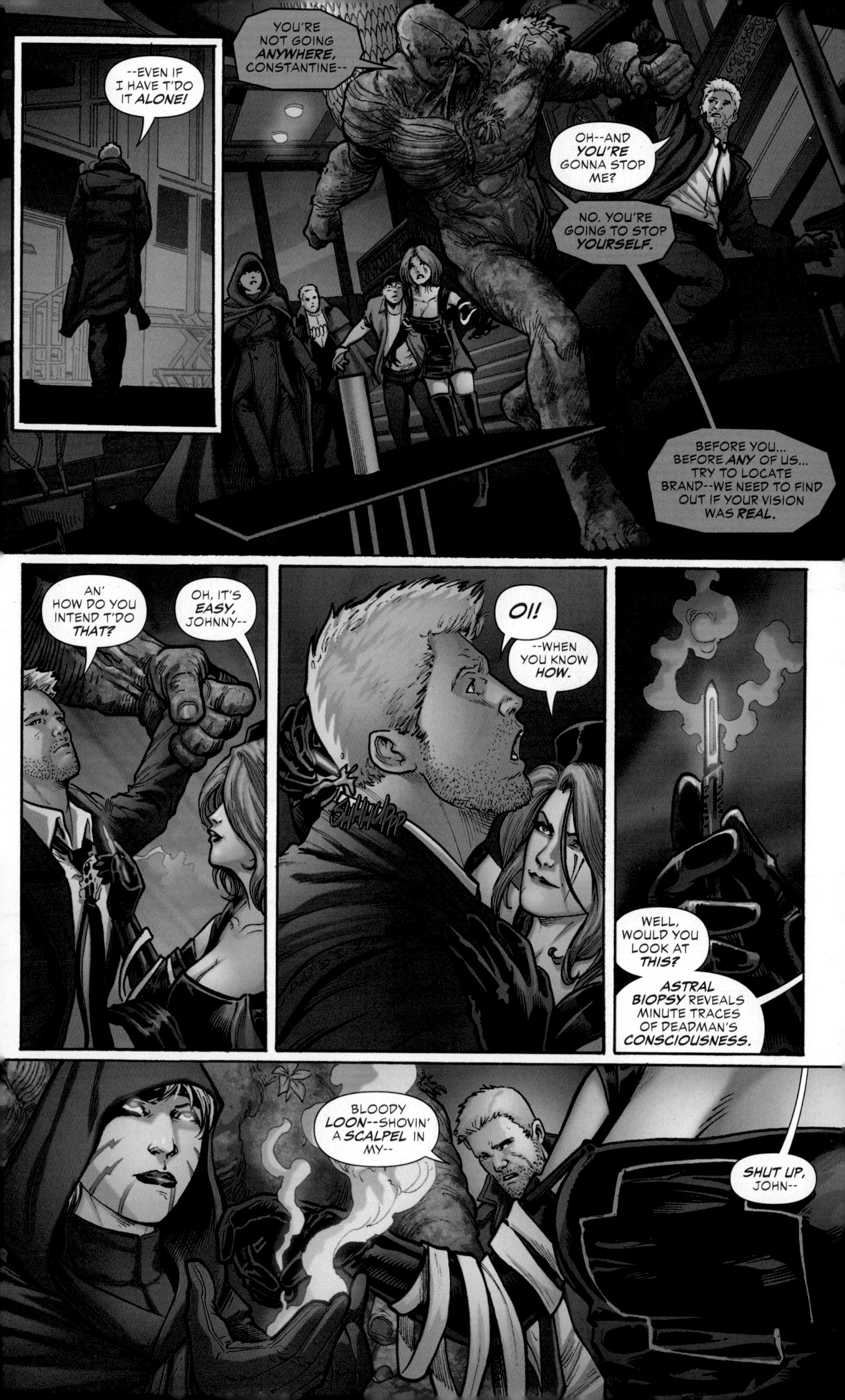
--EVEN IF I HAVE T'DO IT *ALONE!*
YOU'RE NOT GOING *ANYWHERE,* CONSTANTINE--
OH--AND *YOU'RE* GONNA STOP ME?
NO. YOU'RE GOING TO STOP *YOURSELF.*
BEFORE YOU... BEFORE *ANY* OF US... TRY TO LOCATE BRAND--WE NEED TO FIND OUT IF YOUR VISION WAS *REAL.*
AN' HOW DO YOU INTEND T'DO *THAT?*
OH, IT'S *EASY,* JOHNNY--
OI!
--WHEN YOU KNOW *HOW.*
WELL, WOULD YOU LOOK AT *THIS?*
ASTRAL BIOPSY REVEALS MINUTE TRACES OF DEADMAN'S *CONSCIOUSNESS.*
BLOODY *LOON*--SHOVIN' A *SCALPEL* IN MY--
SHUT UP, JOHN--

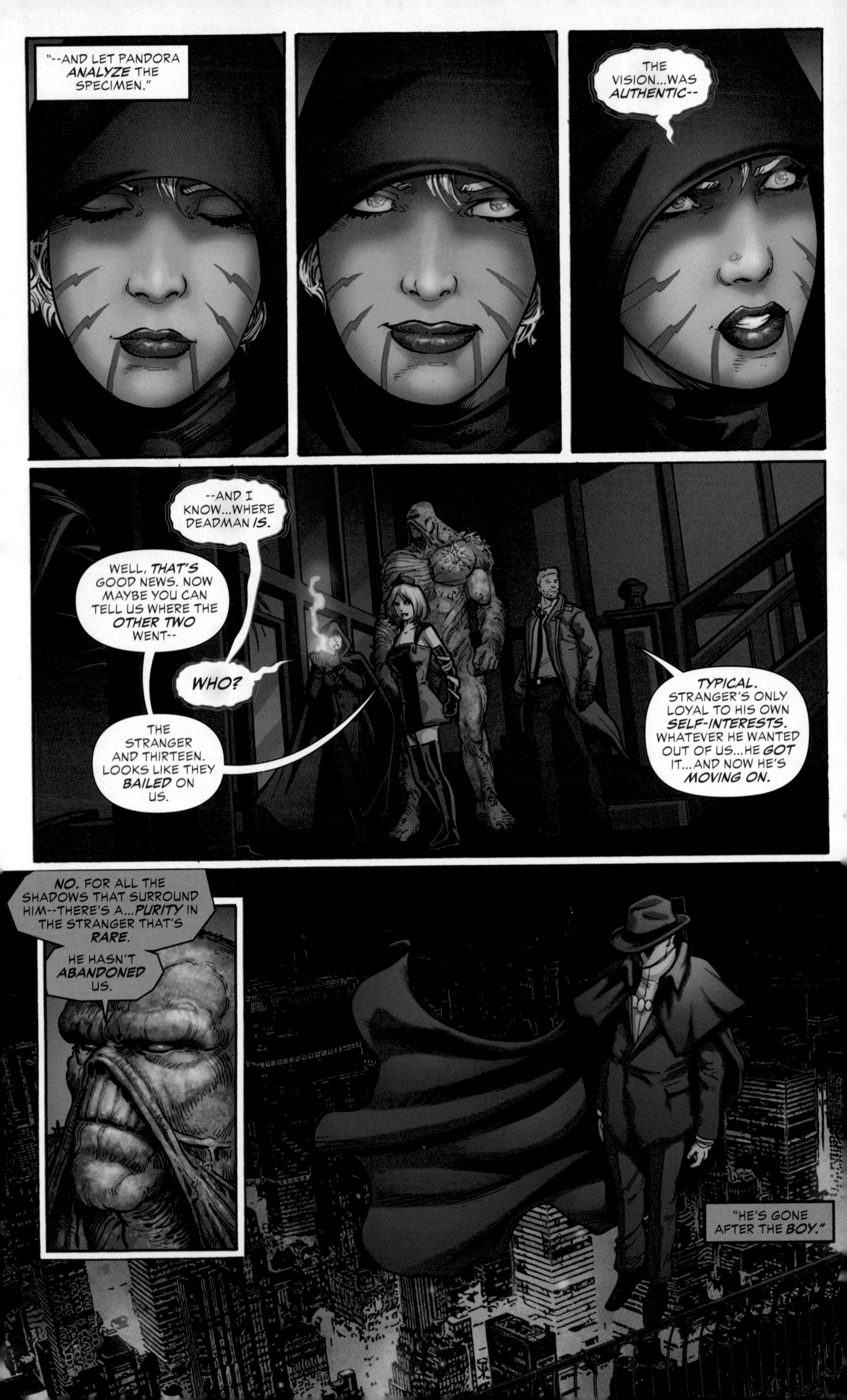
"--AND LET PANDORA ANALYZE THE SPECIMEN."
THE VISION...WAS AUTHENTIC--
--AND I KNOW...WHERE DEADMAN IS.
WELL, THAT'S GOOD NEWS. NOW MAYBE YOU CAN TELL US WHERE THE OTHER TWO WENT--
WHO?
THE STRANGER AND THIRTEEN. LOOKS LIKE THEY BAILED ON US.
TYPICAL. STRANGER'S ONLY LOYAL TO HIS OWN SELF-INTERESTS. WHATEVER HE WANTED OUT OF US...HE GOT IT...AND NOW HE'S MOVING ON.
NO. FOR ALL THE SHADOWS THAT SURROUND HIM--THERE'S A...PURITY IN THE STRANGER THAT'S RARE.
HE HASN'T ABANDONED US.
"HE'S GONE AFTER THE BOY."

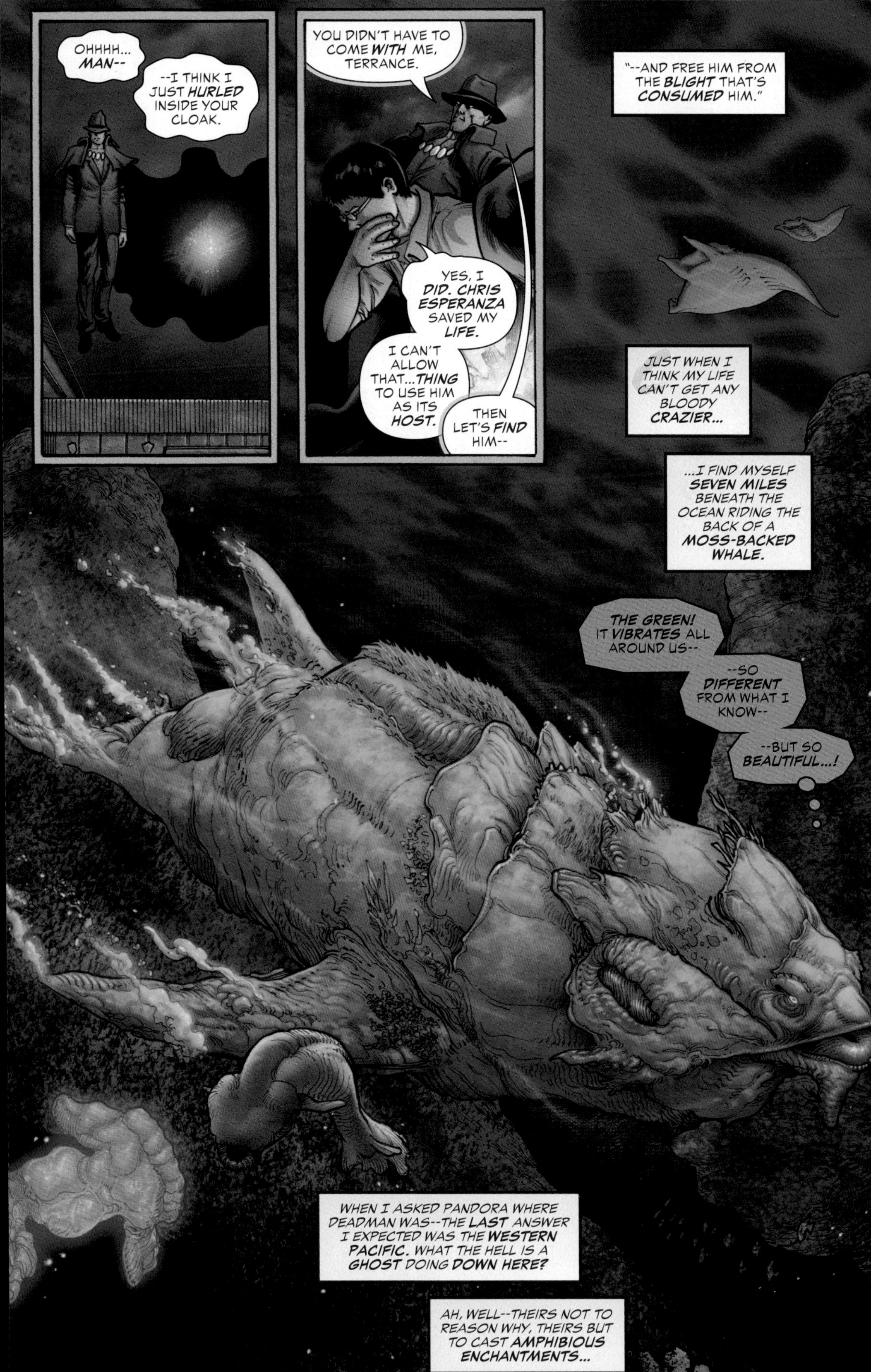
OHHHH... MAN--
--I THINK I JUST HURLED INSIDE YOUR CLOAK.
YOU DIDN'T HAVE TO COME WITH ME, TERRANCE.
YES, I DID. CHRIS ESPERANZA SAVED MY LIFE.
I CAN'T ALLOW THAT...THING TO USE HIM AS ITS HOST.
THEN LET'S FIND HIM--
"--AND FREE HIM FROM THE BLIGHT THAT'S CONSUMED HIM."
JUST WHEN I THINK MY LIFE CAN'T GET ANY BLOODY CRAZIER...
...I FIND MYSELF SEVEN MILES BENEATH THE OCEAN RIDING THE BACK OF A MOSS-BACKED WHALE.
THE GREEN! IT VIBRATES ALL AROUND US--
--SO DIFFERENT FROM WHAT I KNOW--
--BUT SO BEAUTIFUL...!
WHEN I ASKED PANDORA WHERE DEADMAN WAS--THE LAST ANSWER I EXPECTED WAS THE WESTERN PACIFIC. WHAT THE HELL IS A GHOST DOING DOWN HERE?
AH, WELL--THEIRS NOT TO REASON WHY, THEIRS BUT TO CAST AMPHIBIOUS ENCHANTMENTS...

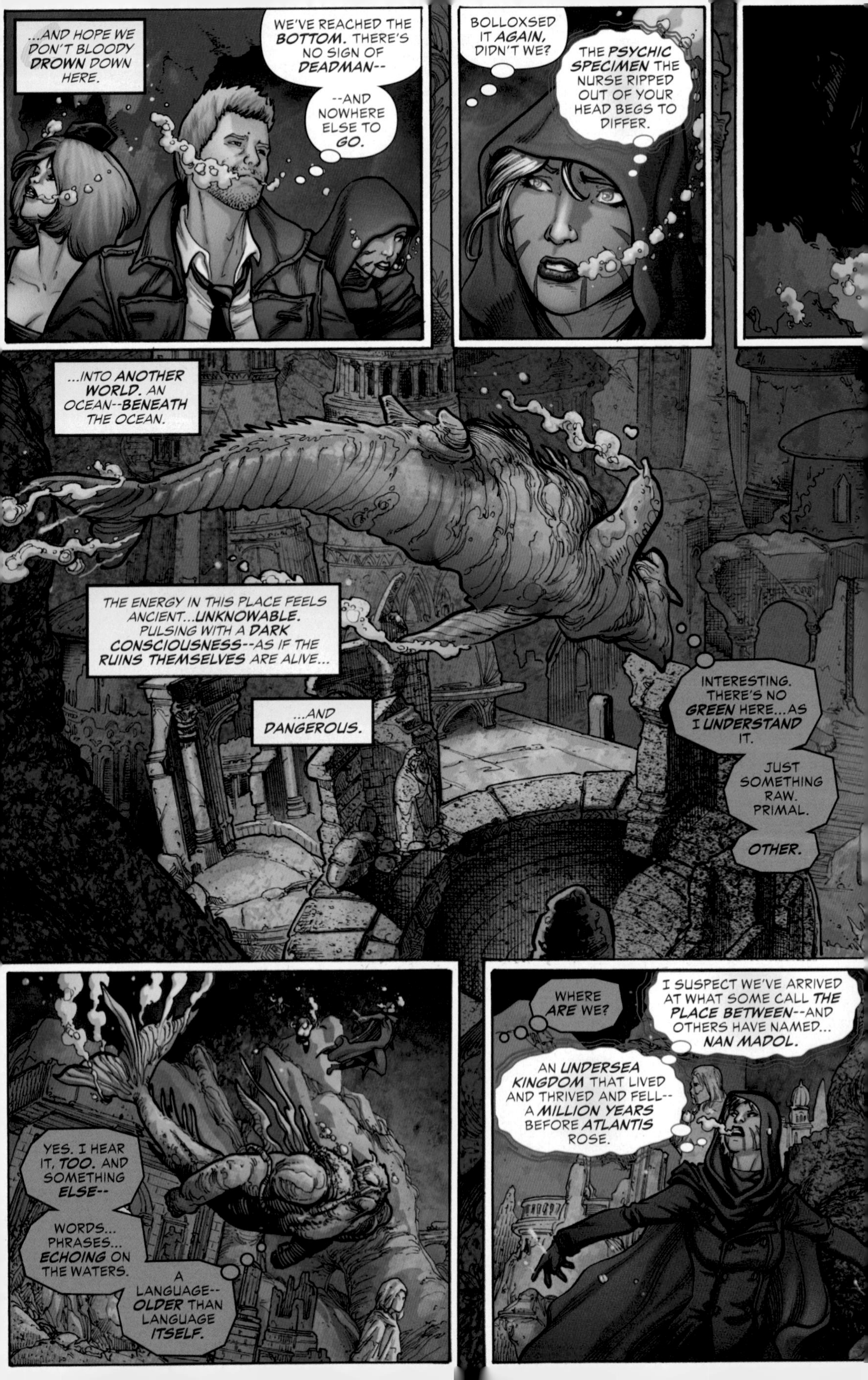
...AND HOPE WE DON'T BLOODY DROWN DOWN HERE.
WE'VE REACHED THE BOTTOM. THERE'S NO SIGN OF DEADMAN--
--AND NOWHERE ELSE TO GO.
BOLLOXSED IT AGAIN, DIDN'T WE?
THE PSYCHIC SPECIMEN THE NURSE RIPPED OUT OF YOUR HEAD BEGS TO DIFFER.
...INTO ANOTHER WORLD. AN OCEAN--BENEATH THE OCEAN.
THE ENERGY IN THIS PLACE FEELS ANCIENT...UNKNOWABLE. PULSING WITH A DARK CONSCIOUSNESS--AS IF THE RUINS THEMSELVES ARE ALIVE...
...AND DANGEROUS.
INTERESTING. THERE'S NO GREEN HERE...AS I UNDERSTAND IT.
JUST SOMETHING RAW. PRIMAL.
OTHER.
YES. I HEAR IT, TOO. AND SOMETHING ELSE--
WORDS... PHRASES... ECHOING ON THE WATERS.
A LANGUAGE--OLDER THAN LANGUAGE ITSELF.
WHERE ARE WE?
I SUSPECT WE'VE ARRIVED AT WHAT SOME CALL THE PLACE BETWEEN--AND OTHERS HAVE NAMED... NAN MADOL.
AN UNDERSEA KINGDOM THAT LIVED AND THRIVED AND FELL--A MILLION YEARS BEFORE ATLANTIS ROSE.

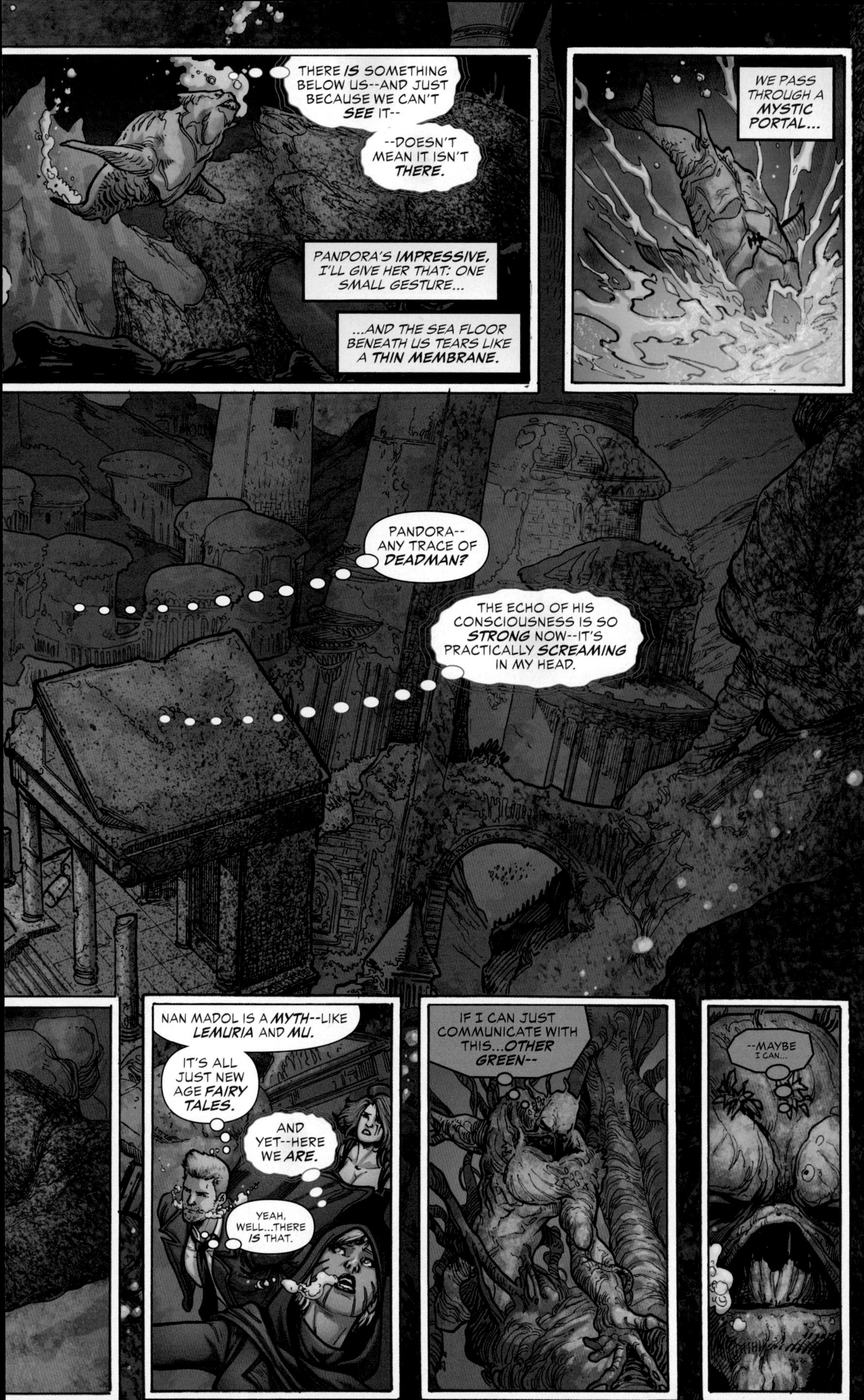

THERE IS SOMETHING BELOW US--AND JUST BECAUSE WE CAN'T SEE IT--
--DOESN'T MEAN IT ISN'T THERE.
PANDORA'S IMPRESSIVE, I'LL GIVE HER THAT: ONE SMALL GESTURE...
...AND THE SEA FLOOR BENEATH US TEARS LIKE A THIN MEMBRANE.
WE PASS THROUGH A MYSTIC PORTAL...
PANDORA-- ANY TRACE OF DEADMAN?
THE ECHO OF HIS CONSCIOUSNESS IS SO STRONG NOW--IT'S PRACTICALLY SCREAMING IN MY HEAD.
NAN MADOL IS A MYTH--LIKE LEMURIA AND MU.
IT'S ALL JUST NEW AGE FAIRY TALES.
AND YET--HERE WE ARE.
YEAH, WELL...THERE IS THAT.
IF I CAN JUST COMMUNICATE WITH THIS...OTHER GREEN--
--MAYBE I CAN...

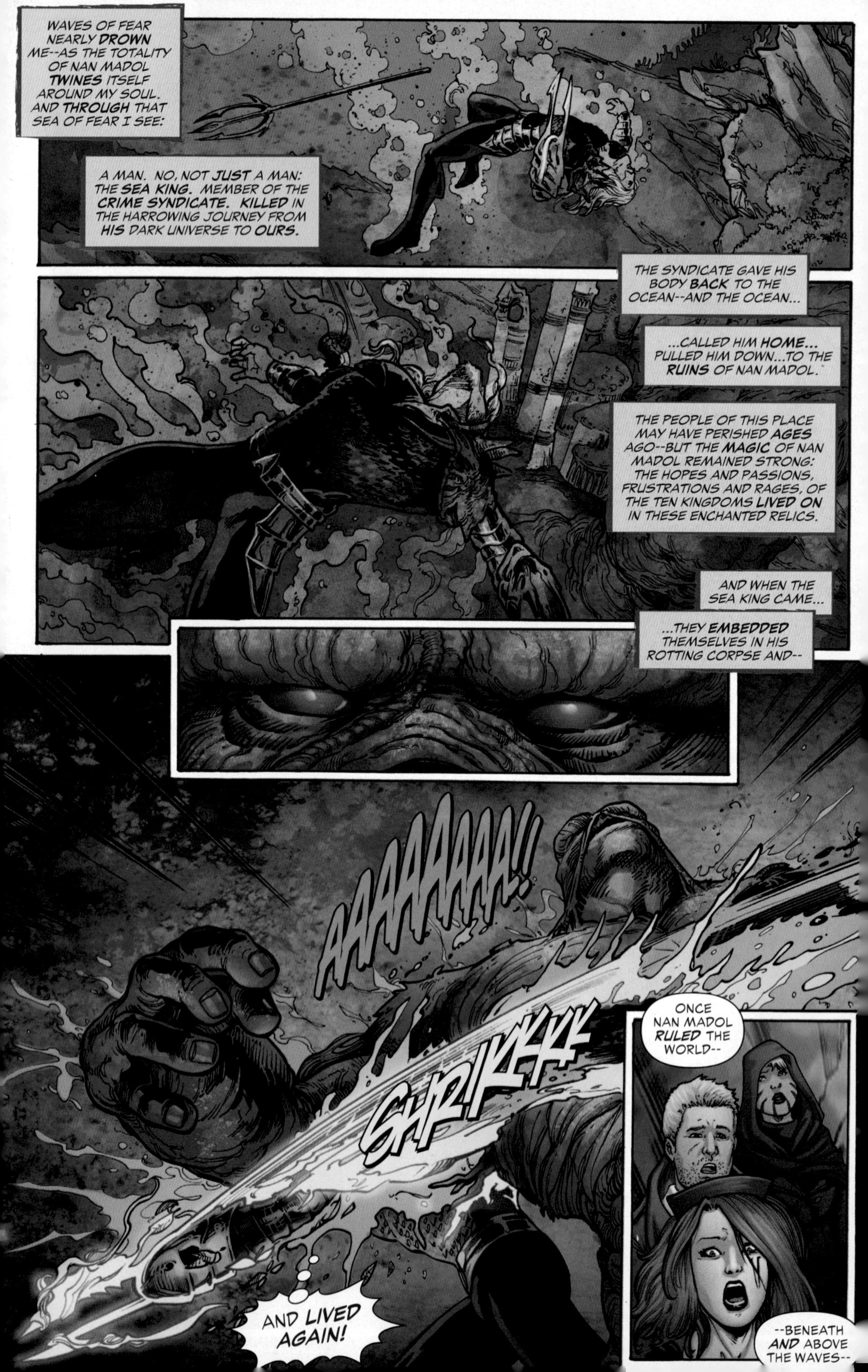
WAVES OF FEAR NEARLY DROWN ME--AS THE TOTALITY OF NAN MADOL TWINES ITSELF AROUND MY SOUL. AND THROUGH THAT SEA OF FEAR I SEE:
A MAN. NO, NOT JUST A MAN: THE SEA KING. MEMBER OF THE CRIME SYNDICATE. KILLED IN THE HARROWING JOURNEY FROM HIS DARK UNIVERSE TO OURS.
THE SYNDICATE GAVE HIS BODY BACK TO THE OCEAN--AND THE OCEAN...
...CALLED HIM HOME... PULLED HIM DOWN...TO THE RUINS OF NAN MADOL.
THE PEOPLE OF THIS PLACE MAY HAVE PERISHED AGES AGO--BUT THE MAGIC OF NAN MADOL REMAINED STRONG: THE HOPES AND PASSIONS, FRUSTRATIONS AND RAGES, OF THE TEN KINGDOMS LIVED ON IN THESE ENCHANTED RELICS.
AND WHEN THE SEA KING CAME...
...THEY EMBEDDED THEMSELVES IN HIS ROTTING CORPSE AND--
AAAAAAA!!
SHRKKK
AND LIVED AGAIN!
ONCE NAN MADOL RULED THE WORLD--
--BENEATH AND ABOVE THE WAVES--

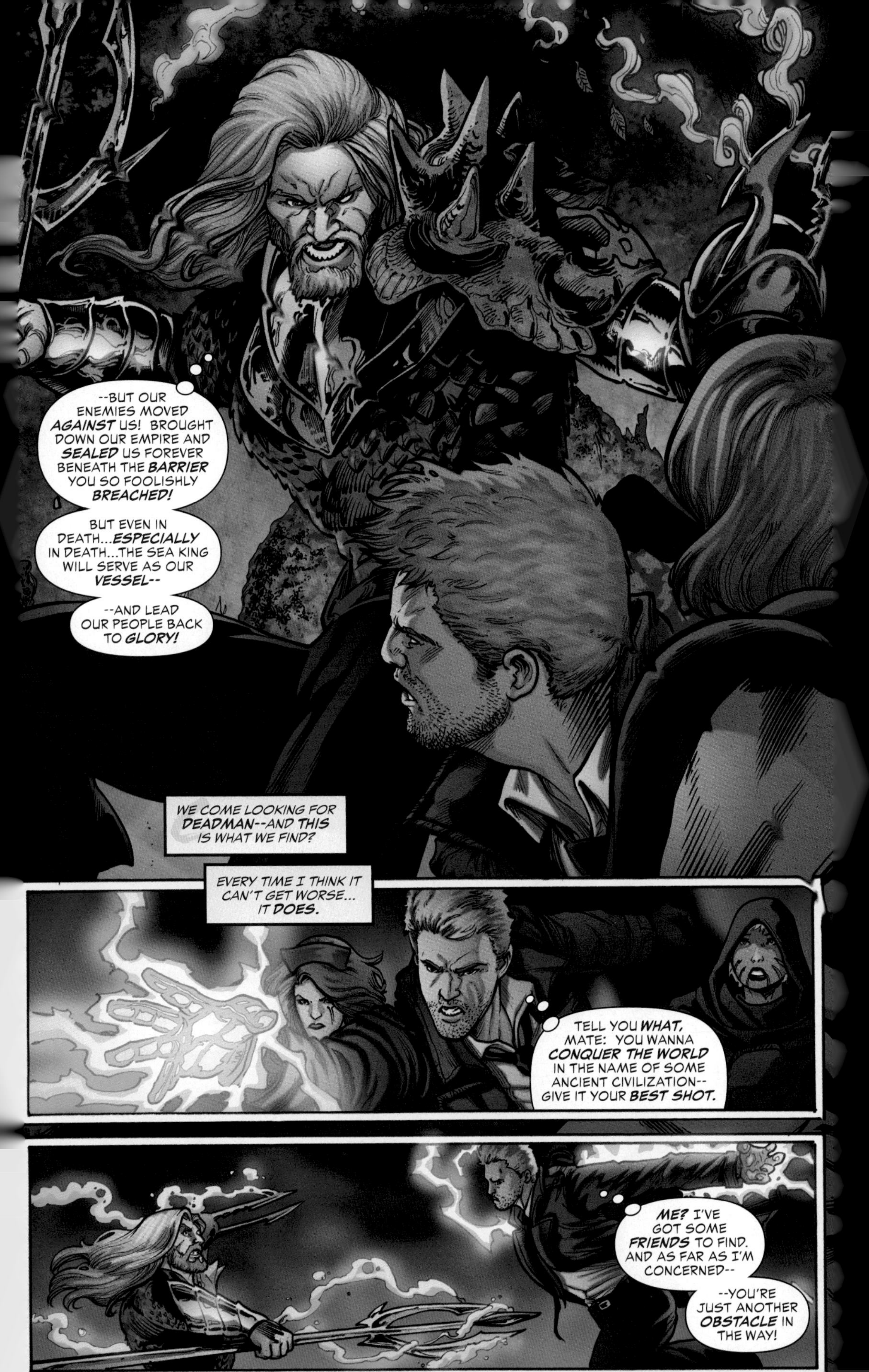
--BUT OUR ENEMIES MOVED AGAINST US! BROUGHT DOWN OUR EMPIRE AND SEALED US FOREVER BENEATH THE BARRIER YOU SO FOOLISHLY BREACHED!
BUT EVEN IN DEATH...ESPECIALLY IN DEATH...THE SEA KING WILL SERVE AS OUR VESSEL--
--AND LEAD OUR PEOPLE BACK TO GLORY!
WE COME LOOKING FOR DEADMAN--AND THIS IS WHAT WE FIND?
EVERY TIME I THINK IT CAN'T GET WORSE... IT DOES.
TELL YOU WHAT, MATE: YOU WANNA CONQUER THE WORLD IN THE NAME OF SOME ANCIENT CIVILIZATION-- GIVE IT YOUR BEST SHOT.
ME? I'VE GOT SOME FRIENDS TO FIND. AND AS FAR AS I'M CONCERNED--
--YOU'RE JUST ANOTHER OBSTACLE IN THE WAY!

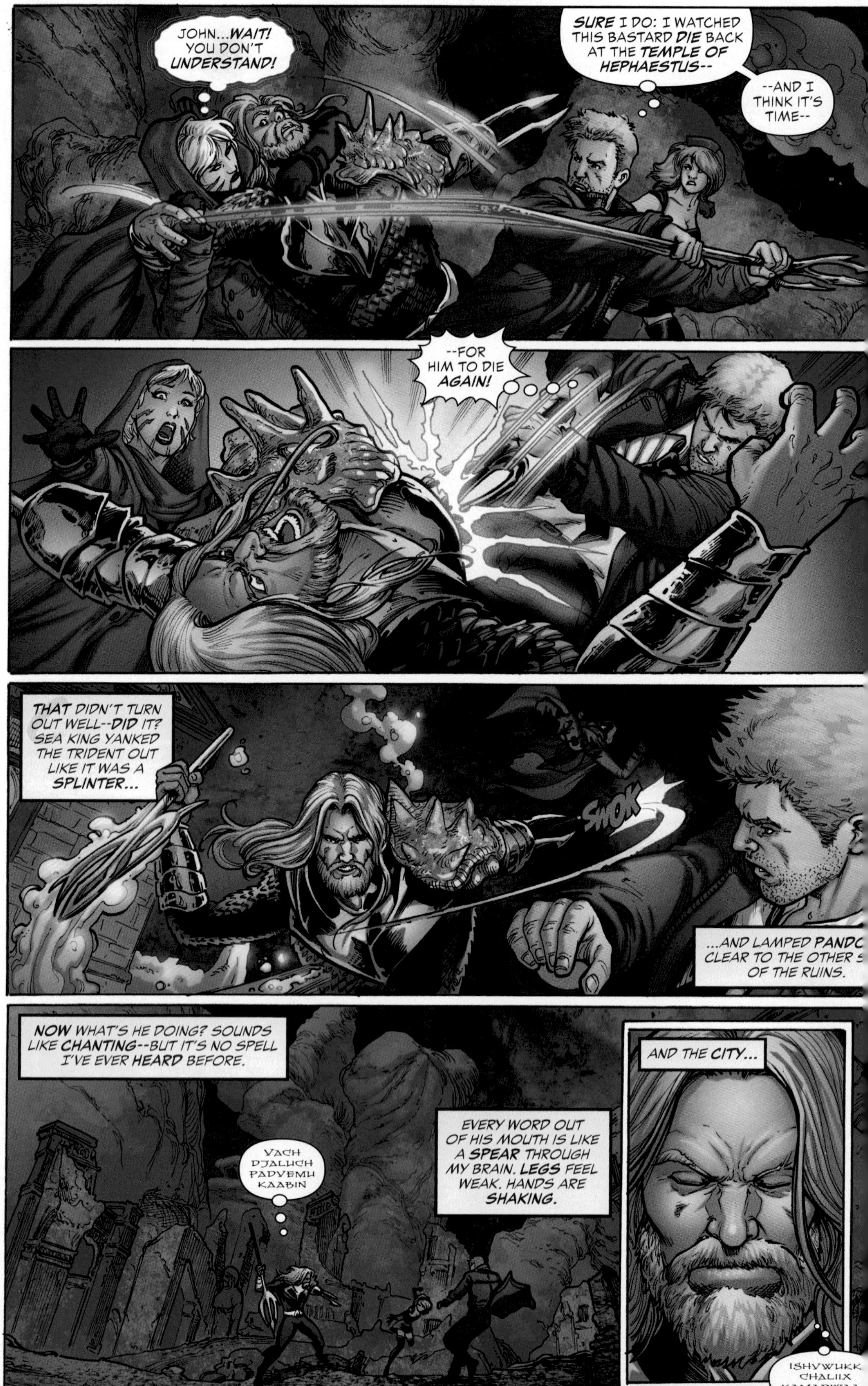

JOHN...WAIT! YOU DON'T UNDERSTAND!
SURE I DO: I WATCHED THIS BASTARD DIE BACK AT THE TEMPLE OF HEPHAESTUS--
--AND I THINK IT'S TIME--
--FOR HIM TO DIE AGAIN!
THAT DIDN'T TURN OUT WELL--DID IT? SEA KING YANKED THE TRIDENT OUT LIKE IT WAS A SPLINTER...
SMOK
...AND LAMPED PANDO CLEAR TO THE OTHER S OF THE RUINS.
NOW WHAT'S HE DOING? SOUNDS LIKE CHANTING--BUT IT'S NO SPELL I'VE EVER HEARD BEFORE.
YACH DJALUCH PADVEMU KAABIN
EVERY WORD OUT OF HIS MOUTH IS LIKE A SPEAR THROUGH MY BRAIN. LEGS FEEL WEAK. HANDS ARE SHAKING.
AND THE CITY...
ISHYWUKK CHALIIX KAMARWAA

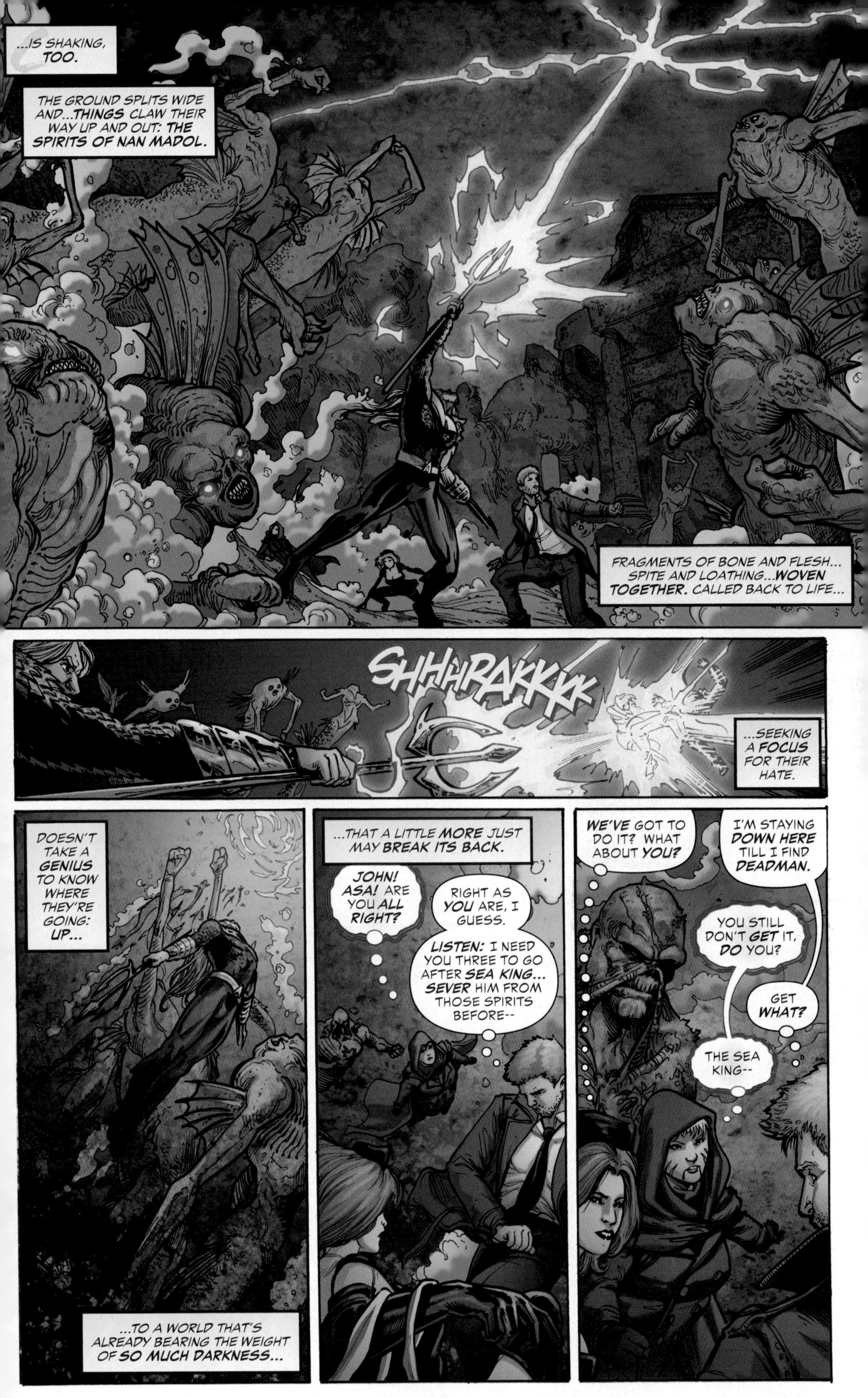
...IS SHAKING, TOO.
THE GROUND SPLITS WIDE AND...THINGS CLAW THEIR WAY UP AND OUT: THE SPIRITS OF NAN MADOL.
FRAGMENTS OF BONE AND FLESH... SPITE AND LOATHING...WOVEN TOGETHER. CALLED BACK TO LIFE...
SHHHRAKKKK
...SEEKING A FOCUS FOR THEIR HATE.
DOESN'T TAKE A GENIUS TO KNOW WHERE THEY'RE GOING: UP...
...TO A WORLD THAT'S ALREADY BEARING THE WEIGHT OF SO MUCH DARKNESS...
...THAT A LITTLE MORE JUST MAY BREAK ITS BACK.
JOHN! ASA! ARE YOU ALL RIGHT?
RIGHT AS YOU ARE, I GUESS.
LISTEN: I NEED YOU THREE TO GO AFTER SEA KING... SEVER HIM FROM THOSE SPIRITS BEFORE--
WE'VE GOT TO DO IT? WHAT ABOUT YOU?
I'M STAYING DOWN HERE TILL I FIND DEADMAN.
YOU STILL DON'T GET IT, DO YOU?
GET WHAT?
THE SEA KING--

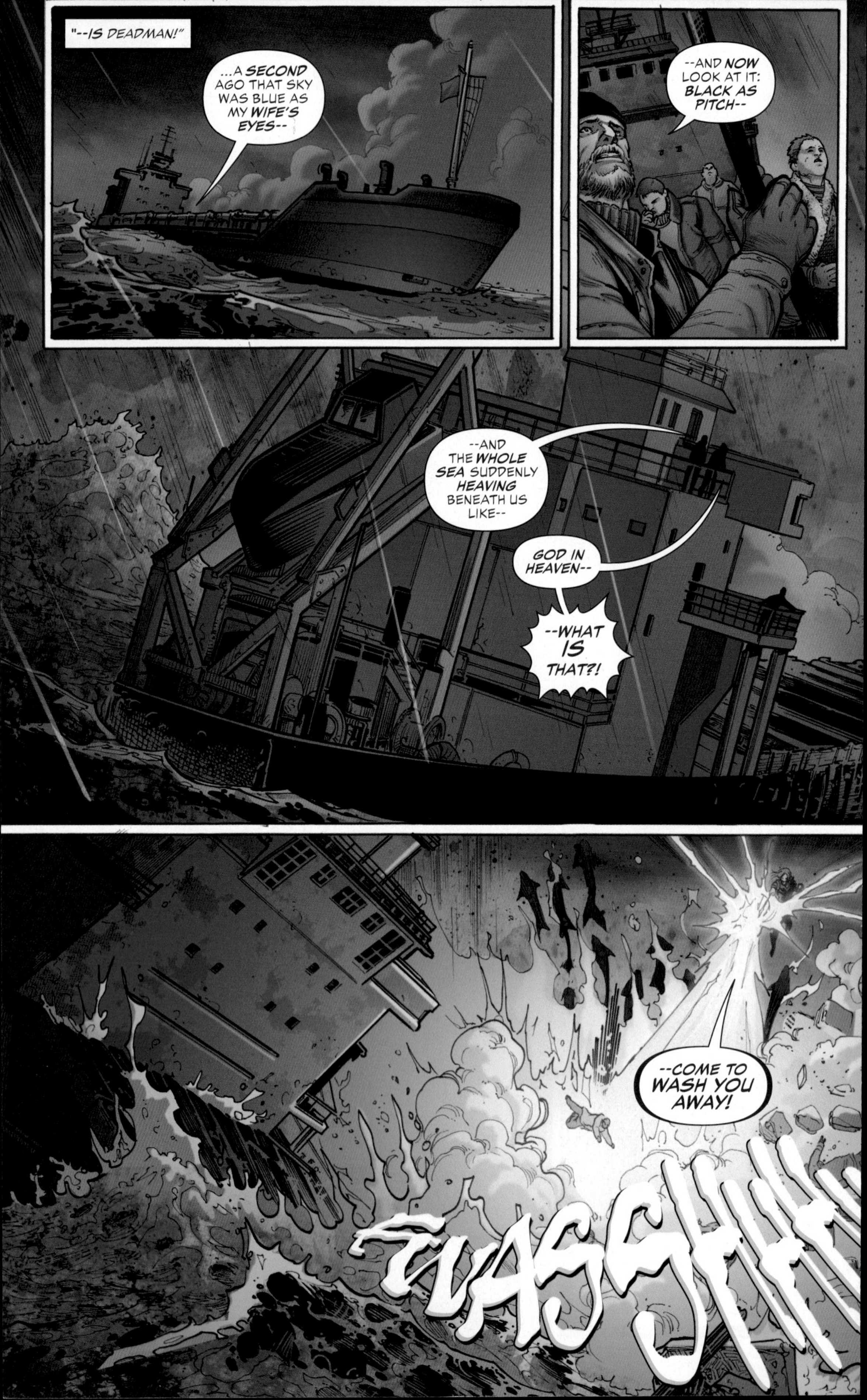
"--IS DEADMAN!"
...A SECOND AGO THAT SKY WAS BLUE AS MY WIFE'S EYES--
--AND NOW LOOK AT IT: BLACK AS PITCH--
--AND THE WHOLE SEA SUDDENLY HEAVING BENEATH US LIKE--
GOD IN HEAVEN--
--WHAT IS THAT?!
--COME TO WASH YOU AWAY!
TWASSHHH

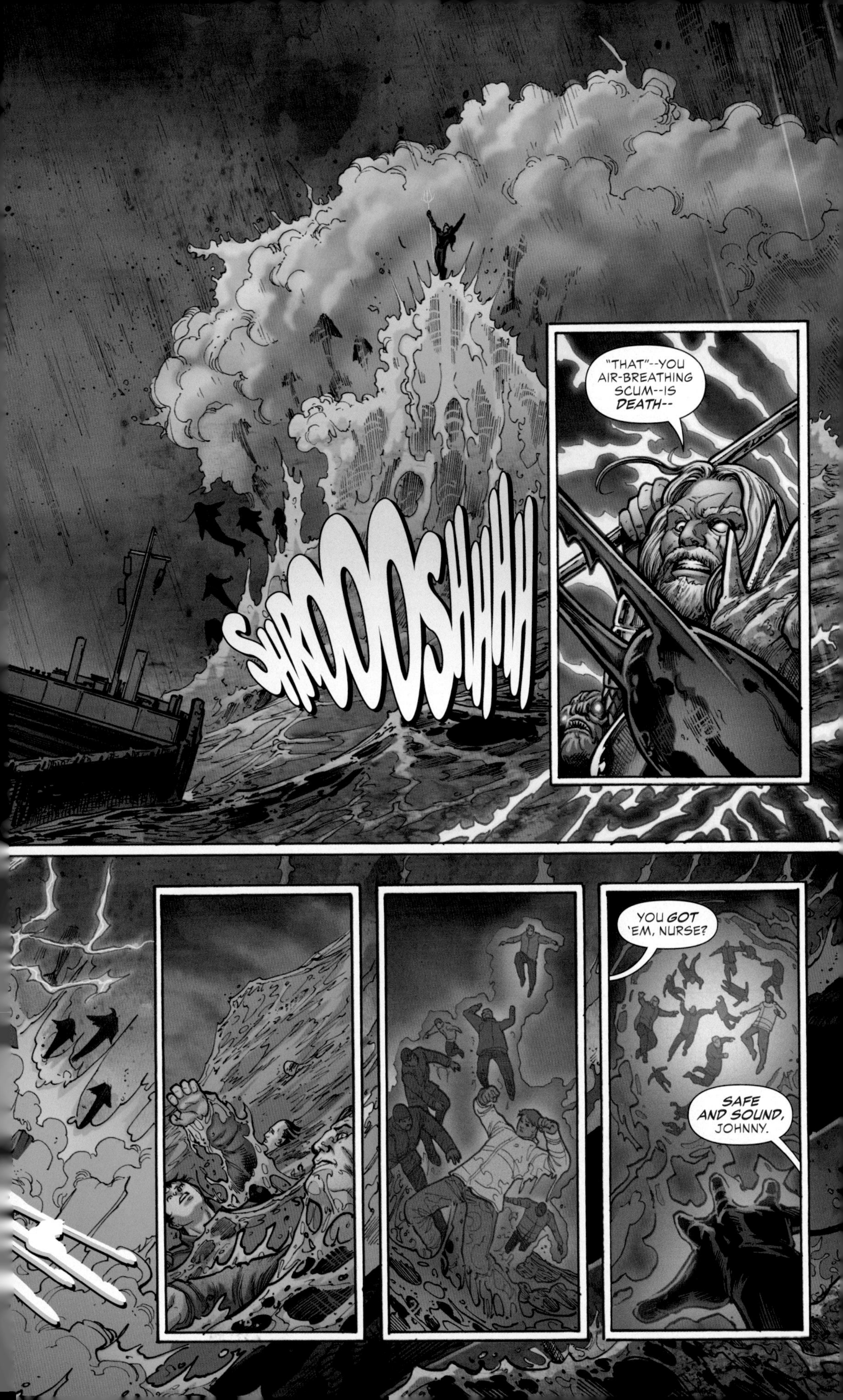
SHROOOOSHHHH
"THAT"--YOU AIR-BREATHING SCUM--IS *DEATH*--
YOU *GOT* 'EM, NURSE?
SAFE AND SOUND, JOHNNY.

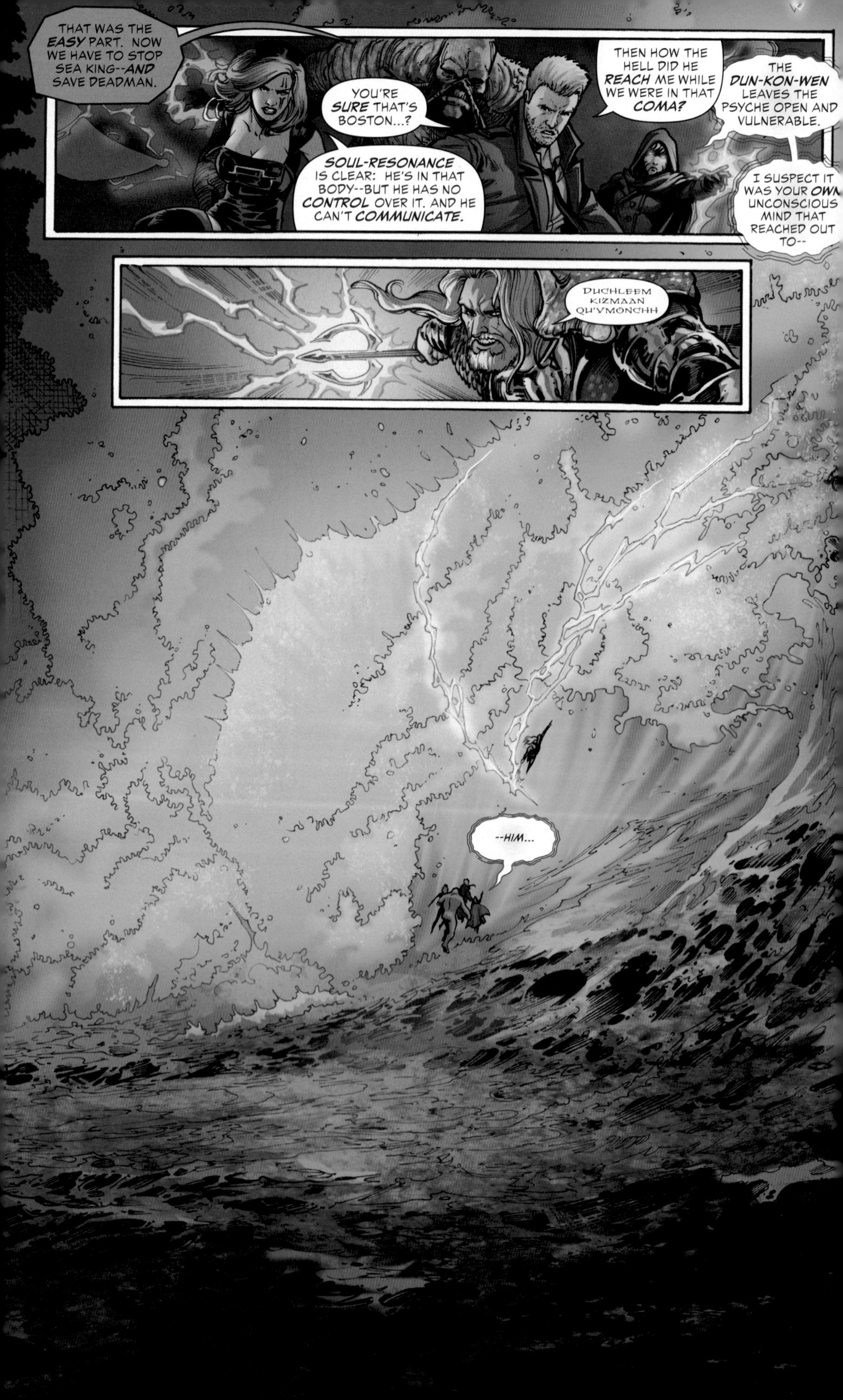
THAT WAS THE EASY PART. NOW WE HAVE TO STOP SEA KING--AND SAVE DEADMAN.
YOU'RE SURE THAT'S BOSTON...?
SOUL-RESONANCE IS CLEAR: HE'S IN THAT BODY--BUT HE HAS NO CONTROL OVER IT. AND HE CAN'T COMMUNICATE.
THEN HOW THE HELL DID HE REACH ME WHILE WE WERE IN THAT COMA?
THE DUN-KON-WEN LEAVES THE PSYCHE OPEN AND VULNERABLE.
I SUSPECT IT WAS YOUR OWN UNCONSCIOUS MIND THAT REACHED OUT TO--
DUCHLEEM KIZMAAN QU'YMONCHH
--HIM...

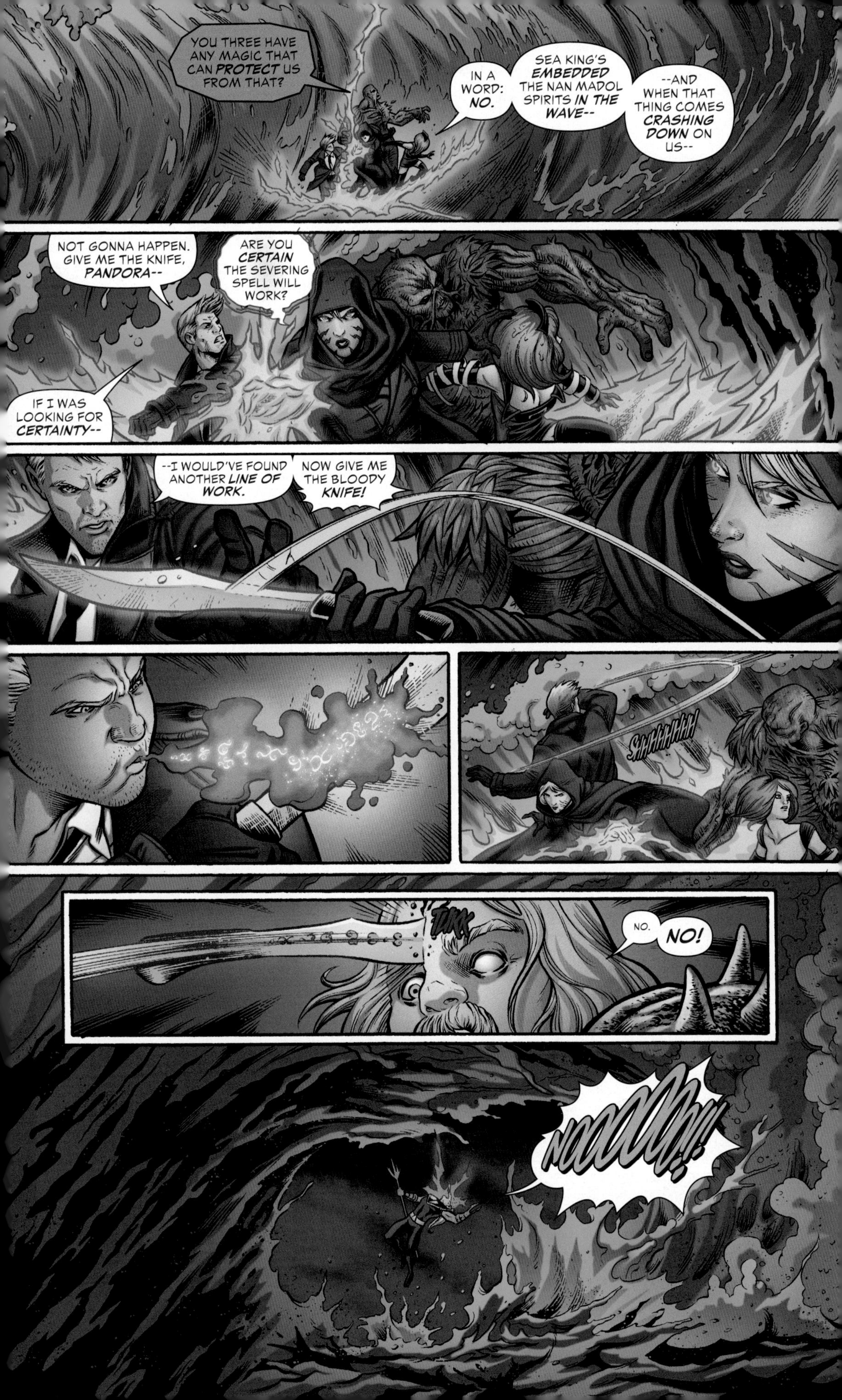
YOU THREE HAVE ANY MAGIC THAT CAN PROTECT US FROM THAT?
IN A WORD: NO.
SEA KING'S EMBEDDED THE NAN MADOL SPIRITS IN THE WAVE--
--AND WHEN THAT THING COMES CRASHING DOWN ON US--
NOT GONNA HAPPEN. GIVE ME THE KNIFE, PANDORA--
ARE YOU CERTAIN THE SEVERING SPELL WILL WORK?
IF I WAS LOOKING FOR CERTAINTY--
--I WOULD'VE FOUND ANOTHER LINE OF WORK.
NOW GIVE ME THE BLOODY KNIFE!
SHHHHHHH
TUKK
NO.
NO!
NOOOOO!!

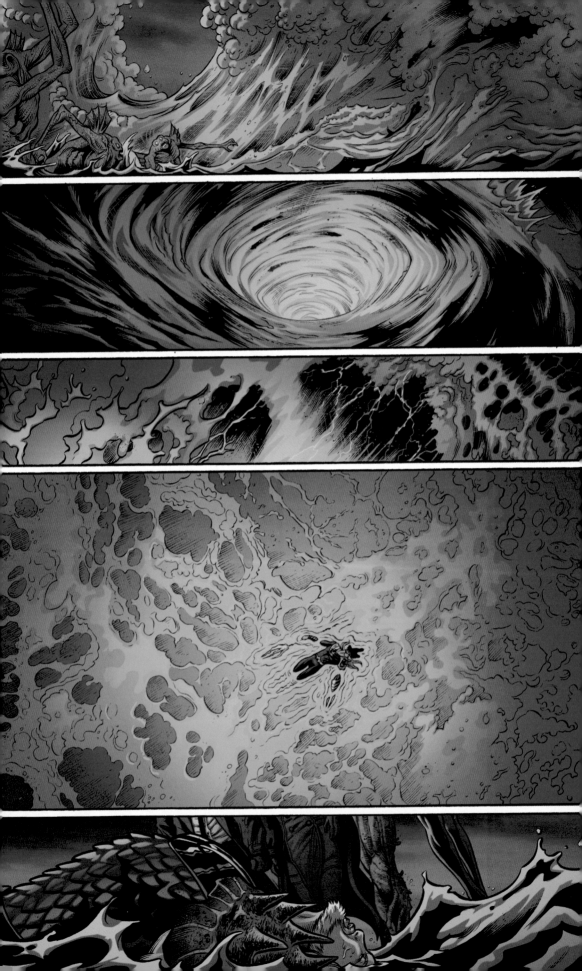

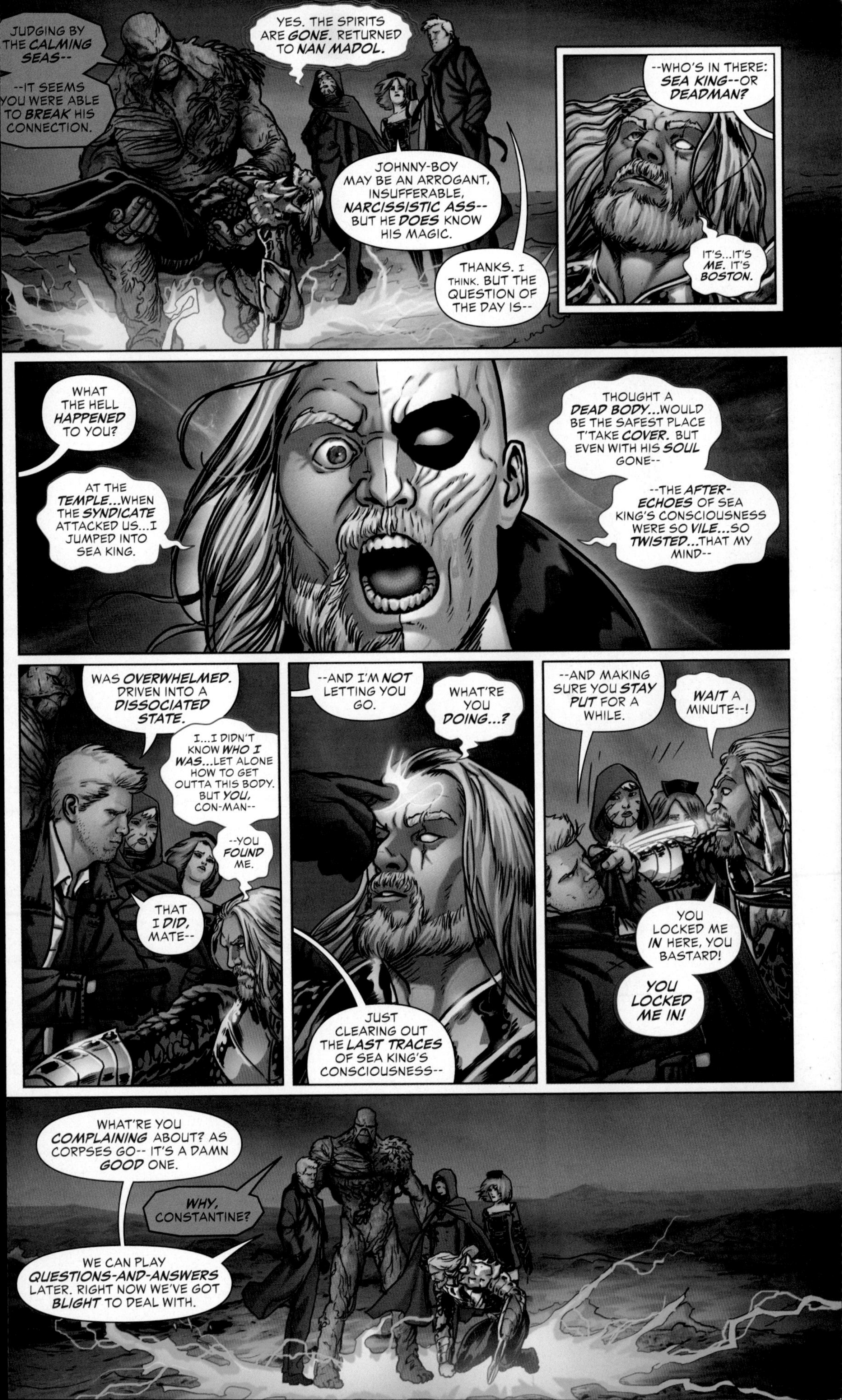

JUDGING BY THE CALMING SEAS--
--IT SEEMS YOU WERE ABLE TO BREAK HIS CONNECTION.
YES. THE SPIRITS ARE GONE. RETURNED TO NAN MADOL.
JOHNNY-BOY MAY BE AN ARROGANT, INSUFFERABLE, NARCISSISTIC ASS-- BUT HE DOES KNOW HIS MAGIC.
THANKS. I THINK. BUT THE QUESTION OF THE DAY IS--
--WHO'S IN THERE: SEA KING--OR DEADMAN?
IT'S...IT'S ME. IT'S BOSTON.
WHAT THE HELL HAPPENED TO YOU?
AT THE TEMPLE...WHEN THE SYNDICATE ATTACKED US...I JUMPED INTO SEA KING.
THOUGHT A DEAD BODY...WOULD BE THE SAFEST PLACE T'TAKE COVER. BUT EVEN WITH HIS SOUL GONE--
--THE AFTER-ECHOES OF SEA KING'S CONSCIOUSNESS WERE SO VILE...SO TWISTED...THAT MY MIND--
WAS OVERWHELMED. DRIVEN INTO A DISSOCIATED STATE.
I...I DIDN'T KNOW WHO I WAS...LET ALONE HOW TO GET OUTTA THIS BODY. BUT YOU, CON-MAN--
--YOU FOUND ME.
THAT I DID, MATE--
--AND I'M NOT LETTING YOU GO.
WHAT'RE YOU DOING...?
JUST CLEARING OUT THE LAST TRACES OF SEA KING'S CONSCIOUSNESS--
--AND MAKING SURE YOU STAY PUT FOR A WHILE.
WAIT A MINUTE--!
YOU LOCKED ME IN HERE, YOU BASTARD!
YOU LOCKED ME IN!
WHAT'RE YOU COMPLAINING ABOUT? AS CORPSES GO-- IT'S A DAMN GOOD ONE.
WHY, CONSTANTINE?
WE CAN PLAY QUESTIONS-AND-ANSWERS LATER. RIGHT NOW WE'VE GOT BLIGHT TO DEAL WITH.

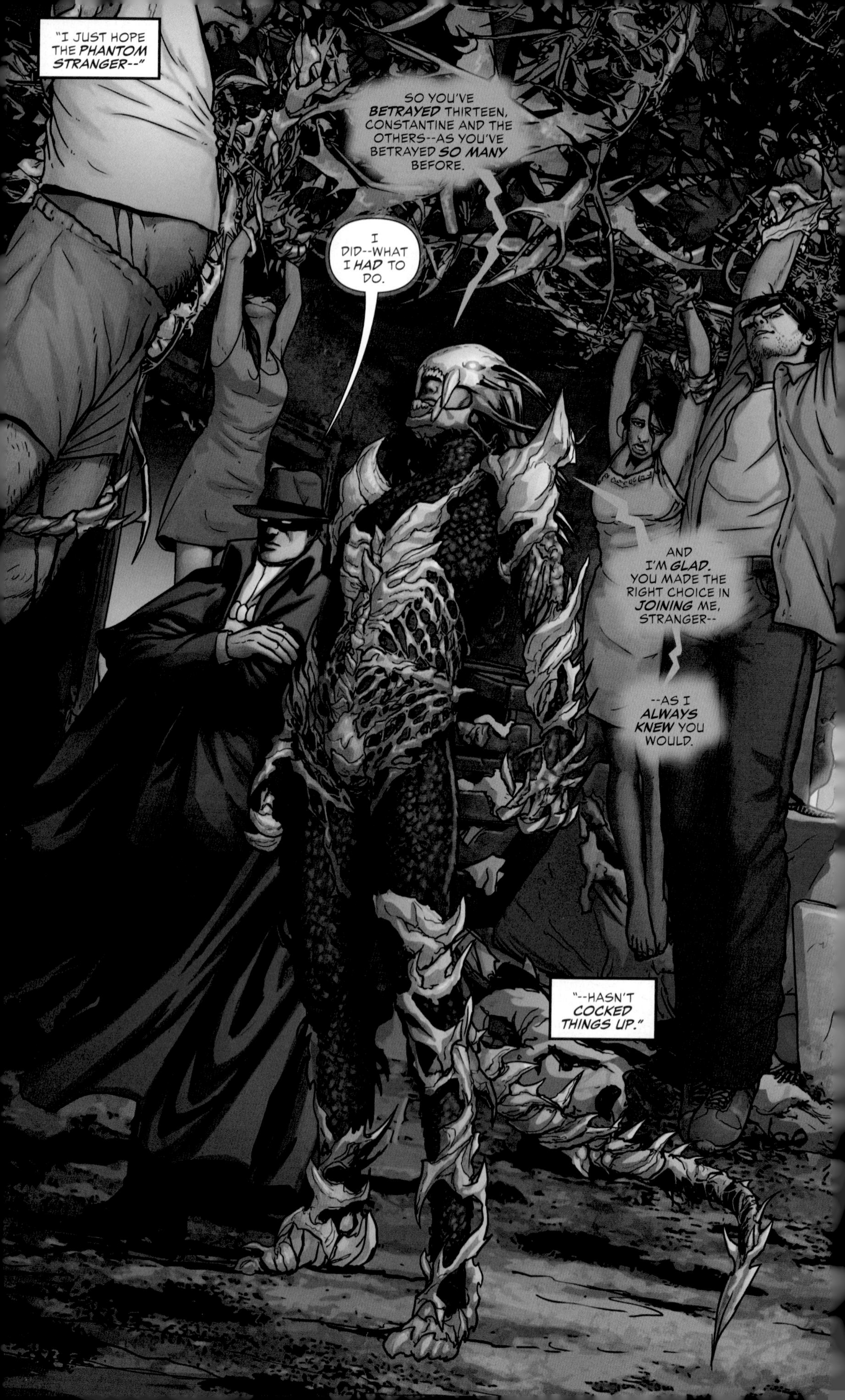
"I JUST HOPE THE PHANTOM STRANGER--"
SO YOU'VE BETRAYED THIRTEEN, CONSTANTINE AND THE OTHERS--AS YOU'VE BETRAYED SO MANY BEFORE.
I DID--WHAT I HAD TO DO.
AND I'M GLAD. YOU MADE THE RIGHT CHOICE IN JOINING ME, STRANGER--
--AS I ALWAYS KNEW YOU WOULD.
"--HASN'T COCKED THINGS UP."

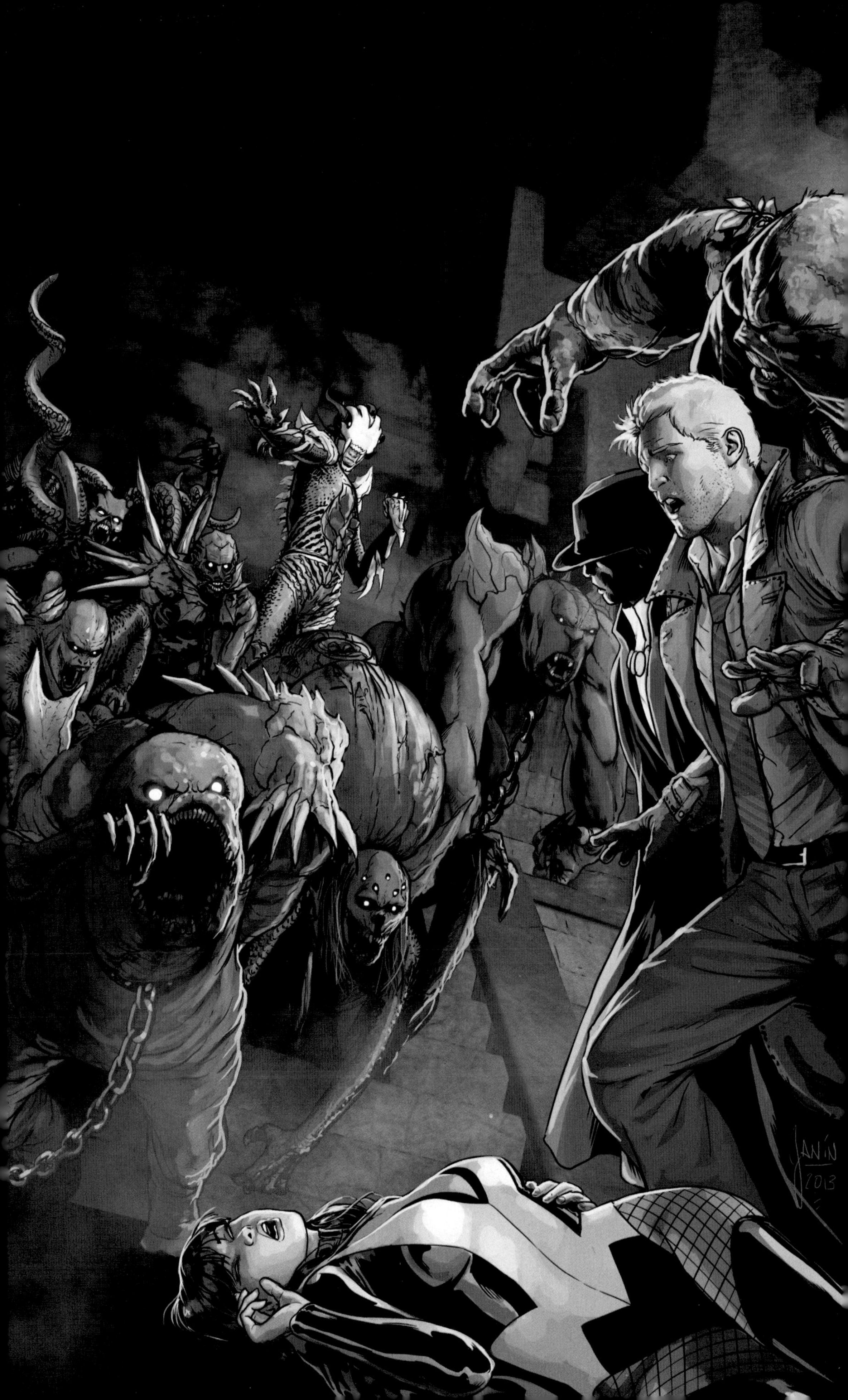
JANÍN
2013

J. M. DeMATTEIS
writer

MIKEL JANIN
penciller & graytone artist

VICENTE CIFUENTES & GUILLERMO ORTEGO
inkers

MIKEL JANIN
cover artist

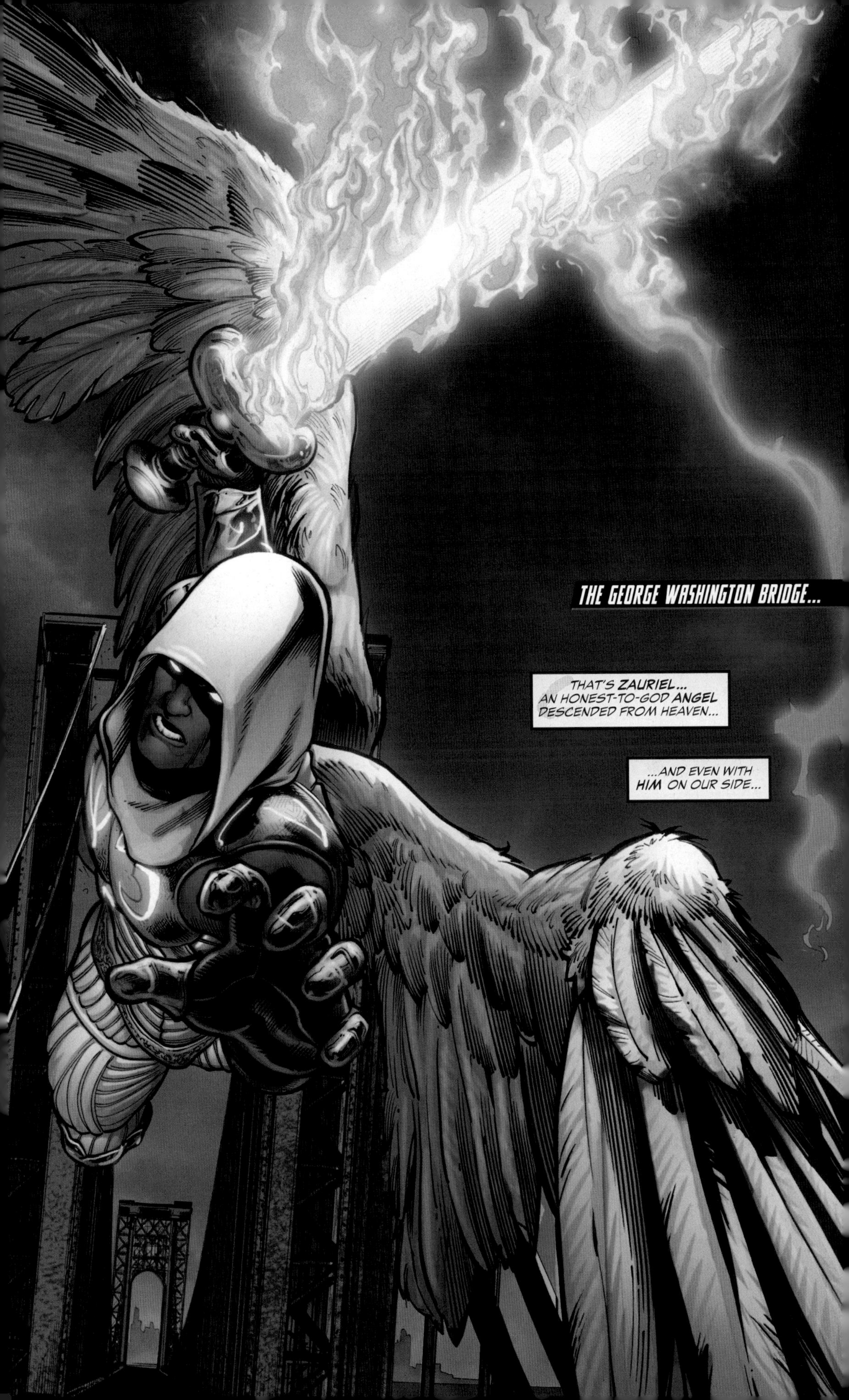
THE GEORGE WASHINGTON BRIDGE...
THAT'S ZAURIEL... AN HONEST-TO-GOD ANGEL DESCENDED FROM HEAVEN...
...AND EVEN WITH HIM ON OUR SIDE...

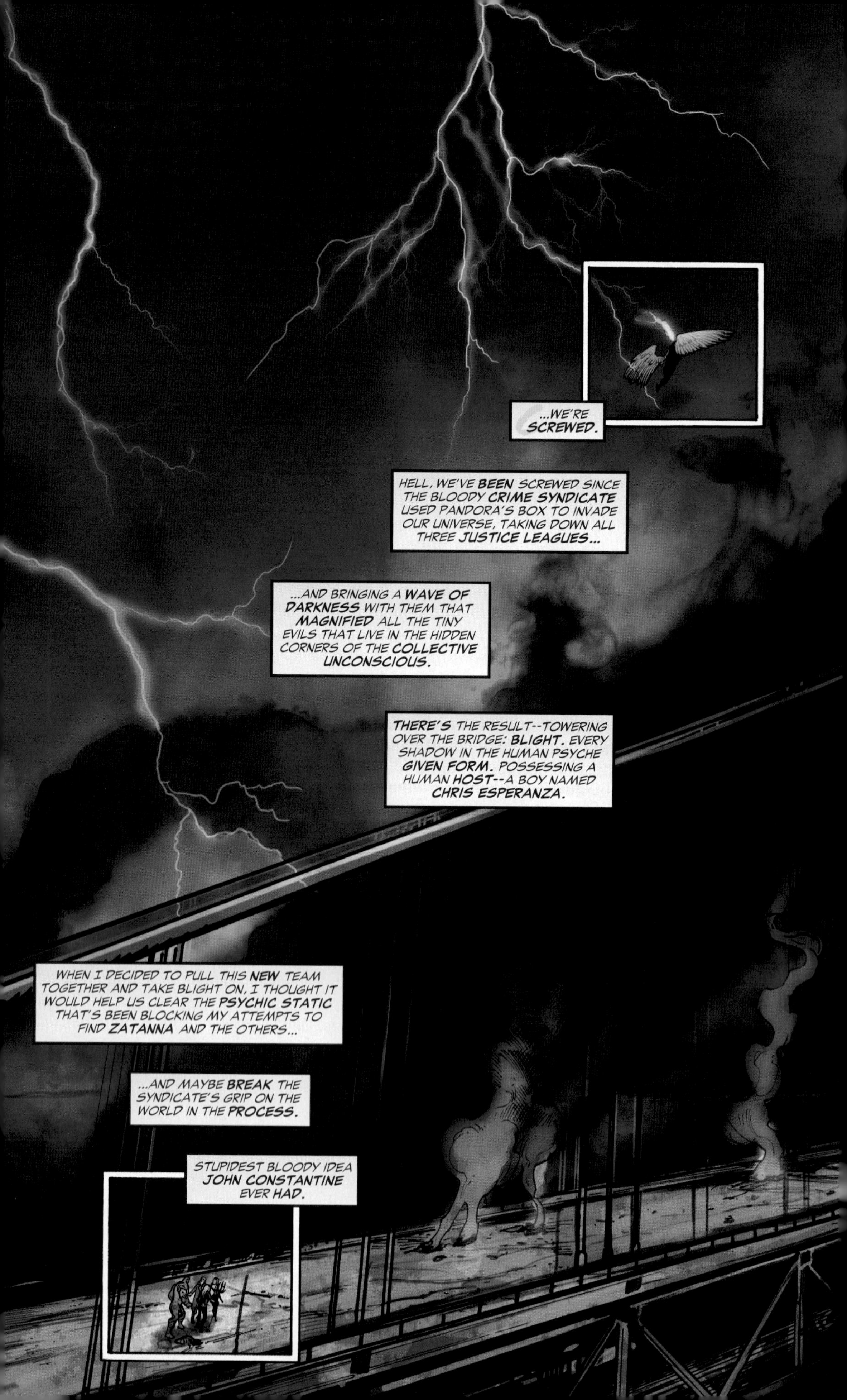
...WE'RE SCREWED.
HELL, WE'VE BEEN SCREWED SINCE THE BLOODY CRIME SYNDICATE USED PANDORA'S BOX TO INVADE OUR UNIVERSE, TAKING DOWN ALL THREE JUSTICE LEAGUES...
...AND BRINGING A WAVE OF DARKNESS WITH THEM THAT MAGNIFIED ALL THE TINY EVILS THAT LIVE IN THE HIDDEN CORNERS OF THE COLLECTIVE UNCONSCIOUS.
THERE'S THE RESULT--TOWERING OVER THE BRIDGE: BLIGHT. EVERY SHADOW IN THE HUMAN PSYCHE GIVEN FORM. POSSESSING A HUMAN HOST--A BOY NAMED CHRIS ESPERANZA.
WHEN I DECIDED TO PULL THIS NEW TEAM TOGETHER AND TAKE BLIGHT ON, I THOUGHT IT WOULD HELP US CLEAR THE PSYCHIC STATIC THAT'S BEEN BLOCKING MY ATTEMPTS TO FIND ZATANNA AND THE OTHERS...
...AND MAYBE BREAK THE SYNDICATE'S GRIP ON THE WORLD IN THE PROCESS.
STUPIDEST BLOODY IDEA JOHN CONSTANTINE EVER HAD.

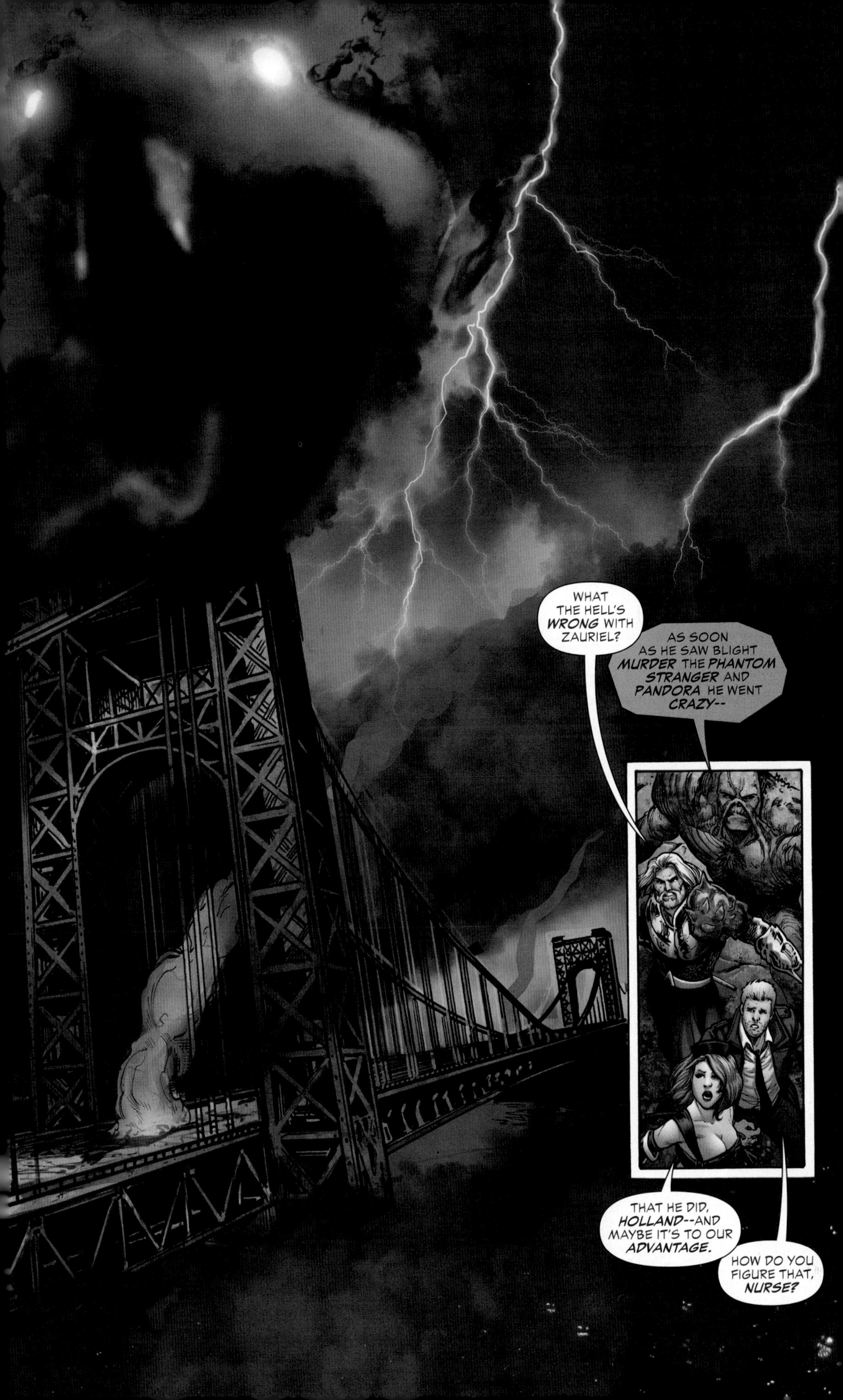
WHAT THE HELL'S WRONG WITH ZAURIEL?
AS SOON AS HE SAW BLIGHT MURDER THE PHANTOM STRANGER AND PANDORA HE WENT CRAZY--
THAT HE DID, HOLLAND--AND MAYBE IT'S TO OUR ADVANTAGE.
HOW DO YOU FIGURE THAT, NURSE?

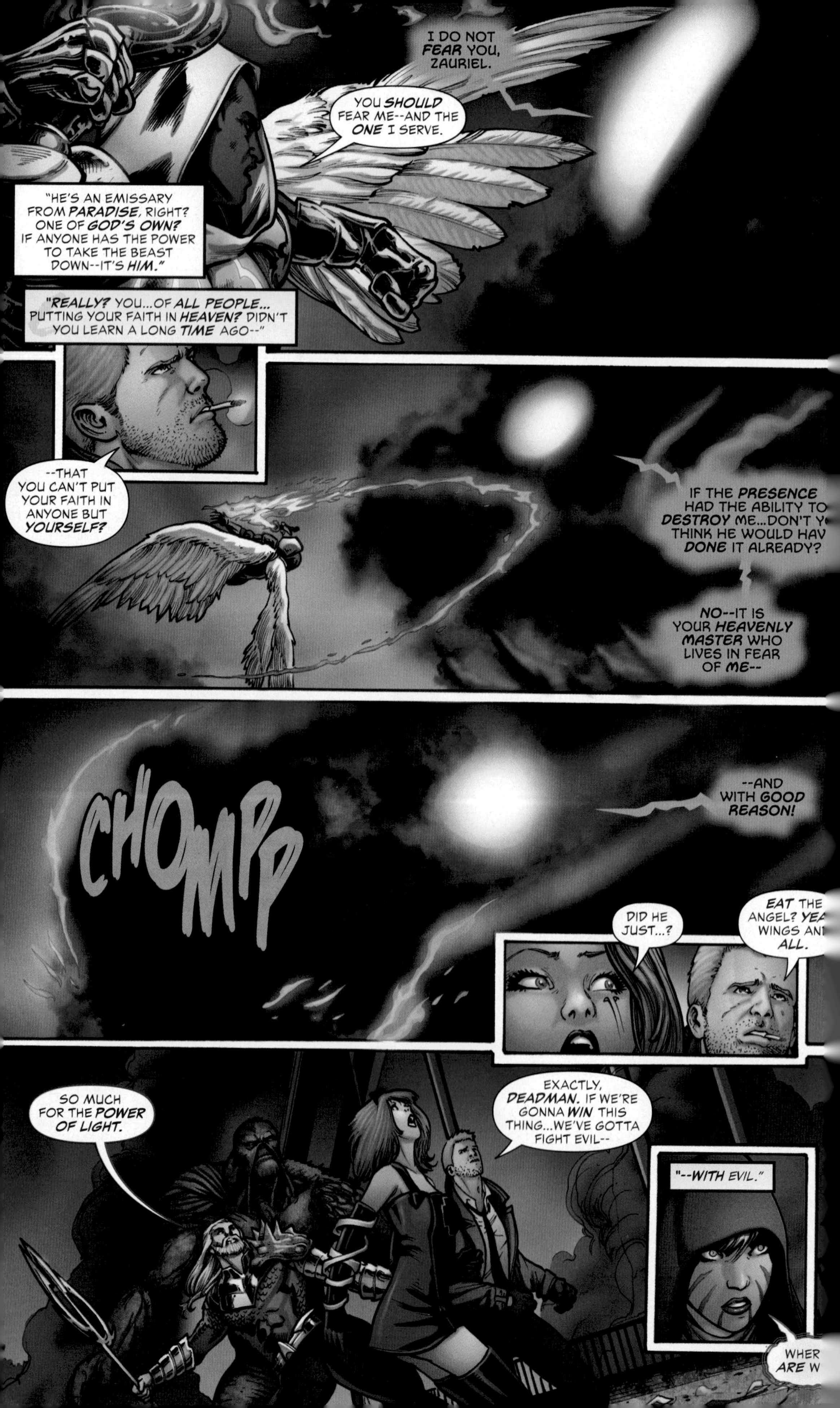
I DO NOT FEAR YOU, ZAURIEL.
YOU SHOULD FEAR ME--AND THE ONE I SERVE.
"HE'S AN EMISSARY FROM PARADISE, RIGHT? ONE OF GOD'S OWN? IF ANYONE HAS THE POWER TO TAKE THE BEAST DOWN--IT'S HIM."
"REALLY? YOU...OF ALL PEOPLE... PUTTING YOUR FAITH IN HEAVEN? DIDN'T YOU LEARN A LONG TIME AGO--"
--THAT YOU CAN'T PUT YOUR FAITH IN ANYONE BUT YOURSELF?
IF THE PRESENCE HAD THE ABILITY TO DESTROY ME...DON'T Y THINK HE WOULD HAV DONE IT ALREADY?
NO--IT IS YOUR HEAVENLY MASTER WHO LIVES IN FEAR OF ME--
CHOMP
--AND WITH GOOD REASON!
DID HE JUST...?
EAT THE ANGEL? YEA WINGS AN ALL.
SO MUCH FOR THE POWER OF LIGHT.
EXACTLY, DEADMAN. IF WE'RE GONNA WIN THIS THING...WE'VE GOTTA FIGHT EVIL--
"--WITH EVIL."
WHER ARE W

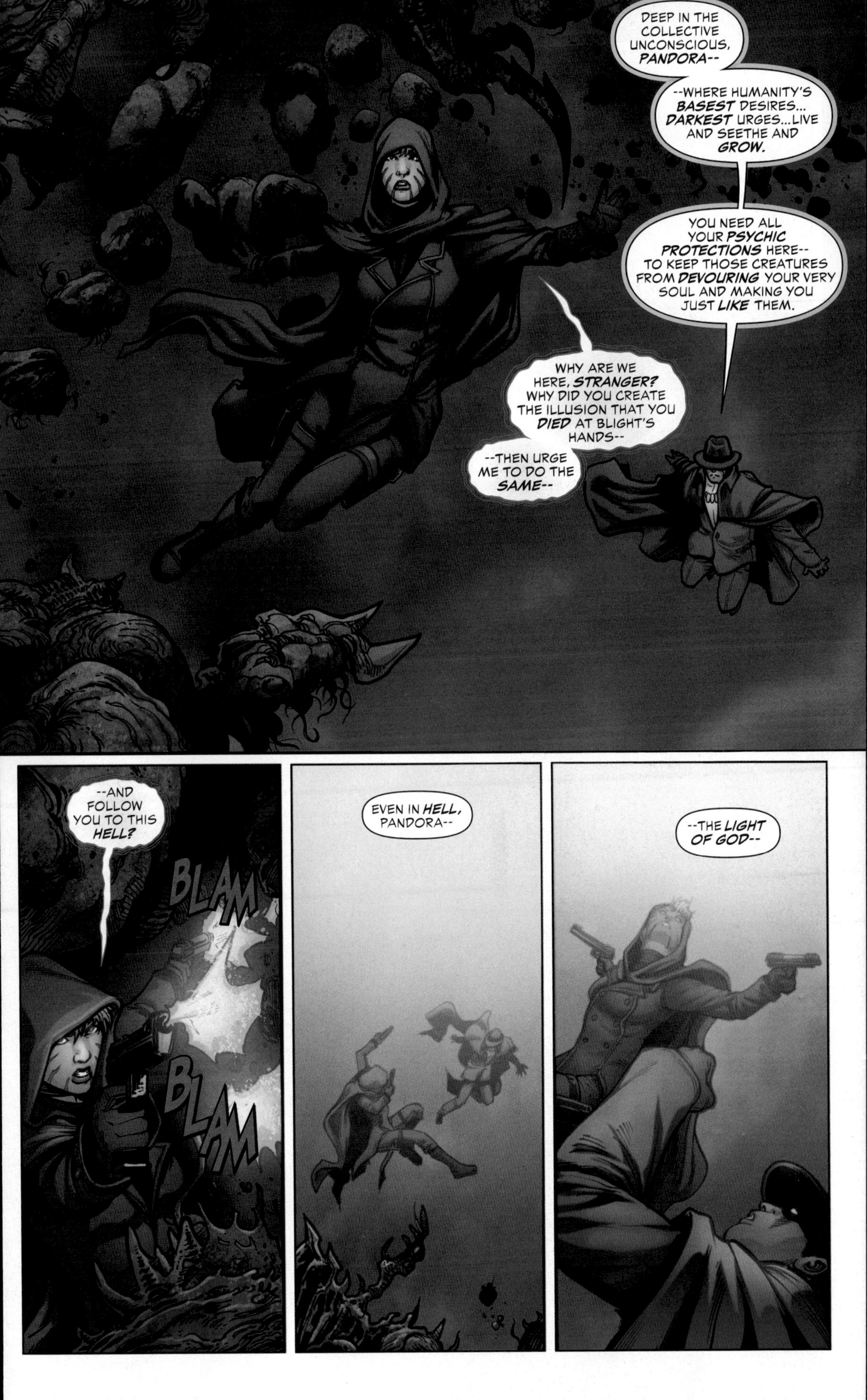
DEEP IN THE COLLECTIVE UNCONSCIOUS, PANDORA--
--WHERE HUMANITY'S BASEST DESIRES... DARKEST URGES...LIVE AND SEETHE AND GROW.
YOU NEED ALL YOUR PSYCHIC PROTECTIONS HERE-- TO KEEP THOSE CREATURES FROM DEVOURING YOUR VERY SOUL AND MAKING YOU JUST LIKE THEM.
WHY ARE WE HERE, STRANGER? WHY DID YOU CREATE THE ILLUSION THAT YOU DIED AT BLIGHT'S HANDS--
--THEN URGE ME TO DO THE SAME--
--AND FOLLOW YOU TO THIS HELL?
BLAM
BLAM
EVEN IN HELL, PANDORA--
--THE LIGHT OF GOD--

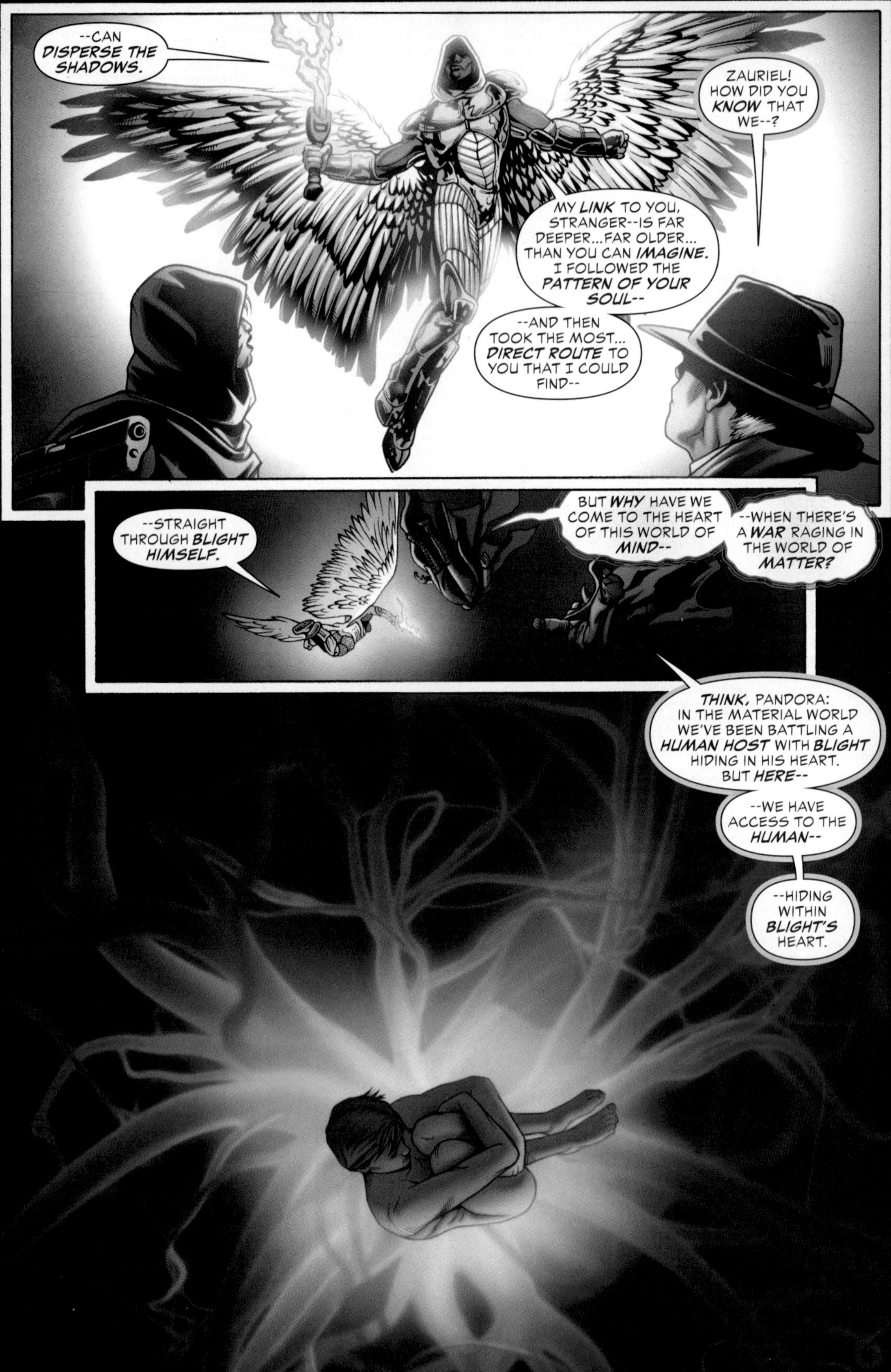
--CAN DISPERSE THE SHADOWS.
ZAURIEL! HOW DID YOU KNOW THAT WE--?
MY LINK TO YOU, STRANGER--IS FAR DEEPER...FAR OLDER... THAN YOU CAN IMAGINE. I FOLLOWED THE PATTERN OF YOUR SOUL--
--AND THEN TOOK THE MOST... DIRECT ROUTE TO YOU THAT I COULD FIND--
--STRAIGHT THROUGH BLIGHT HIMSELF.
BUT WHY HAVE WE COME TO THE HEART OF THIS WORLD OF MIND--
--WHEN THERE'S A WAR RAGING IN THE WORLD OF MATTER?
THINK, PANDORA: IN THE MATERIAL WORLD WE'VE BEEN BATTLING A HUMAN HOST WITH BLIGHT HIDING IN HIS HEART. BUT HERE--
--WE HAVE ACCESS TO THE HUMAN--
--HIDING WITHIN BLIGHT'S HEART.

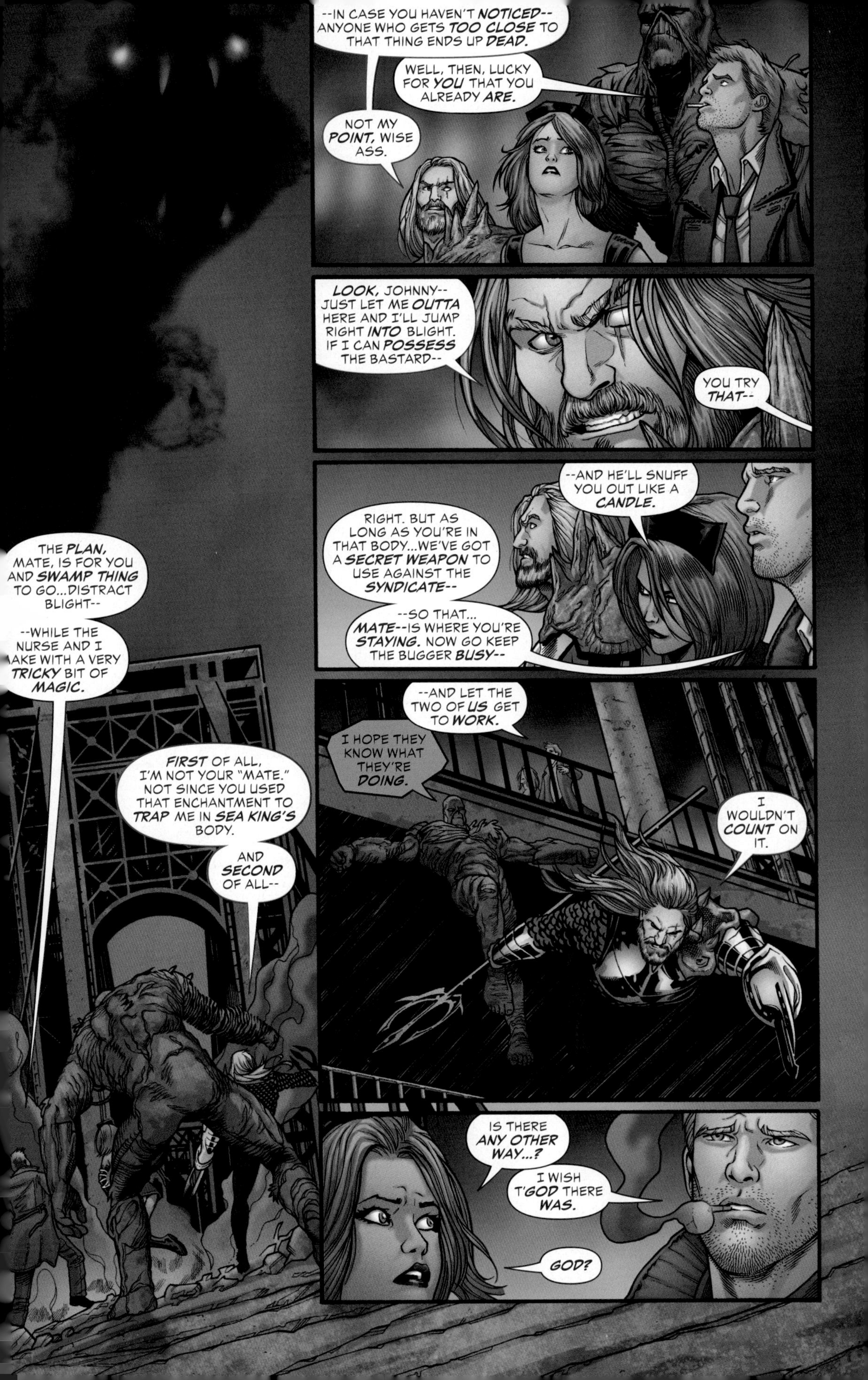
--IN CASE YOU HAVEN'T NOTICED-- ANYONE WHO GETS TOO CLOSE TO THAT THING ENDS UP DEAD.
WELL, THEN, LUCKY FOR YOU THAT YOU ALREADY ARE.
NOT MY POINT, WISE ASS.
LOOK, JOHNNY-- JUST LET ME OUTTA HERE AND I'LL JUMP RIGHT INTO BLIGHT. IF I CAN POSSESS THE BASTARD--
YOU TRY THAT--
--AND HE'LL SNUFF YOU OUT LIKE A CANDLE.
RIGHT. BUT AS LONG AS YOU'RE IN THAT BODY...WE'VE GOT A SECRET WEAPON TO USE AGAINST THE SYNDICATE--
--SO THAT... MATE--IS WHERE YOU'RE STAYING. NOW GO KEEP THE BUGGER BUSY--
--AND LET THE TWO OF US GET TO WORK.
I HOPE THEY KNOW WHAT THEY'RE DOING.
I WOULDN'T COUNT ON IT.
THE PLAN, MATE, IS FOR YOU AND SWAMP THING TO GO...DISTRACT BLIGHT--
--WHILE THE NURSE AND I MAKE WITH A VERY TRICKY BIT OF MAGIC.
FIRST OF ALL, I'M NOT YOUR "MATE." NOT SINCE YOU USED THAT ENCHANTMENT TO TRAP ME IN SEA KING'S BODY.
AND SECOND OF ALL--
IS THERE ANY OTHER WAY...?
I WISH T'GOD THERE WAS.
GOD?

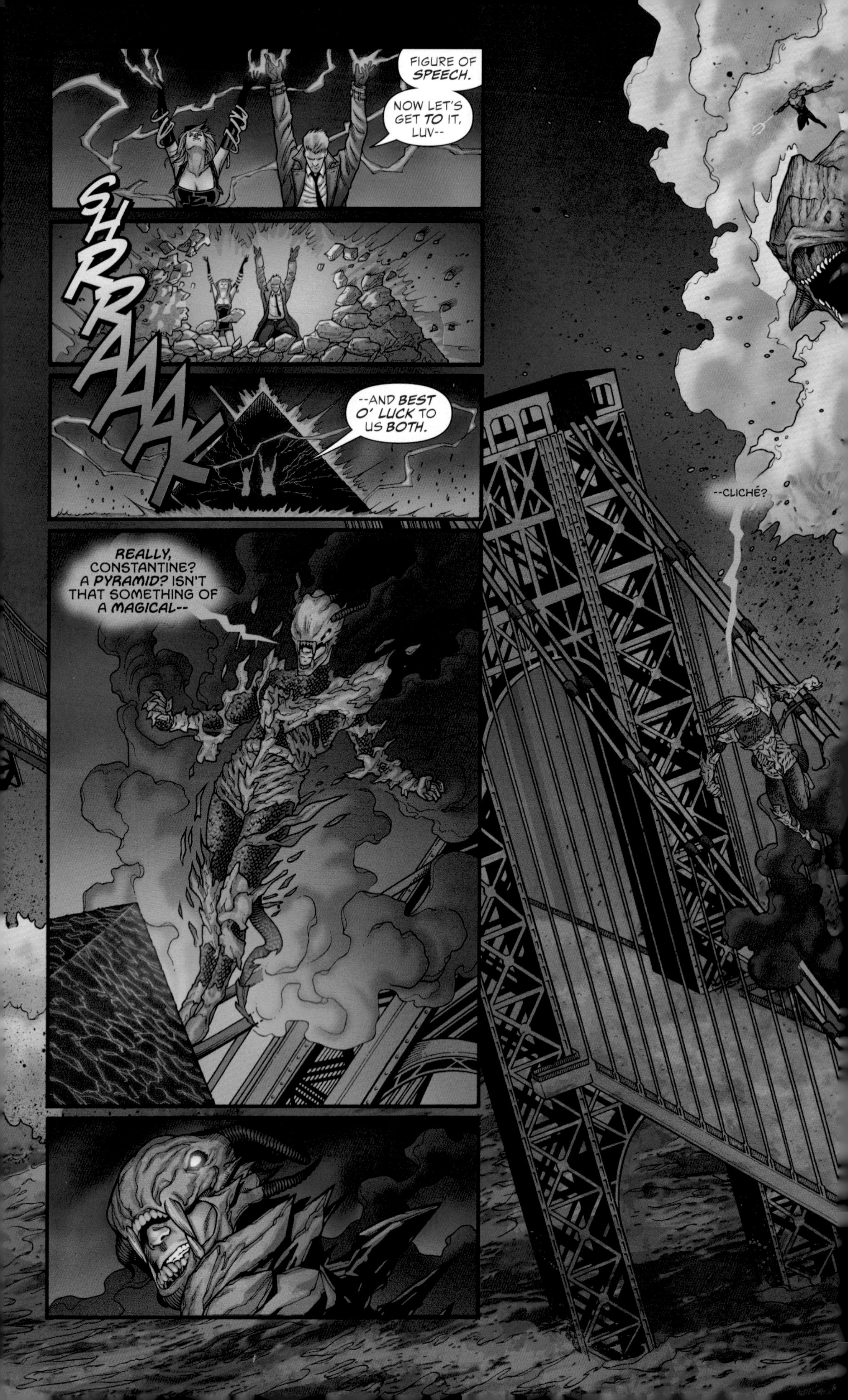
FIGURE OF SPEECH.
NOW LET'S GET TO IT, LUV--
SHRAAAAK
--AND BEST O' LUCK TO US BOTH.
REALLY, CONSTANTINE? A PYRAMID? ISN'T THAT SOMETHING OF A MAGICAL--
--CLICHÉ?

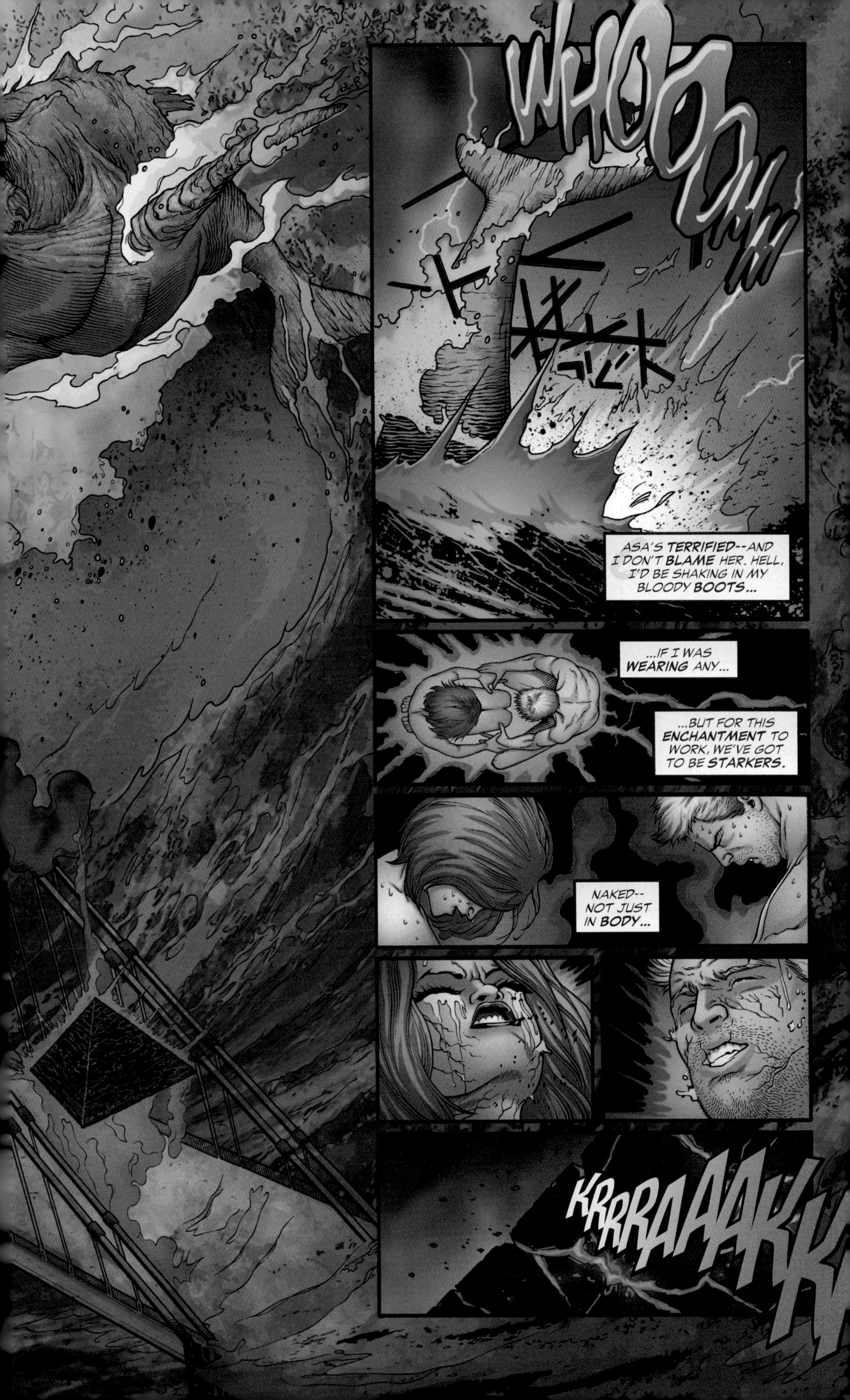
WHOOOOOM
ASA'S TERRIFIED--AND I DON'T BLAME HER. HELL, I'D BE SHAKING IN MY BLOODY BOOTS...
...IF I WAS WEARING ANY...
...BUT FOR THIS ENCHANTMENT TO WORK, WE'VE GOT TO BE STARKERS.
NAKED--NOT JUST IN BODY...
KRRRAAAKK

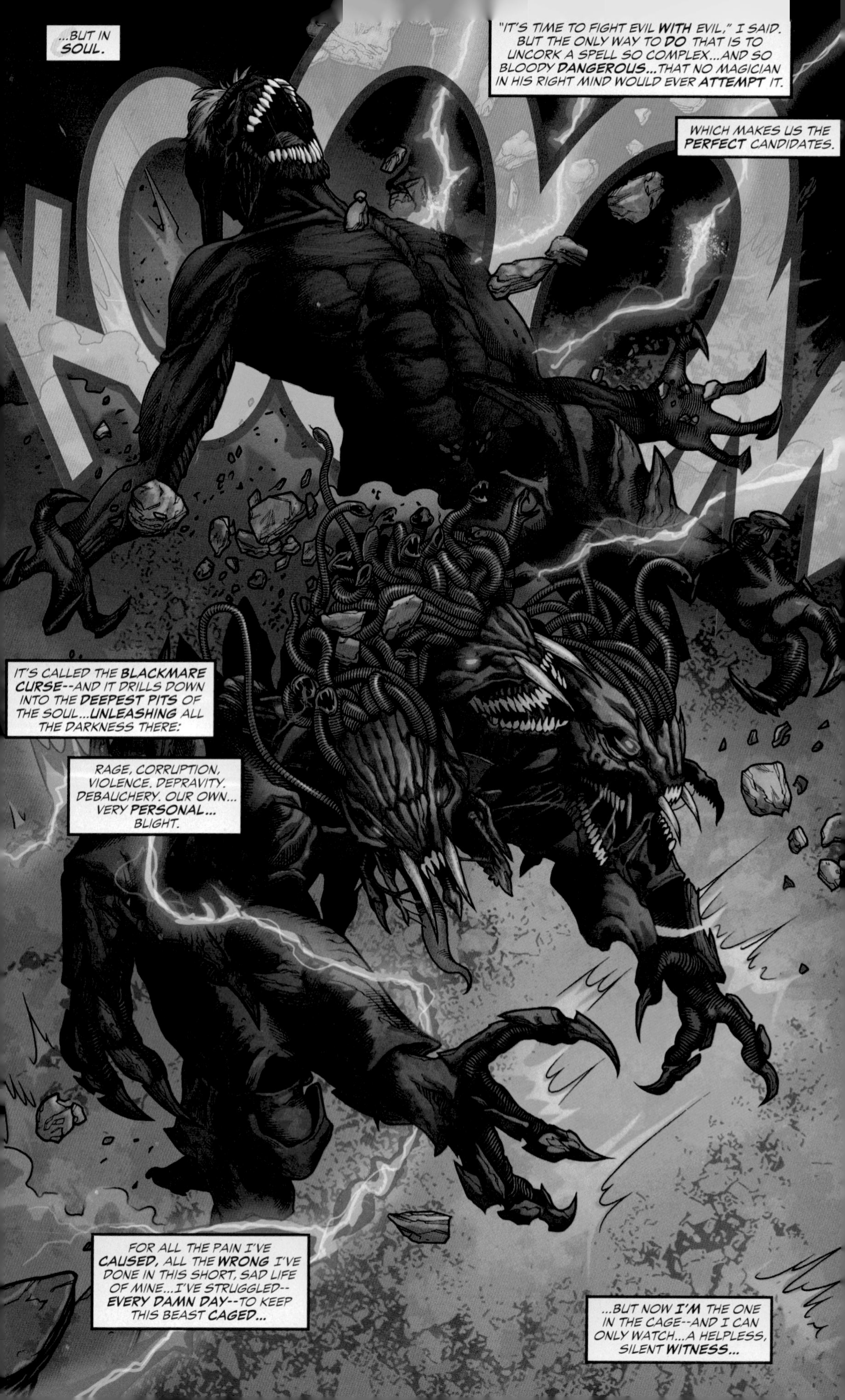
...BUT IN SOUL.
"IT'S TIME TO FIGHT EVIL WITH EVIL," I SAID. BUT THE ONLY WAY TO DO THAT IS TO UNCORK A SPELL SO COMPLEX...AND SO BLOODY DANGEROUS...THAT NO MAGICIAN IN HIS RIGHT MIND WOULD EVER ATTEMPT IT.
WHICH MAKES US THE PERFECT CANDIDATES.
IT'S CALLED THE BLACKMARE CURSE--AND IT DRILLS DOWN INTO THE DEEPEST PITS OF THE SOUL...UNLEASHING ALL THE DARKNESS THERE:
RAGE, CORRUPTION, VIOLENCE. DEPRAVITY. DEBAUCHERY. OUR OWN... VERY PERSONAL... BLIGHT.
FOR ALL THE PAIN I'VE CAUSED, ALL THE WRONG I'VE DONE IN THIS SHORT, SAD LIFE OF MINE...I'VE STRUGGLED-- EVERY DAMN DAY--TO KEEP THIS BEAST CAGED...
...BUT NOW I'M THE ONE IN THE CAGE--AND I CAN ONLY WATCH...A HELPLESS, SILENT WITNESS...

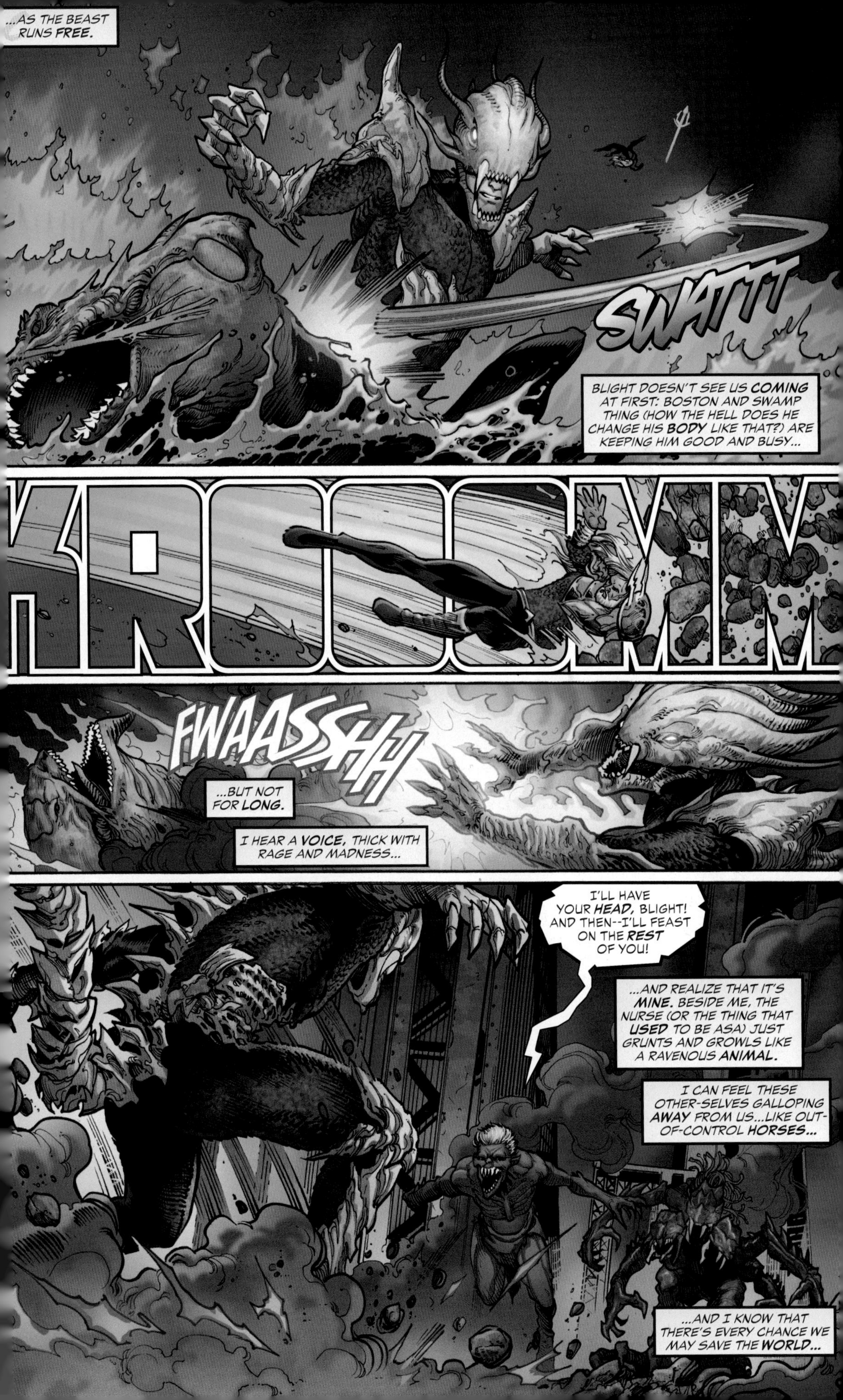
...AS THE BEAST RUNS FREE.
SWATTT
BLIGHT DOESN'T SEE US COMING AT FIRST: BOSTON AND SWAMP THING (HOW THE HELL DOES HE CHANGE HIS BODY LIKE THAT?) ARE KEEPING HIM GOOD AND BUSY...
KROOOMM
FWAASSHH
...BUT NOT FOR LONG.
I HEAR A VOICE, THICK WITH RAGE AND MADNESS...
I'LL HAVE YOUR HEAD, BLIGHT! AND THEN--I'LL FEAST ON THE REST OF YOU!
...AND REALIZE THAT IT'S MINE. BESIDE ME, THE NURSE (OR THE THING THAT USED TO BE ASA) JUST GRUNTS AND GROWLS LIKE A RAVENOUS ANIMAL.
I CAN FEEL THESE OTHER-SELVES GALLOPING AWAY FROM US...LIKE OUT-OF-CONTROL HORSES...
...AND I KNOW THAT THERE'S EVERY CHANCE WE MAY SAVE THE WORLD...

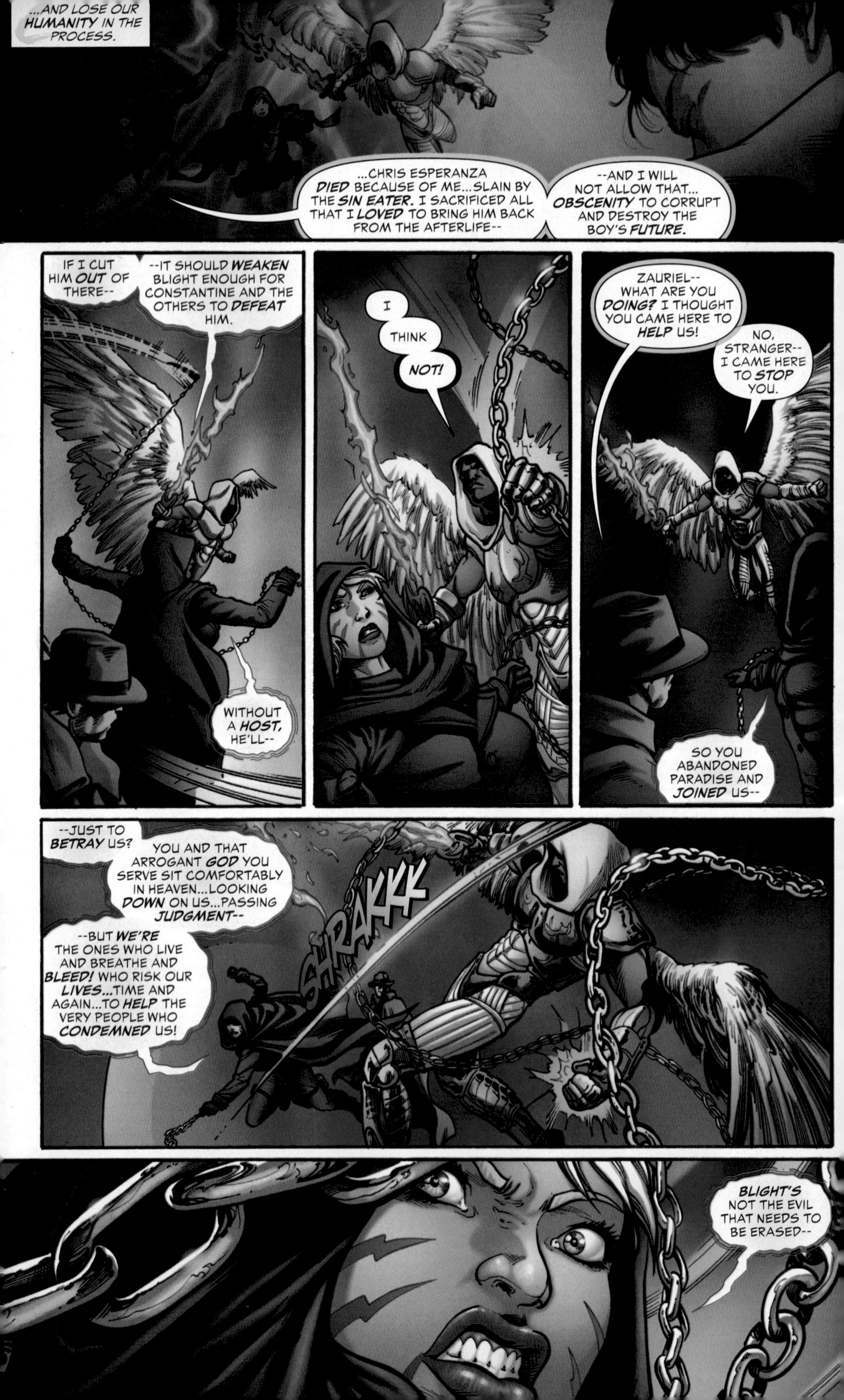
...AND LOSE OUR HUMANITY IN THE PROCESS.
...CHRIS ESPERANZA DIED BECAUSE OF ME...SLAIN BY THE SIN EATER. I SACRIFICED ALL THAT I LOVED TO BRING HIM BACK FROM THE AFTERLIFE--
--AND I WILL NOT ALLOW THAT... OBSCENITY TO CORRUPT AND DESTROY THE BOY'S FUTURE.
IF I CUT HIM OUT OF THERE--
--IT SHOULD WEAKEN BLIGHT ENOUGH FOR CONSTANTINE AND THE OTHERS TO DEFEAT HIM.
WITHOUT A HOST, HE'LL--
I THINK NOT!
ZAURIEL-- WHAT ARE YOU DOING? I THOUGHT YOU CAME HERE TO HELP US!
NO, STRANGER-- I CAME HERE TO STOP YOU.
SO YOU ABANDONED PARADISE AND JOINED US--
--JUST TO BETRAY US?
YOU AND THAT ARROGANT GOD YOU SERVE SIT COMFORTABLY IN HEAVEN...LOOKING DOWN ON US...PASSING JUDGMENT--
--BUT WE'RE THE ONES WHO LIVE AND BREATHE AND BLEED! WHO RISK OUR LIVES...TIME AND AGAIN...TO HELP THE VERY PEOPLE WHO CONDEMNED US!
SHRAKKK
BLIGHT'S NOT THE EVIL THAT NEEDS TO BE ERASED--

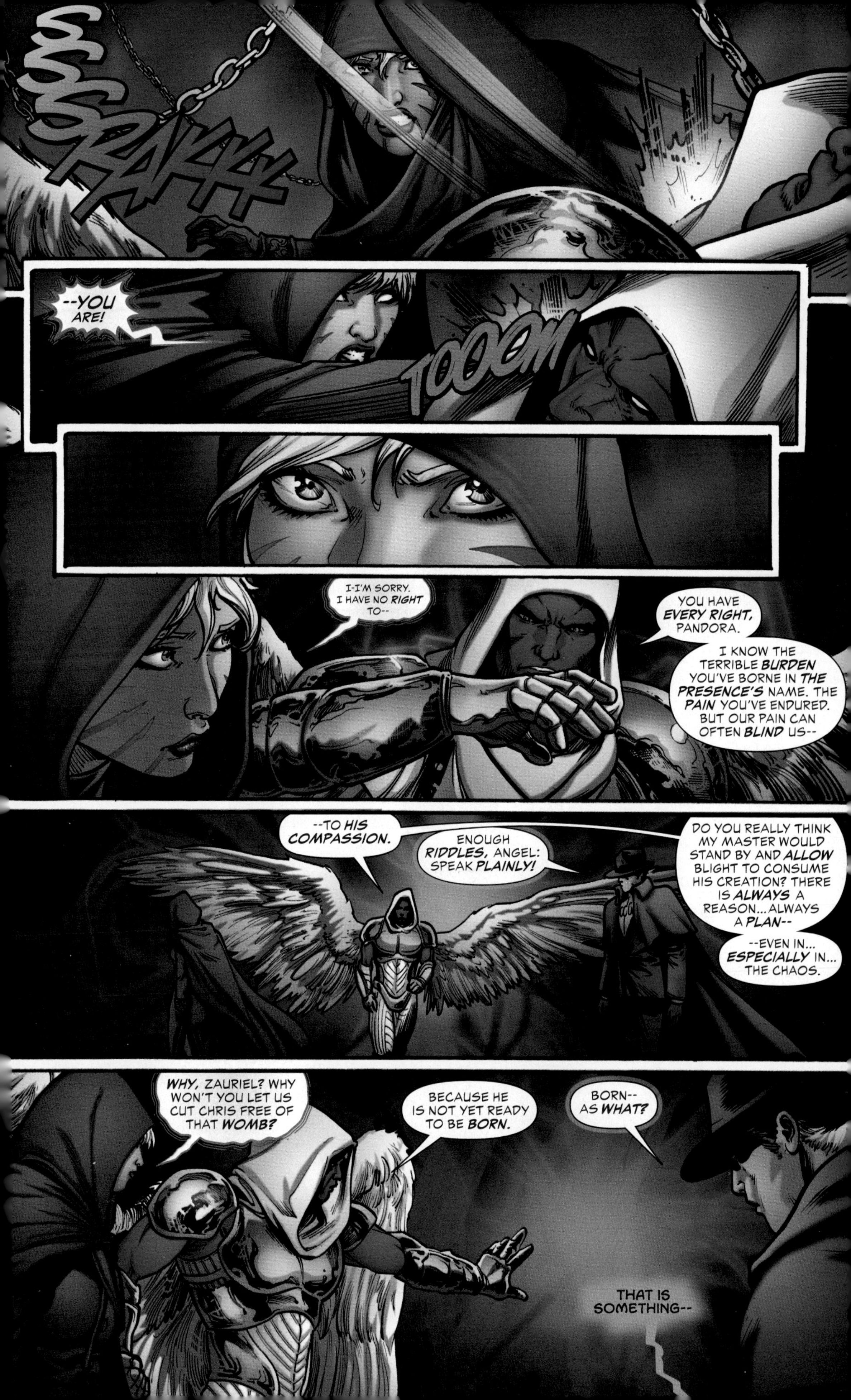
SSSSRAKKK
--YOU ARE!
TOOOM
I-I'M SORRY. I HAVE NO RIGHT TO--
YOU HAVE EVERY RIGHT, PANDORA.
I KNOW THE TERRIBLE BURDEN YOU'VE BORNE IN THE PRESENCE'S NAME. THE PAIN YOU'VE ENDURED. BUT OUR PAIN CAN OFTEN BLIND US--
--TO HIS COMPASSION.
ENOUGH RIDDLES, ANGEL: SPEAK PLAINLY!
DO YOU REALLY THINK MY MASTER WOULD STAND BY AND ALLOW BLIGHT TO CONSUME HIS CREATION? THERE IS ALWAYS A REASON...ALWAYS A PLAN--
--EVEN IN... ESPECIALLY IN... THE CHAOS.
WHY, ZAURIEL? WHY WON'T YOU LET US CUT CHRIS FREE OF THAT WOMB?
BECAUSE HE IS NOT YET READY TO BE BORN.
BORN-- AS WHAT?
THAT IS SOMETHING--

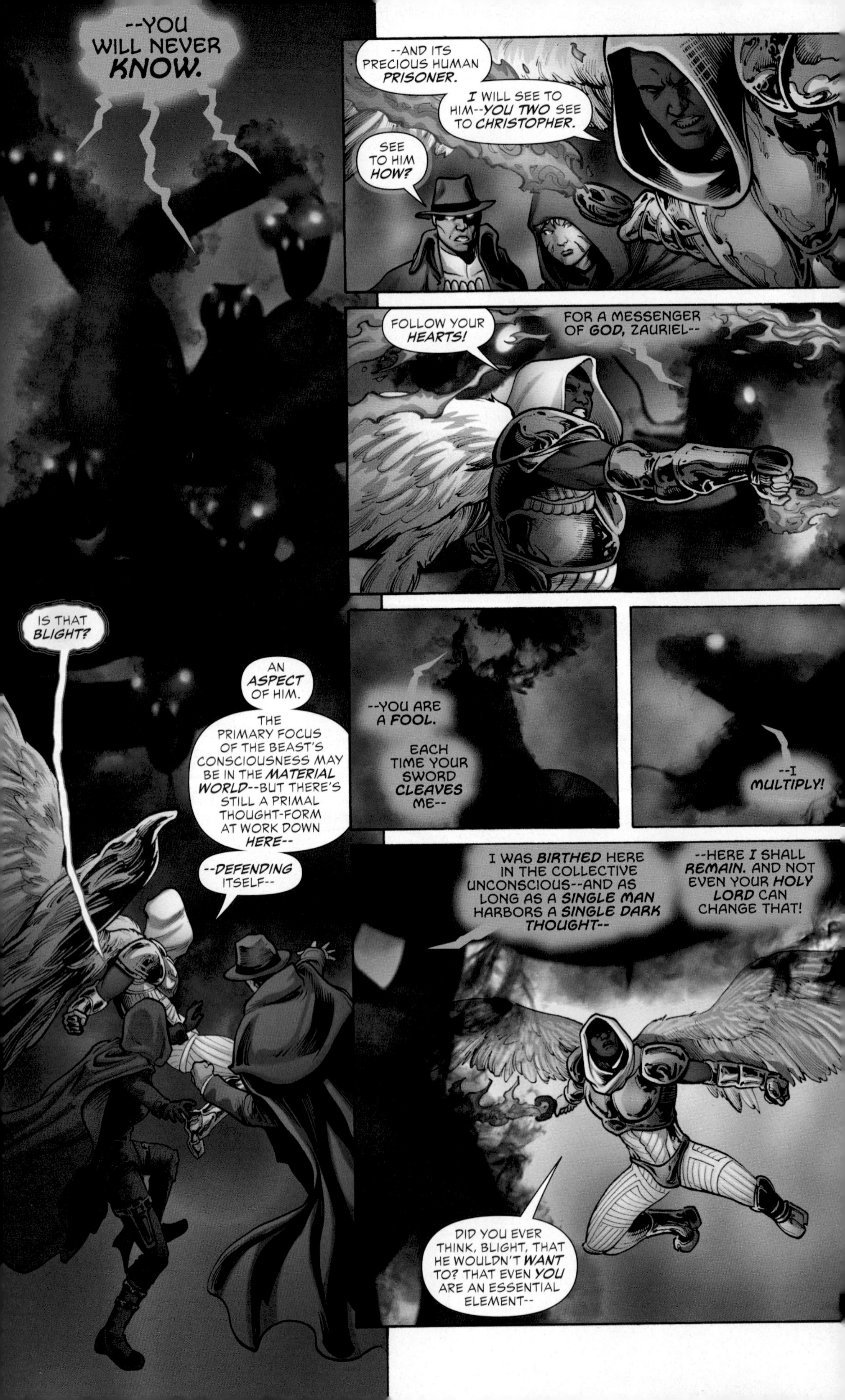
--YOU WILL NEVER KNOW.
--AND ITS PRECIOUS HUMAN PRISONER.
I WILL SEE TO HIM--YOU TWO SEE TO CHRISTOPHER.
SEE TO HIM HOW?
FOLLOW YOUR HEARTS!
FOR A MESSENGER OF GOD, ZAURIEL--
IS THAT BLIGHT?
AN ASPECT OF HIM.
THE PRIMARY FOCUS OF THE BEAST'S CONSCIOUSNESS MAY BE IN THE MATERIAL WORLD--BUT THERE'S STILL A PRIMAL THOUGHT-FORM AT WORK DOWN HERE--
--DEFENDING ITSELF--
--YOU ARE A FOOL.
EACH TIME YOUR SWORD CLEAVES ME--
--I MULTIPLY!
I WAS BIRTHED HERE IN THE COLLECTIVE UNCONSCIOUS--AND AS LONG AS A SINGLE MAN HARBORS A SINGLE DARK THOUGHT--
--HERE I SHALL REMAIN. AND NOT EVEN YOUR HOLY LORD CAN CHANGE THAT!
DID YOU EVER THINK, BLIGHT, THAT HE WOULDN'T WANT TO? THAT EVEN YOU ARE AN ESSENTIAL ELEMENT--

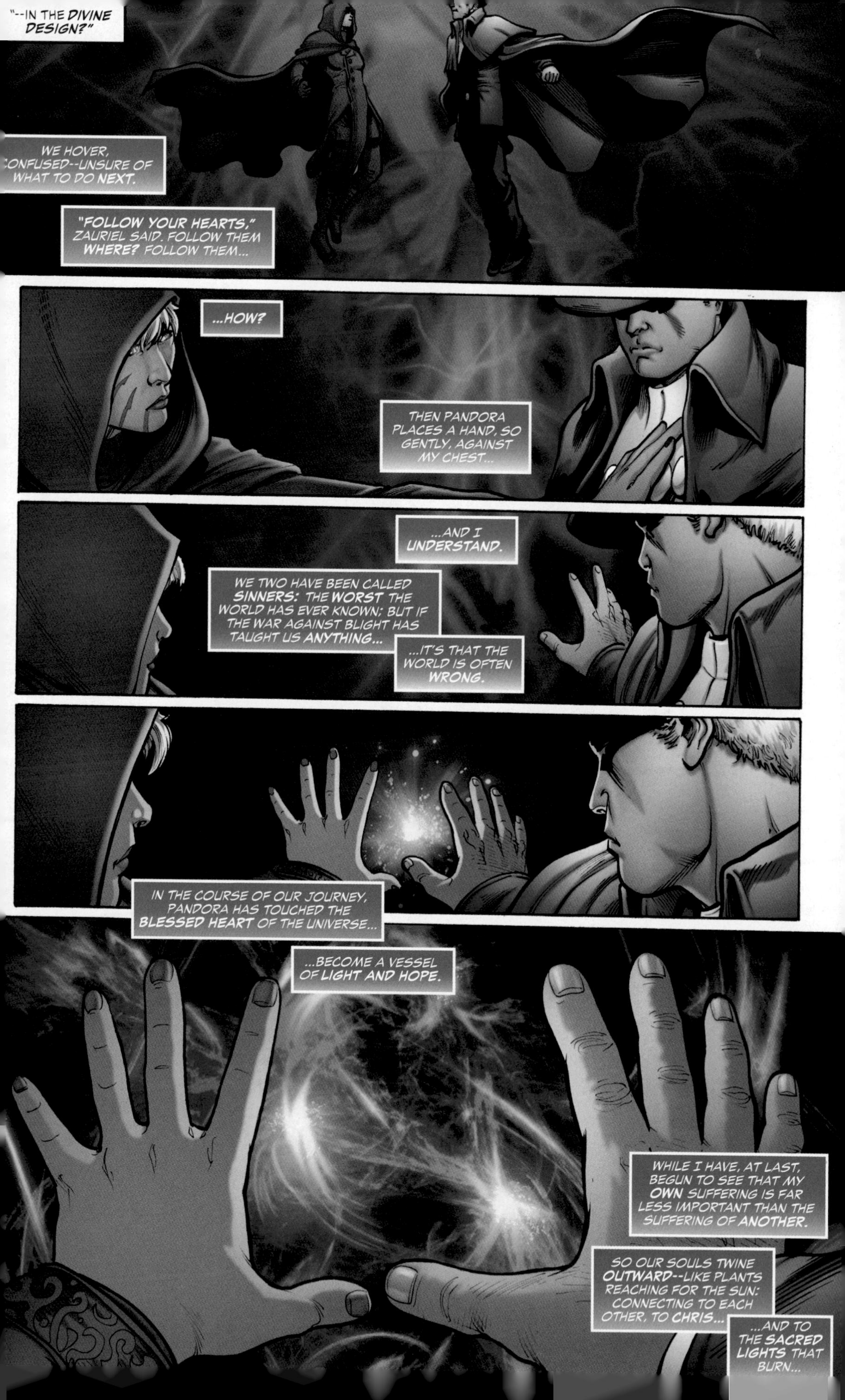
"--IN THE DIVINE DESIGN?"
WE HOVER, CONFUSED--UNSURE OF WHAT TO DO NEXT.
"FOLLOW YOUR HEARTS," ZAURIEL SAID. FOLLOW THEM WHERE? FOLLOW THEM...
...HOW?
THEN PANDORA PLACES A HAND, SO GENTLY, AGAINST MY CHEST...
...AND I UNDERSTAND.
WE TWO HAVE BEEN CALLED SINNERS: THE WORST THE WORLD HAS EVER KNOWN; BUT IF THE WAR AGAINST BLIGHT HAS TAUGHT US ANYTHING...
...IT'S THAT THE WORLD IS OFTEN WRONG.
IN THE COURSE OF OUR JOURNEY, PANDORA HAS TOUCHED THE BLESSED HEART OF THE UNIVERSE...
...BECOME A VESSEL OF LIGHT AND HOPE.
WHILE I HAVE, AT LAST, BEGUN TO SEE THAT MY OWN SUFFERING IS FAR LESS IMPORTANT THAN THE SUFFERING OF ANOTHER.
SO OUR SOULS TWINE OUTWARD--LIKE PLANTS REACHING FOR THE SUN: CONNECTING TO EACH OTHER, TO CHRIS...
...AND TO THE SACRED LIGHTS THAT BURN...

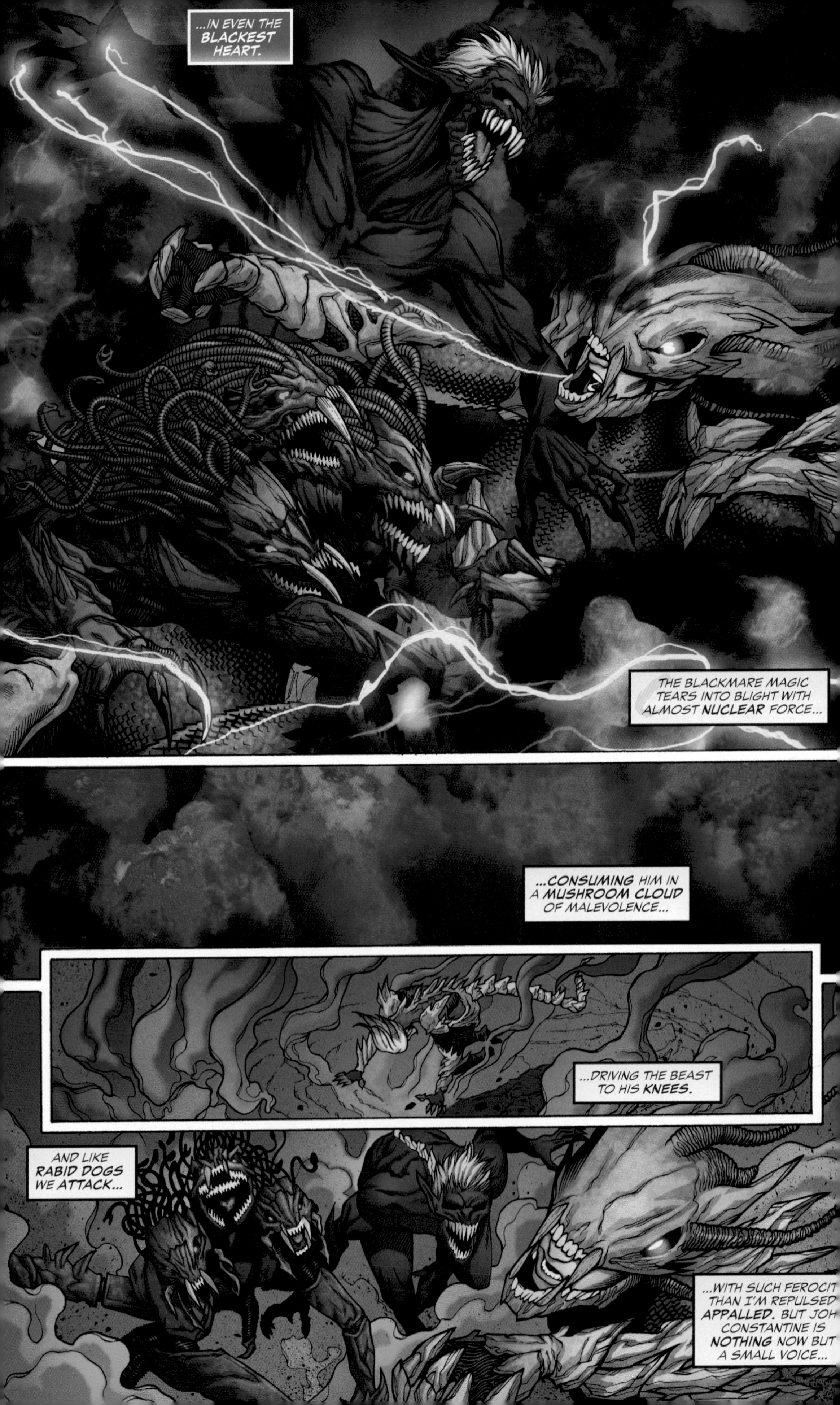
...IN EVEN THE BLACKEST HEART.
THE BLACKMARE MAGIC TEARS INTO BLIGHT WITH ALMOST NUCLEAR FORCE...
...CONSUMING HIM IN A MUSHROOM CLOUD OF MALEVOLENCE...
...DRIVING THE BEAST TO HIS KNEES.
AND LIKE RABID DOGS WE ATTACK...
...WITH SUCH FEROCIT THAN I'M REPULSED APPALLED. BUT JOH CONSTANTINE IS NOTHING NOW BUT A SMALL VOICE...

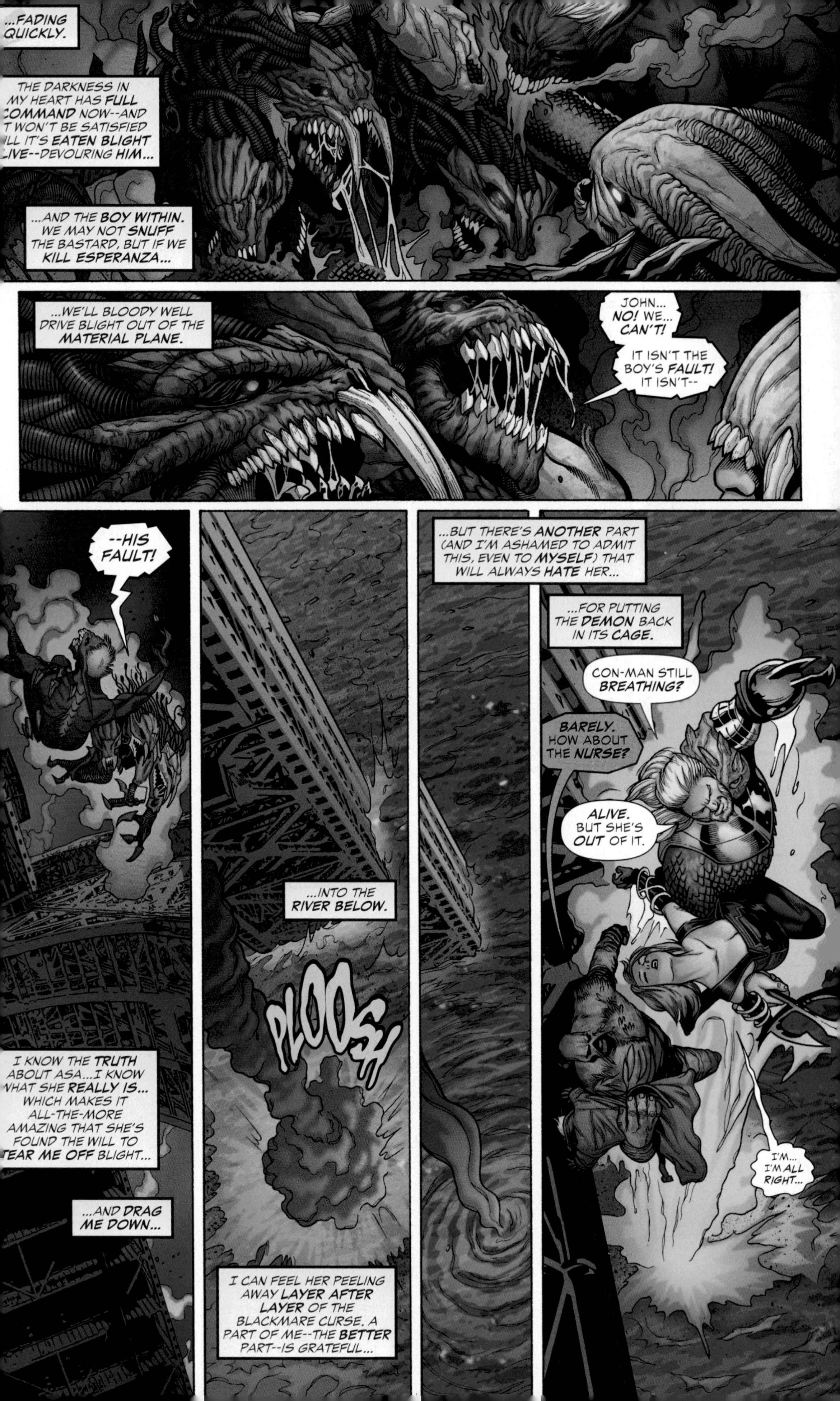

...FADING QUICKLY.
THE DARKNESS IN MY HEART HAS FULL COMMAND NOW--AND IT WON'T BE SATISFIED TILL IT'S EATEN BLIGHT ALIVE--DEVOURING HIM...
...AND THE BOY WITHIN. WE MAY NOT SNUFF THE BASTARD, BUT IF WE KILL ESPERANZA...
...WE'LL BLOODY WELL DRIVE BLIGHT OUT OF THE MATERIAL PLANE.
JOHN... NO! WE... CAN'T!
IT ISN'T THE BOY'S FAULT! IT ISN'T--
--HIS FAULT!
I KNOW THE TRUTH ABOUT ASA...I KNOW WHAT SHE REALLY IS... WHICH MAKES IT ALL-THE-MORE AMAZING THAT SHE'S FOUND THE WILL TO TEAR ME OFF BLIGHT...
...AND DRAG ME DOWN...
...INTO THE RIVER BELOW.
PLOOSH
I CAN FEEL HER PEELING AWAY LAYER AFTER LAYER OF THE BLACKMARE CURSE. A PART OF ME--THE BETTER PART--IS GRATEFUL...
...BUT THERE'S ANOTHER PART (AND I'M ASHAMED TO ADMIT THIS, EVEN TO MYSELF) THAT WILL ALWAYS HATE HER...
...FOR PUTTING THE DEMON BACK IN ITS CAGE.
CON-MAN STILL BREATHING?
BARELY. HOW ABOUT THE NURSE?
ALIVE. BUT SHE'S OUT OF IT.
I'M... I'M ALL RIGHT...

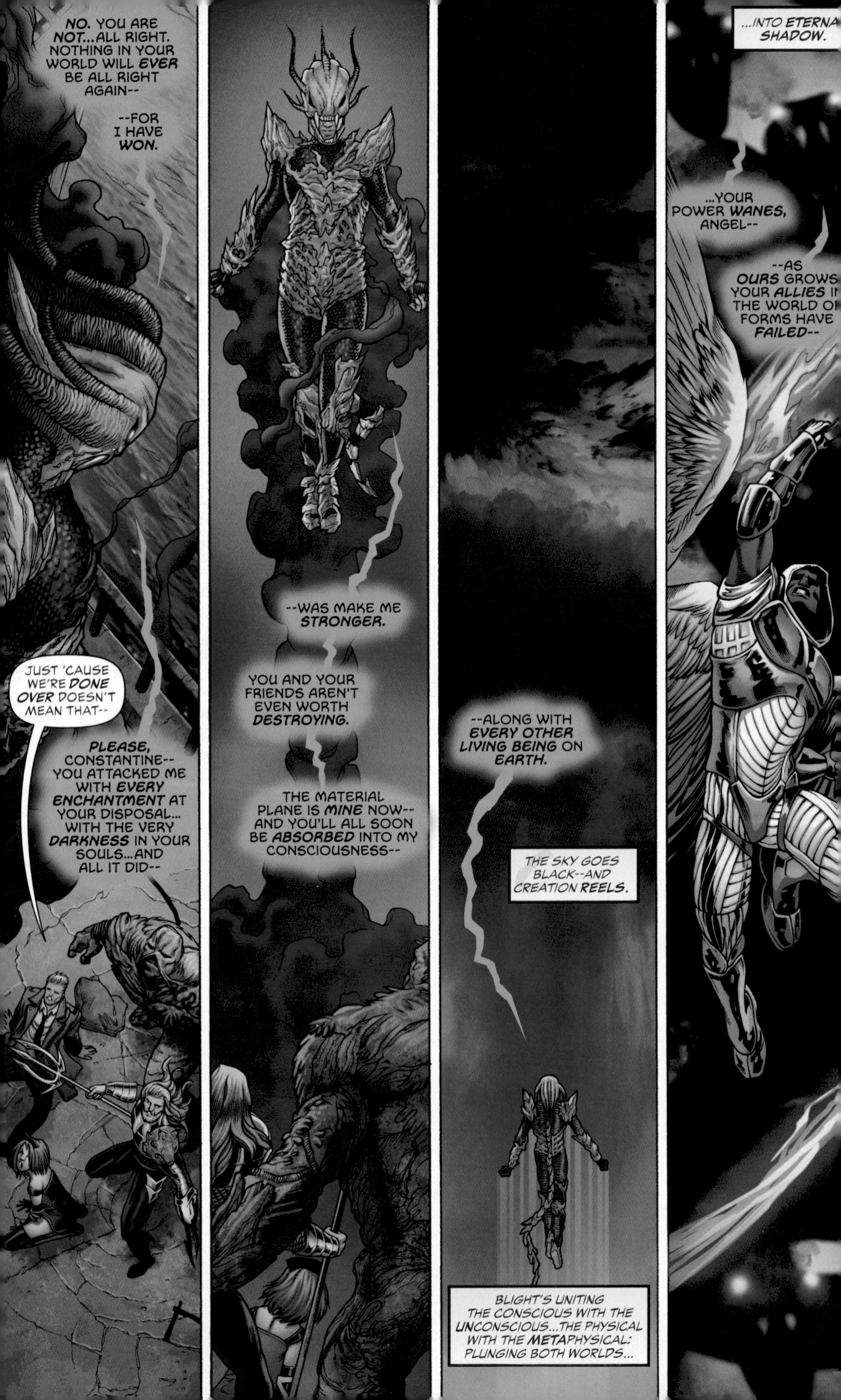
NO. YOU ARE NOT...ALL RIGHT. NOTHING IN YOUR WORLD WILL EVER BE ALL RIGHT AGAIN--
--FOR I HAVE WON.
JUST 'CAUSE WE'RE DONE OVER DOESN'T MEAN THAT--
PLEASE, CONSTANTINE--YOU ATTACKED ME WITH EVERY ENCHANTMENT AT YOUR DISPOSAL...WITH THE VERY DARKNESS IN YOUR SOULS...AND ALL IT DID--
--WAS MAKE ME STRONGER.
YOU AND YOUR FRIENDS AREN'T EVEN WORTH DESTROYING.
THE MATERIAL PLANE IS MINE NOW--AND YOU'LL ALL SOON BE ABSORBED INTO MY CONSCIOUSNESS--
--ALONG WITH EVERY OTHER LIVING BEING ON EARTH.
THE SKY GOES BLACK--AND CREATION REELS.
BLIGHT'S UNITING THE CONSCIOUS WITH THE UNCONSCIOUS...THE PHYSICAL WITH THE METAPHYSICAL: PLUNGING BOTH WORLDS...
...INTO ETERNA
SHADOW.
...YOUR POWER WANES, ANGEL--
--AS OURS GROWS
YOUR ALLIES I
THE WORLD O
FORMS HAVE FAILED--

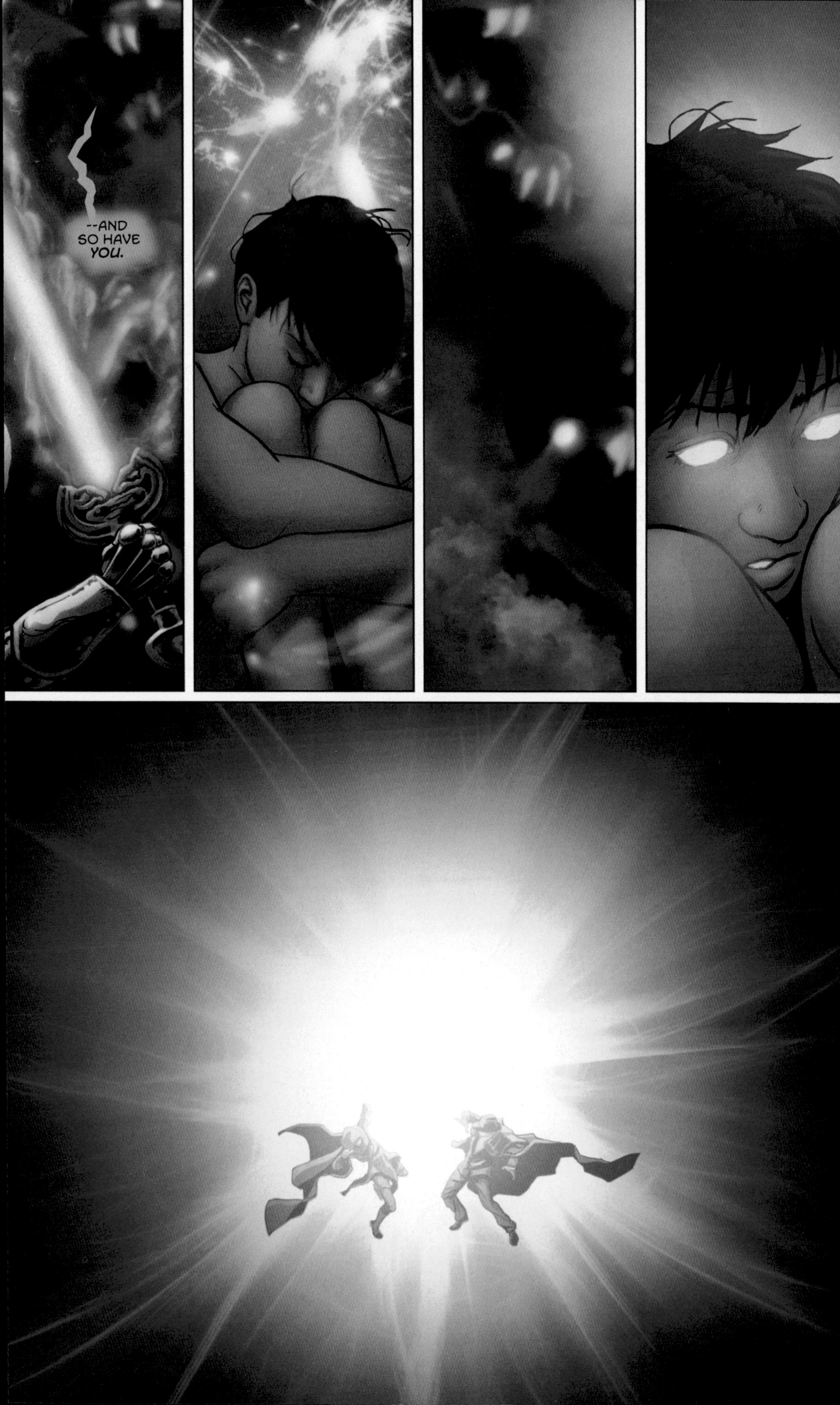
--AND SO HAVE YOU.

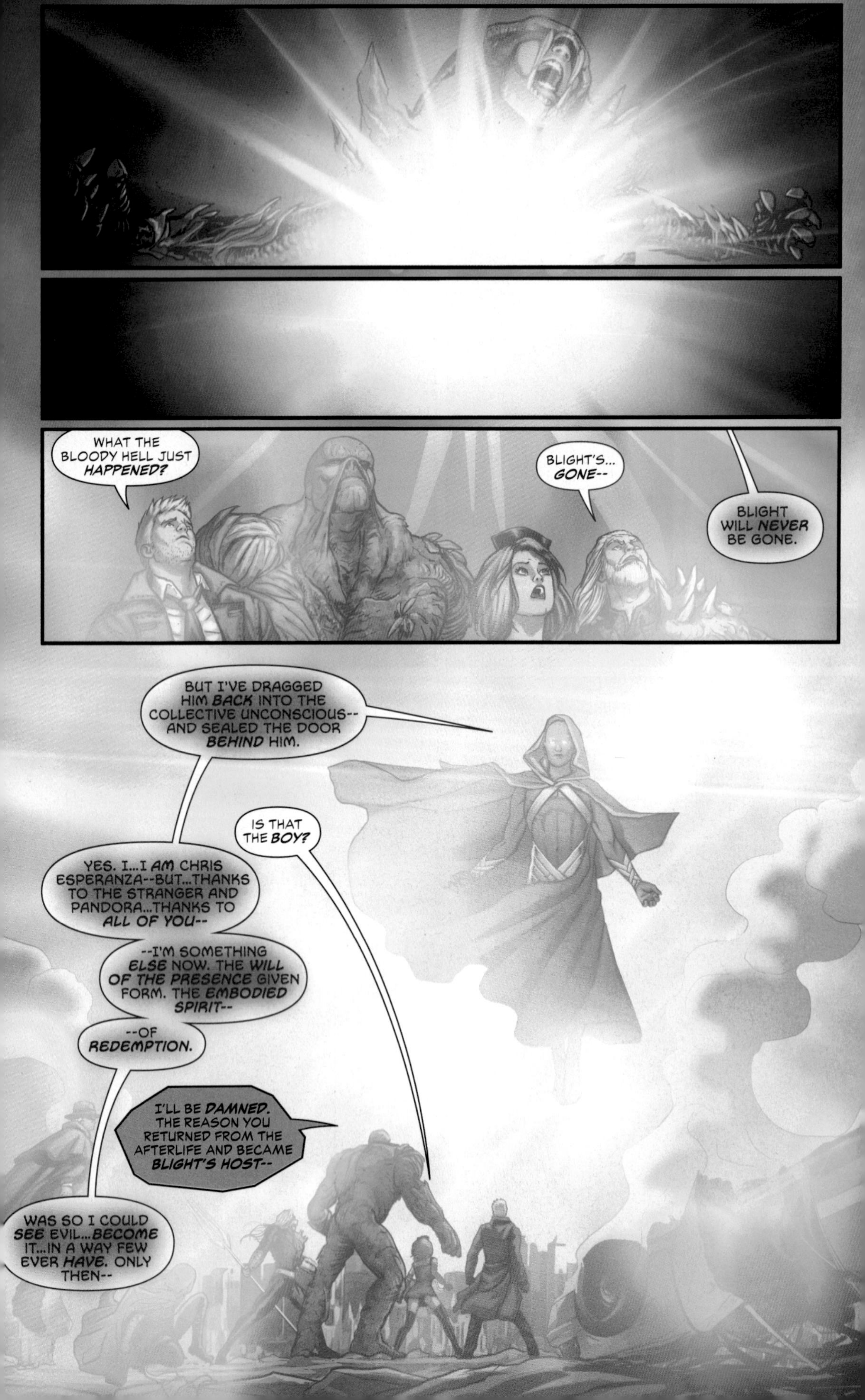

WHAT THE BLOODY HELL JUST HAPPENED?
BLIGHT'S... GONE--
BLIGHT WILL NEVER BE GONE.
BUT I'VE DRAGGED HIM BACK INTO THE COLLECTIVE UNCONSCIOUS-- AND SEALED THE DOOR BEHIND HIM.
IS THAT THE BOY?
YES. I...I AM CHRIS ESPERANZA--BUT...THANKS TO THE STRANGER AND PANDORA...THANKS TO ALL OF YOU--
--I'M SOMETHING ELSE NOW. THE WILL OF THE PRESENCE GIVEN FORM. THE EMBODIED SPIRIT--
--OF REDEMPTION.
I'LL BE DAMNED. THE REASON YOU RETURNED FROM THE AFTERLIFE AND BECAME BLIGHT'S HOST--
WAS SO I COULD SEE EVIL...BECOME IT...IN A WAY FEW EVER HAVE. ONLY THEN--

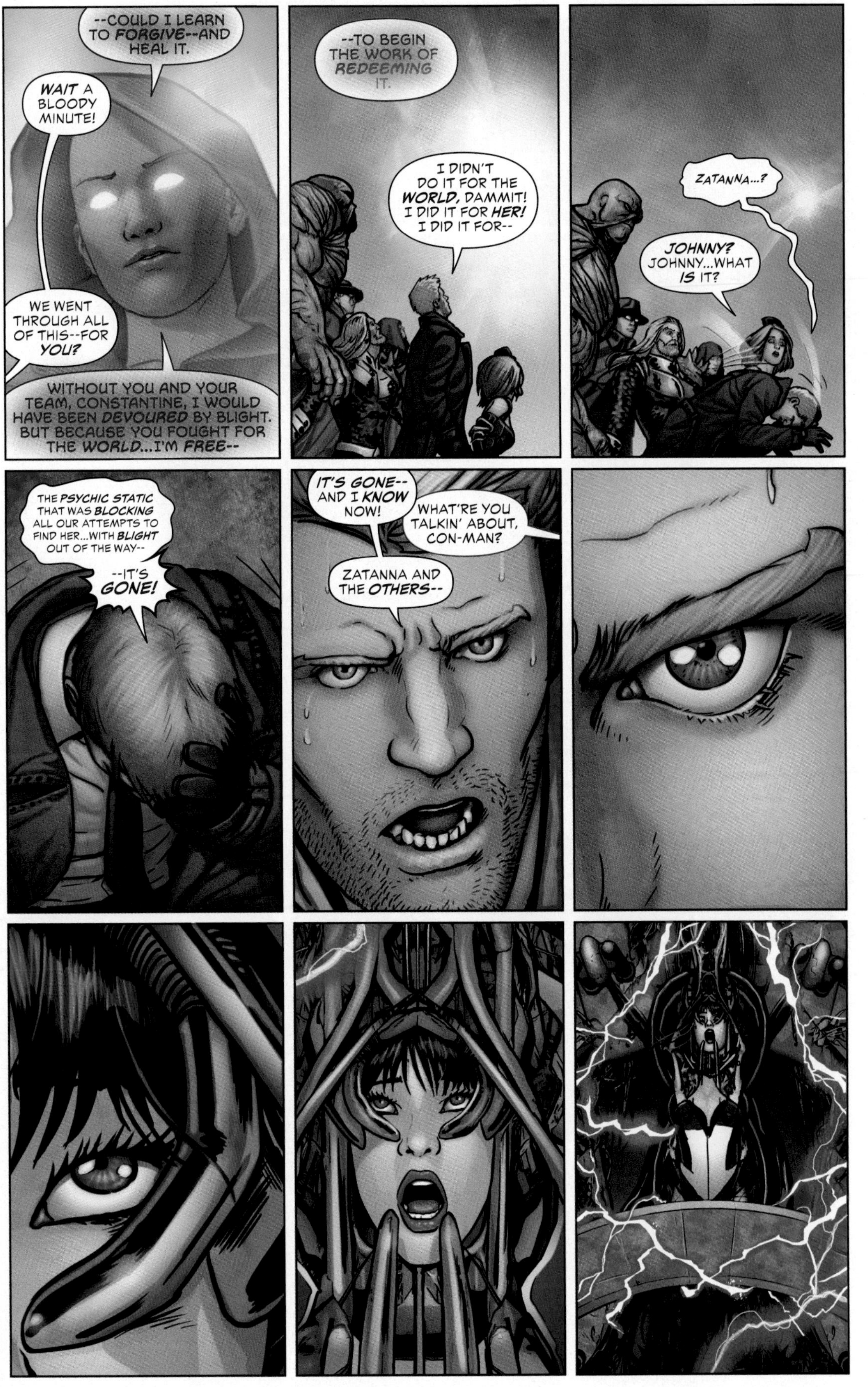
--COULD I LEARN TO FORGIVE--AND HEAL IT.
WAIT A BLOODY MINUTE!
WE WENT THROUGH ALL OF THIS--FOR YOU?
WITHOUT YOU AND YOUR TEAM, CONSTANTINE, I WOULD HAVE BEEN DEVOURED BY BLIGHT. BUT BECAUSE YOU FOUGHT FOR THE WORLD...I'M FREE--
--TO BEGIN THE WORK OF REDEEMING IT.
I DIDN'T DO IT FOR THE WORLD, DAMMIT! I DID IT FOR HER! I DID IT FOR--
ZATANNA...?
JOHNNY? JOHNNY...WHAT IS IT?
THE PSYCHIC STATIC THAT WAS BLOCKING ALL OUR ATTEMPTS TO FIND HER...WITH BLIGHT OUT OF THE WAY--
--IT'S GONE!
IT'S GONE--AND I KNOW NOW!
WHAT'RE YOU TALKIN' ABOUT, CON-MAN?
ZATANNA AND THE OTHERS--

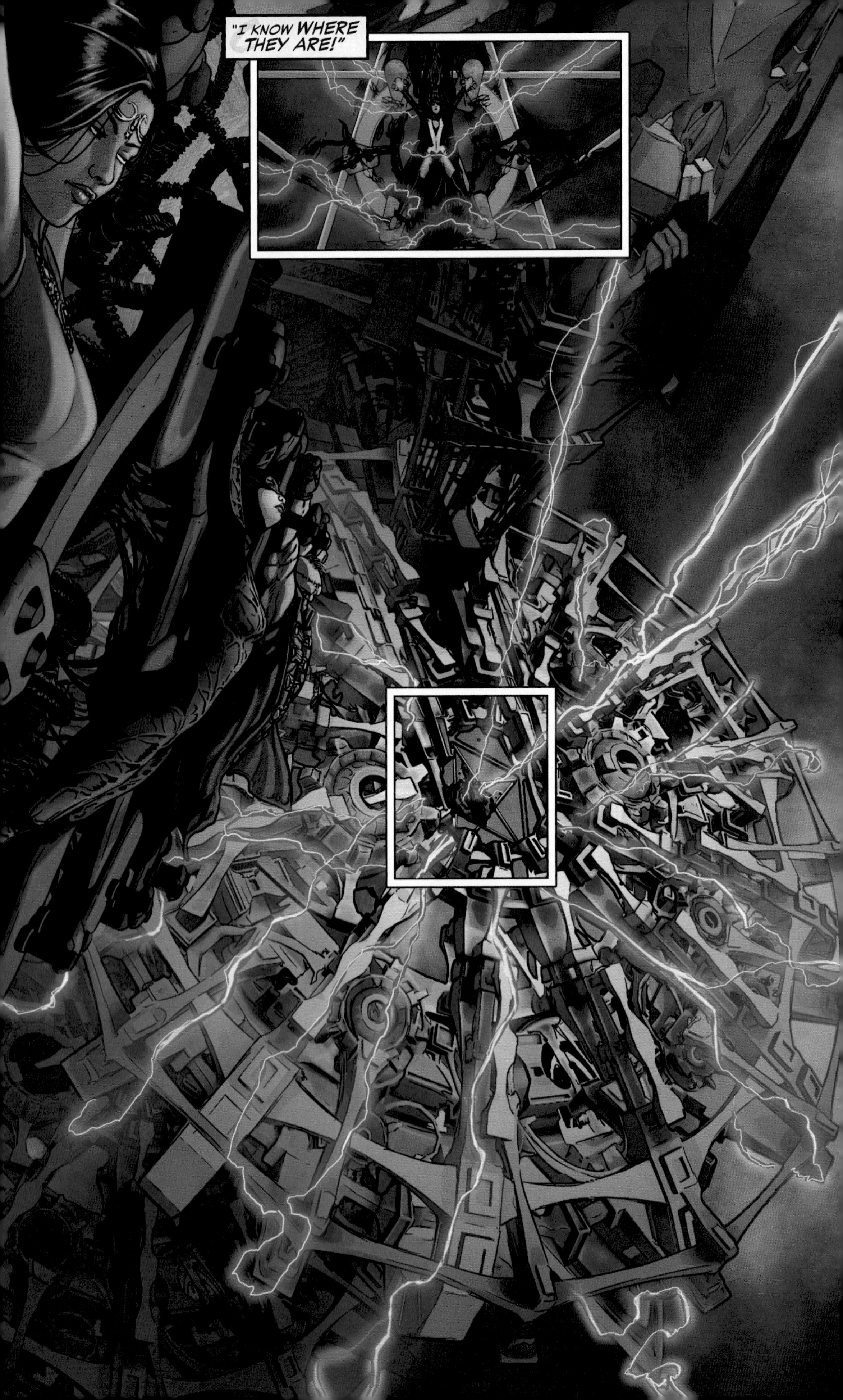
"I KNOW WHERE THEY ARE!"

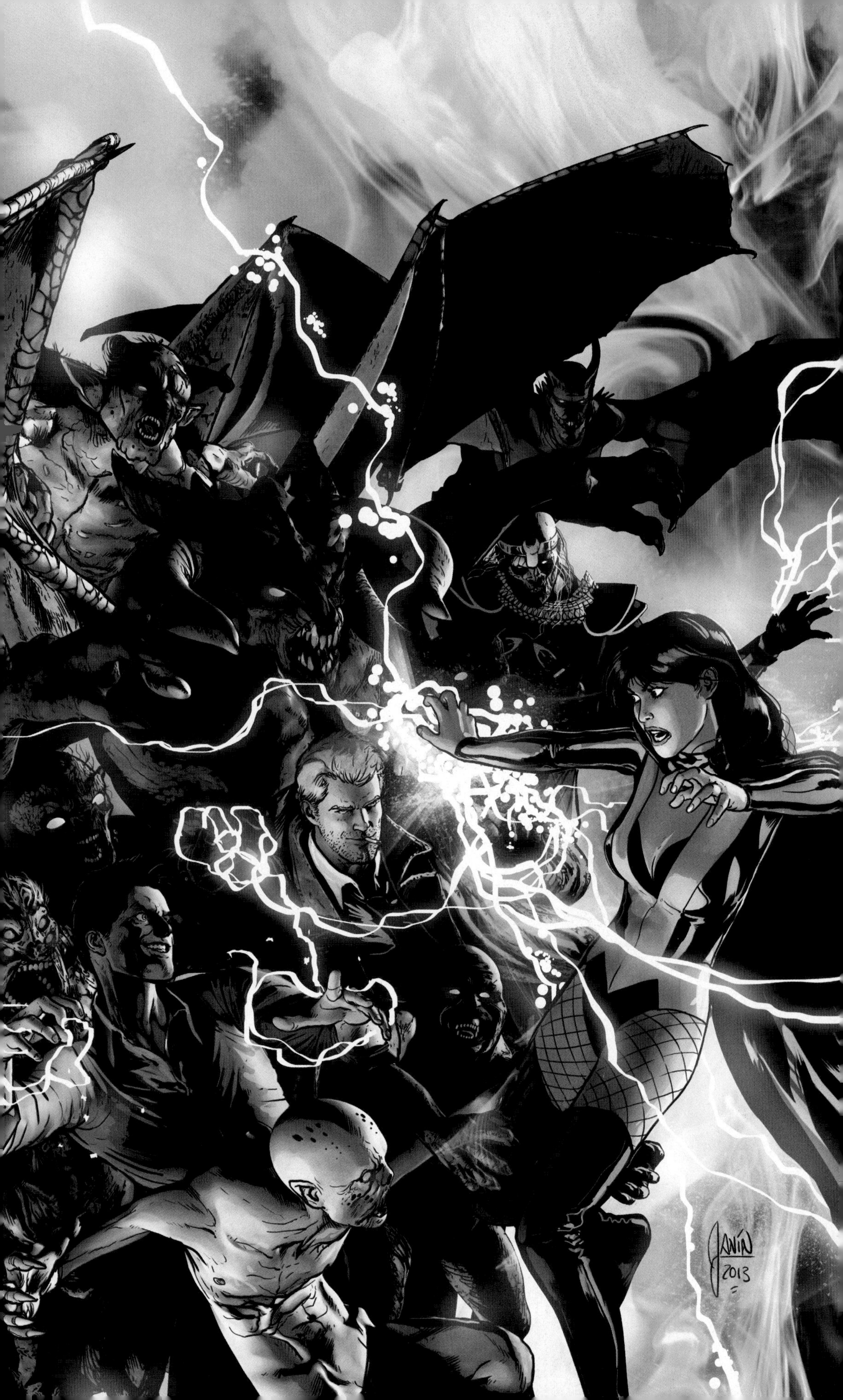
JANÍN
2013

J. M. DeMATTEIS
writer

VINCENTE CIFUENTES
artist

DAN JURGENS
breakdown artist

MIKEL JANIN
cover artist

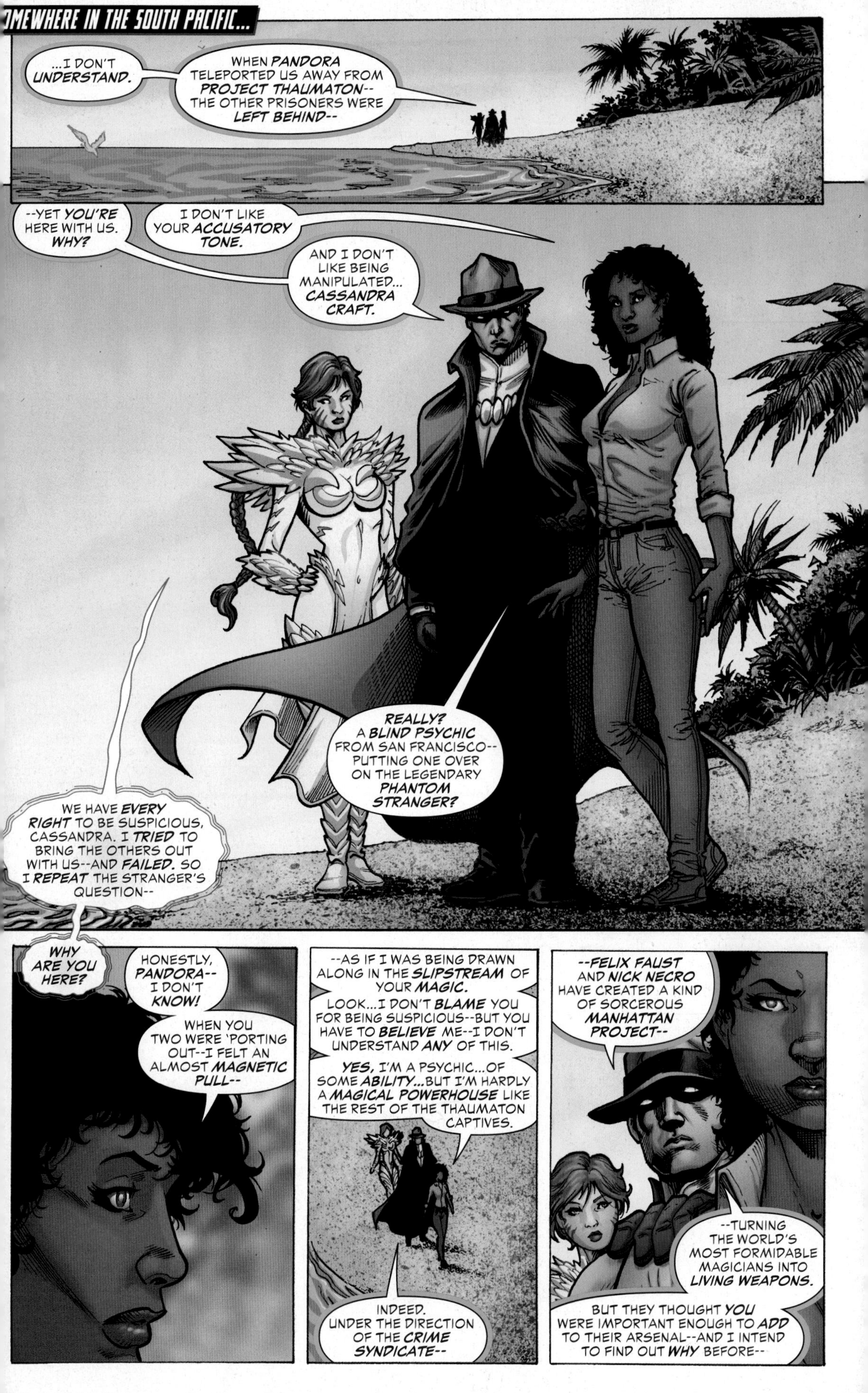

OMEWHERE IN THE SOUTH PACIFIC...
...I DON'T UNDERSTAND.
WHEN PANDORA TELEPORTED US AWAY FROM PROJECT THAUMATON-- THE OTHER PRISONERS WERE LEFT BEHIND--
--YET YOU'RE HERE WITH US. WHY?
I DON'T LIKE YOUR ACCUSATORY TONE.
AND I DON'T LIKE BEING MANIPULATED... CASSANDRA CRAFT.
REALLY? A BLIND PSYCHIC FROM SAN FRANCISCO-- PUTTING ONE OVER ON THE LEGENDARY PHANTOM STRANGER?
WE HAVE EVERY RIGHT TO BE SUSPICIOUS, CASSANDRA. I TRIED TO BRING THE OTHERS OUT WITH US--AND FAILED. SO I REPEAT THE STRANGER'S QUESTION--
WHY ARE YOU HERE?
HONESTLY, PANDORA-- I DON'T KNOW!
WHEN YOU TWO WERE 'PORTING OUT--I FELT AN ALMOST MAGNETIC PULL--
--AS IF I WAS BEING DRAWN ALONG IN THE SLIPSTREAM OF YOUR MAGIC.
LOOK...I DON'T BLAME YOU FOR BEING SUSPICIOUS--BUT YOU HAVE TO BELIEVE ME--I DON'T UNDERSTAND ANY OF THIS.
YES, I'M A PSYCHIC...OF SOME ABILITY...BUT I'M HARDLY A MAGICAL POWERHOUSE LIKE THE REST OF THE THAUMATON CAPTIVES.
INDEED. UNDER THE DIRECTION OF THE CRIME SYNDICATE--
--FELIX FAUST AND NICK NECRO HAVE CREATED A KIND OF SORCEROUS MANHATTAN PROJECT--
--TURNING THE WORLD'S MOST FORMIDABLE MAGICIANS INTO LIVING WEAPONS.
BUT THEY THOUGHT YOU WERE IMPORTANT ENOUGH TO ADD TO THEIR ARSENAL--AND I INTEND TO FIND OUT WHY BEFORE--

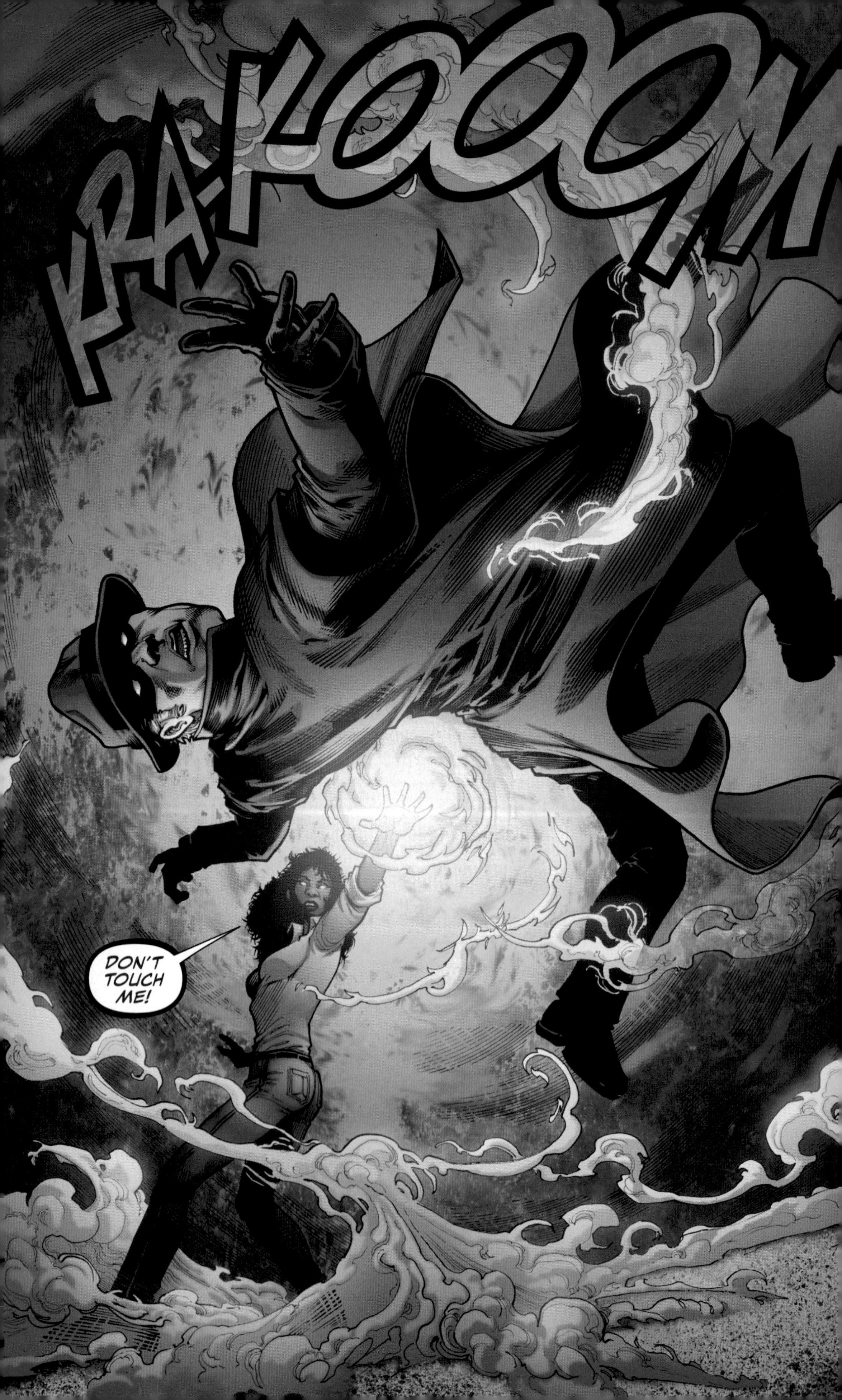
KRAKOOOM
DON'T TOUCH ME!

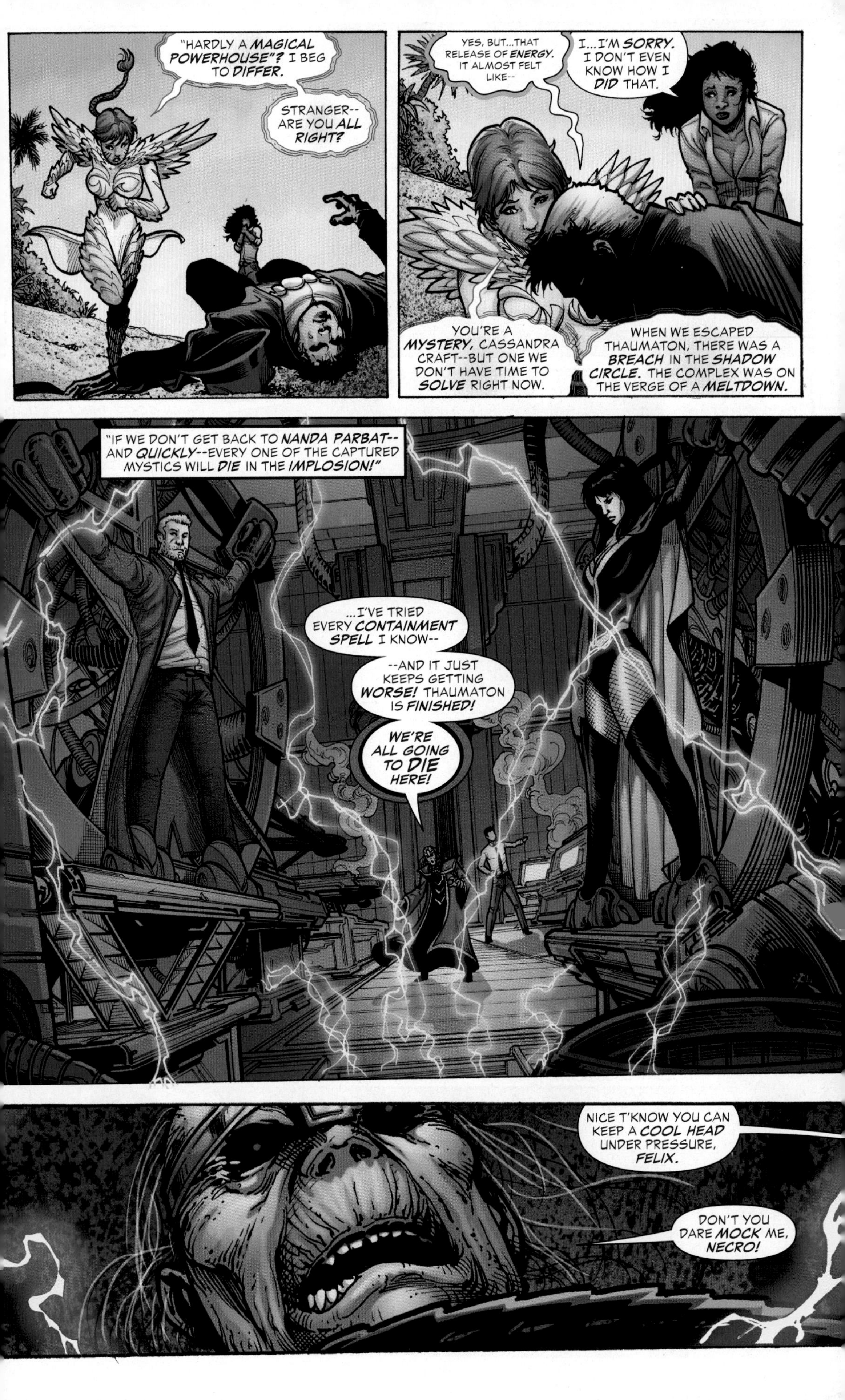

"HARDLY A MAGICAL POWERHOUSE"? I BEG TO DIFFER.
STRANGER-- ARE YOU ALL RIGHT?
I...I'M SORRY. I DON'T EVEN KNOW HOW I DID THAT.
YES, BUT...THAT RELEASE OF ENERGY. IT ALMOST FELT LIKE--
YOU'RE A MYSTERY, CASSANDRA CRAFT--BUT ONE WE DON'T HAVE TIME TO SOLVE RIGHT NOW.
WHEN WE ESCAPED THAUMATON, THERE WAS A BREACH IN THE SHADOW CIRCLE. THE COMPLEX WAS ON THE VERGE OF A MELTDOWN.
"IF WE DON'T GET BACK TO NANDA PARBAT-- AND QUICKLY--EVERY ONE OF THE CAPTURED MYSTICS WILL DIE IN THE IMPLOSION!"
...I'VE TRIED EVERY CONTAINMENT SPELL I KNOW--
--AND IT JUST KEEPS GETTING WORSE! THAUMATON IS FINISHED!
WE'RE ALL GOING TO DIE HERE!
NICE T'KNOW YOU CAN KEEP A COOL HEAD UNDER PRESSURE, FELIX.
DON'T YOU DARE MOCK ME, NECRO!

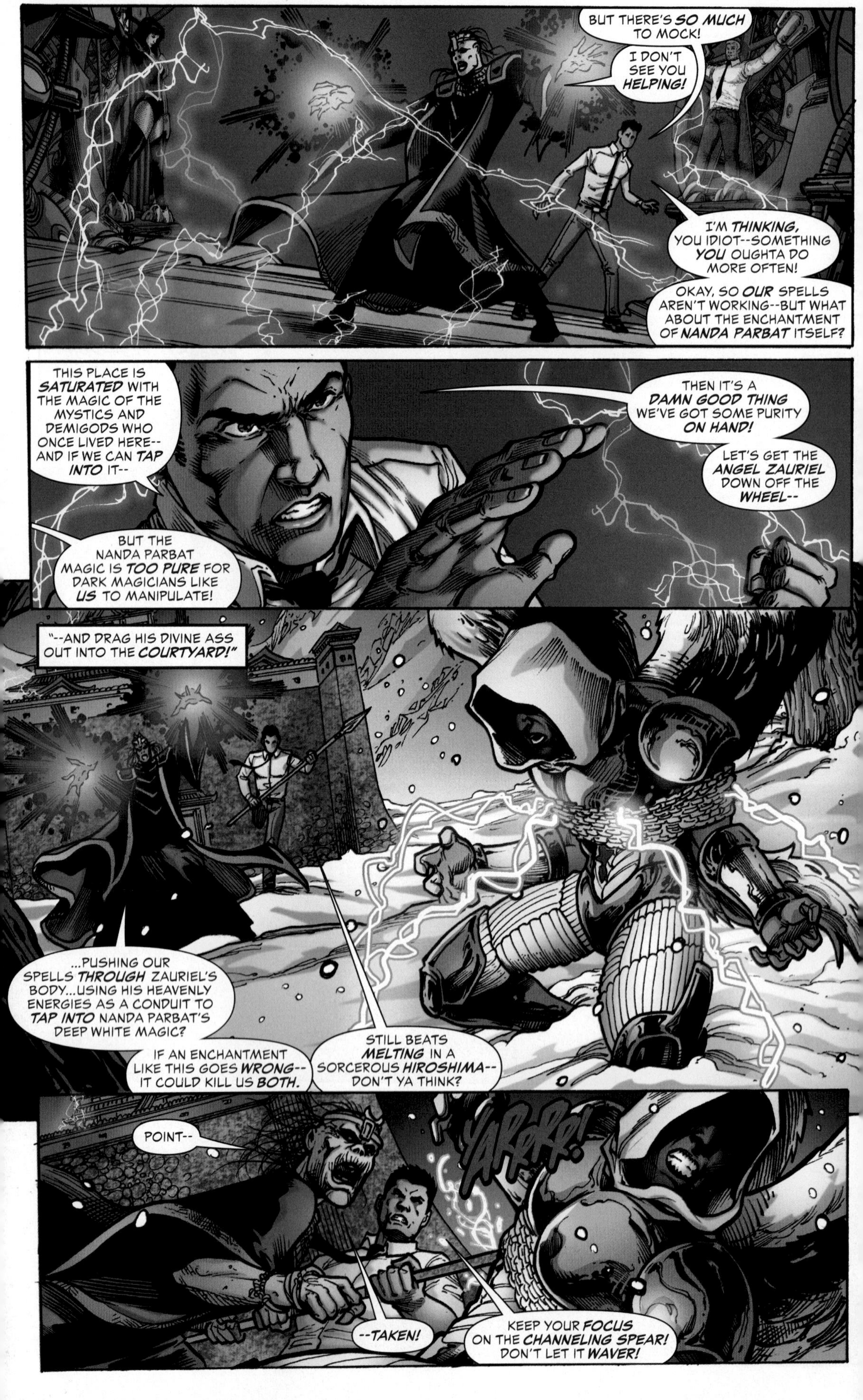

BUT THERE'S SO MUCH TO MOCK!
I DON'T SEE YOU HELPING!
I'M THINKING, YOU IDIOT--SOMETHING YOU OUGHTA DO MORE OFTEN!
OKAY, SO OUR SPELLS AREN'T WORKING--BUT WHAT ABOUT THE ENCHANTMENT OF NANDA PARBAT ITSELF?
THIS PLACE IS SATURATED WITH THE MAGIC OF THE MYSTICS AND DEMIGODS WHO ONCE LIVED HERE--AND IF WE CAN TAP INTO IT--
BUT THE NANDA PARBAT MAGIC IS TOO PURE FOR DARK MAGICIANS LIKE US TO MANIPULATE!
THEN IT'S A DAMN GOOD THING WE'VE GOT SOME PURITY ON HAND!
LET'S GET THE ANGEL ZAURIEL DOWN OFF THE WHEEL--
"--AND DRAG HIS DIVINE ASS OUT INTO THE COURTYARD!"
...PUSHING OUR SPELLS THROUGH ZAURIEL'S BODY...USING HIS HEAVENLY ENERGIES AS A CONDUIT TO TAP INTO NANDA PARBAT'S DEEP WHITE MAGIC?
IF AN ENCHANTMENT LIKE THIS GOES WRONG--IT COULD KILL US BOTH.
STILL BEATS MELTING IN A SORCEROUS HIROSHIMA--DON'T YA THINK?
POINT--
YARRRR!
--TAKEN!
KEEP YOUR FOCUS ON THE CHANNELING SPEAR! DON'T LET IT WAVER!

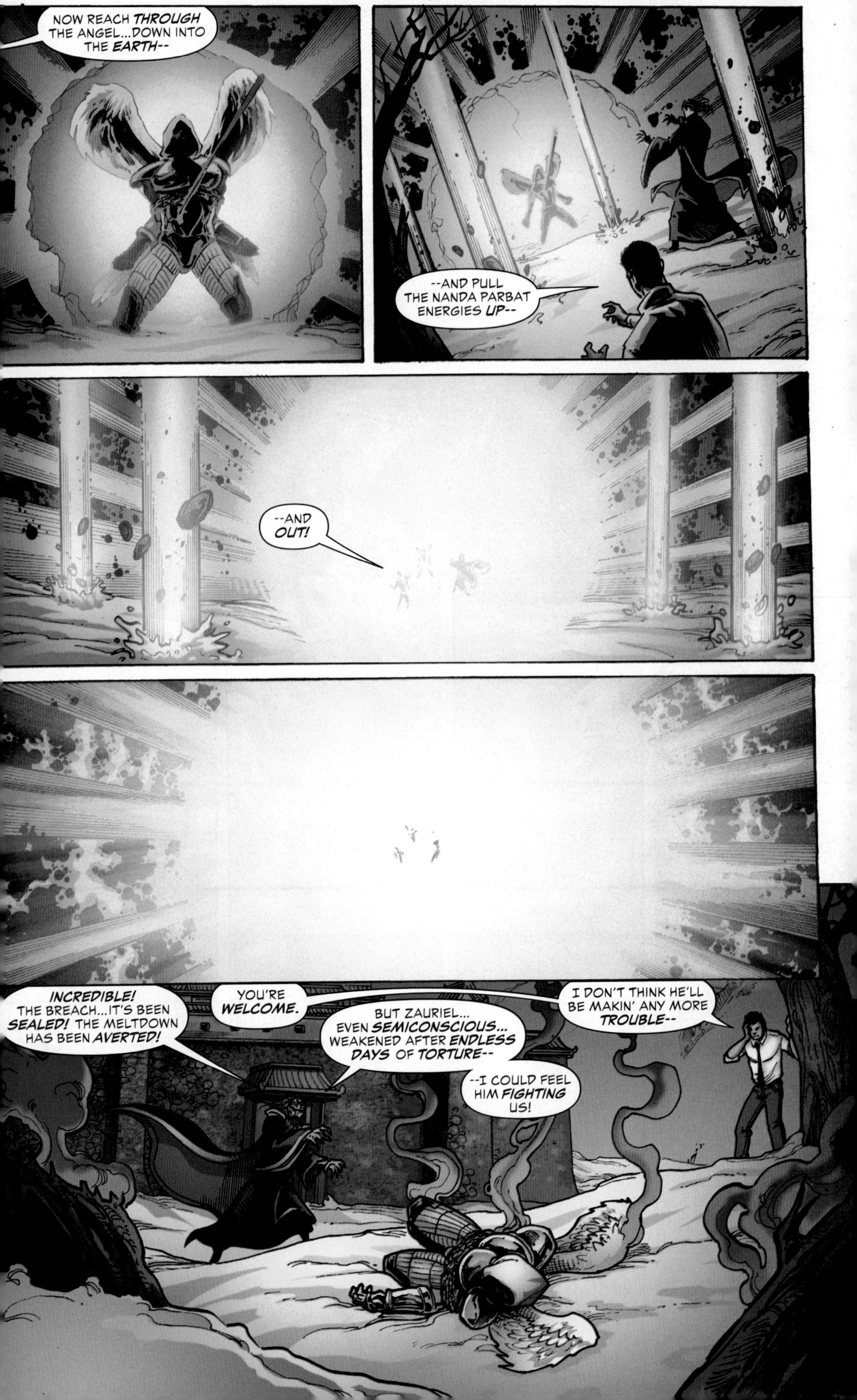
NOW REACH THROUGH THE ANGEL...DOWN INTO THE EARTH--
--AND PULL THE NANDA PARBAT ENERGIES UP--
--AND OUT!
INCREDIBLE! THE BREACH...IT'S BEEN SEALED! THE MELTDOWN HAS BEEN AVERTED!
YOU'RE WELCOME.
I DON'T THINK HE'LL BE MAKIN' ANY MORE TROUBLE--
BUT ZAURIEL... EVEN SEMICONSCIOUS... WEAKENED AFTER ENDLESS DAYS OF TORTURE--
--I COULD FEEL HIM FIGHTING US!

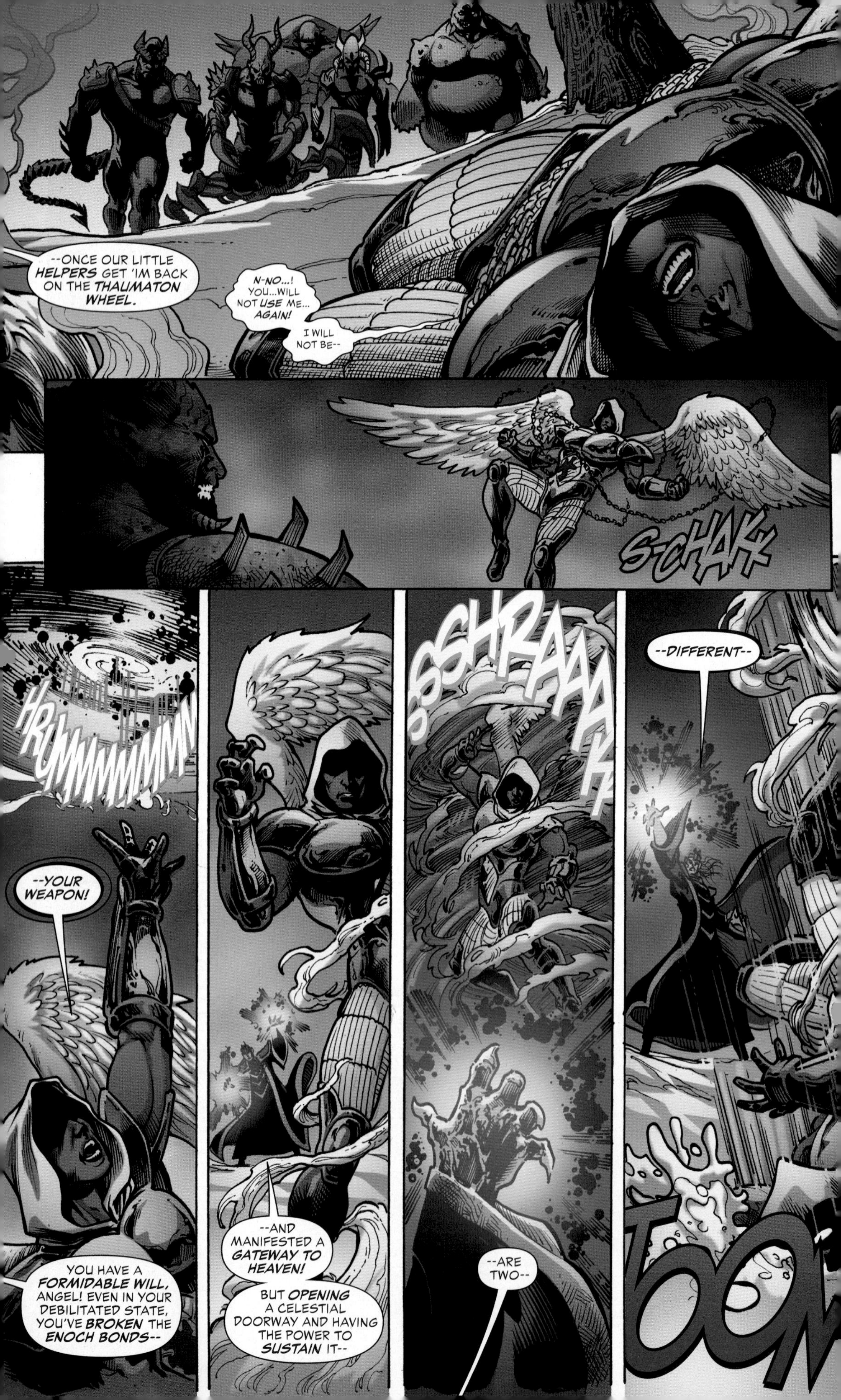
--ONCE OUR LITTLE HELPERS GET 'IM BACK ON THE THAUMATON WHEEL.
N-NO...! YOU...WILL NOT USE ME... AGAIN!
I WILL NOT BE--
S-CHAKK
HRUMMMMMMN
--YOUR WEAPON!
YOU HAVE A FORMIDABLE WILL, ANGEL! EVEN IN YOUR DEBILITATED STATE, YOU'VE BROKEN THE ENOCH BONDS--
--AND MANIFESTED A GATEWAY TO HEAVEN!
BUT OPENING A CELESTIAL DOORWAY AND HAVING THE POWER TO SUSTAIN IT--
SSHRAAAAKK
--ARE TWO--
--DIFFERENT--
TOOM

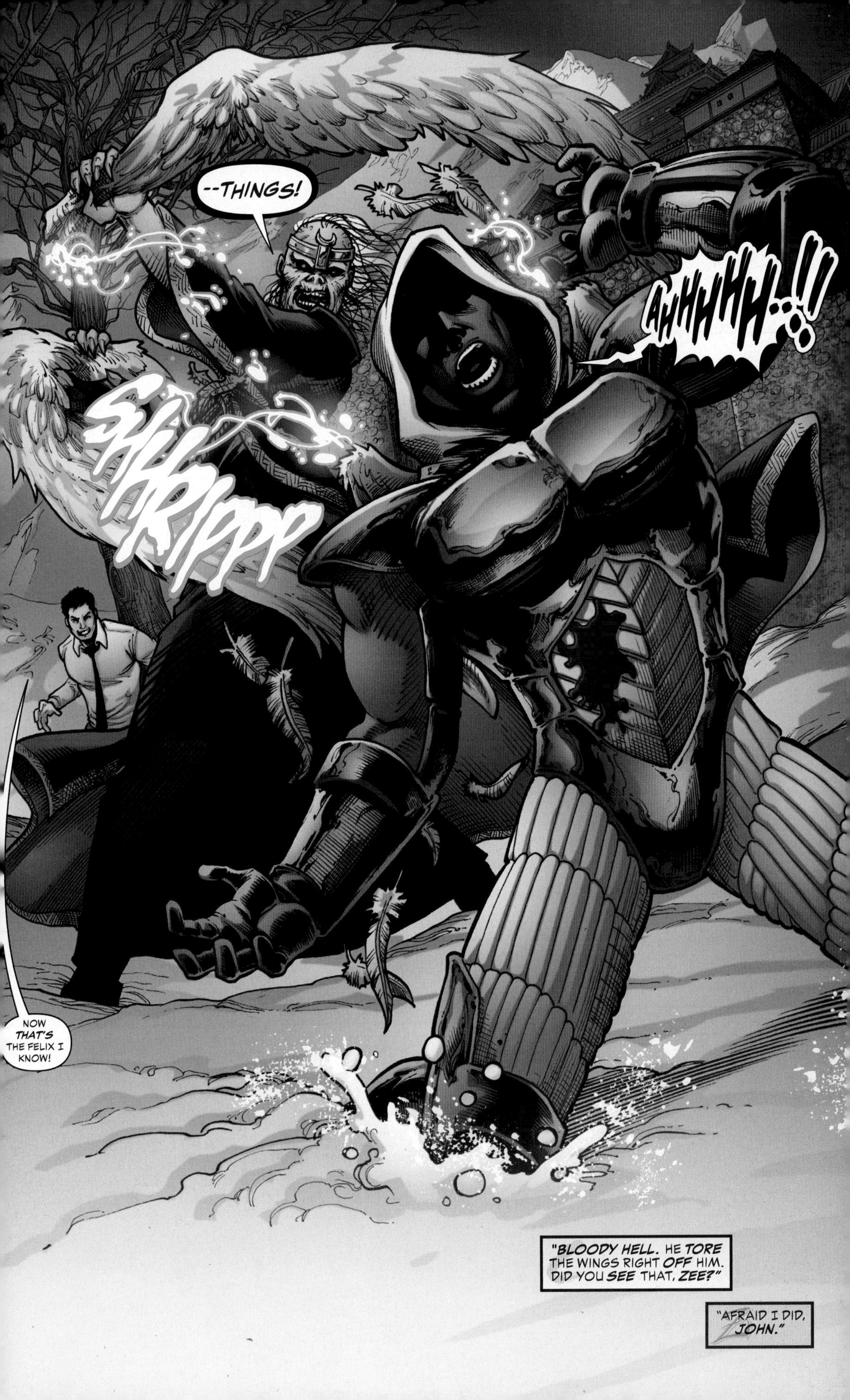
--THINGS!
AHHHHH--!!!
SHHRIPPP
NOW THAT'S THE FELIX I KNOW!
"BLOODY HELL. HE TORE THE WINGS RIGHT OFF HIM. DID YOU SEE THAT, ZEE?"
"AFRAID I DID, JOHN."

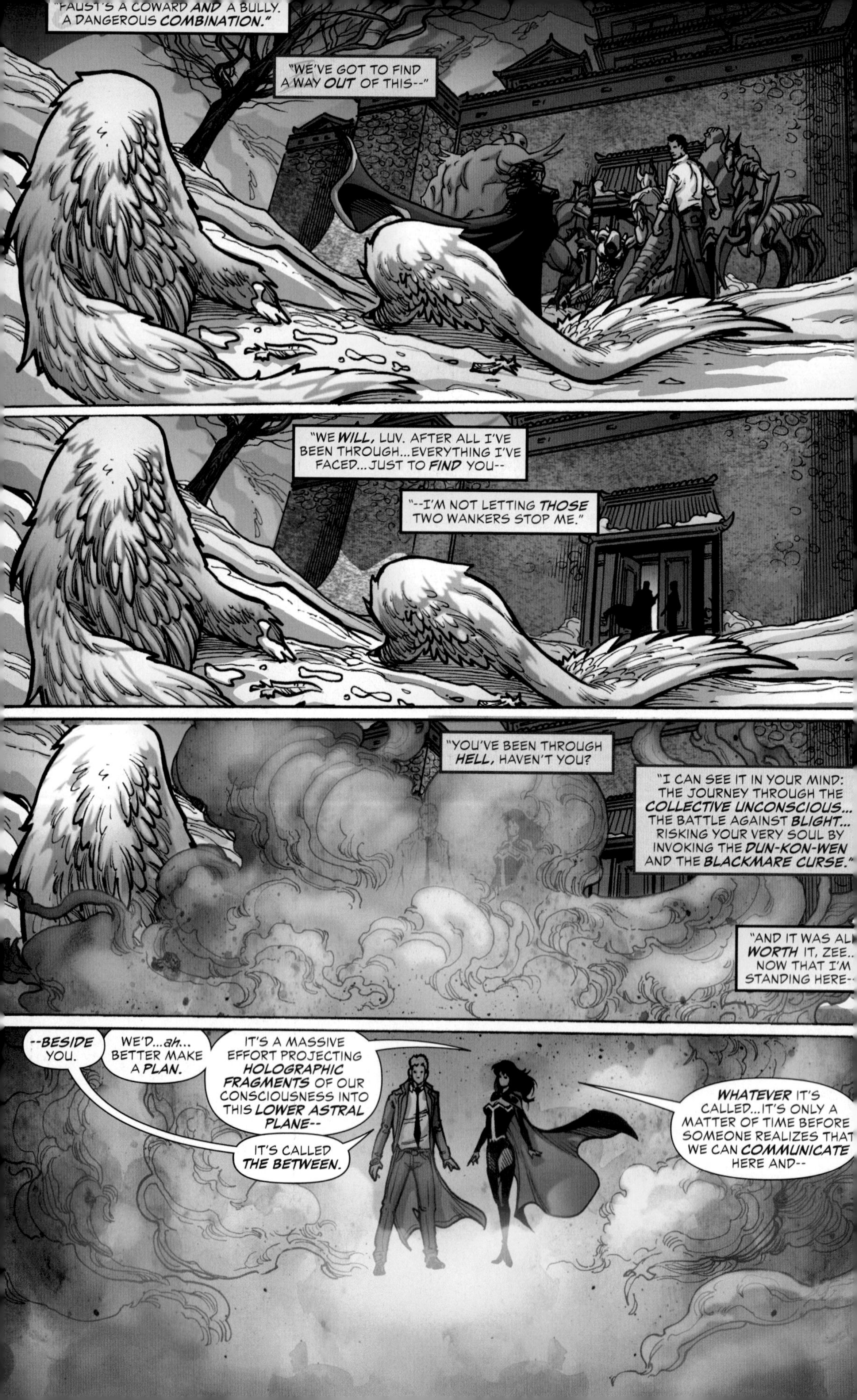
"FAUST'S A COWARD AND A BULLY. A DANGEROUS COMBINATION."
"WE'VE GOT TO FIND A WAY OUT OF THIS--"
"WE WILL, LUV. AFTER ALL I'VE BEEN THROUGH...EVERYTHING I'VE FACED...JUST TO FIND YOU--
"--I'M NOT LETTING THOSE TWO WANKERS STOP ME."
"YOU'VE BEEN THROUGH HELL, HAVEN'T YOU?
"I CAN SEE IT IN YOUR MIND: THE JOURNEY THROUGH THE COLLECTIVE UNCONSCIOUS... THE BATTLE AGAINST BLIGHT... RISKING YOUR VERY SOUL BY INVOKING THE DUN-KON-WEN AND THE BLACKMARE CURSE."
"AND IT WAS AL WORTH IT, ZEE.. NOW THAT I'M STANDING HERE--
--BESIDE YOU.
WE'D...ah... BETTER MAKE A PLAN.
IT'S A MASSIVE EFFORT PROJECTING HOLOGRAPHIC FRAGMENTS OF OUR CONSCIOUSNESS INTO THIS LOWER ASTRAL PLANE--
IT'S CALLED THE BETWEEN.
WHATEVER IT'S CALLED...IT'S ONLY A MATTER OF TIME BEFORE SOMEONE REALIZES THAT WE CAN COMMUNICATE HERE AND--

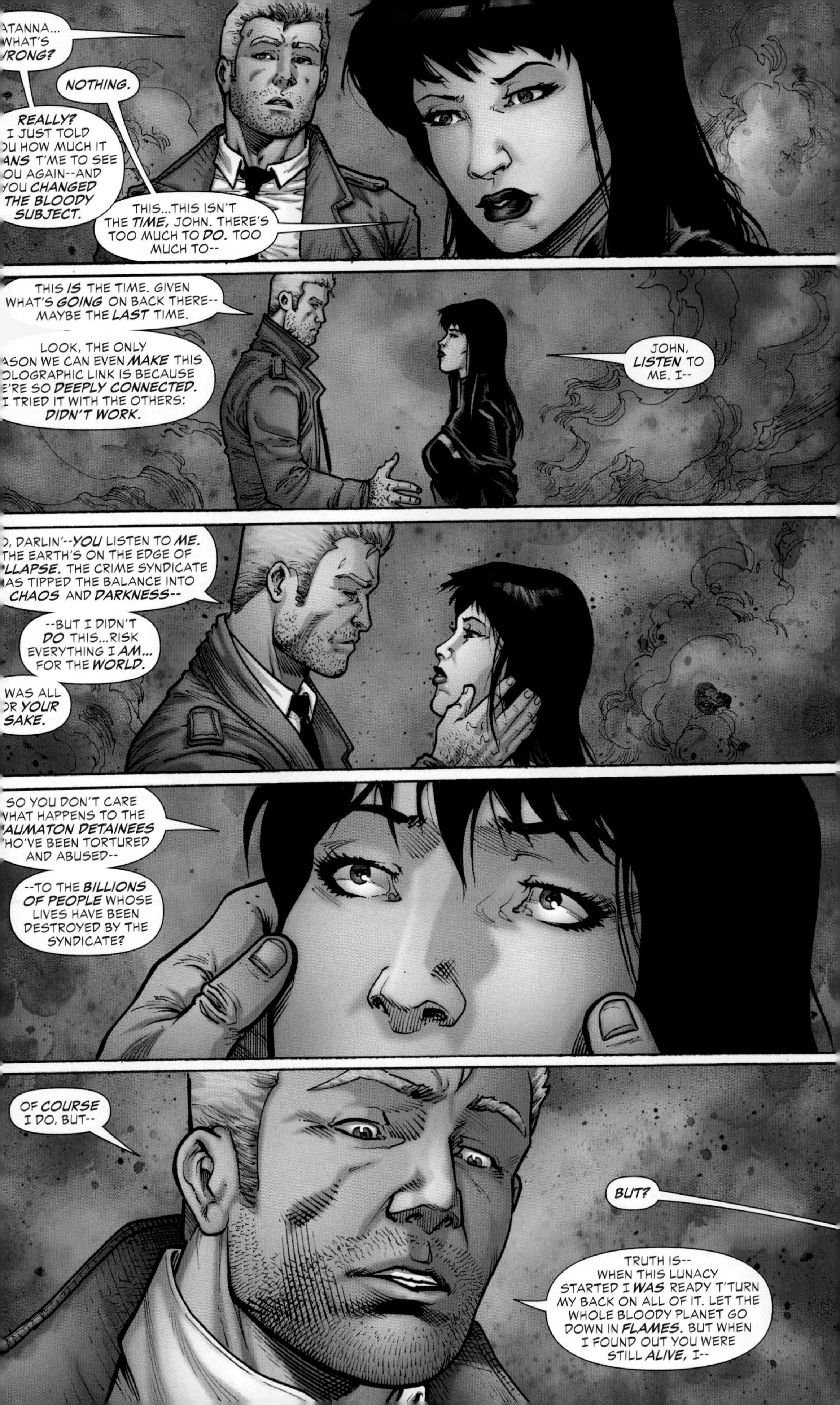
ATANNA... WHAT'S WRONG?
NOTHING.
REALLY? I JUST TOLD OU HOW MUCH IT ANS T'ME TO SEE OU AGAIN--AND YOU CHANGED THE BLOODY SUBJECT.
THIS...THIS ISN'T THE TIME, JOHN. THERE'S TOO MUCH TO DO. TOO MUCH TO--
THIS IS THE TIME. GIVEN WHAT'S GOING ON BACK THERE-- MAYBE THE LAST TIME.
LOOK, THE ONLY ASON WE CAN EVEN MAKE THIS OLOGRAPHIC LINK IS BECAUSE E'RE SO DEEPLY CONNECTED. I TRIED IT WITH THE OTHERS: DIDN'T WORK.
JOHN, LISTEN TO ME. I--
O, DARLIN'--YOU LISTEN TO ME. THE EARTH'S ON THE EDGE OF LLAPSE. THE CRIME SYNDICATE AS TIPPED THE BALANCE INTO CHAOS AND DARKNESS--
--BUT I DIDN'T DO THIS...RISK EVERYTHING I AM... FOR THE WORLD.
WAS ALL OR YOUR SAKE.
SO YOU DON'T CARE WHAT HAPPENS TO THE AUMATON DETAINEES HO'VE BEEN TORTURED AND ABUSED--
--TO THE BILLIONS OF PEOPLE WHOSE LIVES HAVE BEEN DESTROYED BY THE SYNDICATE?
OF COURSE I DO, BUT--
BUT?
TRUTH IS-- WHEN THIS LUNACY STARTED I WAS READY T'TURN MY BACK ON ALL OF IT. LET THE WHOLE BLOODY PLANET GO DOWN IN FLAMES. BUT WHEN I FOUND OUT YOU WERE STILL ALIVE, I--

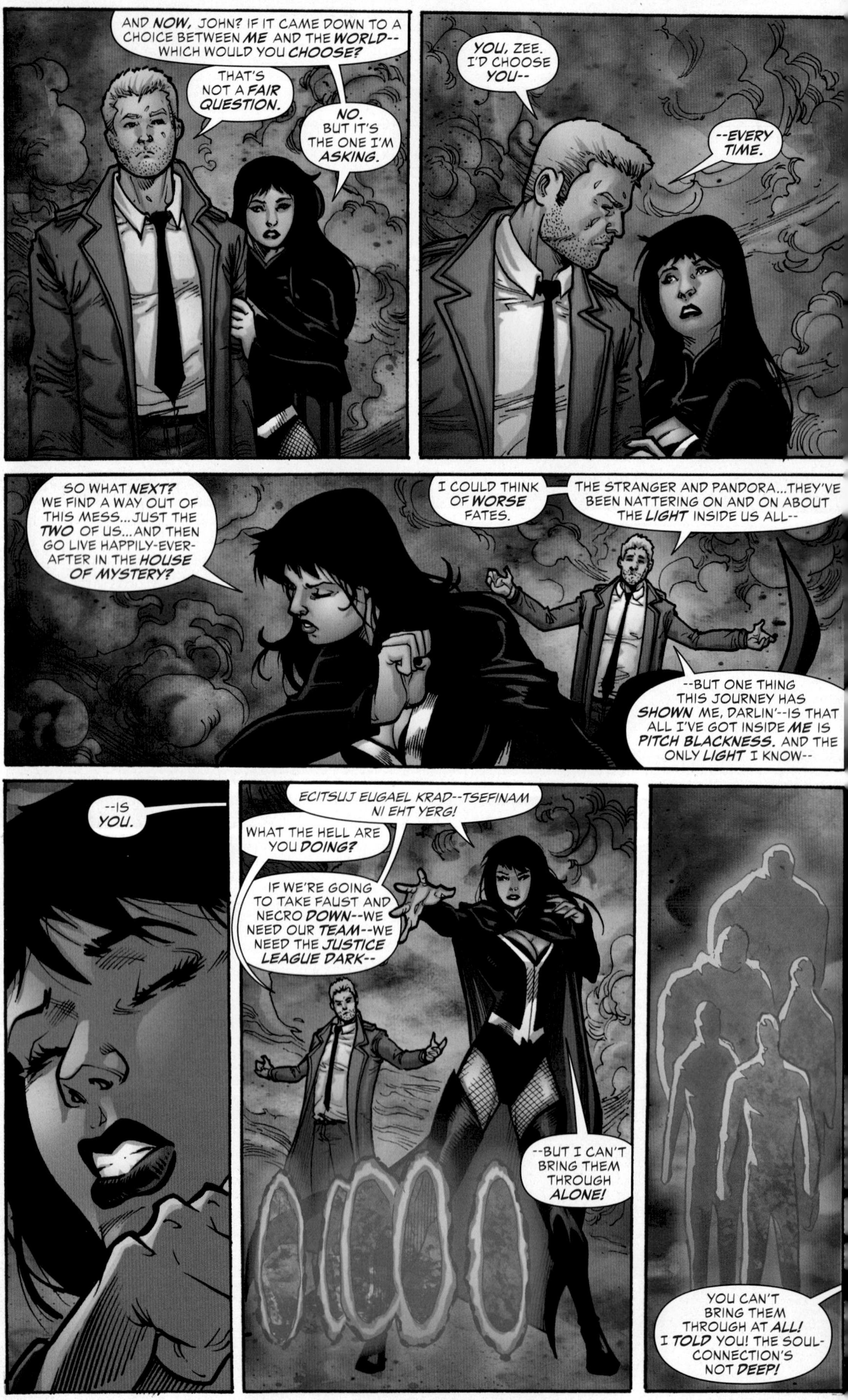

AND NOW, JOHN? IF IT CAME DOWN TO A CHOICE BETWEEN ME AND THE WORLD-- WHICH WOULD YOU CHOOSE?
THAT'S NOT A FAIR QUESTION.
NO. BUT IT'S THE ONE I'M ASKING.
YOU, ZEE. I'D CHOOSE YOU--
--EVERY TIME.
SO WHAT NEXT? WE FIND A WAY OUT OF THIS MESS...JUST THE TWO OF US...AND THEN GO LIVE HAPPILY-EVER-AFTER IN THE HOUSE OF MYSTERY?
I COULD THINK OF WORSE FATES.
THE STRANGER AND PANDORA...THEY'VE BEEN NATTERING ON AND ON ABOUT THE LIGHT INSIDE US ALL--
--BUT ONE THING THIS JOURNEY HAS SHOWN ME, DARLIN'--IS THAT ALL I'VE GOT INSIDE ME IS PITCH BLACKNESS. AND THE ONLY LIGHT I KNOW--
--IS YOU.
ECITSUJ EUGAEL KRAD--TSEFINAM NI EHT YERG!
WHAT THE HELL ARE YOU DOING?
IF WE'RE GOING TO TAKE FAUST AND NECRO DOWN--WE NEED OUR TEAM--WE NEED THE JUSTICE LEAGUE DARK--
--BUT I CAN'T BRING THEM THROUGH ALONE!
YOU CAN'T BRING THEM THROUGH AT ALL! I TOLD YOU! THE SOUL-CONNECTION'S NOT DEEP!

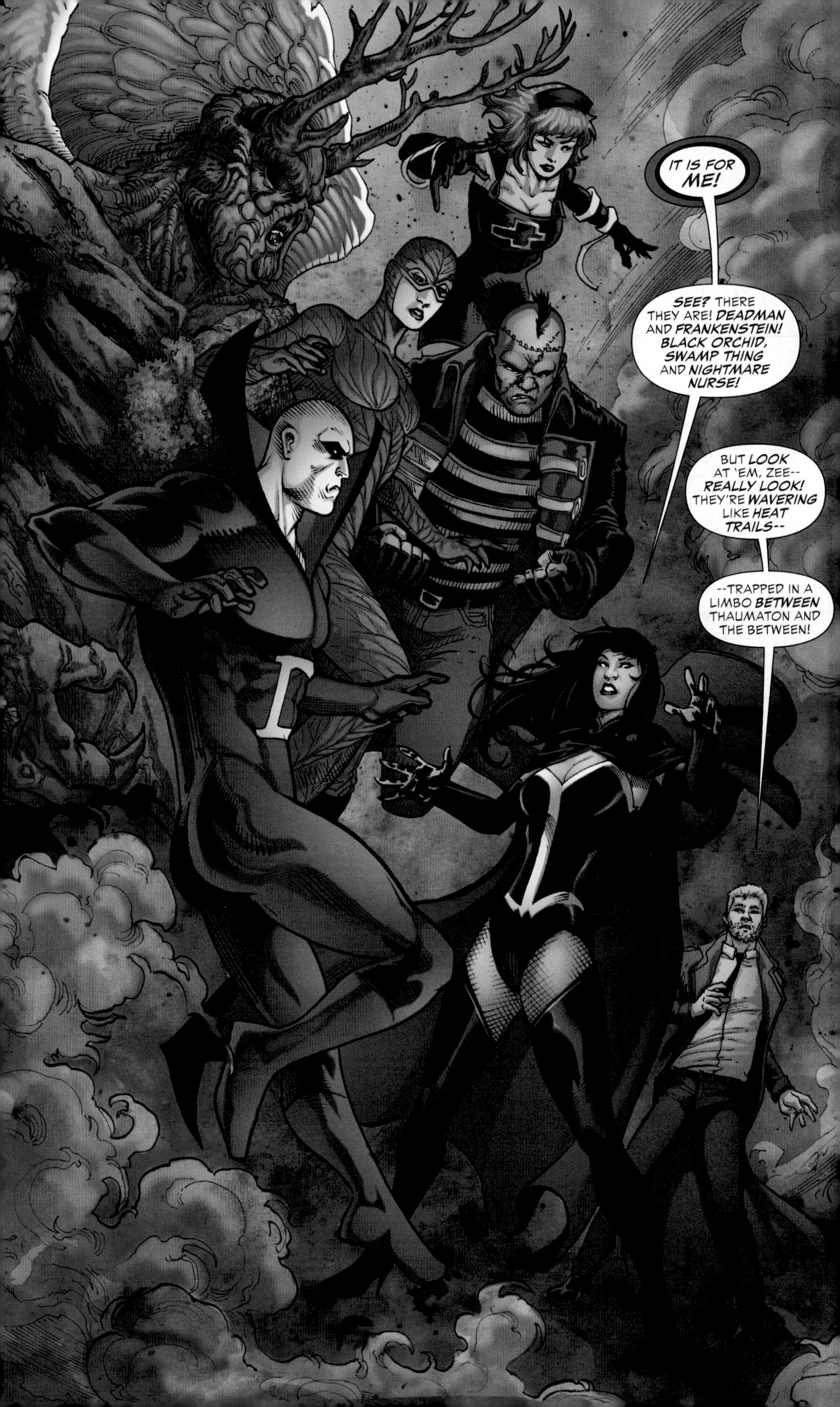
IT IS FOR ME!
SEE? THERE THEY ARE! DEADMAN AND FRANKENSTEIN! BLACK ORCHID, SWAMP THING AND NIGHTMARE NURSE!
BUT LOOK AT 'EM, ZEE-- REALLY LOOK! THEY'RE WAVERING LIKE HEAT TRAILS--
--TRAPPED IN A LIMBO BETWEEN THAUMATON AND THE BETWEEN!

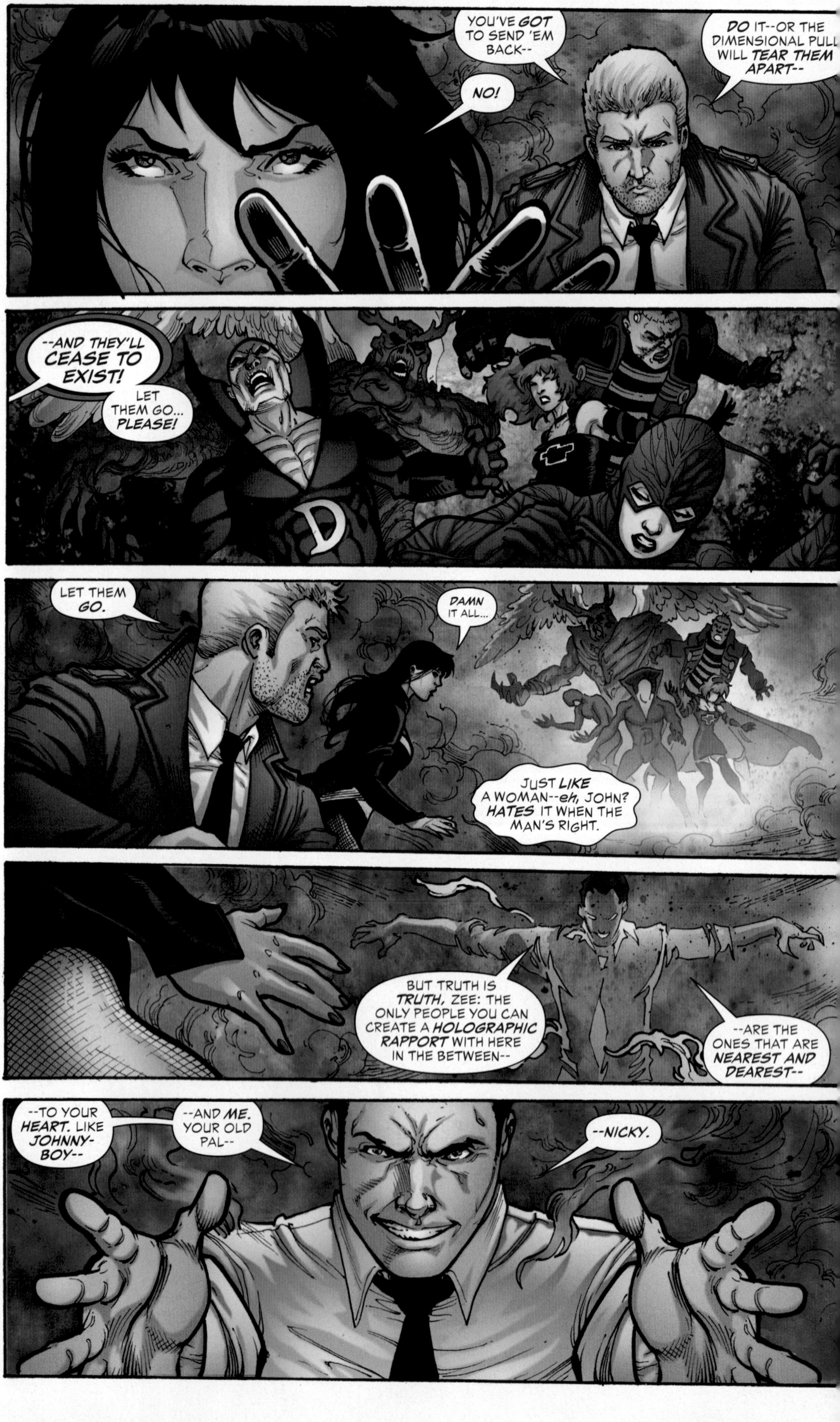

YOU'VE GOT TO SEND 'EM BACK--
NO!
DO IT--OR THE DIMENSIONAL PULL WILL TEAR THEM APART--
--AND THEY'LL CEASE TO EXIST!
LET THEM GO... PLEASE!
LET THEM GO.
DAMN IT ALL...
JUST LIKE A WOMAN--eh, JOHN? HATES IT WHEN THE MAN'S RIGHT.
BUT TRUTH IS TRUTH, ZEE: THE ONLY PEOPLE YOU CAN CREATE A HOLOGRAPHIC RAPPORT WITH HERE IN THE BETWEEN--
--ARE THE ONES THAT ARE NEAREST AND DEAREST--
--TO YOUR HEART. LIKE JOHNNY-BOY--
--AND ME. YOUR OLD PAL--
--NICKY.

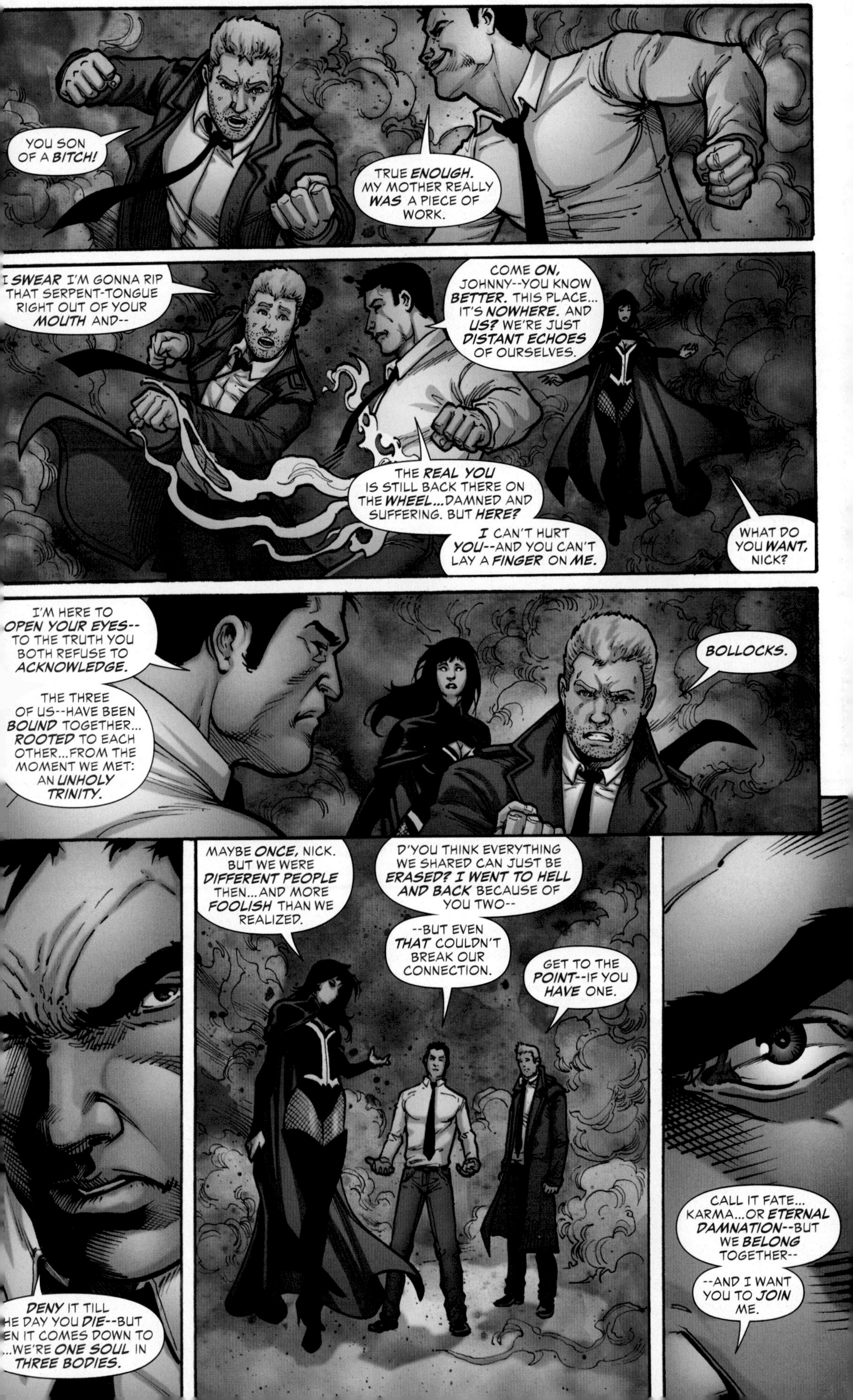

YOU SON OF A BITCH!
TRUE ENOUGH. MY MOTHER REALLY WAS A PIECE OF WORK.
I SWEAR I'M GONNA RIP THAT SERPENT-TONGUE RIGHT OUT OF YOUR MOUTH AND--
COME ON, JOHNNY--YOU KNOW BETTER. THIS PLACE... IT'S NOWHERE. AND US? WE'RE JUST DISTANT ECHOES OF OURSELVES.
THE REAL YOU IS STILL BACK THERE ON THE WHEEL...DAMNED AND SUFFERING. BUT HERE?
I CAN'T HURT YOU--AND YOU CAN'T LAY A FINGER ON ME.
WHAT DO YOU WANT, NICK?
I'M HERE TO OPEN YOUR EYES--TO THE TRUTH YOU BOTH REFUSE TO ACKNOWLEDGE.
THE THREE OF US--HAVE BEEN BOUND TOGETHER... ROOTED TO EACH OTHER...FROM THE MOMENT WE MET: AN UNHOLY TRINITY.
BOLLOCKS.
MAYBE ONCE, NICK. BUT WE WERE DIFFERENT PEOPLE THEN...AND MORE FOOLISH THAN WE REALIZED.
D'YOU THINK EVERYTHING WE SHARED CAN JUST BE ERASED? I WENT TO HELL AND BACK BECAUSE OF YOU TWO--
--BUT EVEN THAT COULDN'T BREAK OUR CONNECTION.
GET TO THE POINT--IF YOU HAVE ONE.
DENY IT TILL HE DAY YOU DIE--BUT EN IT COMES DOWN TO ...WE'RE ONE SOUL IN THREE BODIES.
CALL IT FATE... KARMA...OR ETERNAL DAMNATION--BUT WE BELONG TOGETHER--
--AND I WANT YOU TO JOIN ME.

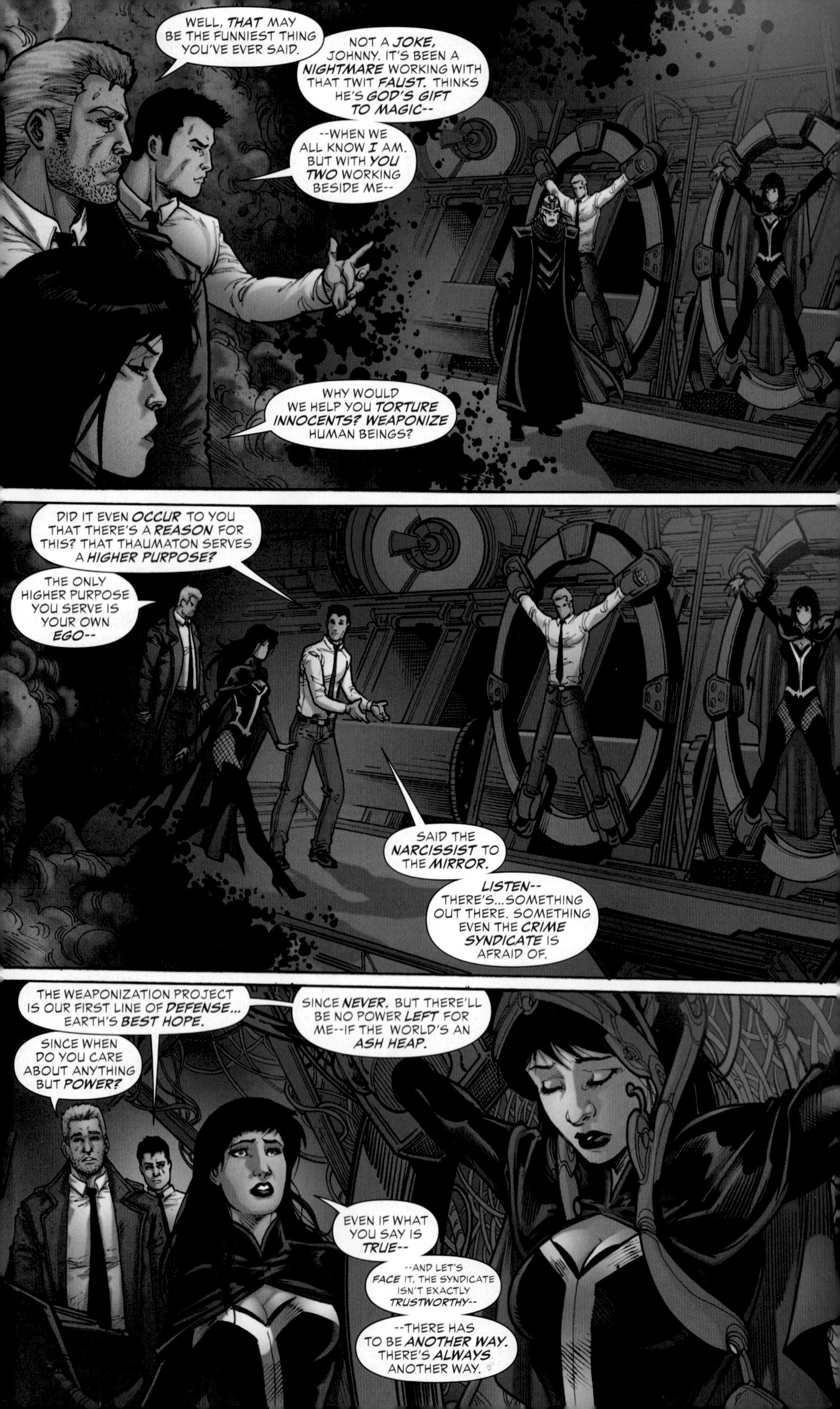
WELL, *THAT* MAY BE THE FUNNIEST THING YOU'VE EVER SAID.
NOT A *JOKE,* JOHNNY. IT'S BEEN A *NIGHTMARE* WORKING WITH THAT TWIT *FAUST.* THINKS HE'S *GOD'S GIFT TO MAGIC*--
--WHEN WE ALL KNOW *I* AM. BUT WITH *YOU TWO* WORKING BESIDE ME--
WHY WOULD WE HELP YOU *TORTURE INNOCENTS? WEAPONIZE* HUMAN BEINGS?
DID IT EVEN *OCCUR* TO YOU THAT THERE'S A *REASON* FOR THIS? THAT THAUMATON SERVES A *HIGHER PURPOSE?*
THE ONLY HIGHER PURPOSE YOU SERVE IS YOUR OWN *EGO*--
SAID THE *NARCISSIST* TO THE *MIRROR.*
LISTEN-- THERE'S...SOMETHING OUT THERE. SOMETHING EVEN THE *CRIME SYNDICATE* IS AFRAID OF.
THE WEAPONIZATION PROJECT IS OUR FIRST LINE OF *DEFENSE*... EARTH'S *BEST HOPE.*
SINCE WHEN DO YOU CARE ABOUT ANYTHING BUT *POWER?*
SINCE *NEVER.* BUT THERE'LL BE NO POWER *LEFT* FOR ME--IF THE WORLD'S AN *ASH HEAP.*
EVEN IF WHAT YOU SAY IS *TRUE*--
--AND LET'S *FACE* IT, THE SYNDICATE ISN'T EXACTLY *TRUSTWORTHY*--
--THERE HAS TO BE *ANOTHER WAY.* THERE'S *ALWAYS* ANOTHER WAY.

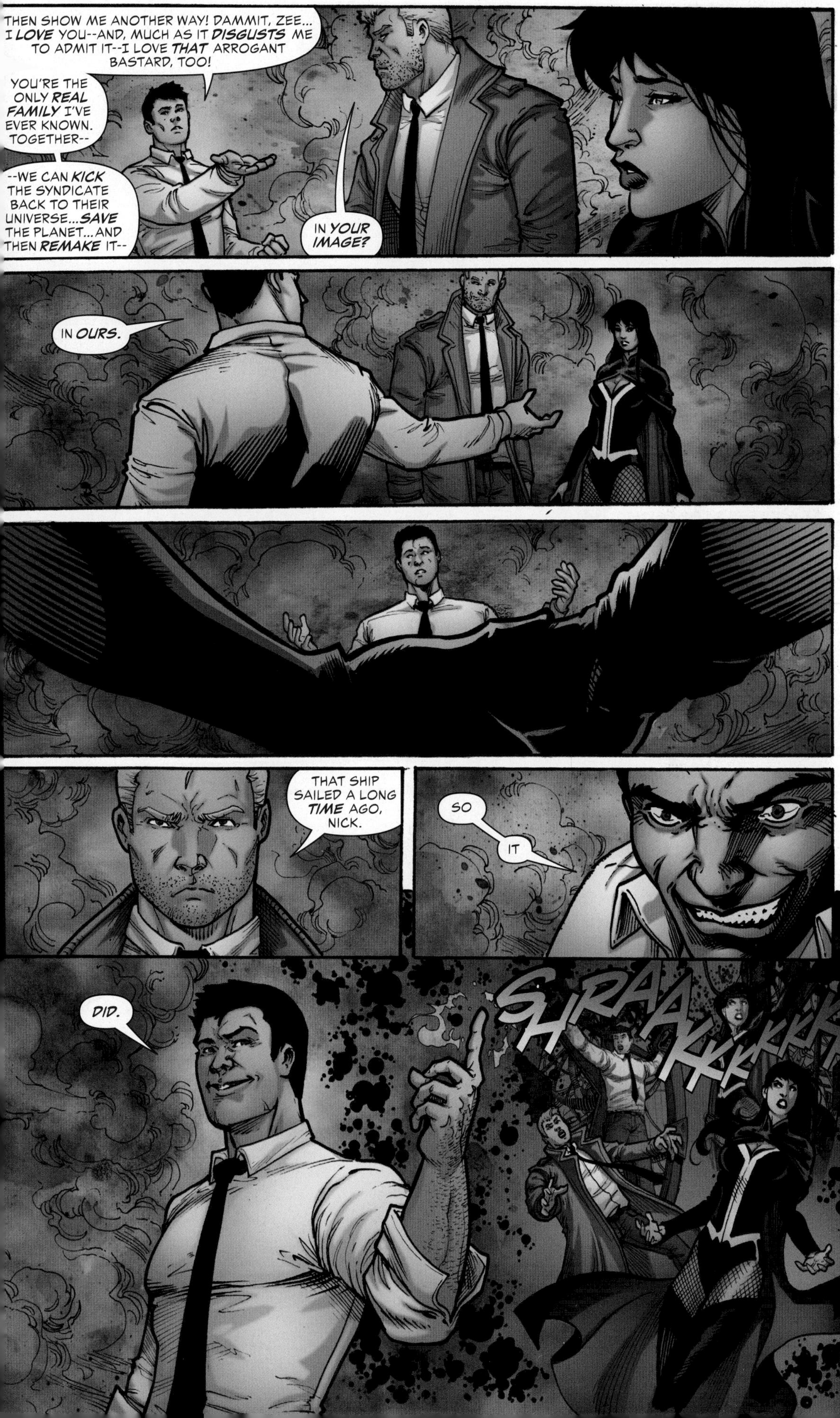
THEN SHOW ME ANOTHER WAY! DAMMIT, ZEE... I LOVE YOU--AND, MUCH AS IT DISGUSTS ME TO ADMIT IT--I LOVE THAT ARROGANT BASTARD, TOO!
YOU'RE THE ONLY REAL FAMILY I'VE EVER KNOWN. TOGETHER--
--WE CAN KICK THE SYNDICATE BACK TO THEIR UNIVERSE...SAVE THE PLANET...AND THEN REMAKE IT--
IN YOUR IMAGE?
IN OURS.
THAT SHIP SAILED A LONG TIME AGO, NICK.
SO
IT
DID.
SHRAAKKKKKK

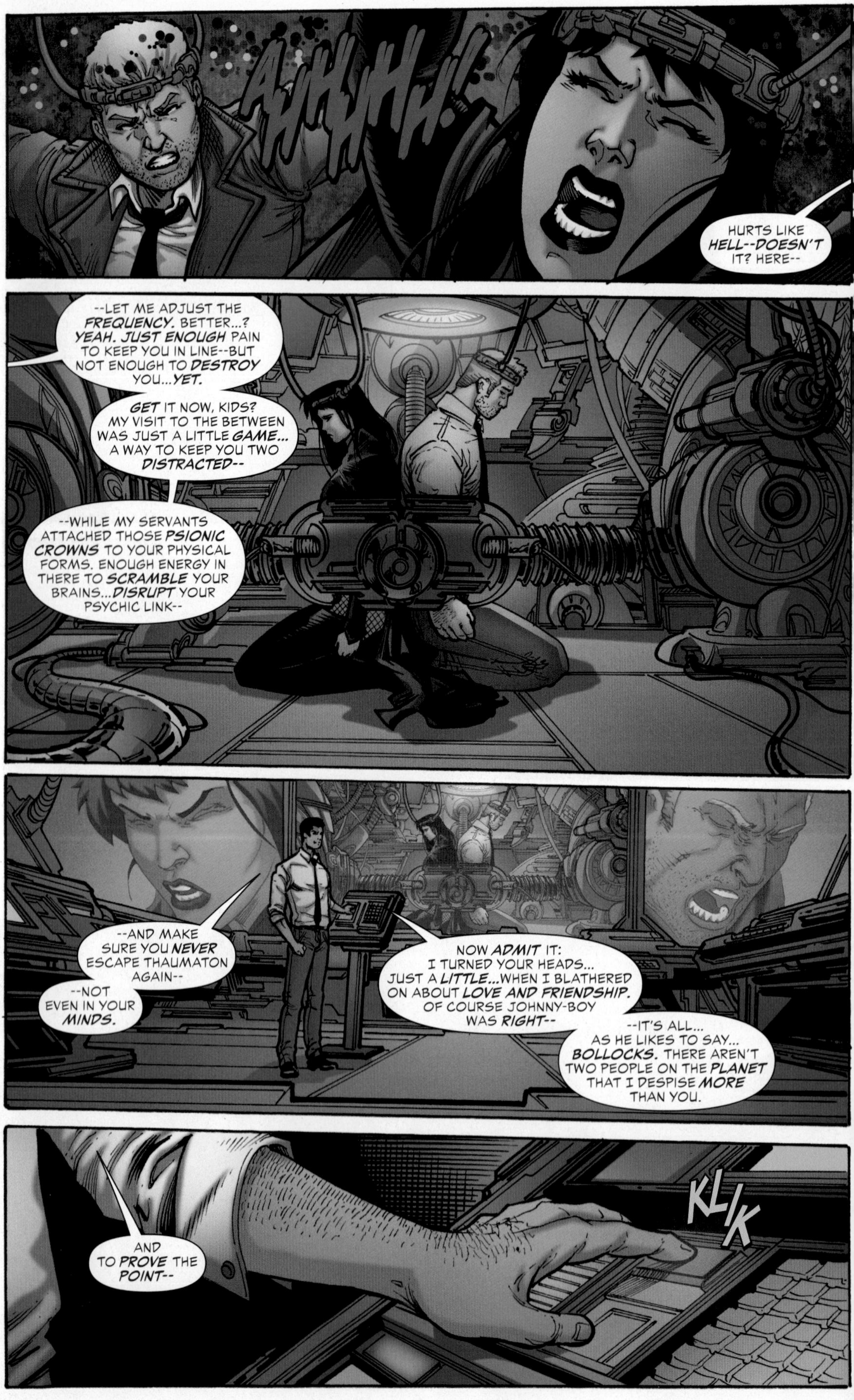
AHHHH!!
HURTS LIKE HELL--DOESN'T IT? HERE--
--LET ME ADJUST THE FREQUENCY. BETTER...? YEAH. JUST ENOUGH PAIN TO KEEP YOU IN LINE--BUT NOT ENOUGH TO DESTROY YOU...YET.
GET IT NOW, KIDS? MY VISIT TO THE BETWEEN WAS JUST A LITTLE GAME... A WAY TO KEEP YOU TWO DISTRACTED--
--WHILE MY SERVANTS ATTACHED THOSE PSIONIC CROWNS TO YOUR PHYSICAL FORMS. ENOUGH ENERGY IN THERE TO SCRAMBLE YOUR BRAINS...DISRUPT YOUR PSYCHIC LINK--
--AND MAKE SURE YOU NEVER ESCAPE THAUMATON AGAIN--
--NOT EVEN IN YOUR MINDS.
NOW ADMIT IT: I TURNED YOUR HEADS... JUST A LITTLE...WHEN I BLATHERED ON ABOUT LOVE AND FRIENDSHIP. OF COURSE JOHNNY-BOY WAS RIGHT--
--IT'S ALL... AS HE LIKES TO SAY... BOLLOCKS. THERE AREN'T TWO PEOPLE ON THE PLANET THAT I DESPISE MORE THAN YOU.
AND TO PROVE THE POINT--
KLIK

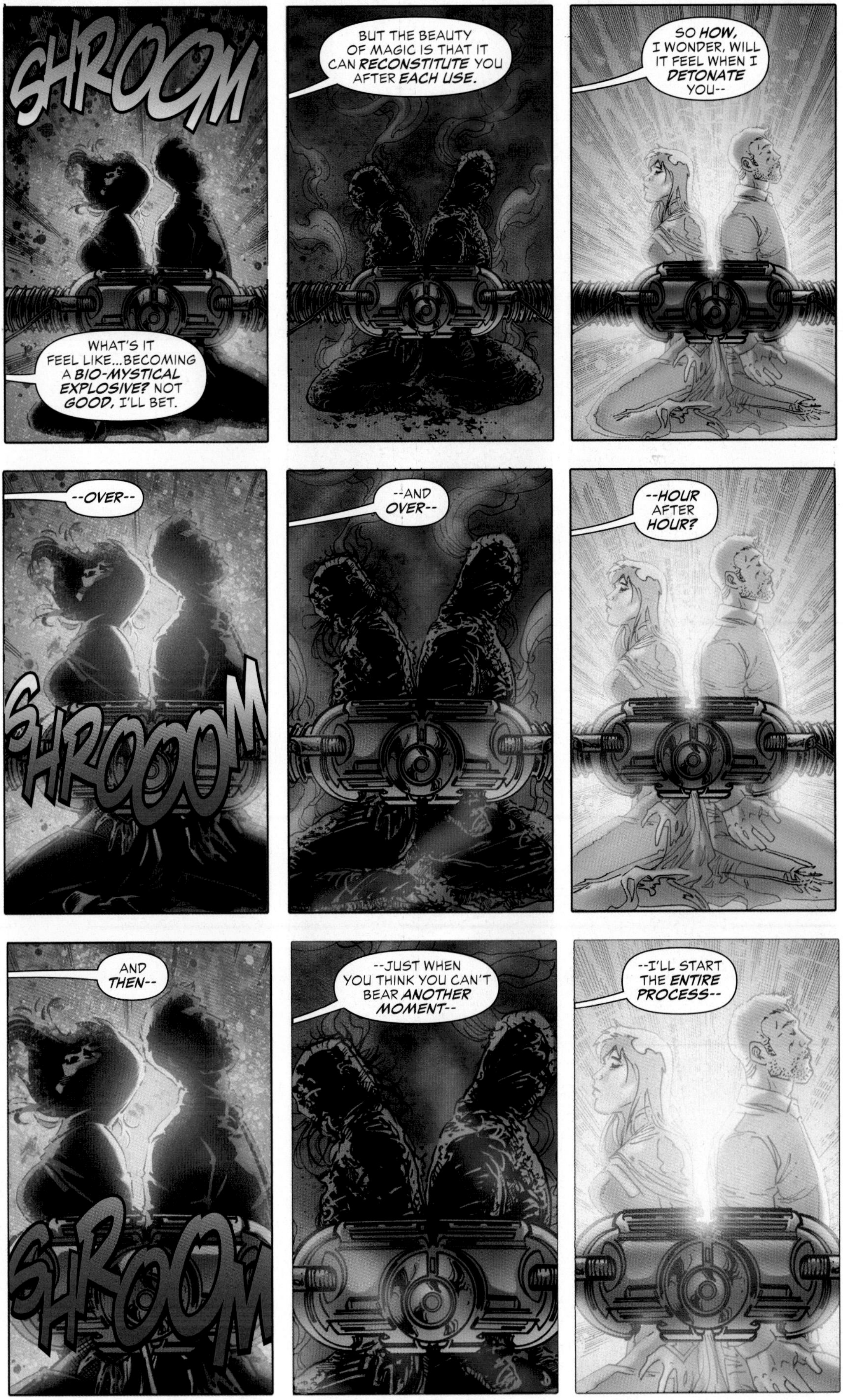
SHROOM
WHAT'S IT FEEL LIKE...BECOMING A BIO-MYSTICAL EXPLOSIVE? NOT GOOD, I'LL BET.
BUT THE BEAUTY OF MAGIC IS THAT IT CAN RECONSTITUTE YOU AFTER EACH USE.
SO HOW, I WONDER, WILL IT FEEL WHEN I DETONATE YOU--
--OVER--
SHROOOM
--AND OVER--
--HOUR AFTER HOUR?
AND THEN--
SHROOM
--JUST WHEN YOU THINK YOU CAN'T BEAR ANOTHER MOMENT--
--I'LL START THE ENTIRE PROCESS--

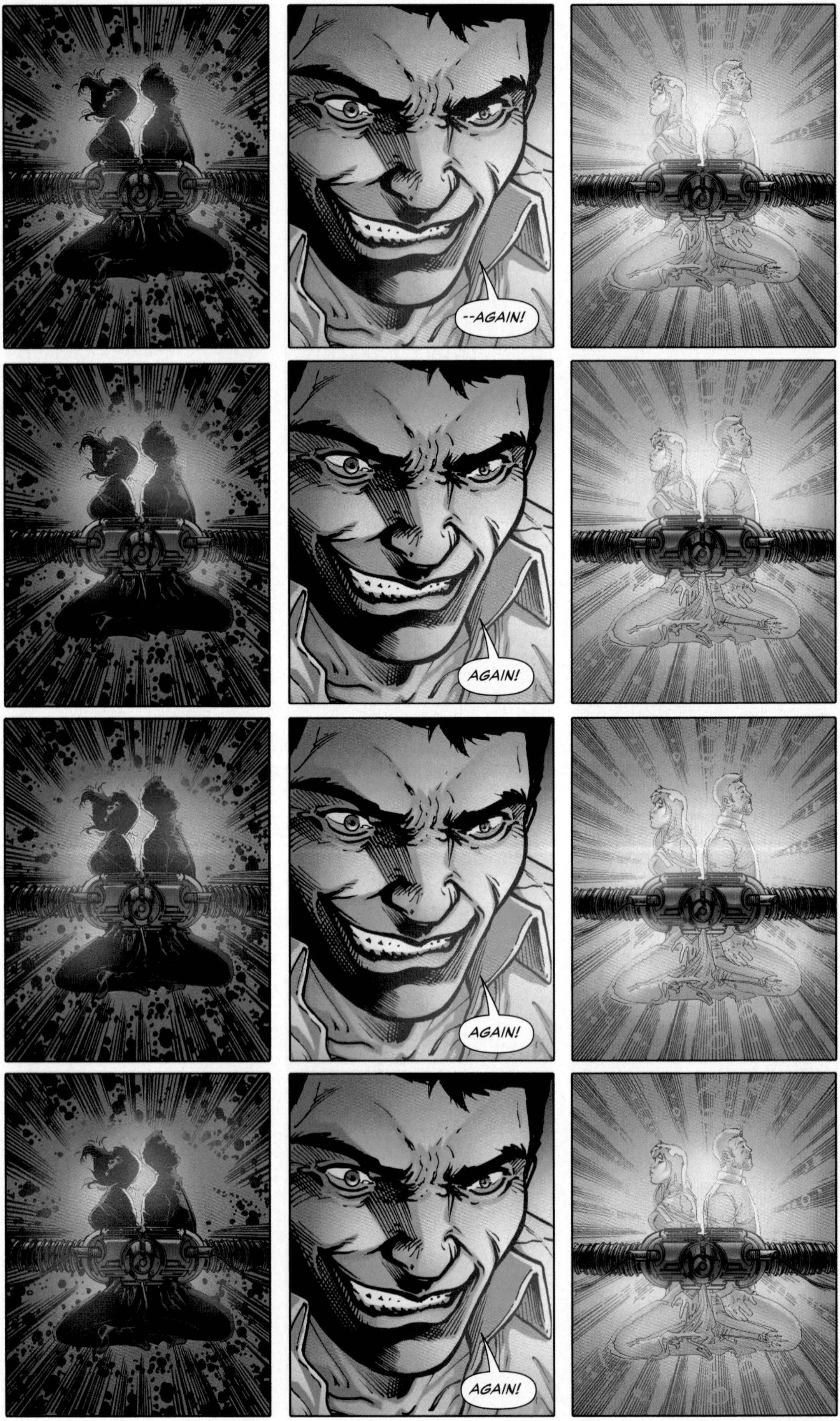
--AGAIN!
AGAIN!
AGAIN!
AGAIN!

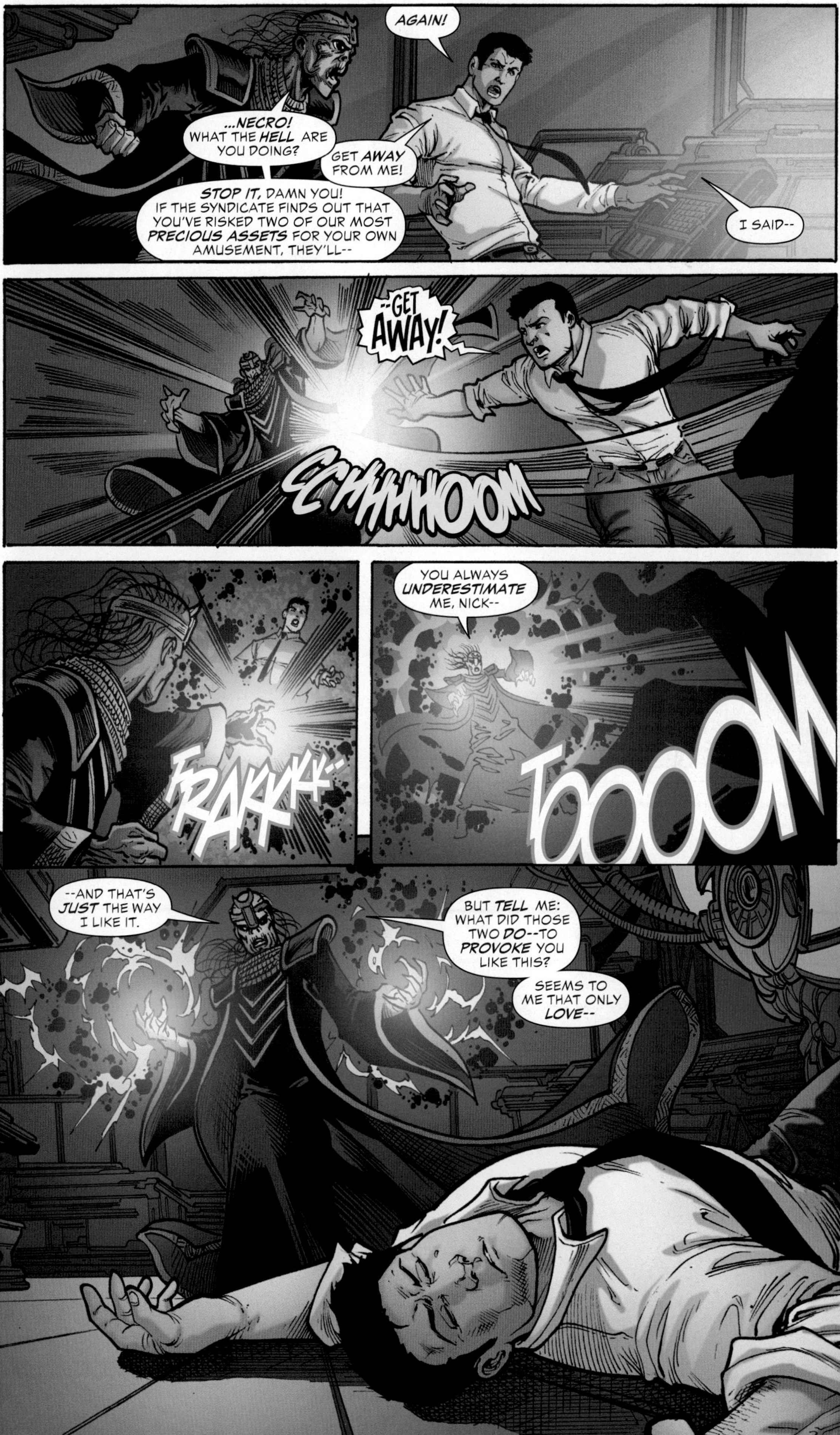
AGAIN!
...NECRO! WHAT THE HELL ARE YOU DOING?
GET AWAY FROM ME!
STOP IT, DAMN YOU! IF THE SYNDICATE FINDS OUT THAT YOU'VE RISKED TWO OF OUR MOST PRECIOUS ASSETS FOR YOUR OWN AMUSEMENT, THEY'LL--
I SAID--
--GET AWAY!
CCHHHHOOM
FRAKKKK--
YOU ALWAYS UNDERESTIMATE ME, NICK--
TOOOOM
--AND THAT'S JUST THE WAY I LIKE IT.
BUT TELL ME: WHAT DID THOSE TWO DO--TO PROVOKE YOU LIKE THIS?
SEEMS TO ME THAT ONLY LOVE--

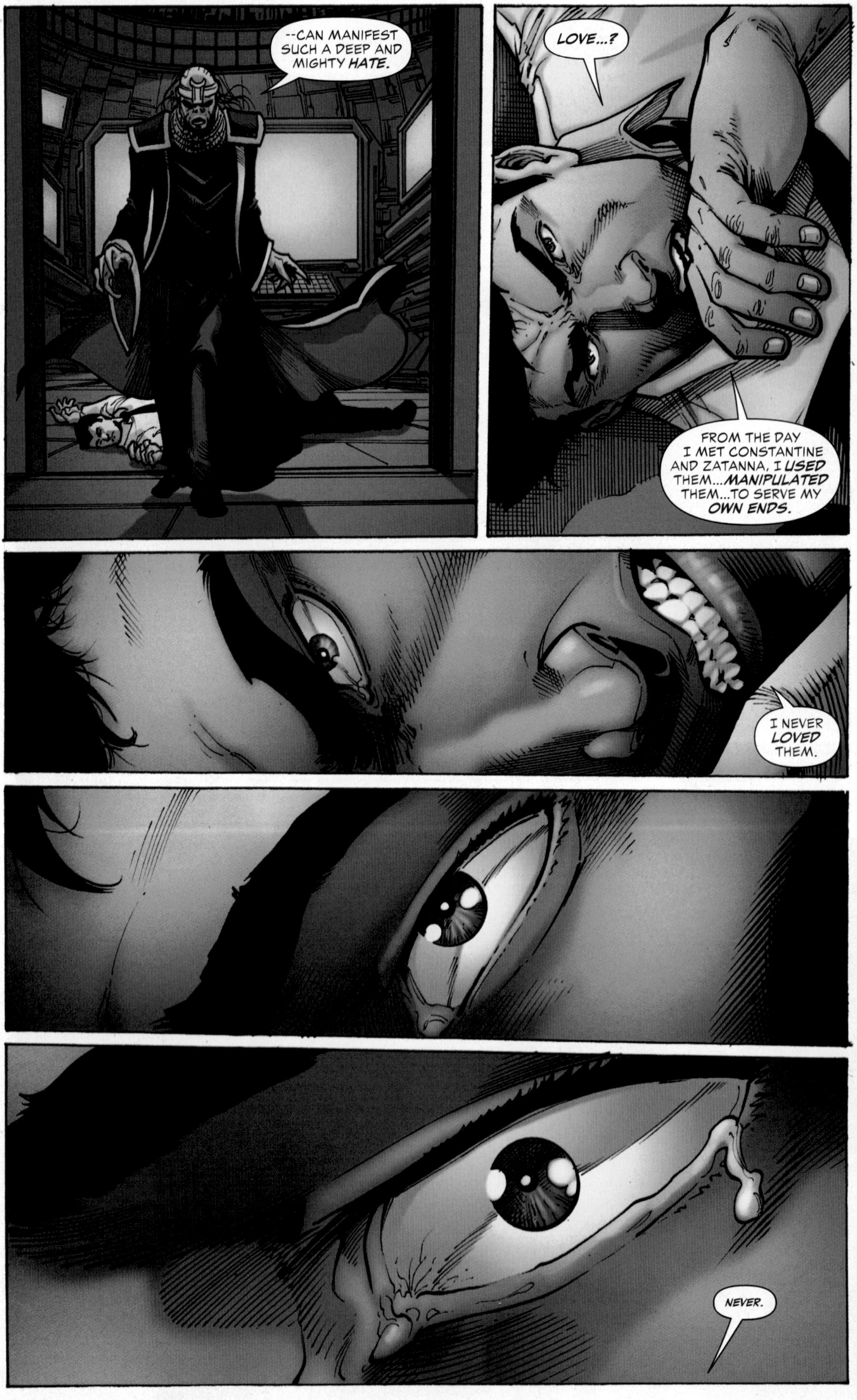
--CAN MANIFEST SUCH A DEEP AND MIGHTY HATE.
LOVE...?
FROM THE DAY I MET CONSTANTINE AND ZATANNA, I USED THEM...MANIPULATED THEM...TO SERVE MY OWN ENDS.
I NEVER LOVED THEM.
NEVER.

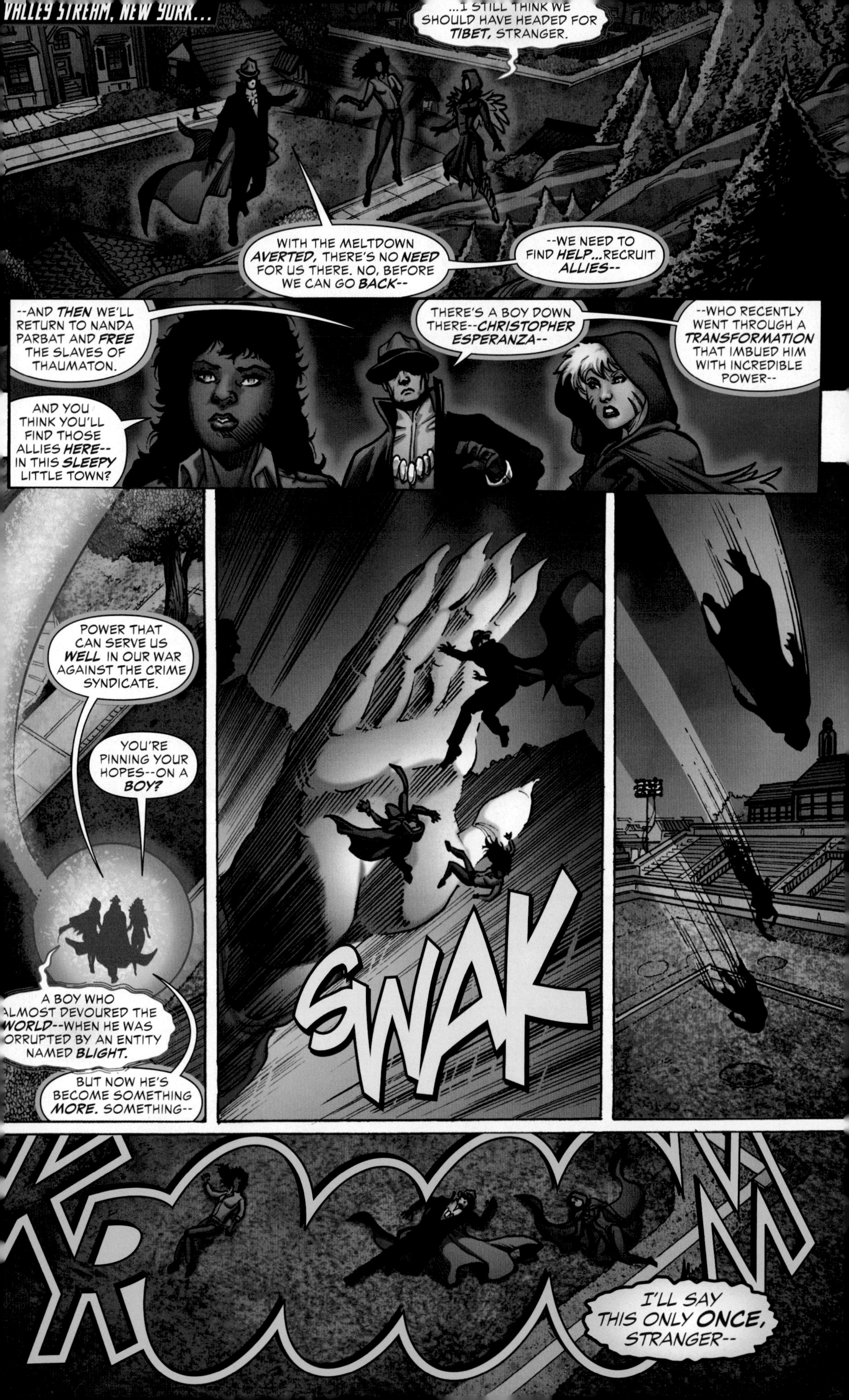
VALLEY STREAM, NEW YORK...
...I STILL THINK WE SHOULD HAVE HEADED FOR TIBET, STRANGER.
WITH THE MELTDOWN AVERTED, THERE'S NO NEED FOR US THERE. NO, BEFORE WE CAN GO BACK--
--WE NEED TO FIND HELP...RECRUIT ALLIES--
--AND THEN WE'LL RETURN TO NANDA PARBAT AND FREE THE SLAVES OF THAUMATON.
AND YOU THINK YOU'LL FIND THOSE ALLIES HERE-- IN THIS SLEEPY LITTLE TOWN?
THERE'S A BOY DOWN THERE--CHRISTOPHER ESPERANZA--
--WHO RECENTLY WENT THROUGH A TRANSFORMATION THAT IMBUED HIM WITH INCREDIBLE POWER--
POWER THAT CAN SERVE US WELL IN OUR WAR AGAINST THE CRIME SYNDICATE.
YOU'RE PINNING YOUR HOPES--ON A BOY?
A BOY WHO ALMOST DEVOURED THE WORLD--WHEN HE WAS CORRUPTED BY AN ENTITY NAMED BLIGHT.
BUT NOW HE'S BECOME SOMETHING MORE. SOMETHING--
SWAK
I'LL SAY THIS ONLY ONCE, STRANGER--

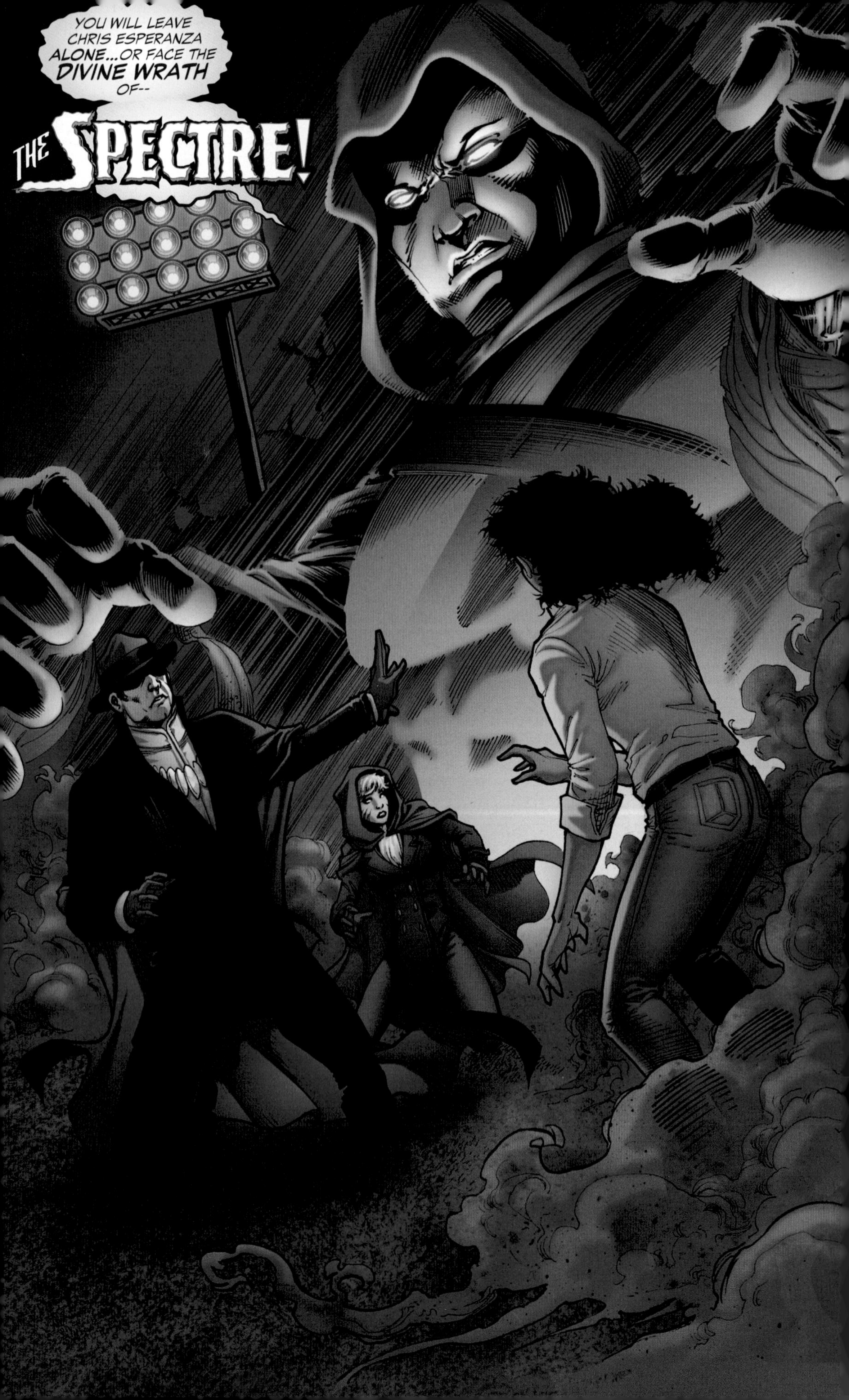
YOU WILL LEAVE CHRIS ESPERANZA ALONE...OR FACE THE DIVINE WRATH OF--
THE SPECTRE!

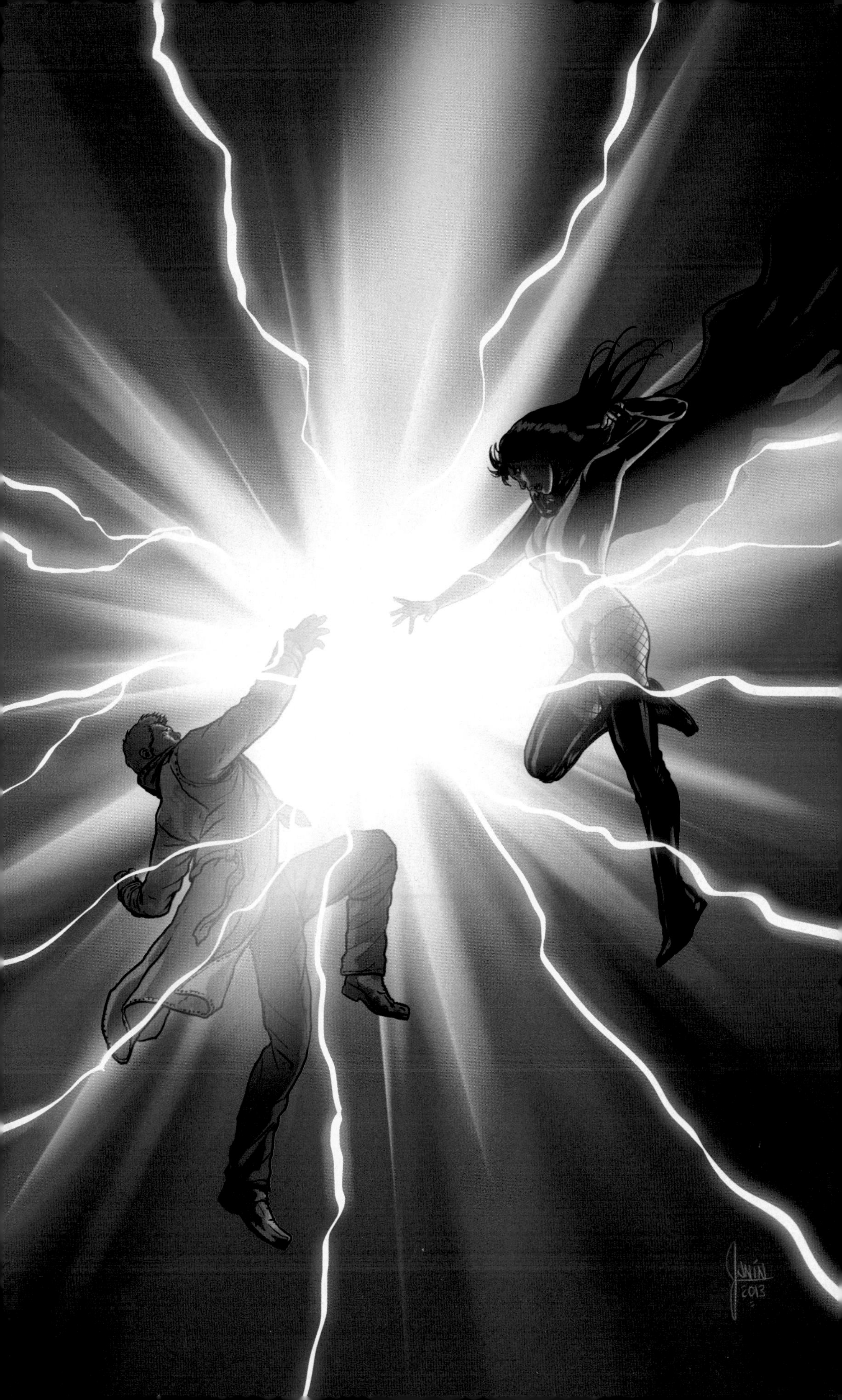

J. M. DeMATTEIS
writer

VINCENTE CIFUENTES
artist

TOM DERENICK
breakdown artist

MIKEL JANIN
cover artist

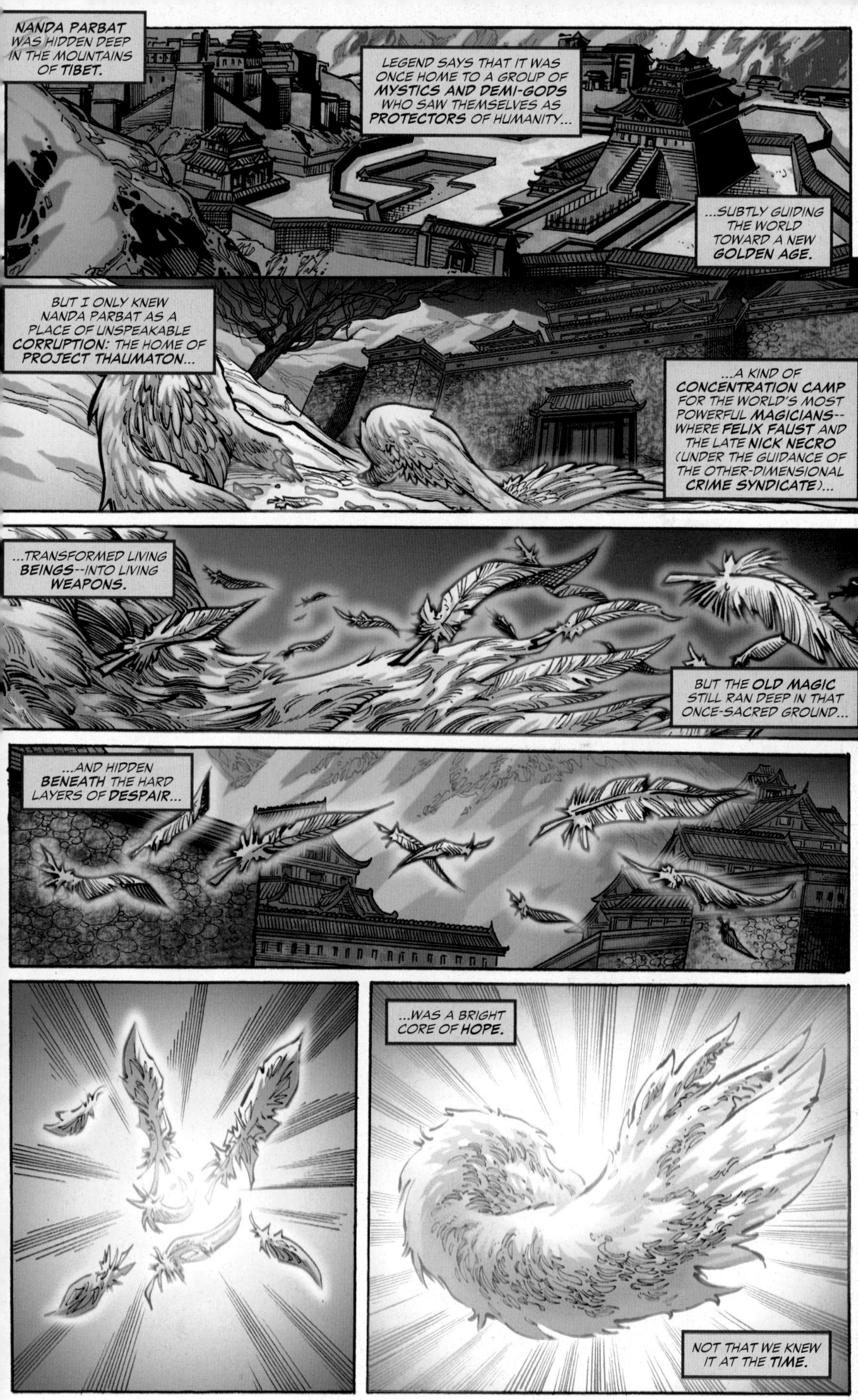
NANDA PARBAT WAS HIDDEN DEEP IN THE MOUNTAINS OF TIBET.
LEGEND SAYS THAT IT WAS ONCE HOME TO A GROUP OF MYSTICS AND DEMI-GODS WHO SAW THEMSELVES AS PROTECTORS OF HUMANITY...
...SUBTLY GUIDING THE WORLD TOWARD A NEW GOLDEN AGE.
BUT I ONLY KNEW NANDA PARBAT AS A PLACE OF UNSPEAKABLE CORRUPTION: THE HOME OF PROJECT THAUMATON...
...A KIND OF CONCENTRATION CAMP FOR THE WORLD'S MOST POWERFUL MAGICIANS-- WHERE FELIX FAUST AND THE LATE NICK NECRO (UNDER THE GUIDANCE OF THE OTHER-DIMENSIONAL CRIME SYNDICATE)...
...TRANSFORMED LIVING BEINGS--INTO LIVING WEAPONS.
BUT THE OLD MAGIC STILL RAN DEEP IN THAT ONCE-SACRED GROUND...
...AND HIDDEN BENEATH THE HARD LAYERS OF DESPAIR...
...WAS A BRIGHT CORE OF HOPE.
NOT THAT WE KNEW IT AT THE TIME.

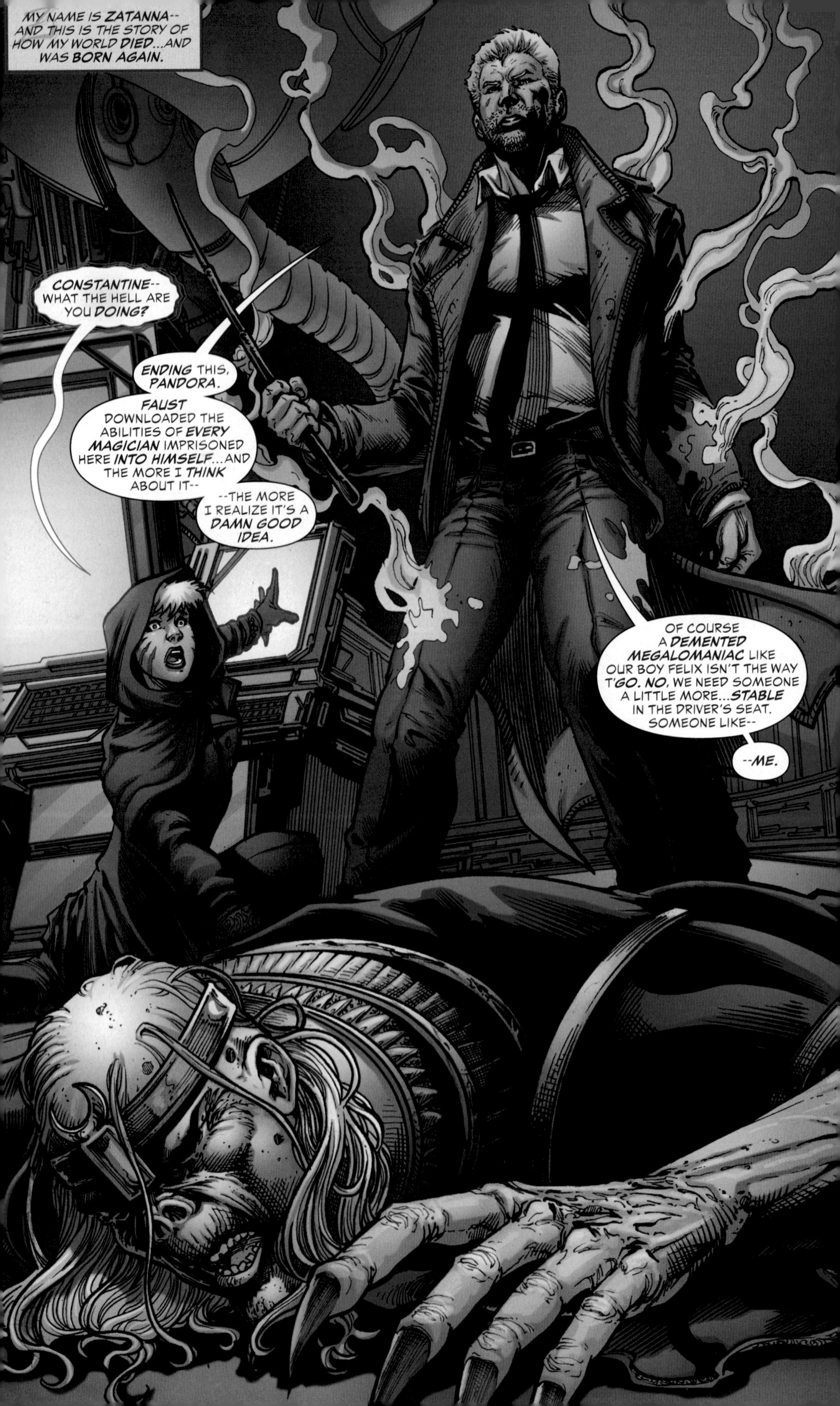

MY NAME IS ZATANNA-- AND THIS IS THE STORY OF HOW MY WORLD DIED...AND WAS BORN AGAIN.
CONSTANTINE-- WHAT THE HELL ARE YOU DOING?
ENDING THIS, PANDORA.
FAUST DOWNLOADED THE ABILITIES OF EVERY MAGICIAN IMPRISONED HERE INTO HIMSELF...AND THE MORE I THINK ABOUT IT--
--THE MORE I REALIZE IT'S A DAMN GOOD IDEA.
OF COURSE A DEMENTED MEGALOMANIAC LIKE OUR BOY FELIX ISN'T THE WAY T'GO. NO, WE NEED SOMEONE A LITTLE MORE...STABLE IN THE DRIVER'S SEAT. SOMEONE LIKE--
--ME.

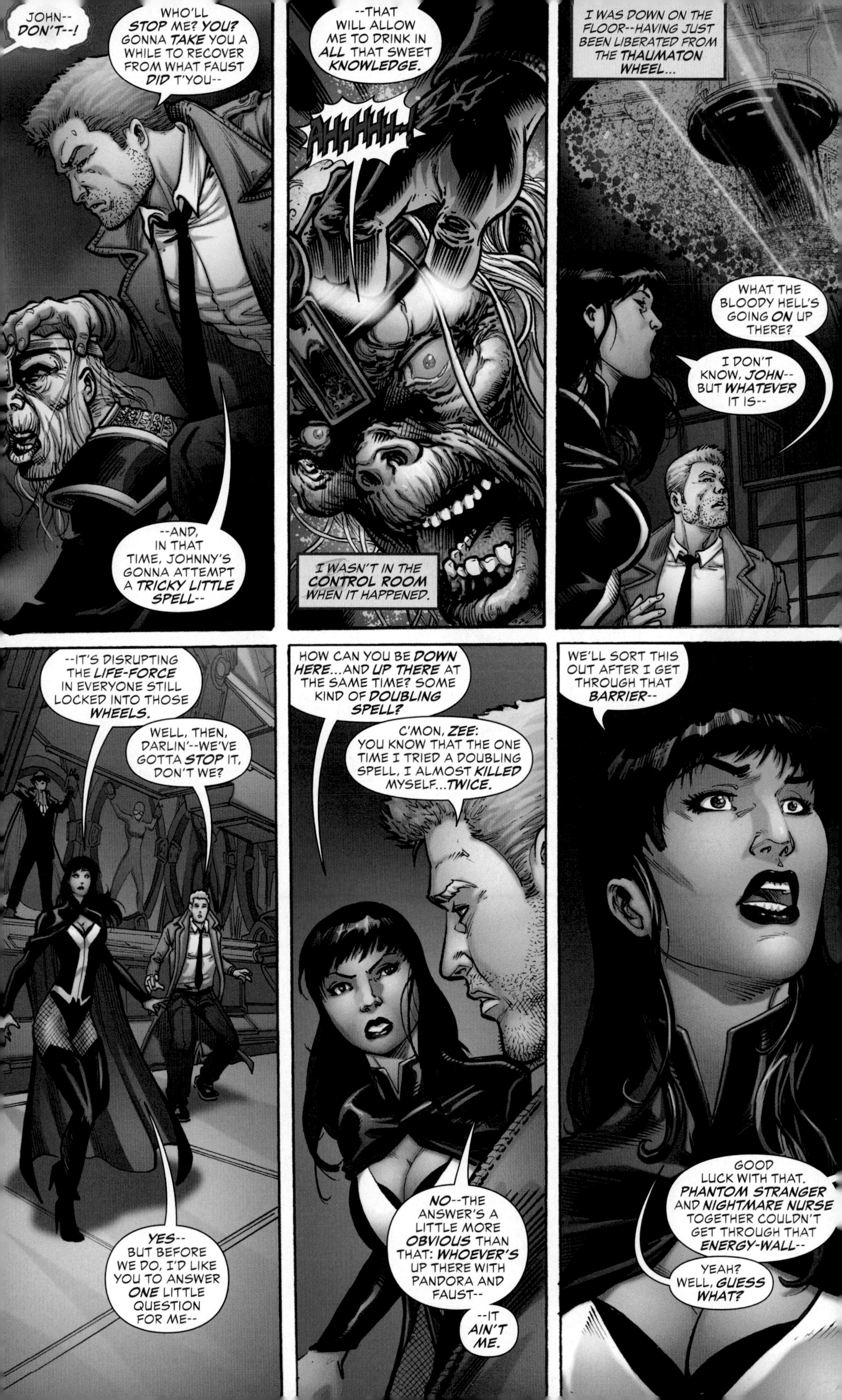

JOHN-- DON'T--!
WHO'LL STOP ME? YOU? GONNA TAKE YOU A WHILE TO RECOVER FROM WHAT FAUST DID T'YOU--
--AND, IN THAT TIME, JOHNNY'S GONNA ATTEMPT A TRICKY LITTLE SPELL--
--THAT WILL ALLOW ME TO DRINK IN ALL THAT SWEET KNOWLEDGE.
AHHHHH--!
I WASN'T IN THE CONTROL ROOM WHEN IT HAPPENED.
I WAS DOWN ON THE FLOOR--HAVING JUST BEEN LIBERATED FROM THE THAUMATON WHEEL...
WHAT THE BLOODY HELL'S GOING ON UP THERE?
I DON'T KNOW, JOHN--BUT WHATEVER IT IS--
--IT'S DISRUPTING THE LIFE-FORCE IN EVERYONE STILL LOCKED INTO THOSE WHEELS.
WELL, THEN, DARLIN'--WE'VE GOTTA STOP IT, DON'T WE?
YES--BUT BEFORE WE DO, I'D LIKE YOU TO ANSWER ONE LITTLE QUESTION FOR ME--
HOW CAN YOU BE DOWN HERE...AND UP THERE AT THE SAME TIME? SOME KIND OF DOUBLING SPELL?
C'MON, ZEE: YOU KNOW THAT THE ONE TIME I TRIED A DOUBLING SPELL, I ALMOST KILLED MYSELF...TWICE.
NO--THE ANSWER'S A LITTLE MORE OBVIOUS THAN THAT: WHOEVER'S UP THERE WITH PANDORA AND FAUST--
--IT AIN'T ME.
WE'LL SORT THIS OUT AFTER I GET THROUGH THAT BARRIER--
GOOD LUCK WITH THAT. PHANTOM STRANGER AND NIGHTMARE NURSE TOGETHER COULDN'T GET THROUGH THAT ENERGY-WALL--
YEAH? WELL, GUESS WHAT?

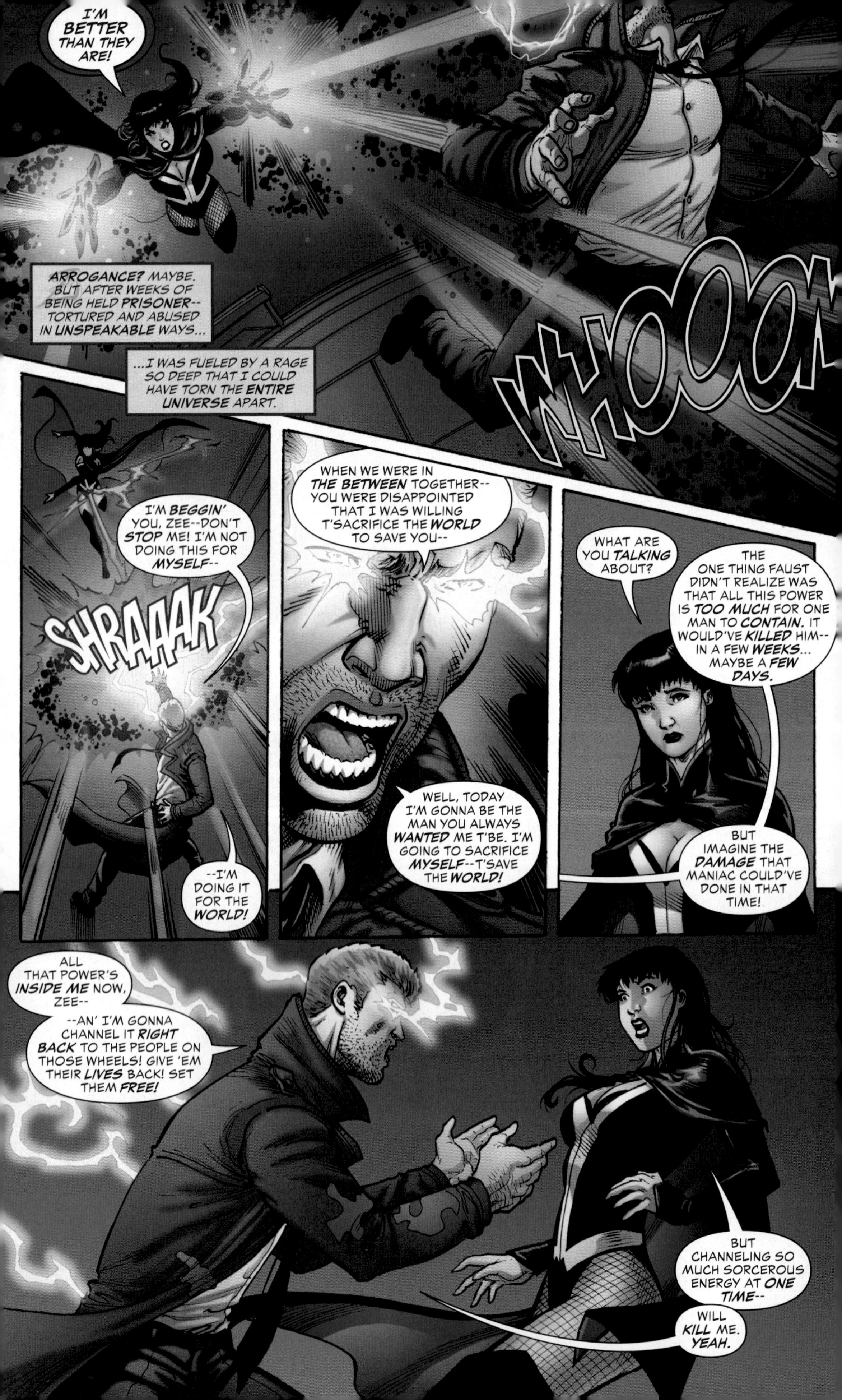
I'M BETTER THAN THEY ARE!
ARROGANCE? MAYBE. BUT AFTER WEEKS OF BEING HELD PRISONER-- TORTURED AND ABUSED IN UNSPEAKABLE WAYS...
...I WAS FUELED BY A RAGE SO DEEP THAT I COULD HAVE TORN THE ENTIRE UNIVERSE APART.
WHOOOOM
I'M BEGGIN' YOU, ZEE--DON'T STOP ME! I'M NOT DOING THIS FOR MYSELF--
SHRAAAK
--I'M DOING IT FOR THE WORLD!
WHEN WE WERE IN THE BETWEEN TOGETHER-- YOU WERE DISAPPOINTED THAT I WAS WILLING T'SACRIFICE THE WORLD TO SAVE YOU--
WELL, TODAY I'M GONNA BE THE MAN YOU ALWAYS WANTED ME T'BE. I'M GOING TO SACRIFICE MYSELF--T'SAVE THE WORLD!
WHAT ARE YOU TALKING ABOUT?
THE ONE THING FAUST DIDN'T REALIZE WAS THAT ALL THIS POWER IS TOO MUCH FOR ONE MAN TO CONTAIN. IT WOULD'VE KILLED HIM-- IN A FEW WEEKS... MAYBE A FEW DAYS.
BUT IMAGINE THE DAMAGE THAT MANIAC COULD'VE DONE IN THAT TIME!
ALL THAT POWER'S INSIDE ME NOW, ZEE--
--AN' I'M GONNA CHANNEL IT RIGHT BACK TO THE PEOPLE ON THOSE WHEELS! GIVE 'EM THEIR LIVES BACK! SET THEM FREE!
BUT CHANNELING SO MUCH SORCEROUS ENERGY AT ONE TIME--
WILL KILL ME. YEAH.

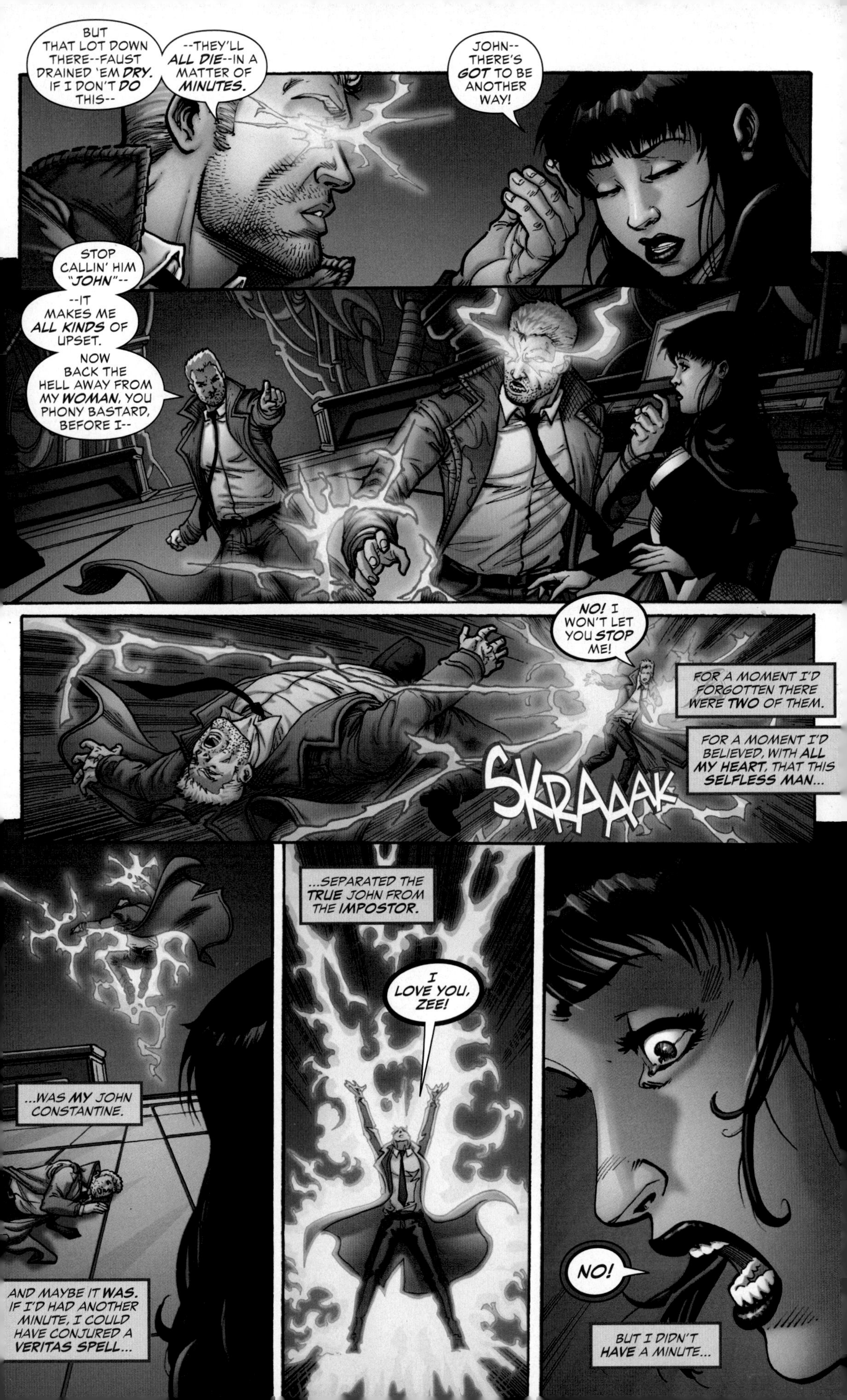
BUT THAT LOT DOWN THERE--FAUST DRAINED 'EM DRY. IF I DON'T DO THIS--
--THEY'LL ALL DIE--IN A MATTER OF MINUTES.
JOHN--THERE'S GOT TO BE ANOTHER WAY!
STOP CALLIN' HIM "JOHN"--
--IT MAKES ME ALL KINDS OF UPSET.
NOW BACK THE HELL AWAY FROM MY WOMAN, YOU PHONY BASTARD, BEFORE I--
NO! I WON'T LET YOU STOP ME!
FOR A MOMENT I'D FORGOTTEN THERE WERE TWO OF THEM.
FOR A MOMENT I'D BELIEVED, WITH ALL MY HEART, THAT THIS SELFLESS MAN...
SKRAAAK
...WAS MY JOHN CONSTANTINE.
AND MAYBE IT WAS. IF I'D HAD ANOTHER MINUTE, I COULD HAVE CONJURED A VERITAS SPELL...
...SEPARATED THE TRUE JOHN FROM THE IMPOSTOR.
I LOVE YOU, ZEE!
NO!
BUT I DIDN'T HAVE A MINUTE...

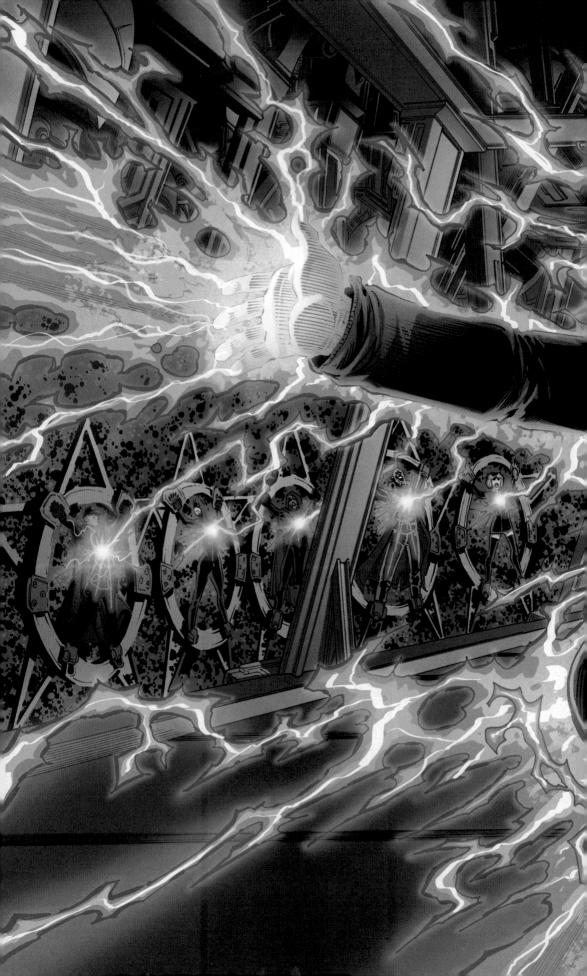

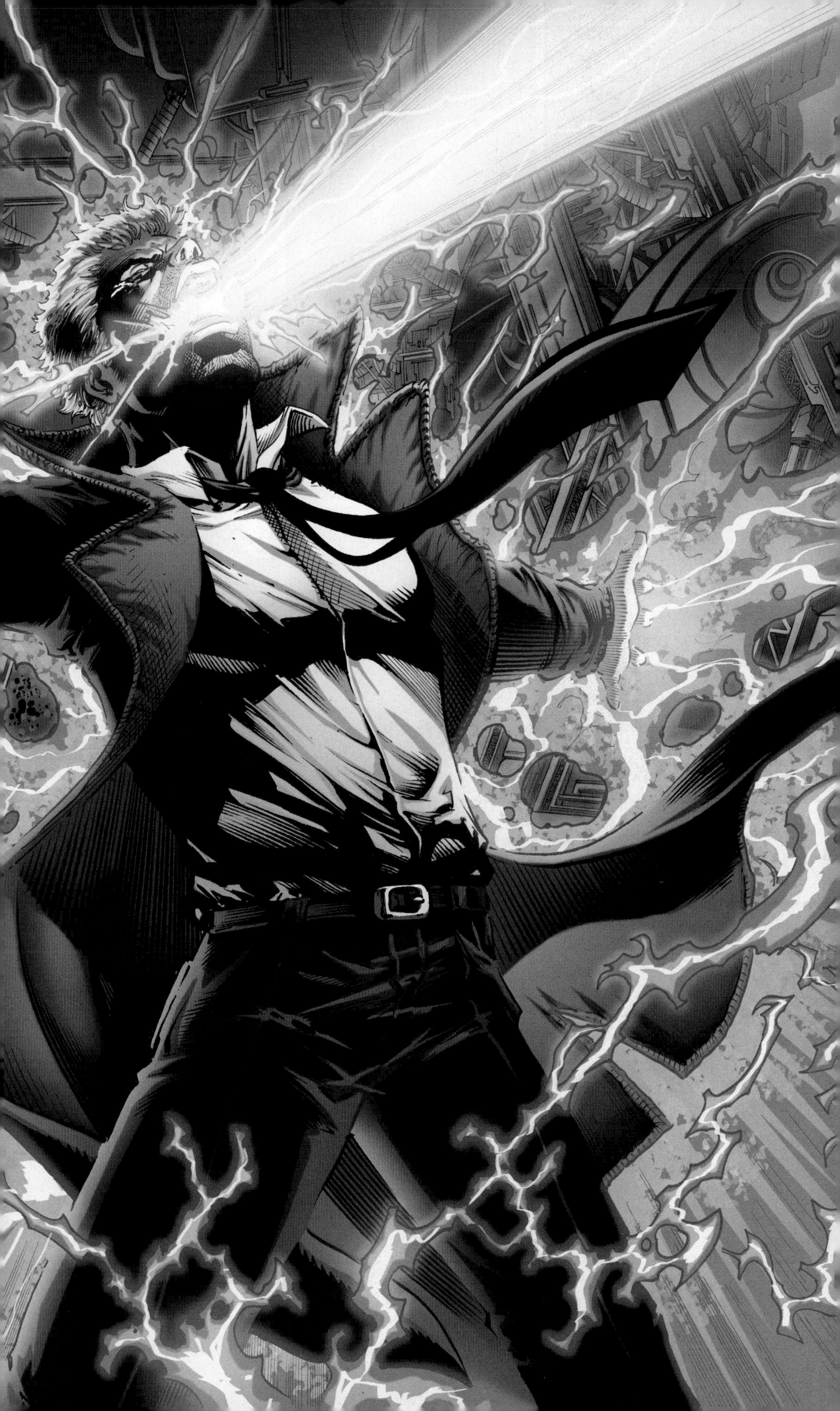

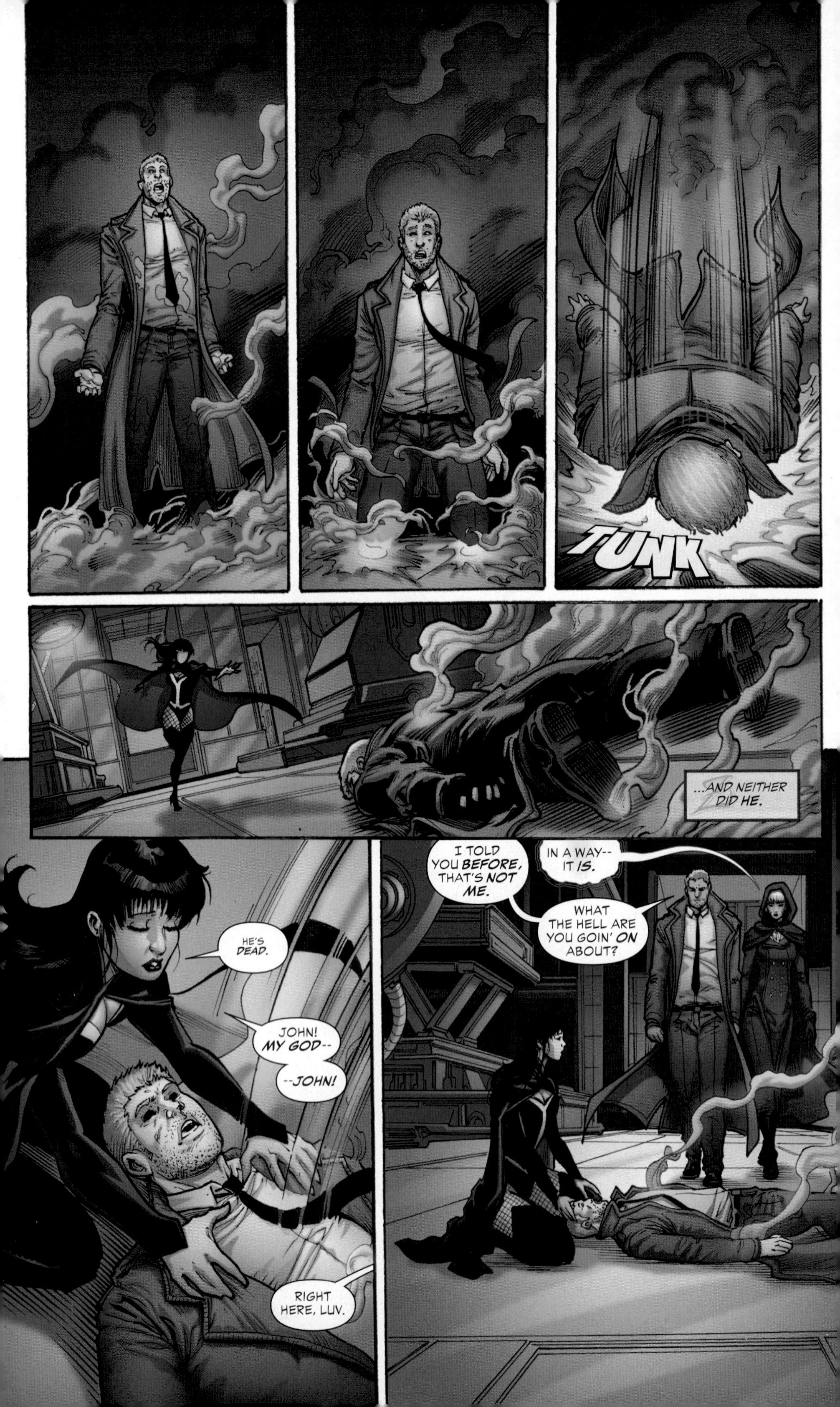
TUNK
...AND NEITHER DID HE.
HE'S DEAD.
JOHN! MY GOD--
--JOHN!
RIGHT HERE, LUV.
I TOLD YOU BEFORE, THAT'S NOT ME.
IN A WAY-- IT IS.
WHAT THE HELL ARE YOU GOIN' ON ABOUT?

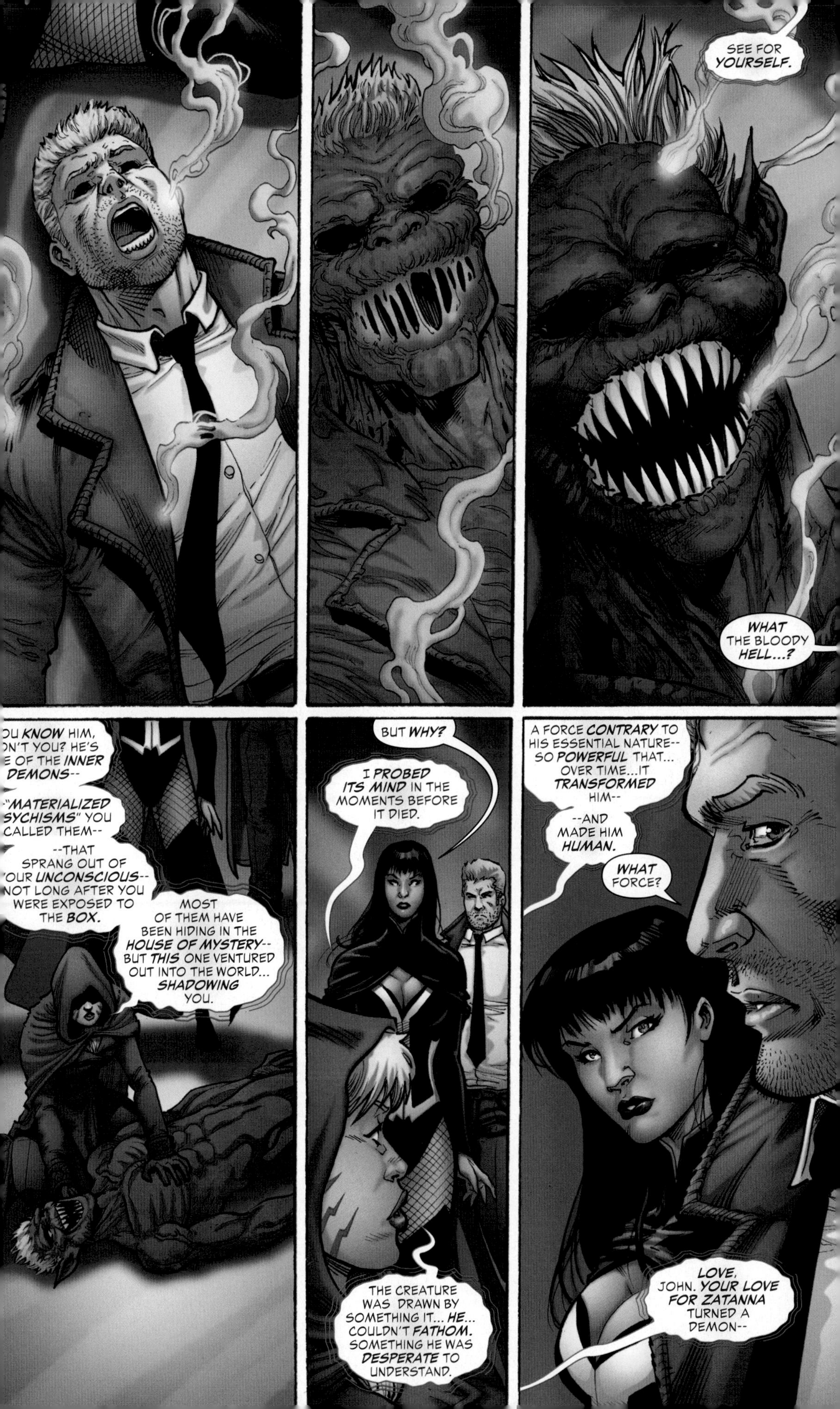
SEE FOR YOURSELF.
WHAT THE BLOODY HELL...?
OU KNOW HIM, ON'T YOU? HE'S E OF THE INNER DEMONS--
"MATERIALIZED SYCHISMS" YOU CALLED THEM--
--THAT SPRANG OUT OF OUR UNCONSCIOUS-- NOT LONG AFTER YOU WERE EXPOSED TO THE BOX.
MOST OF THEM HAVE BEEN HIDING IN THE HOUSE OF MYSTERY-- BUT THIS ONE VENTURED OUT INTO THE WORLD... SHADOWING YOU.
BUT WHY?
I PROBED ITS MIND IN THE MOMENTS BEFORE IT DIED.
THE CREATURE WAS DRAWN BY SOMETHING IT... HE... COULDN'T FATHOM. SOMETHING HE WAS DESPERATE TO UNDERSTAND.
A FORCE CONTRARY TO HIS ESSENTIAL NATURE-- SO POWERFUL THAT... OVER TIME...IT TRANSFORMED HIM--
--AND MADE HIM HUMAN.
WHAT FORCE?
LOVE. JOHN. YOUR LOVE FOR ZATANNA TURNED A DEMON--

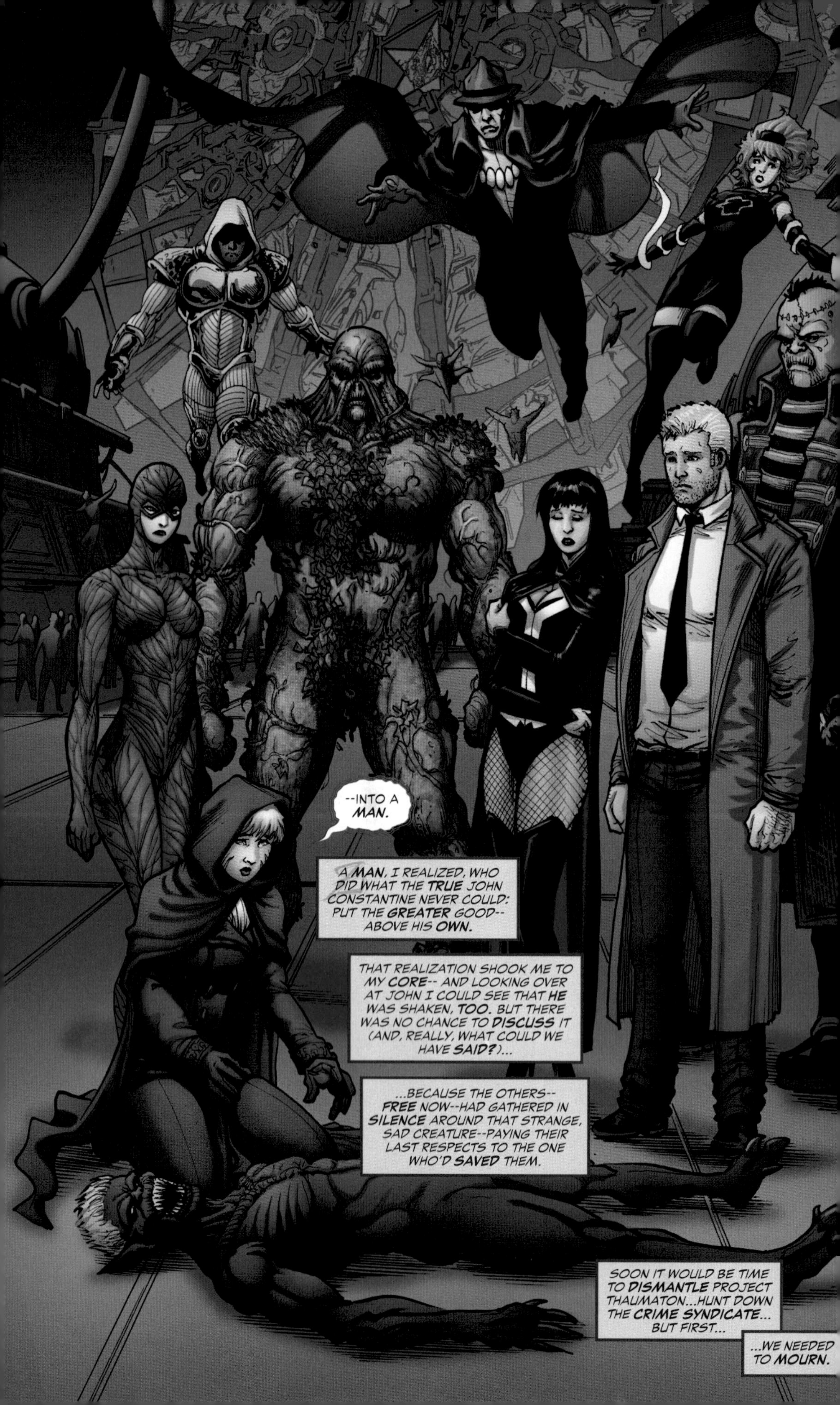
--INTO A MAN.
A MAN, I REALIZED, WHO DID WHAT THE TRUE JOHN CONSTANTINE NEVER COULD: PUT THE GREATER GOOD-- ABOVE HIS OWN.
THAT REALIZATION SHOOK ME TO MY CORE-- AND LOOKING OVER AT JOHN I COULD SEE THAT HE WAS SHAKEN, TOO. BUT THERE WAS NO CHANCE TO DISCUSS IT (AND, REALLY, WHAT COULD WE HAVE SAID?)...
...BECAUSE THE OTHERS-- FREE NOW--HAD GATHERED IN SILENCE AROUND THAT STRANGE, SAD CREATURE--PAYING THEIR LAST RESPECTS TO THE ONE WHO'D SAVED THEM.
SOON IT WOULD BE TIME TO DISMANTLE PROJECT THAUMATON...HUNT DOWN THE CRIME SYNDICATE... BUT FIRST...
...WE NEEDED TO MOURN.

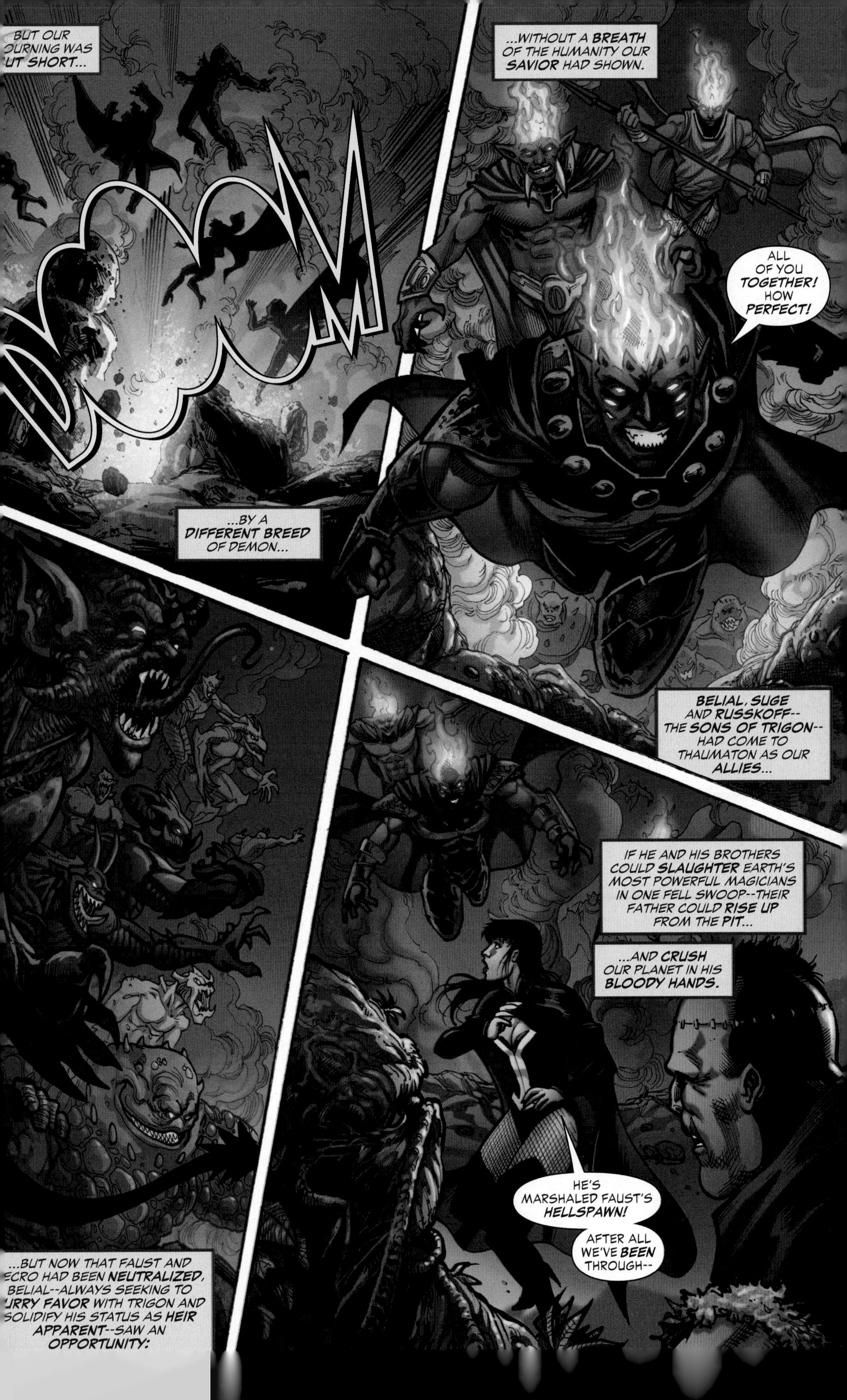
BUT OUR
OURNING WAS
UT SHORT...
...BY A
DIFFERENT BREED
OF DEMON...
...WITHOUT A BREATH
OF THE HUMANITY OUR
SAVIOR HAD SHOWN.
ALL
OF YOU
TOGETHER!
HOW
PERFECT!
BELIAL, SUGE
AND RUSSKOFF--
THE SONS OF TRIGON--
HAD COME TO
THAUMATON AS OUR
ALLIES...
...BUT NOW THAT FAUST AND
ECRO HAD BEEN NEUTRALIZED,
BELIAL--ALWAYS SEEKING TO
URRY FAVOR WITH TRIGON AND
SOLIDIFY HIS STATUS AS HEIR
APPARENT--SAW AN
OPPORTUNITY:
IF HE AND HIS BROTHERS
COULD SLAUGHTER EARTH'S
MOST POWERFUL MAGICIANS
IN ONE FELL SWOOP--THEIR
FATHER COULD RISE UP
FROM THE PIT...
...AND CRUSH
OUR PLANET IN HIS
BLOODY HANDS.
HE'S
MARSHALED FAUST'S
HELLSPAWN!
AFTER ALL
WE'VE BEEN
THROUGH--

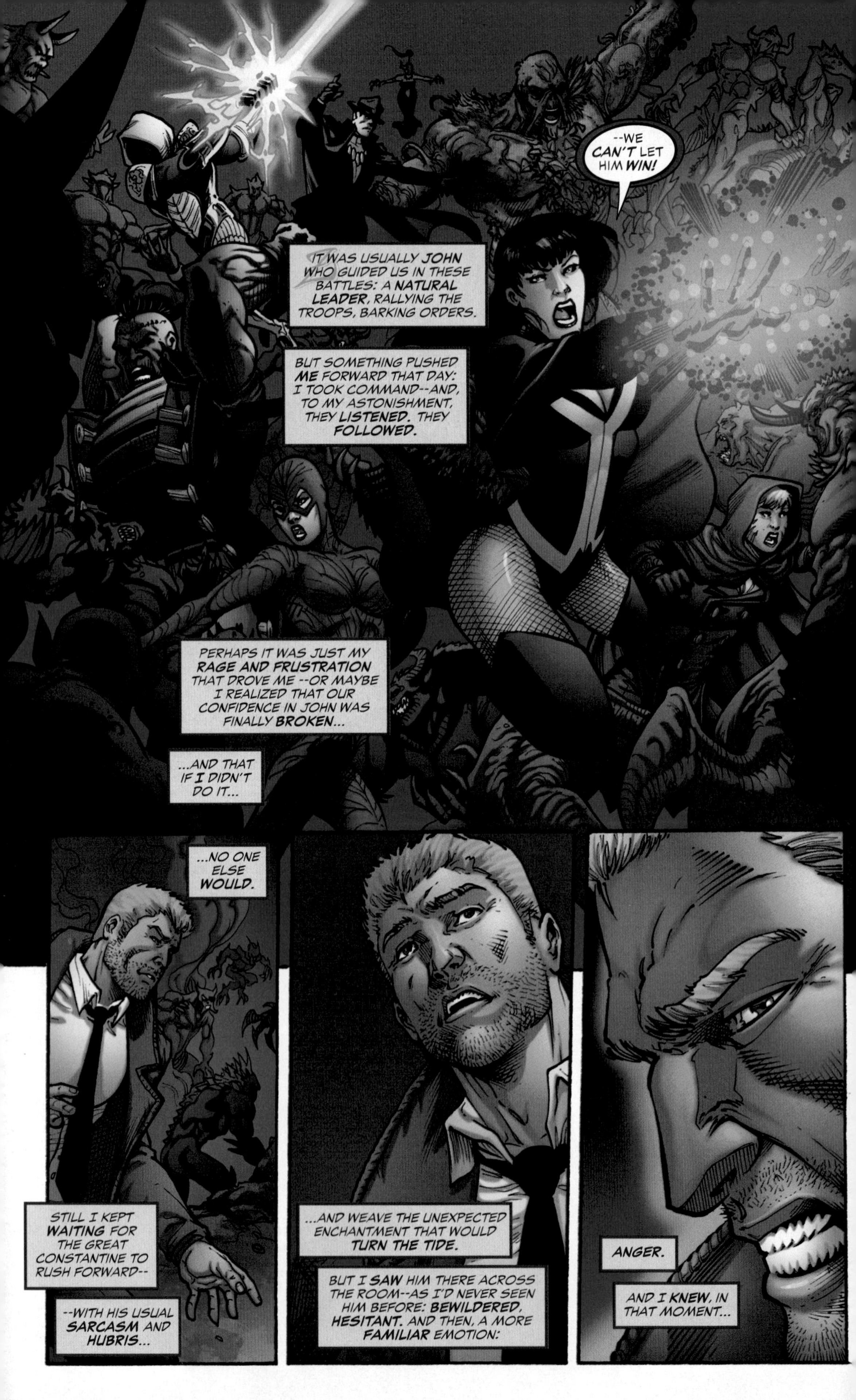
--WE CAN'T LET HIM WIN!
IT WAS USUALLY JOHN WHO GUIDED US IN THESE BATTLES: A NATURAL LEADER, RALLYING THE TROOPS, BARKING ORDERS.
BUT SOMETHING PUSHED ME FORWARD THAT DAY: I TOOK COMMAND--AND, TO MY ASTONISHMENT, THEY LISTENED. THEY FOLLOWED.
PERHAPS IT WAS JUST MY RAGE AND FRUSTRATION THAT DROVE ME --OR MAYBE I REALIZED THAT OUR CONFIDENCE IN JOHN WAS FINALLY BROKEN...
...AND THAT IF I DIDN'T DO IT...
...NO ONE ELSE WOULD.
STILL I KEPT WAITING FOR THE GREAT CONSTANTINE TO RUSH FORWARD--
--WITH HIS USUAL SARCASM AND HUBRIS...
...AND WEAVE THE UNEXPECTED ENCHANTMENT THAT WOULD TURN THE TIDE.
BUT I SAW HIM THERE ACROSS THE ROOM--AS I'D NEVER SEEN HIM BEFORE: BEWILDERED, HESITANT. AND THEN, A MORE FAMILIAR EMOTION:
ANGER.
AND I KNEW, IN THAT MOMENT...

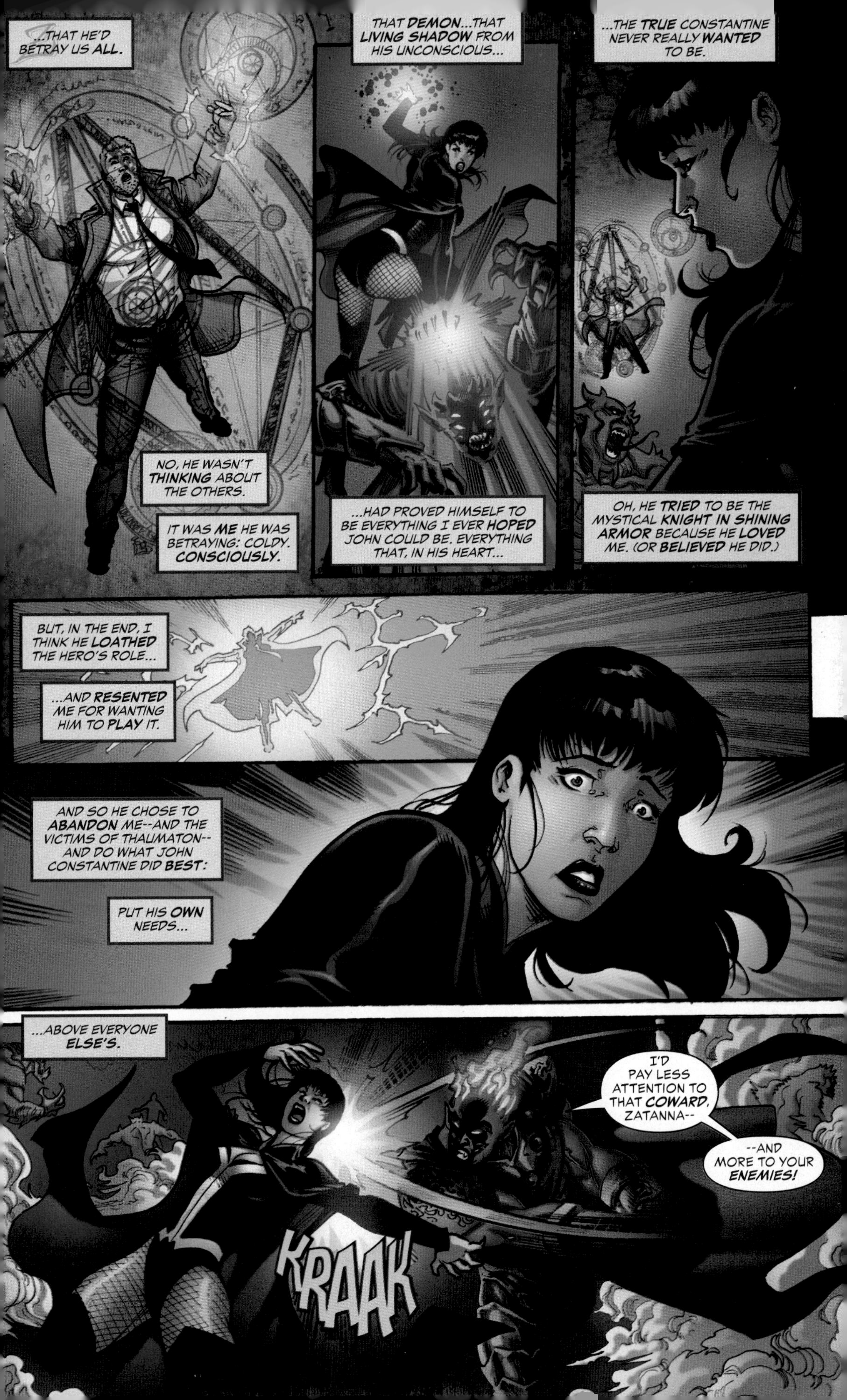

...THAT HE'D BETRAY US ALL.
NO, HE WASN'T THINKING ABOUT THE OTHERS.
IT WAS ME HE WAS BETRAYING: COLDY. CONSCIOUSLY.
THAT DEMON...THAT LIVING SHADOW FROM HIS UNCONSCIOUS...
...HAD PROVED HIMSELF TO BE EVERYTHING I EVER HOPED JOHN COULD BE. EVERYTHING THAT, IN HIS HEART...
...THE TRUE CONSTANTINE NEVER REALLY WANTED TO BE.
OH, HE TRIED TO BE THE MYSTICAL KNIGHT IN SHINING ARMOR BECAUSE HE LOVED ME. (OR BELIEVED HE DID.)
BUT, IN THE END, I THINK HE LOATHED THE HERO'S ROLE...
...AND RESENTED ME FOR WANTING HIM TO PLAY IT.
AND SO HE CHOSE TO ABANDON ME--AND THE VICTIMS OF THAUMATON--AND DO WHAT JOHN CONSTANTINE DID BEST:
PUT HIS OWN NEEDS...
...ABOVE EVERYONE ELSE'S.
I'D PAY LESS ATTENTION TO THAT COWARD, ZATANNA--
--AND MORE TO YOUR ENEMIES!
KRAAK

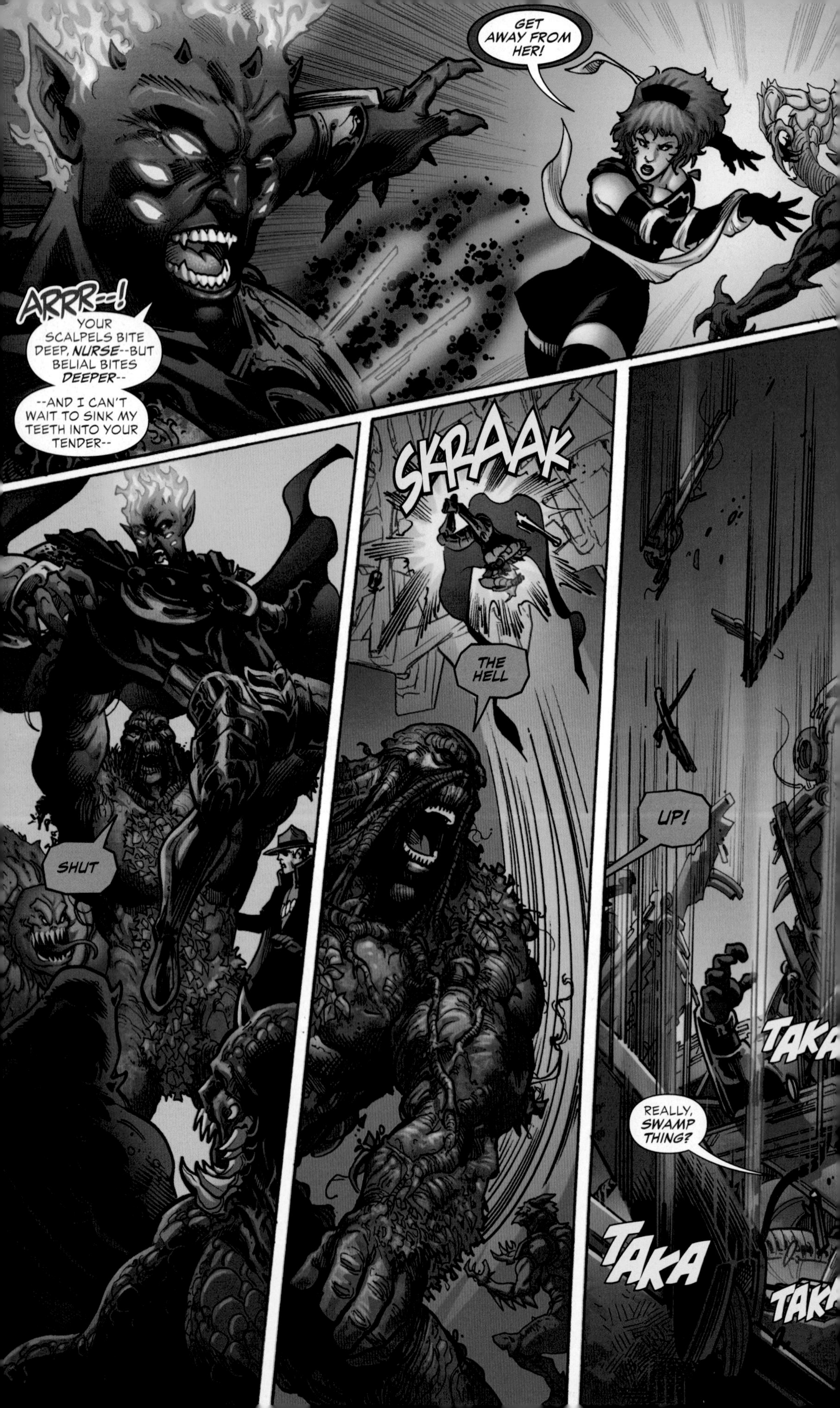
GET AWAY FROM HER!
ARRR--!
YOUR SCALPELS BITE DEEP, NURSE--BUT BELIAL BITES DEEPER--
--AND I CAN'T WAIT TO SINK MY TEETH INTO YOUR TENDER--
SHUT
SKRAAK
THE HELL
UP!
TAKA
REALLY, SWAMP THING?
TAKA

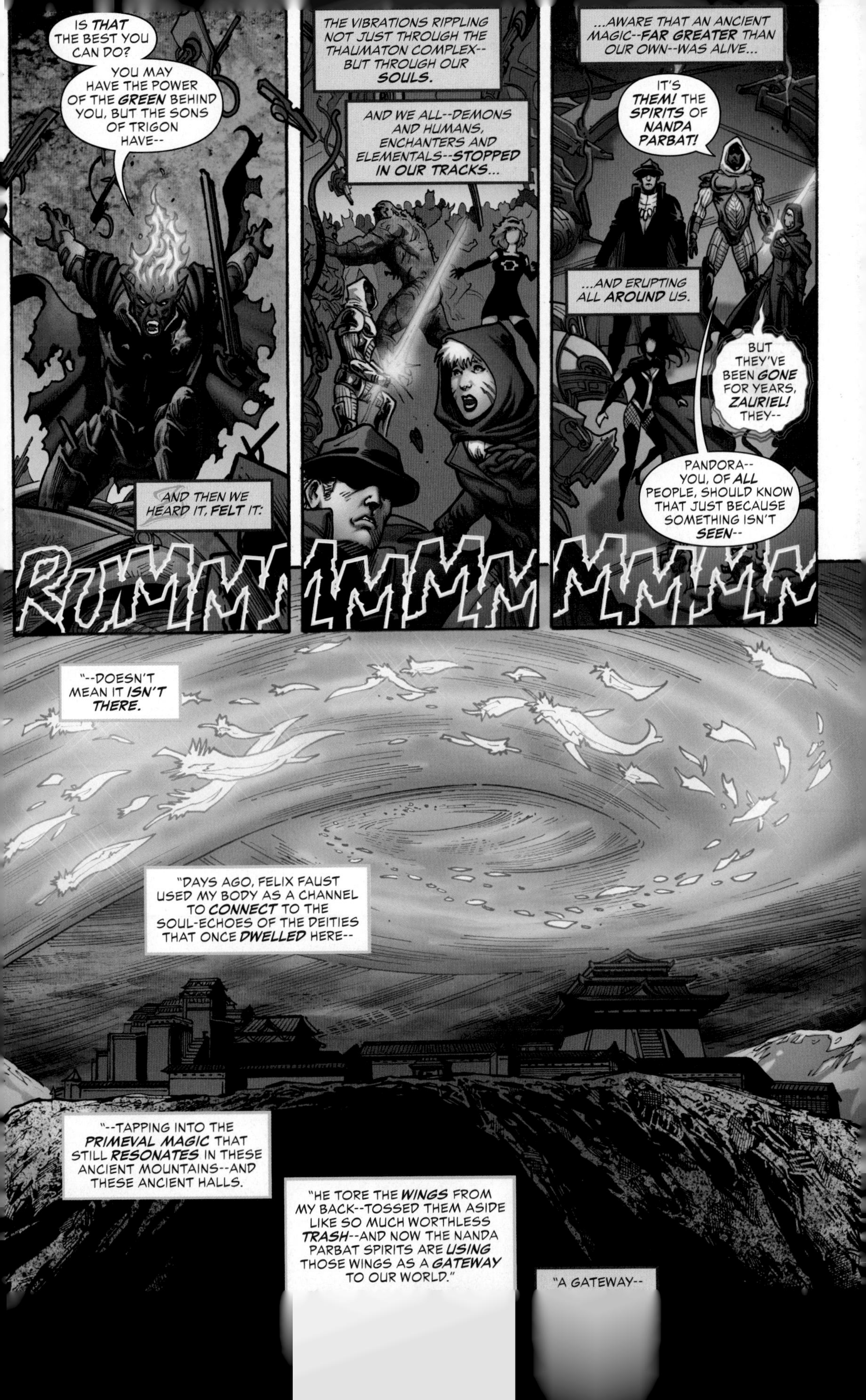
IS THAT THE BEST YOU CAN DO?
YOU MAY HAVE THE POWER OF THE GREEN BEHIND YOU, BUT THE SONS OF TRIGON HAVE--
AND THEN WE HEARD IT, FELT IT:
THE VIBRATIONS RIPPLING NOT JUST THROUGH THE THAUMATON COMPLEX--BUT THROUGH OUR SOULS.
AND WE ALL--DEMONS AND HUMANS, ENCHANTERS AND ELEMENTALS--STOPPED IN OUR TRACKS...
...AWARE THAT AN ANCIENT MAGIC--FAR GREATER THAN OUR OWN--WAS ALIVE...
IT'S THEM! THE SPIRITS OF NANDA PARBAT!
...AND ERUPTING ALL AROUND US.
BUT THEY'VE BEEN GONE FOR YEARS, ZAURIEL! THEY--
PANDORA--YOU, OF ALL PEOPLE, SHOULD KNOW THAT JUST BECAUSE SOMETHING ISN'T SEEN--
RUMMMMMMMMMMMMMN
"--DOESN'T MEAN IT ISN'T THERE.
"DAYS AGO, FELIX FAUST USED MY BODY AS A CHANNEL TO CONNECT TO THE SOUL-ECHOES OF THE DEITIES THAT ONCE DWELLED HERE--
"--TAPPING INTO THE PRIMEVAL MAGIC THAT STILL RESONATES IN THESE ANCIENT MOUNTAINS--AND THESE ANCIENT HALLS.
"HE TORE THE WINGS FROM MY BACK--TOSSED THEM ASIDE LIKE SO MUCH WORTHLESS TRASH--AND NOW THE NANDA PARBAT SPIRITS ARE USING THOSE WINGS AS A GATEWAY TO OUR WORLD."
"A GATEWAY--

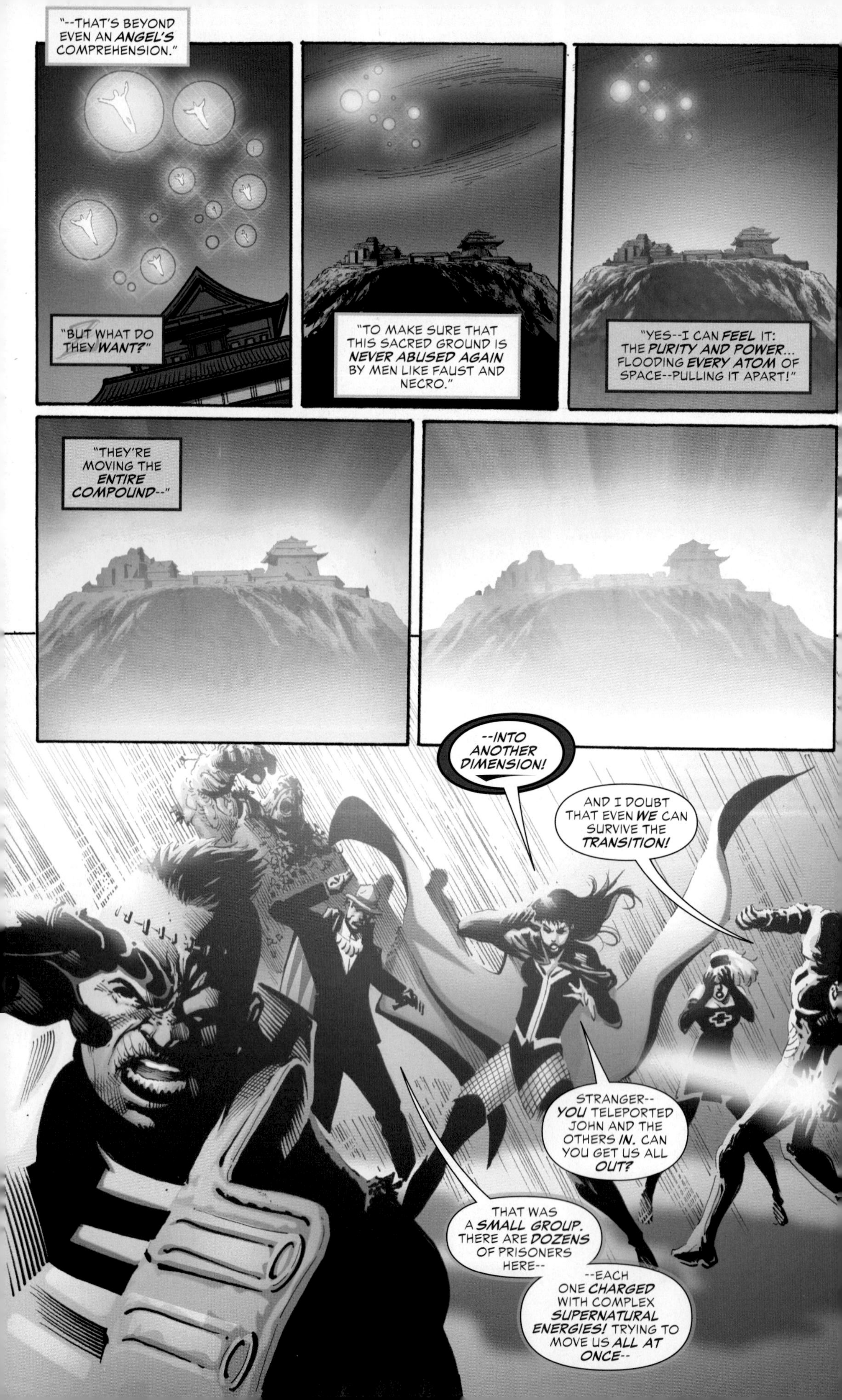

"--THAT'S BEYOND EVEN AN ANGEL'S COMPREHENSION."
"BUT WHAT DO THEY WANT?"
"TO MAKE SURE THAT THIS SACRED GROUND IS NEVER ABUSED AGAIN BY MEN LIKE FAUST AND NECRO."
"YES--I CAN FEEL IT: THE PURITY AND POWER... FLOODING EVERY ATOM OF SPACE--PULLING IT APART!"
"THEY'RE MOVING THE ENTIRE COMPOUND--"
--INTO ANOTHER DIMENSION!
AND I DOUBT THAT EVEN WE CAN SURVIVE THE TRANSITION!
STRANGER-- YOU TELEPORTED JOHN AND THE OTHERS IN. CAN YOU GET US ALL OUT?
THAT WAS A SMALL GROUP. THERE ARE DOZENS OF PRISONERS HERE--
--EACH ONE CHARGED WITH COMPLEX SUPERNATURAL ENERGIES! TRYING TO MOVE US ALL AT ONCE--

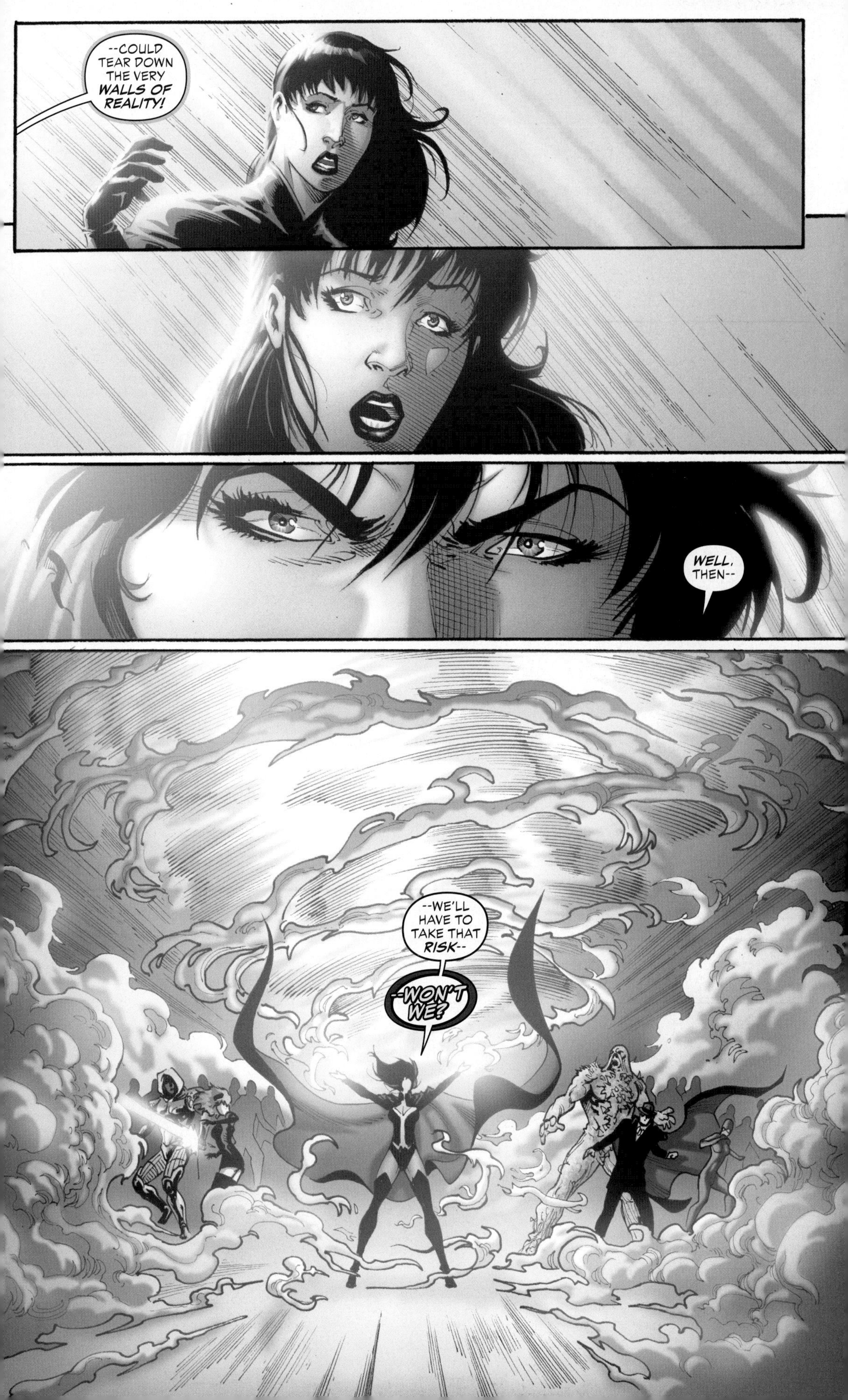
--COULD TEAR DOWN THE VERY WALLS OF REALITY!
WELL, THEN--
--WE'LL HAVE TO TAKE THAT RISK--
--WON'T WE?

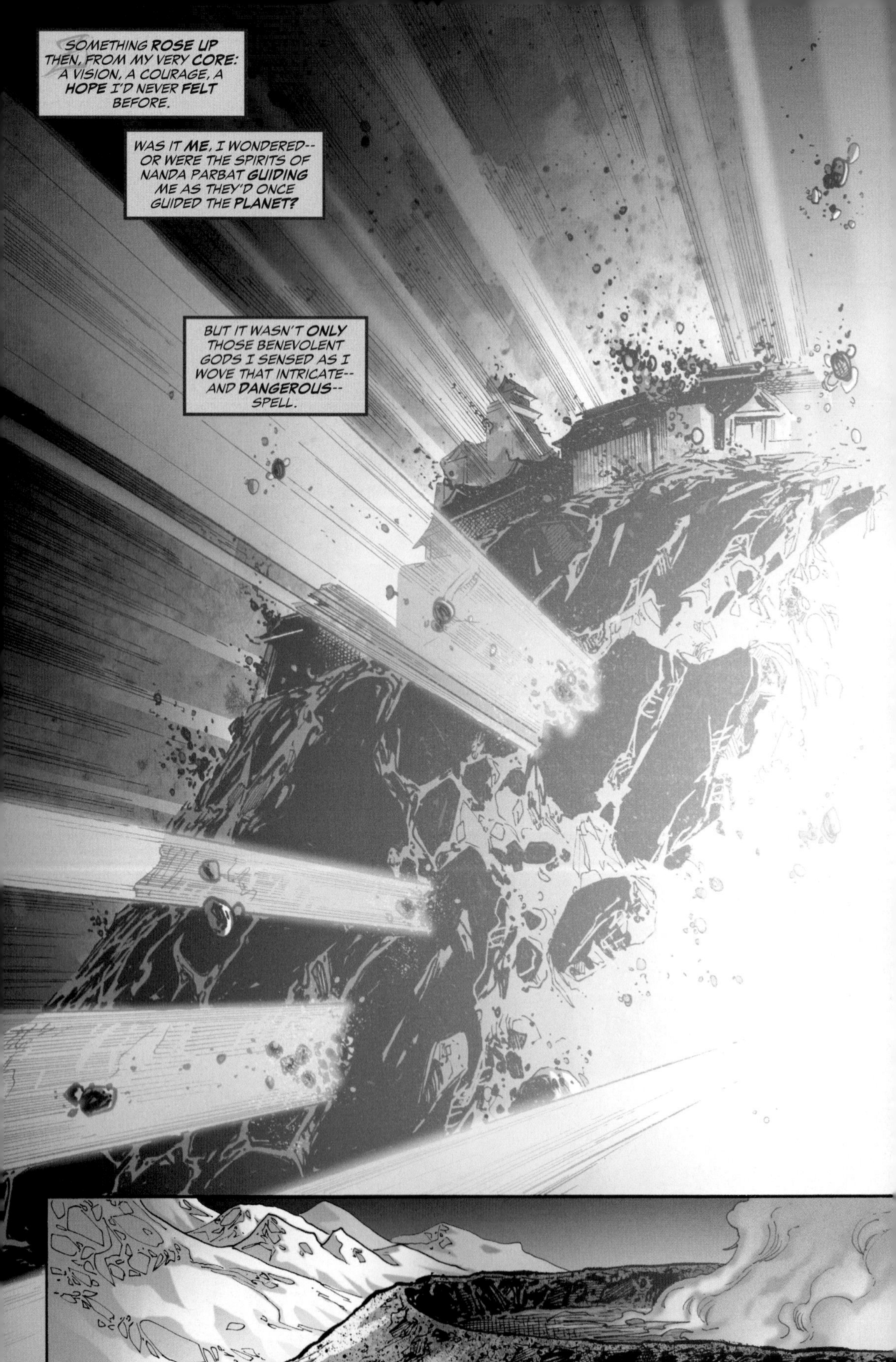
SOMETHING ROSE UP THEN, FROM MY VERY CORE: A VISION, A COURAGE, A HOPE I'D NEVER FELT BEFORE.
WAS IT ME, I WONDERED--OR WERE THE SPIRITS OF NANDA PARBAT GUIDING ME AS THEY'D ONCE GUIDED THE PLANET?
BUT IT WASN'T ONLY THOSE BENEVOLENT GODS I SENSED AS I WOVE THAT INTRICATE--AND DANGEROUS--SPELL.
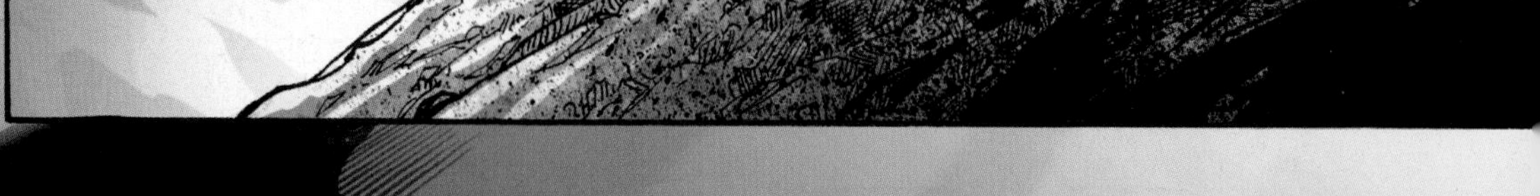

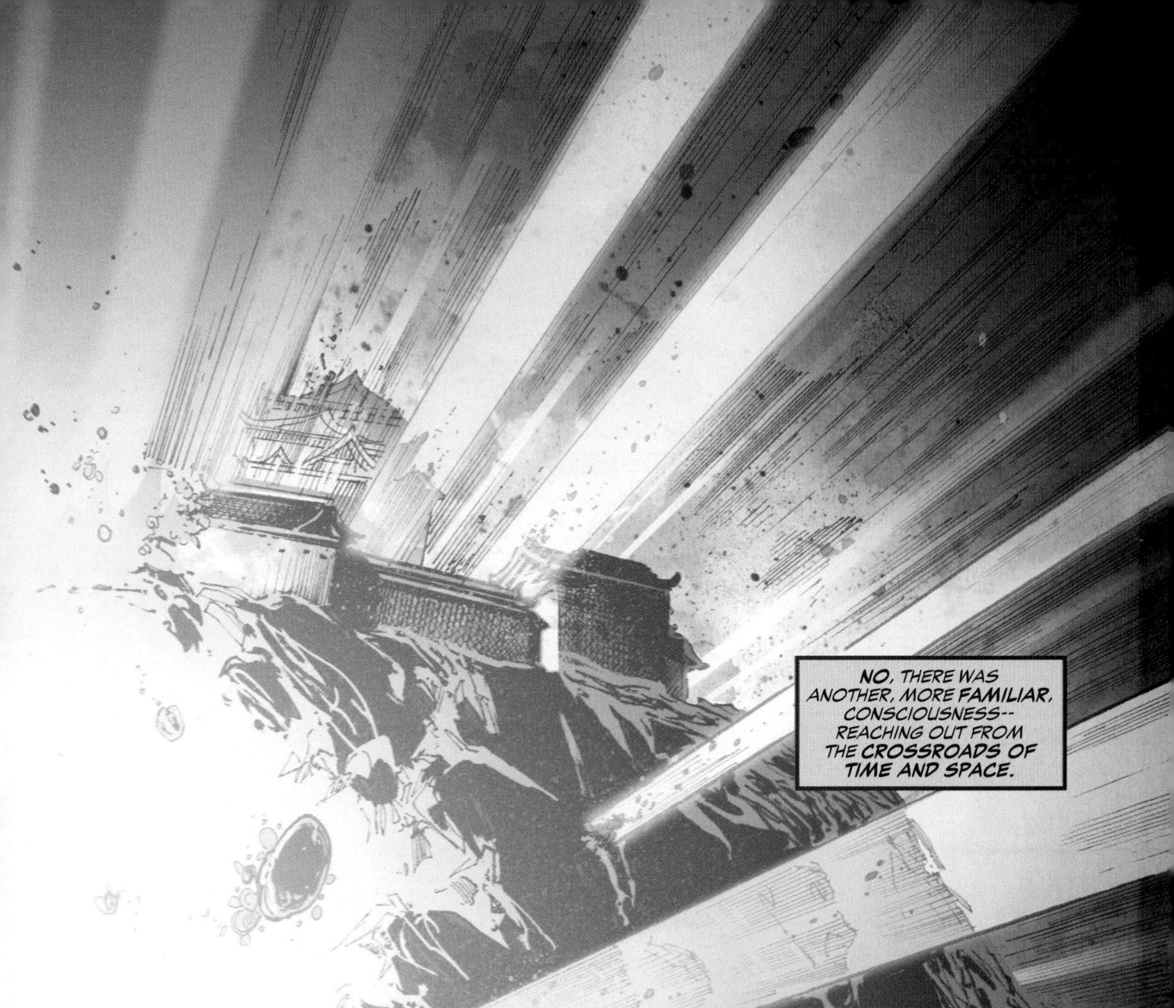
NO, THERE WAS ANOTHER, MORE FAMILIAR, CONSCIOUSNESS-- REACHING OUT FROM THE CROSSROADS OF TIME AND SPACE.

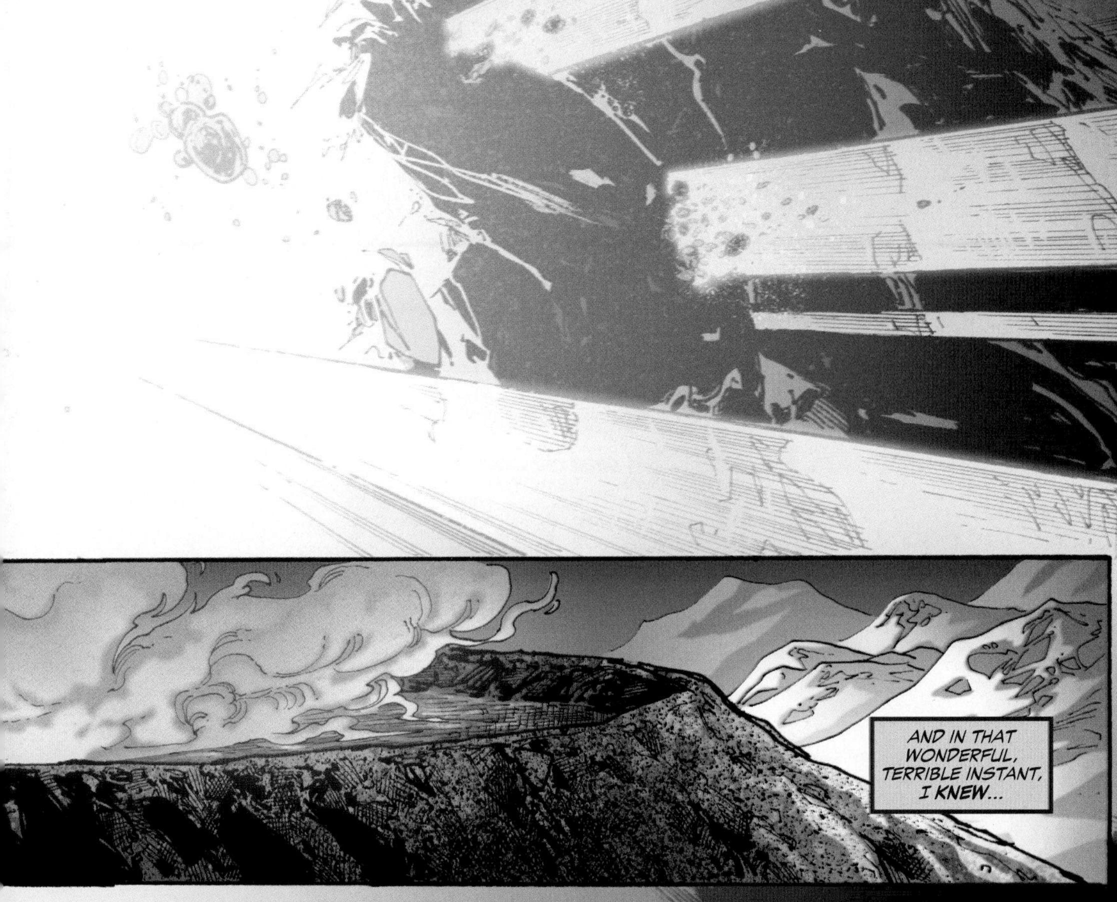
AND IN THAT WONDERFUL, TERRIBLE INSTANT, I KNEW...

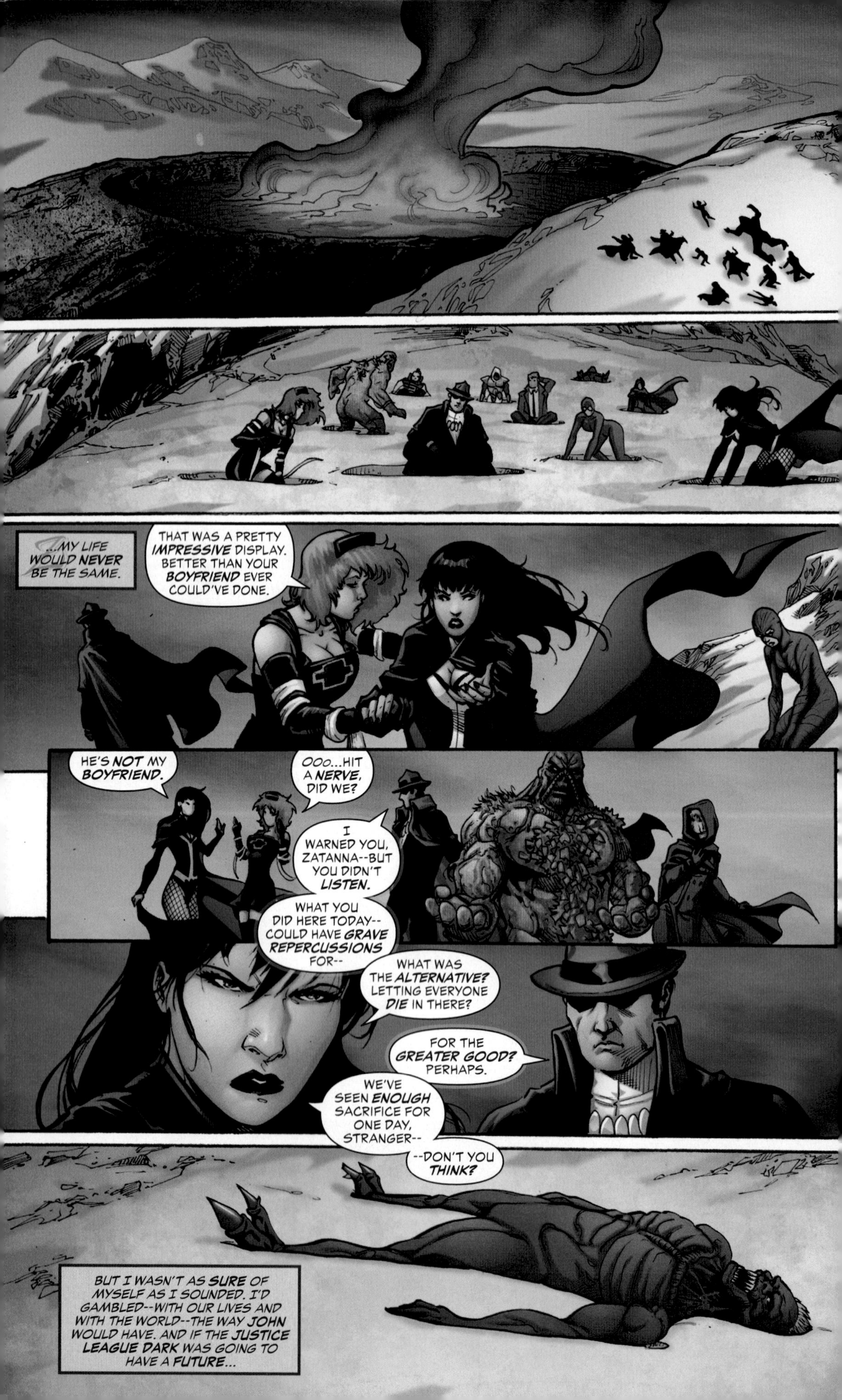
...MY LIFE WOULD NEVER BE THE SAME.
THAT WAS A PRETTY IMPRESSIVE DISPLAY. BETTER THAN YOUR BOYFRIEND EVER COULD'VE DONE.
HE'S NOT MY BOYFRIEND.
OOO...HIT A NERVE, DID WE?
I WARNED YOU, ZATANNA--BUT YOU DIDN'T LISTEN.
WHAT YOU DID HERE TODAY--COULD HAVE GRAVE REPERCUSSIONS FOR--
WHAT WAS THE ALTERNATIVE? LETTING EVERYONE DIE IN THERE?
FOR THE GREATER GOOD? PERHAPS.
WE'VE SEEN ENOUGH SACRIFICE FOR ONE DAY, STRANGER--
--DON'T YOU THINK?
BUT I WASN'T AS SURE OF MYSELF AS I SOUNDED. I'D GAMBLED--WITH OUR LIVES AND WITH THE WORLD--THE WAY JOHN WOULD HAVE. AND IF THE JUSTICE LEAGUE DARK WAS GOING TO HAVE A FUTURE...

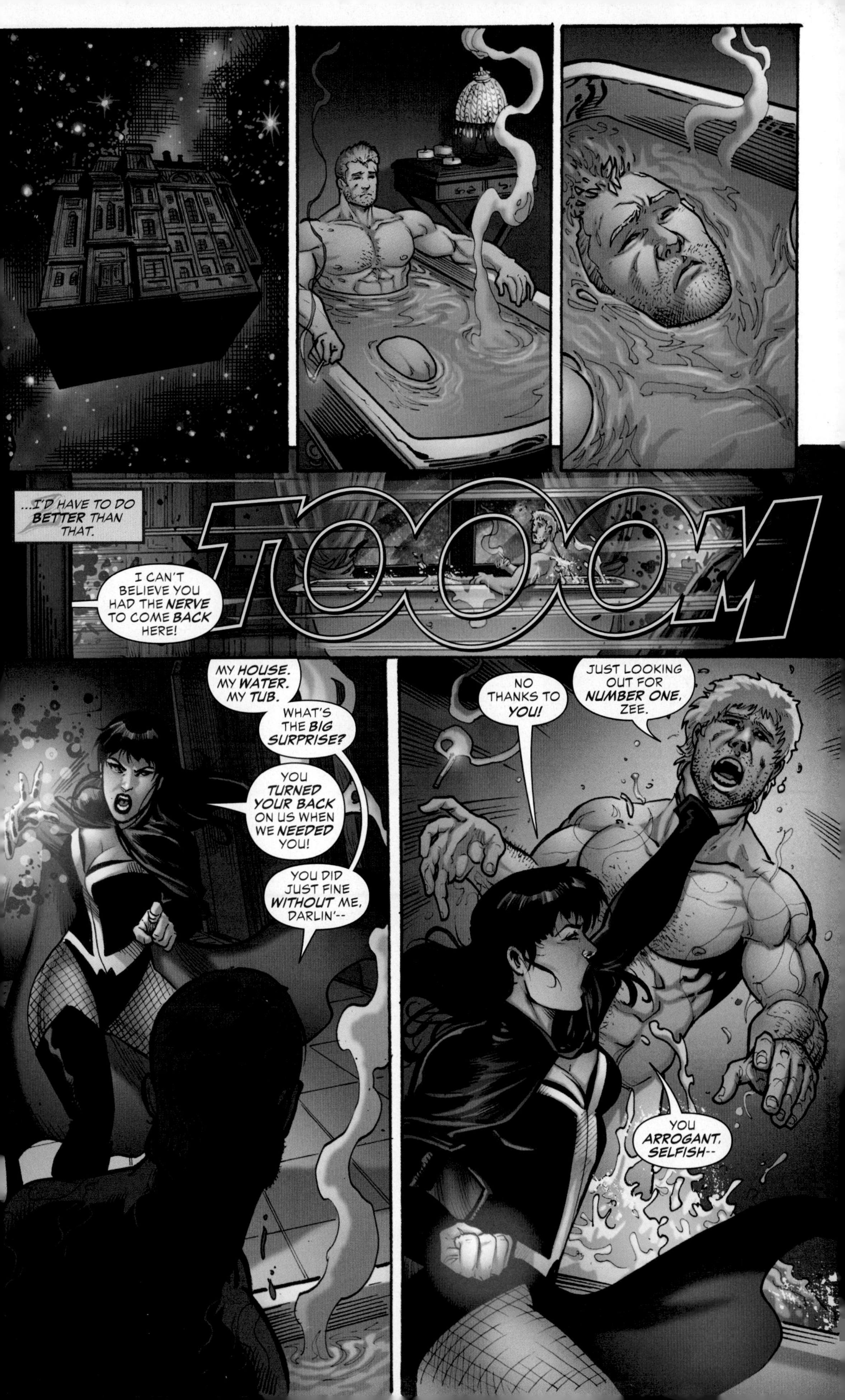

...I'D HAVE TO DO BETTER THAN THAT.
TOOOM
I CAN'T BELIEVE YOU HAD THE NERVE TO COME BACK HERE!
MY HOUSE. MY WATER. MY TUB.
WHAT'S THE BIG SURPRISE?
YOU TURNED YOUR BACK ON US WHEN WE NEEDED YOU!
YOU DID JUST FINE WITHOUT ME, DARLIN'--
NO THANKS TO YOU!
JUST LOOKING OUT FOR NUMBER ONE, ZEE.
YOU ARROGANT, SELFISH--

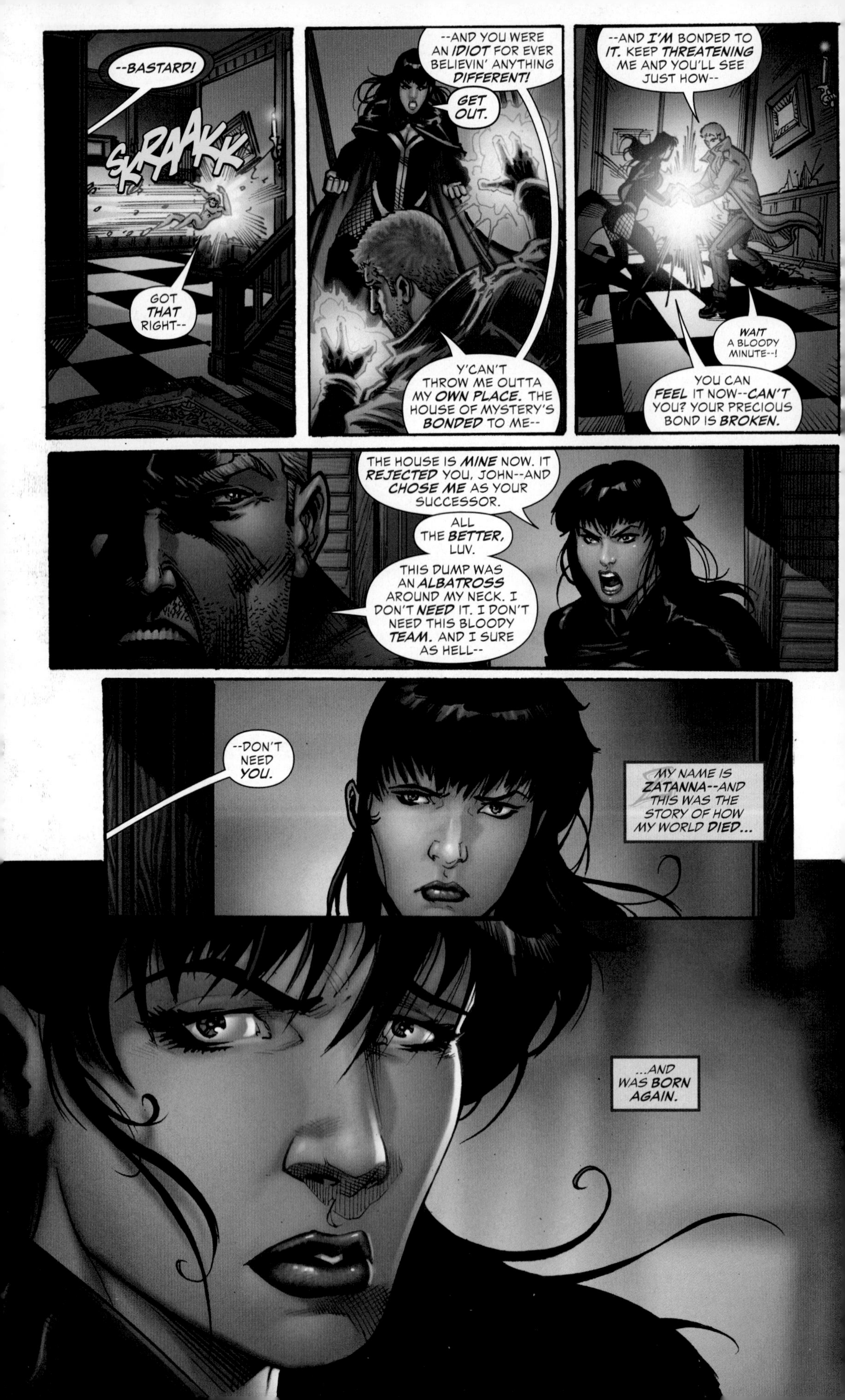
--BASTARD!
SKRAAKK
GOT THAT RIGHT--
--AND YOU WERE AN IDIOT FOR EVER BELIEVIN' ANYTHING DIFFERENT!
GET OUT.
Y'CAN'T THROW ME OUTTA MY OWN PLACE. THE HOUSE OF MYSTERY'S BONDED TO ME--
--AND I'M BONDED TO IT. KEEP THREATENING ME AND YOU'LL SEE JUST HOW--
WAIT A BLOODY MINUTE--!
YOU CAN FEEL IT NOW--CAN'T YOU? YOUR PRECIOUS BOND IS BROKEN.
THE HOUSE IS MINE NOW. IT REJECTED YOU, JOHN--AND CHOSE ME AS YOUR SUCCESSOR.
ALL THE BETTER, LUV.
THIS DUMP WAS AN ALBATROSS AROUND MY NECK. I DON'T NEED IT. I DON'T NEED THIS BLOODY TEAM. AND I SURE AS HELL--
--DON'T NEED YOU.
MY NAME IS ZATANNA--AND THIS WAS THE STORY OF HOW MY WORLD DIED...
...AND WAS BORN AGAIN.

JUSTICE LEAGUE DARK #22
Variant cover by Brett Booth, Norm Rapmund & Andrew Dalhouse

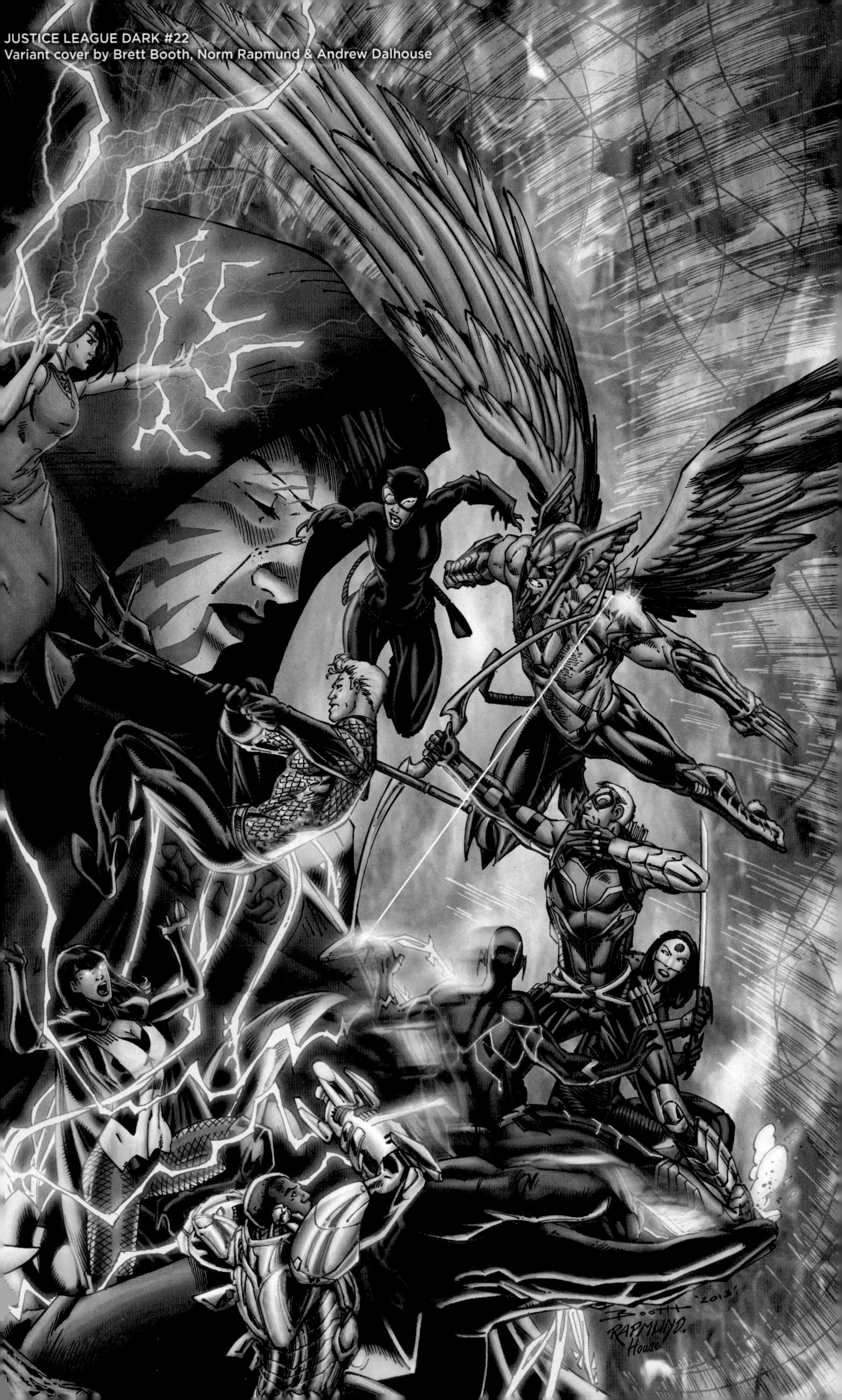

BOOTH '2013'
RAPMUND.
House

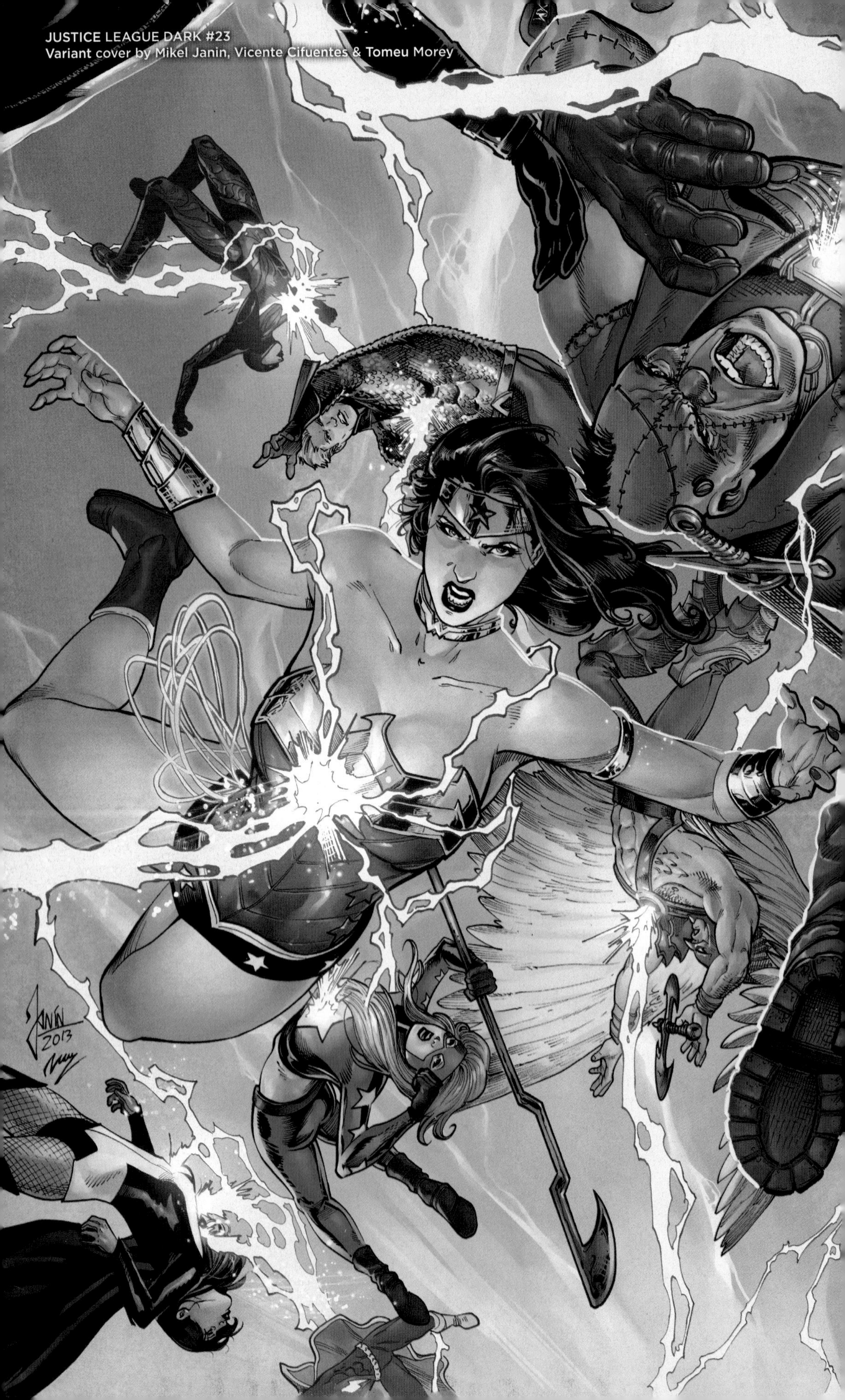
Janin
2013
JUSTICE LEAGUE DARK #23
Variant cover by Mikel Janin, Vicente Cifuentes & Tomeu Morey

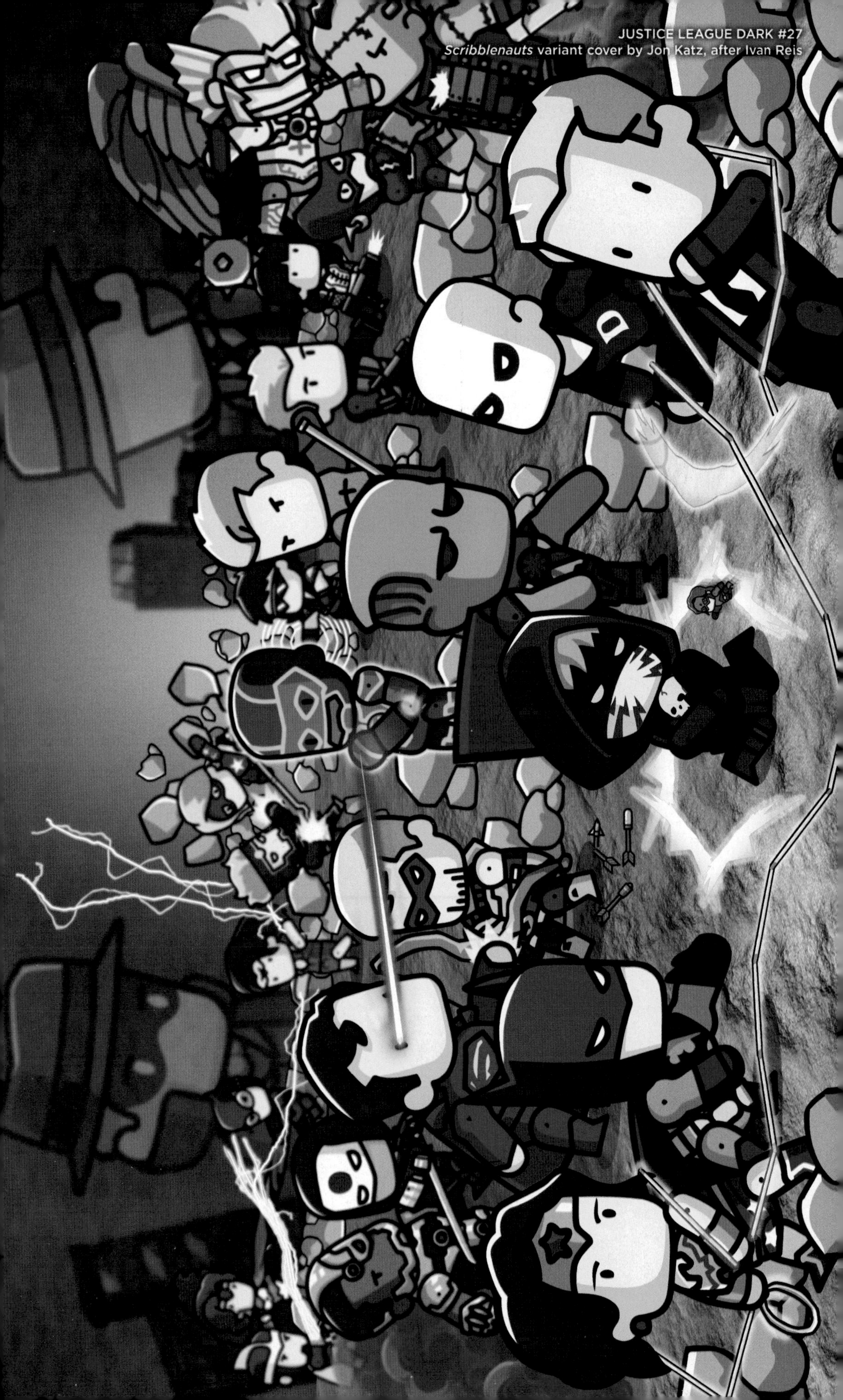

JUSTICE LEAGUE DARK #27
Scribblenauts variant cover by Jon Katz, after Ivan Reis

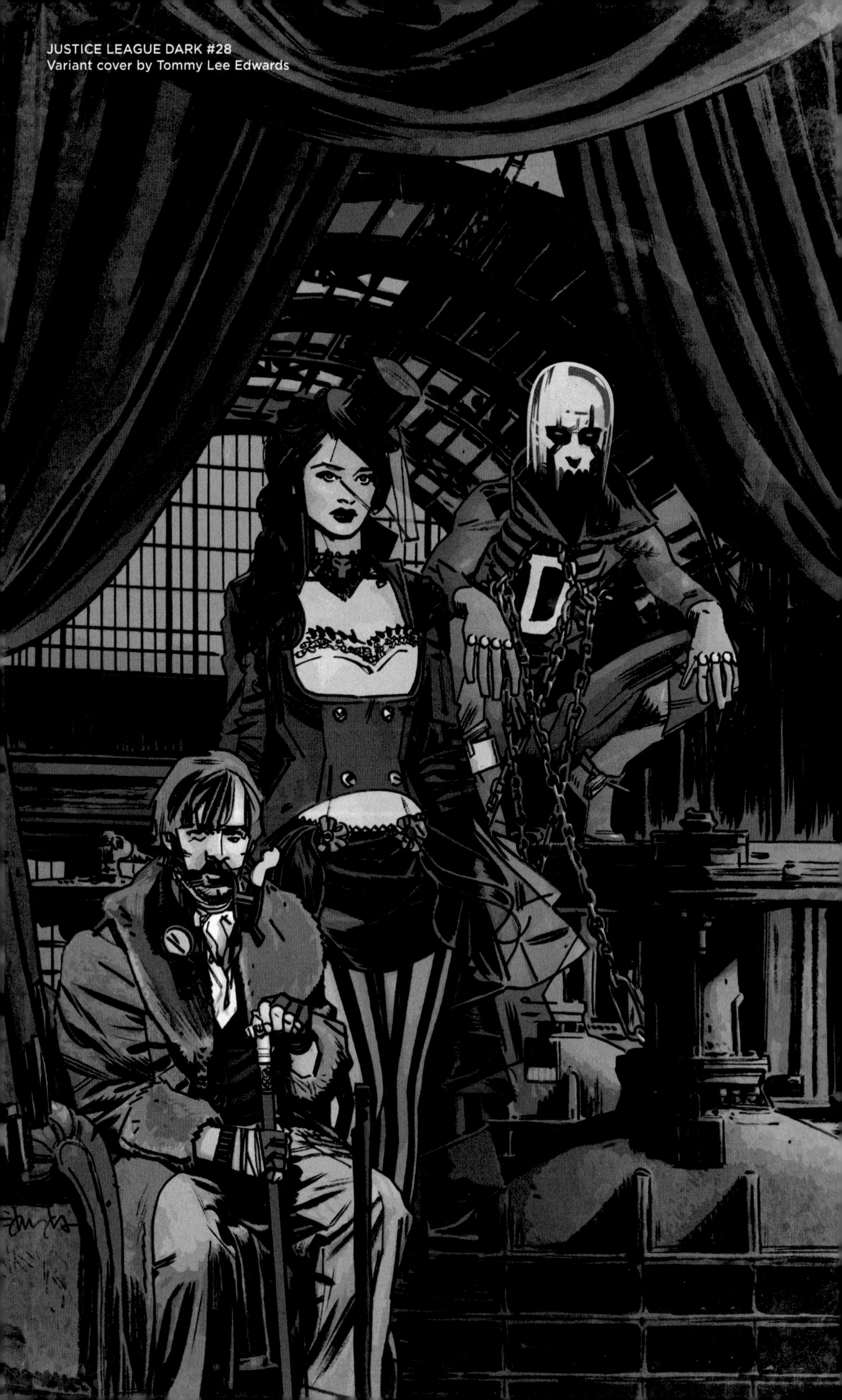

JUSTICE LEAGUE DARK #28
Variant cover by Tommy Lee Edwards

JUSTICE LEAGUE DARK #29
Robot Chicken variant cover by RC Stoodios

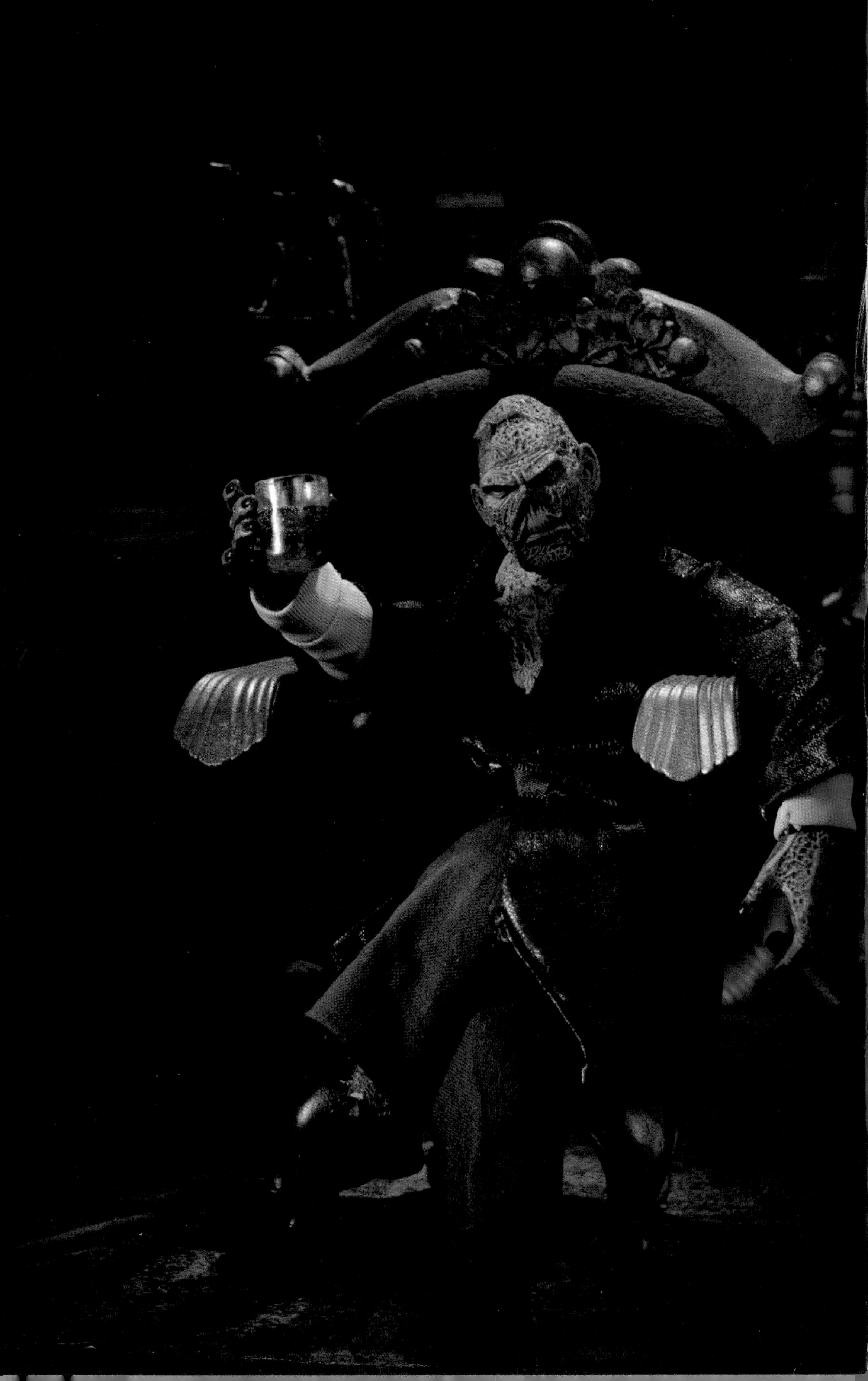

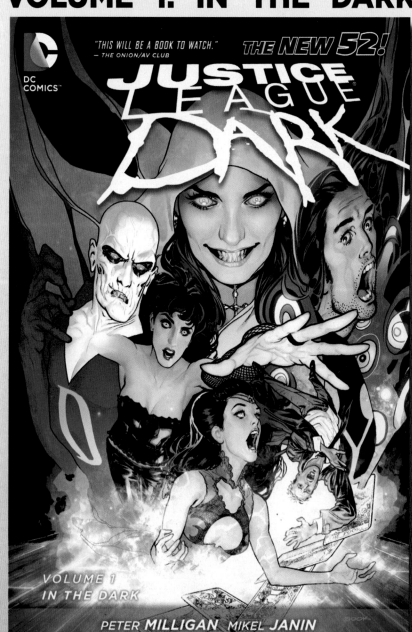